LEISURE COUNSELING

LEISURE COUNSELING

Concepts and Applications

Edited by

E. Thomas Dowd, Ph.D., ABPP

Diplomate in Counseling Psychology
American Board of Professional Psychology, Inc.

CHARLES C THOMAS • PUBLISHER
Springfield • Illinois • U.S.A.

Published and Distributed Throughout the World by

CHARLES C THOMAS • PUBLISHER

2600 South First Street

Springfield, Illinois 62717

© *1984 by* CHARLES C THOMAS • PUBLISHER

ISBN 0-398-0-398-04824-X

Library of Congress Catalog Card Number: 82-25625

With THOMAS BOOKS *careful attention is given to all details of manufacturing and
design. It is the Publisher's desire to present books that are satisfactory as to their physical
qualities and artistic possibilities and appropriate for their particular use.* THOMAS
BOOKS *will be true to those laws of quality that assure a good name and good will.*

Printed in the United States of America
Q-R-3

Library of Congress Cataloging in Publication Data

Main entry under title:

Leisure counseling.
   Bibliography: p.
   Includes indexes.
    1. Leisure counseling--Addresses, essays, lectures.
I. Dowd, E. Thomas.
GV181.42.L44   1984   790'.01   82-25625
ISBN 0-398-04824-X

To my wife Terri, my daughter Kathy, and my son Michael,
who have been optimally arousing and intrinsically motivating.

CONTRIBUTORS

Donald H. Blocher is Professor of Counseling Psychology at the State University of New York at Albany. He has held professorships at the University of Minnesota and the University of Western Ontario. He has been visiting professor at Utah State University, the University of Colorado, the University of British Columbia, and the University of Keele in the United Kingdom. Dr. Blocher is a past president of the Division of Counseling Psychology of the American Psychological Association. He is author or co-author of several books including *Developmental Counseling*. He is the author of numerous journal articles and is a Fellow of the American Psychological Association.

E. Thomas Dowd received his Ph.D. in Counseling and Student Personnel Psychology from the University of Minnesota in 1971. He was a VA psychologist and was on the Counseling faculty of Florida State University from 1973 to 1981. He is currently a professor in the Counseling Psychology program at the University of Nebraska. He is a Diplomate in Counseling Psychology, American Board of Professional Psychology, and a member of the National Register of Health Service Providers in Psychology. He has contributed numerous scholarly papers and book chapters to the professional community in the areas of Cognitive Behavior Therapy, social influence processes, counseling and leisure counseling and is particularly interested in career/leisure concerns of adults.

Gary Ellis is a research associate in the Division of Recreation and Leisure Studies at North Texas State University. He expects to receive his Ph.D. in 1983 in College Teaching.

Gerald S. Fain received his Ph.D in Recreation and Leisure with a minor in Counseling from the University of Maryland in 1976. He is currently associate Professor and Coordinator of Human Service Programs, Leisure Studies, and Health Education at Boston University. He has been employed as a recreation therapist at the North Carolina Memorial Hospital in Chapel Hill, North Carolina.

Arnold H. Grossman is an Associate Professor of Recreation and Leisure Studies and Chairman of the Department of Recreation and Leisure Studies in the School of Education, Health, Nursing, and Arts Professions, New York University. He received his B.S. (Sociology) from the City College of New York and his M.S.W. (Social Group Work) and Ph.D. (Human Relations) from New York University. Before coming to N.Y.U., he worked for over 15 years in community center, social agency, and camping programs providing recreation, leisure, and social services.

Robert W. Herron received his Ph.D. in Family Relations and Marriage

Counseling from the University of Minnesota in 1975. He is a clinical member of the American Association for Marriage and Family Therapy (AAMFT) and is a Certified Marriage and Family Therapist in North Carolina. He is currently the Executive Director of the Presbyterian Counseling Center in Greensboro, North Carolina.

Christine Z. Howe received her Ph.D. in Leisure Studies from the University of Illinois at Urbana-Champaign in 1978. She is an Associate Professor in the Department of Recreation and Leisure Studies at the University of Georgia and previously taught at Virginia Commonwealth University. Howe's academic interests include research and evaluation in leisure, future studies, and aging. She is presently writing a textbook in the area of leisure programming, proposing a cyclical approach to that process.

Seppo E. Iso-Ahola received his undergraduate training from the University of Jyväskyla (Finland), his masters degree from the same institution, and his Ph.D. from the University of Illinois in 1976. His academic area is social psychology and leisure studies. He taught at the University of Iowa from 1976 to 1981 and is currently an associate professor at the University of Maryland.

Joan H. Kindy is a Professor of Counselor Education in the Department of Counselor Education, School of Education, Health, Nursing, and Arts Professions, New York University. She received her B.A. (Latin) from Bucknell University and her M.S. and Ed.D. degrees in Counseling/Higher Education from Indiana University. She has worked as a university counselor and an administrator in both student services and faculty and staff personnel.

Larry C. Loesch is currently a Professor and Graduate Coordinator in the Department of Counselor Education at the University of Florida, where he has been employed since 1973. He received his doctorate in Counselor Education from Kent State University in 1973. Prior to that he had worked as a mathematics teacher in a high school, school counselor in a K-12 school, and a computer programmer. Dr. Loesch is the current president of the Association for Measurement and Evaluation in Guidance and has served as editor of the AMEG journal, *Measurement and Evaluation in Guidance*. He is currently serving as the advisor for examination development for the National Board for Certified Counselors, Inc., an APGA corporate affiliate coordinating national counselor certification. He was a co-founder of the Florida AMEG and, in 1976, a recipient of a Distinguished Service Award from Florida ACES. He has had a feature article on leisure counseling in *The Counseling Psychologist* and has recently co-authored the book, *Principles of Leisure Counseling*. His primary professional interests center on research, measurement and evaluation, leisure counseling, and counselor education.

C. Forrest McDowell received his Ph.D. in Leisure Services and Counseling Psychology from the University of Utah in 1975. He was on the faculty of the University of Oregon from 1975 to 1977 and has held several guest professorships. He currently directs his own Consulting Center, Leisure/Health

Associates. His current interests involve the integration of wellness with leisure life-style and spiritual and philosophical aspects of leisure, with specific attention to Eastern Cultures. Dr. McDowell has a keen interest in leisure in New Age Communities and is an accomplished playright, composer, and musician.

Jane E. Myers received her Ph.D. in counselor education with specializations in rehabilitation and gerontology from the University of Florida in 1978. She is currently an Assistant Professor of Guidance and Counseling and Director of Rehabilitation Counselor Education at Ohio University in Athens. In addition to work experience as a counselor and aging programs administrator, she also has taught at Florida State University and was Director of the National Project on Counseling Older People, a jointly funded project between the American Personnel and Guidance Association and the U.S. Administration on Aging. Her primary research interests are in the areas of gerontological counseling, assessment and appraisal techniques, and rehabilitation of older disabled workers. She is active in professional associations in the areas of counseling, rehabilitation, and gerontology.

Sharon H. Niles is a research associate in the Division of Recreation and Leisure Studies at North Texas State University. She expects to receive her Ph.D. in 1983 in Higher Education.

Dennis K. Orthner received his Ph.D. in Sociology from Florida State University in 1975. He was on the faculty of the Family Research Center at the University of North Carolina-Greensboro from 1975 to 1982 and is currently a consultant with SRA Corporation, Washington, D.C. His primary interests are in family leisure and leisure consultation.

Robin Siegal received her Ph.D. in 1982 in Counseling Psychology at the State University of New York at Albany. She is currently a staff psychologist at the Albany County Mental Health Center, Albany, New York. Her area of interest is Cognitive Developmental Theory.

Diane J. Tinsley is a counseling psychologist within Student Services and adjunct assistant professor of psychology at Southern Illinois University of Carbondale. She received her B.A. in psychology from The University of Pennsylvania and her Ph.D. in psychology from The University of Minnesota in 1972. Dr. Tinsley has authored over 10 publications dealing with counseling psychology, student services, and leisure. She is a member of the American College Personnel Association, the National Vocational Guidance Association, and the Division of Counseling Psychology and the Division of Psychology of Women of the American Psychological Association. Dr. Tinsley is a former chair of the Commission on Career Planning and Placement of the American College of Personnel Association.

Howard E. A. Tinsley is a professor of psychology and director of the graduate training program in counseling psychology at Southern Illinois University at Carbondale. He received his B.A. and M.A. at Western Washington University and obtained his Ph.D. in psychology from the University of Minnesota in 1971.

Dr. Tinsley was formerly assistant professor at the University of Oregon and visiting associate professor at the University of Texas at Austin. He has served as editor of the *Journal of Leisure Research*. Dr. Tinsely has authored over 50 publications dealing with counseling psychology, psychological measurement, and leisure, has contributed chapters to four other books, and is the recipient of the 1976 research award of the American Rehabilitation Counseling Association in recognition of an outstanding contribution to the research literature in rehabilitation counseling. Dr. Tinsley is a Fellow of the Division of Counseling Psychology of the American Psychological Association, Chair of the Commission of Assessment for Student Development of the American College Personnel Association, and a member of the Board of the Council of Counseling Psychology Training Programs.

Peter A. Witt received his Ph.D. in Leisure Studies from the University of Illinois in 1970. He is currently Chairperson and Associate Professor in the Division of Recreation and Leisure Studies at North Texas State University in Denton. Previously he was with the University of Ottawa (Canada).

PREFACE

T HIS book is an outgrowth of the 1981 issue of the *The Counseling Psychologist* on leisure counseling that I edited. As work progressed on that volume, I became increasingly aware that the field of leisure counseling was not being explored in all of its scope and depth. My mounting frustration with the task of trying to comprehensively explore a new field within the confines of what amounted to a monograph led to the conceptualization and final "birth" of the present book.

The book as finally developed is an attempt to provide a comprehensive and multifaceted look at leisure counseling as it presently exists. Especially significant is the attempt in Part I to develop a theoretical psychological foundation for the phenomenon of leisure and the practice of leisure counseling. This theoretical background is then used in Part II for the practice of leisure counseling with selected populations and problems. Part III discusses professional issues and training in leisure counseling.

I was acutely aware during the development of this book that leisure counseling is the province both of counseling psychology and of leisure and recreation. Thus, the chapter authors were chosen to be representative of both fields. The reader will note that some of the individual chapters are themselves collaborations between individuals in both disciplines, a fact which is especially gratifying to me. However, the book is definitely psychologically oriented and should be approached as such.

I was also aware, as I struggled with the conceptualization of the volume, that the *practice* of leisure counseling, that is, the process and interventions, differs little if at all from other types of counseling. What is different are the goals or ends towards which this process moves, as well as a consideration of the psychological meaning of leisure and the societal role that it plays (or could play) in life. A book that focused primarily on leisure counseling intervention techniques would be highly redundant, while one that focused on activities selection would be limited. The reader will therefore note that the majority of the book is devoted to an examination of the theoretical and practical aspects of leisure rather than a discussion of leisure counseling techniques. Only insofar as particular interventions are specific to leisure are they presented in detail.

I was very fortunate in securing some of the most prominent individuals in both fields of counseling psychology and of leisure and recreation as chapter authors. Whatever merit the book may possess, I owe it primarily to them. They have been stimulating to work with and I have learned much from them.

Thanks are also due to Kenneth D. Orton, Department Head of Educational Psychology and Social Foundations at the University of Nebraska, for his encouragement of scholarly and creative endeavor and to Cheryl Carlson for manuscript typing. Finally, I want to thank Charles C Thomas, Publisher who has been supportive from the first and has allowed the book to develop in its own way.

Work on this volume has been meaningful to me as it has provided a framework for collaborative, cross-disciplinary activity, which I value highly. Because, in an ironic twist, I have had significantly less "leisure time" since beginning this project, it is fortunate indeed that it has been intrinsically motivating and has provided me with optimal arousal and a higher level of perceived competence. In that sense this book has truly been a leisure experience.

E. Thomas Dowd
Lincoln, Nebraska

CONTENTS

PART III. PROFESSIONAL ISSUES

LEISURE COUNSELING

Part I
THEORETICAL BACKGROUND

Chapter 1

LEISURE: CONSCIOUSNESS, WELL-BEING, AND COUNSELING

C. FORREST MCDOWELL

WE clearly have a task ahead of us. Even as we attempt to depict leisure within certain norms of activities and behavior, our sense of intuition tells us that the spirit or feeling of leisure is perhaps just as elusive and mystical as the ebb and flow we feel about love, happiness, fulfillment, or even the eternal question, "Who am I?" So, how are we as counselors and psychologists to relate to such a polymorphic, mercurial concept? Do we submit to the doctrine of the work-market society and thus view leisure merely as some activity with some price tag that occurs within some space of time? Do we define it and give it worth as a function of work-vocation? Do we squeeze it into already harried time frames and say, "Now how do you feel about your leisure?" Do we suspect it as the integral key to the decline of productive society, and so must guard people's pursuit of pleasure through leisure? Do we really even care about people's ideas and concerns about leisure? Should we even care? Finally, why should we care?

It is interesting that we know less now, in the course of human history, about the penetrating concept and influence of leisure (and not just as some activity with which to fill time) than we did centuries ago, especially during Grecian times. Perhaps, like the colloquial and faddish phrases of the time ("far out," groovy, etc.), leisure too has passed through phases of inquiry and unconcern. Today, we use the phrase "leisure time" and even "leisure activity." We hear terms "constructive leisure" and "creative leisure." I question why we must use qualifying words when we discuss leisure, and not with other life concepts (such as work time, family time, community activity, constructive work, etc.). I firmly believe that the reason we must continuously tinsel leisure with descriptive words and phrases is because by doing so it allows us to think we know what leisure is really all about.

Actually, for many people leisure has more refined esoteric qualities about it than even the "marketeers of Leisure pursuasion" (Glasser, 1970) realize. In some of my ongoing research, I have been field interviewing numbers of people selected at random who are engaged in what empiricists would describe as "leisure activities." I have been interviewing joggers, weightlifters, bicyclists, connoisseur diners, picnickers, hikers, movie-goers, window shoppers, etc. In

This chapter is based on an article of the same title that originally appeared in *The Counseling Psychologist*, 1981, *9*(3).

almost every case I discover that the activity people select to experience leisure is not a reliable source of experiencing leisure each time they engage in it.

It is difficult to imagine the paradox that exists regarding leisure. We educate and train, focus and delimit our ambitions for and about a type of work-vocation, and the thread of hope exists that this will be our niche for the next twenty years. We select a spouse, mate, friend among the wide choice of availables, and the thread of expectation is that they will be around for some time. We expect that our spiritual beliefs will guide us optimistically toward some end called salvation or peace of mind. What is it that accounts for the fickle nature of experiencing leisure? Why does a sense of leisureliness elude even the best intentions, time schedules, planned vacations, anticipated retirement?

Somehow, the leisure we put into our pursuit of the "good life" seems superficial and candy-coated: it gives us immediate gratification, perhaps pleasure, and a quick escape from the mundane (even as it too becomes mundane). It also quite often leaves us with a sense of dissatisfaction, discomfort, frustration, and guilt over the long run.

The people I have been interviewing all seem to have some inner quest for experiencing leisure. The quest — a fulfillment of some desirable identity — hangs by some gossamer thread of optimism and hope. Perhaps it is this optimism, as it is emitted from some biology of hope (Tiger, 1979), that instills in people the need to keep trying to experience leisure, even if they are not too sure themselves just what experiencing leisure would feel like.

I would like to think that this chapter will stimulate some different thoughts about the concept of leisure — what it is, what it can be, perhaps what it should be for people. There is an obvious risk in presenting the amount of conceptual material that is relatively fresh in nature as it relates to leisure. It is my *hope* that terms such as *leisure consciousness* and *leisure well-being* will do more for solidifying the concepts of leisure and leisure counseling than otherwise might be expected. The first section of this chapter will explore the notion of a leisure consciousness and leisure ideology in relationship to a work-responsibility-dutifulness consciousness and ideology. The conclusions drawn should point to the need for considering the idea of a person's general well-being and their leisure well-being, as explored in the second section. Finally, the third section will speak to the concept of leisure counseling from a more theoretical position. This recognizes the need to explore the conceptual bases upon which to offer counseling, in light of the preponderance of facilitative material that already inundates the field.

LEISURE AND CONSCIOUSNESS

Until recently, psychology studied the mind without a brain, while biology studied the brain without a mind. Presently, there is a landslide of interest in the split-brain phenemonen and the duality of consciousness spun from the right (called the intuitive mode) and the left (called the rational mode) sides of the brain. The brain seeks to function in a complementary relationship of the two sides, in a sense, like a flow of consciousness and functioning. Our thoughts, moods, emotions, and behaviors are in constant transition. We move in and out of consciousness of time, activity, reason and logic, creativity and pleasure, and so forth.

I have every reason to believe that, both culturally and biologically, our interpretations of the differences in work and leisure do in fact support the inherent uniquenesses between the two modes of consciousness. The left side, or the rational mode of consciousness, seems clearly related to aspects of work, responsibility, and dutifulness. The right side, or the intuitive mode of consciousness, seems clearly related to aspects of leisure, play, and the pursuit of pleasure. (The reader who is unfamiliar with the brain and its modes of consciousness should consult the excellent works of Ornstein, 1972; Samples, 1976; Bruner, 1973; Goleman & Davidson, 1979). We can flow in and out of these two modes, and understand more clearly why sometimes leisure is pure unadulterated pleasure/joy and at other times it takes on dimensions of work-obligation; why work can seem like leisure one moment and pure drudgery the next. However, as transitional in nature as the concepts of work and leisure can be in our daily lives, an acculturation of consciousness does affect selection and preference. Only a thorough historical understanding would indicate that modern cultures glorify a work-responsibility-dutifulness consciousness at the expense of the balancing qualities of a leisure consciousness.

The young child is most in touch with fondling a play or leisure spirit of consciousness, before the cultural logic and symbolism of language, time, and responsibility-dutifulness affects and conditions future development of life-style preferences, attitudes, values, and beliefs concerning work, vocation, and the good life. The young child's fondling is very well what Albert Einstein described as the "sacred gift of nature": the intuitive mind. The infant, before language development (what Bruner describes as the most profound learning act in which the child will engage), simply has an inherent psychological link to feelings of timelessness, sensualness, freedom, pleasure-seeking (Buhler's concept of pleasure in functioning), inventiveness, intuitiveness. Before two to four years, the human being is culturally untampered. It does not know clock or calender time, nor structure, routine, duties, responsibilities, reason, or the idea of work. It responds to innate expressions of its own rhythm, its own unstructured cyclical time frame, and the explorations and discoveries of space and freedom of movement. Anything and everything exists within a curious wonderment of experiencing as a whole, not according to some system of logic.

Language development, however, is the child's initial conditioning in the use and preference of the rational mode of consciousness as differentiated from the intuitive mode (Galin, Levy-Agresti, & Sperry, 1968; Tiger, 1979; Samples, 1976). On the surface, there is nothing inherently wrong about such a preference. Although Einstein also addressed it as the faithful servant to the intuitive mind, the rational mind does have as much to do with biological survival as it does with cultural preservation of the individual and the species. It is object-centered and aids in analyzing our position towards the world. It strings together associations in a linear perspective of events enduring in time, in sequence, and in cause-and-effect relationships. Such linearity is essential in the development of an organized culture and can only evolve within two highly refined aspects of this mode of consciousness: language and reason. Within the realm of rational consciousness lies our ability to organize ourselves, to seek order and conformity, to be discrete and logical, to concentrate on the rules and directions, especially as needed in analytical and intellectual formulations associated with language, writing, numbers, and reasoning.

It may be that our need for reason only emerges from our initial and paramount need for freedom, joy, pleasure, and creativity, and passion — all inherent qualities emanating from our right, and intuitive, mode of consciousness; sadly, these qualities seem elusive and unfulfilling in today's society. The child learns at an early age that those natural feelings associated with freedom, pleasure, etc. are primarily manipulations of the symbols of language and reason that are praised and worshipped by a predominantly left consciousness-oriented society. A society that deifies time (be on time, it is time to do this or that, use time wisely, find time), responsibility and dutifulness (clean your room and then you can play, finish your homework and then you can watch television, your play privileges are taken away), work (what are you going to be when you grow up?), rules, logic, and rationality (this is the correct way, there's only one good way, that's a good excuse), and virtuousness in conforming can only be heard through the sound of one hand clapping.

Perhaps many persons desire a fuller applause in their life-style. They do not wish the hand of freedom to be bound by the hand of order or constraint; the hand of joy and pleasure to be bound by the hand of guilt; the hand of creativity to be bound by the hand of logic; the hand of passion to be bound by the hand of reason; the hand of timeless experiencing to be bound by the hand of time, structure, and routine; the hand of playfulness to be bound by the hand of responsibility and dutifulness; and finally, the hand of leisure to be bound by the hand of work.

Certainly the present need is to understand the complementary enriching qualities of both a work-responsibility-dutifulness consciousness and a leisure consciousness — what separates them and what enjoins them.

Indicators of a Work Consciousness and a Leisure Consciousness

Ornstein (1972), Samples (1976), and others have compiled excellent dichotomies of the two modes of consciousness, supported by science and cross-cultural beliefs/myths. From a perusal of the literature, I have developed a tentative dichotomy between work-responsibility-dutifulness consciousness and leisure consciousness (Table 1-I).

Table 1-I

A Tentative Dichotomy Between Work and Leisure Consciousness

Work-Responsibility-Dutifulness Consciousness (Left Mode)	Leisure-Pleasure-Play Consciousness (Right Mode)
Day, Light	Night, Eve, Dark
Masculine	Feminine
Strong	Weak
Righteous	Scornful
Heaven, Spirit	Earth, Nature, Natural
Moral, Ethical	Immoral, Unethical
Busyness, Productive	Laziness, Idleness
Active	Passive
Creation, Construction	Re-creation, Relaxation
Effort, Action	Relaxation, Receptiveness
Time, Schedule, Routine	Timelessness, Space
Activity, Explicit Behavior	Experience, Implicit Behavior
Focal	Diffuse
External	Internal
Reason, Logic, Rules, Analytical, Seriousness	Intuition, Inventive, Pleasure, Fantasies, Dreams
Boundedness	Unboundedness, Freedom
Adultlike	Childlike
Intellectual	Sensual
Conformity	Unconvention
Right-handedness	Left-handedness
Yang	Yin

Some of the dichotomies seem rather blatant in cultural terms, for example, the distinction between day-light and night-dark. In spite of people's natural and varying biorhythms, work for the most part occurs during daylight, and leisure is viewed as what occurs *after* work, or more specifically during the evening or dark side of the day.

The dichotomy between masculine-feminine and strong-weak is also culturally evident. Work historically is associated with manliness, masculinity, and strength. Leisure has often been relegated to a dimension of weakness of the working spirit. An utterly false assumption has also been contrived that because the woman's place is the home, she has more leisure time than her working spouse.

The concepts of busyness and productivity versus laziness and idleness are also culturally blatant. Work is equated with both productive and constructive use of one's time, whereas leisure is viewed through the dogma of "idleness is the Devil's playground." In a similar vein, work is culturally elevated to a righteous-heaven-moral position, whereas leisure is seen as scornful, submitting to earthly pleasures, and immoral. In the sixth century, St. Benedict proclaimed, "Idleness is the enemy of the soul, and work is one's salvation." Indeed, if work is one's salvation, its righteous and moral value over the course of time has indeed promised a sort of heaven on earth. Today this is most apparent in the concept of retirement, a type of salvational heaven on earth given to one as a reward for working hard for many years, just as heaven is promised to the righteous. Leisure, on the other hand, is seen as self-loving and an act of selfishness if done at the expense of hard work, or in excess.

A dissective analysis of the concepts distinguishing work and leisure could be fun and lengthy. It would also serve to alienate the potential for understanding the flow between leisure consciousness and work-responsibility-dutifulness consciousness. I believe the concepts presented in Table 1-I can be reduced to five delicate links, or indicators, within this potential flow:

Time — Timelessness
Effort — Relaxation
Reason — Intuition
Boundedness — Unboundedness
Activity — Experience

Time — Timelessness

Work-responsibility-dutifulness consciousness in today's work-market society is heavily impregnated with the concept of time and duration. This is evident because of four interrelated characteristics of the left, or rational, mode of consciousness:

1. It deals with the concept of time. We learn to do things at a certain time, within a certain time frame. We also learn that time has a value and certain rewards and punishments associated with it.
2. It deals with things one at a time. We learn time is synonymous with doing and activity, both of which must be *structured* within a reasonable amount of time and order.
3. It processes information in a linear manner. We learn that the best way to structure our activities is according to some *schedule* occurring within time and order.
4. It functions according to sequence. We learn that the only way to efficiently run through a schedule of activities is to adopt a *routine*. This routine becomes the confirmation by habit that the order and timing of a set of activities is efficient and productive.

That specific work tasks over the course of history allowed people to engage in trade and barter of goods and wares accounts for much of the linear "programming" of time in people's lives. Divisions of labor are concurrently intertwined with divisions of time: time for labor, time for rest, time for worship, and so forth. However, clock time, calender time, work time, spare time, each artificially schedules our natural rhythms. We use them as means to measure how responsible we are or have been in our activities. Such a consciousness, at the expense of any other mode, merely turns lives into a string of events — Pavlovian stimuli in the form of stoplights, bells, scheduled programs, awaiting retirement. Everything exists in an unending stream of passing from past to future. The present is only a means to get a handle on the time of the future.

A work-market consciousness also creates a similar life-style: we all get up generally at the same time in the morning; perform our body maintenance functions generally in unison; clog the roadways, byways, railways, airways at the same times; have lunch at twelve, dinner at six; en masse watch the same Nielsen-rated shows; and go to bed generally within the same hour or two. The scenario is generally true for all people at all ages (except for those we might label the "leisure class").

Such a consciousness also creates the same blend of attitudes and rationalizations about time. In effect, time becomes the linear scapegoat for not engaging in leisure. The left mode of consciousness can easily rationalize why we don't have the time to do something. It draws conclusions about wasting time, putting in time, or even needing time out.

One of the most powerful elements of leisure-pleasure consciousness, however, is that of timelessness, a beautiful quality of the right, or intuitive, mode of consciousness. One only needs to pause to reflect upon experiences in which time ceased to exist: daydreaming, the pleasureful playing of or listening to music, a three-day weekend filled with many interesting events. When enaged in an activity with a sense of spirit of leisure about it, we become most receptive to the inner feelings of joy, pleasure, and passion emanating from our right brain. Our most filled and pleasurable involvements seem to pass quickly, and remain in memory enduringly. For the moment, time simply does not exist.

Actually, the reason time does not seem to exist is because the nonlineal time characteristics of leisure are also enriched by a present-moment centeredness of quality of the intuitive mode. There appears to be a receptivity to an "infinite present," in which we become so tuned in to the experience at hand that we lose all contact with any aspect of time, either the immediate past or future. I believe that the timeless and present-moment qualities of leisure are what clairifies its existence as a state of mind, whereas the qualities of work-responsibility-dutifulness clairfy their existence as an orientation within the man-made concept of time. Leisure flows from the right mode of consciousness and only then emerges within an activity or experience. For this reason, we feel leisurely, at leisure, and leisurable at something we do. Viewed in this light, work has the potential to be leisure. We can attest to this at those moments when we enthusiastically and intensely get involved in the work we are doing and find pleasure in the experience. When we become conscious of time again, we are amazed at how fast it seemed to have passed.

Leisure, then, is our link with the pleasure of the present-moment. We may attempt to plan or schedule "leisure time," but this alone does not guarantee experiencing leisure, as we all can attest.

Effort — Relaxation

In the rhythm of life there is a natural psycho-physical ebb and flow. Terms such as input-output, stop-go, action-reception, constriction, contraction, and effort-relaxation describe this natural pattern. Over the course of history, however, religious and market ideologies have acculturated the myth/belief that effort-relaxation are bipolar descriptions of work and leisure. Thus, a work-responsibility-dutifulness consciousness is most often associated with hard effort, focused effort, keeping busy and active, productivity, busting one's gut — all of which exclaim the virtuousness of action (as in the belief that "idle hands are the Devil's playground"). It also emphasizes the idea of service to others (allonomous effort) and what is to be earned as a reward for work well done, as indicated in the belief that "you forge your own fortune."

A work consciousness demands that relaxation be earned, that it has little utilitarian value when not associated with work-efort. For this reason, relaxation of effort and receptivity within states of mind such as doing nothing or even quiet contemplation are primarily equated with idleness, apathy, sloth, and laziness.

The complementary effort-relaxation functions of consciousness are innate resources every individual possesses at birth. As such, the cyclical characteristic of effort-relaxation is inherently self-determined, self-initiated, autonomous, autotelic. Martin (1975) suggests that this interrelative concept coincides with Von Bertalanffy's image of man as an active personality system, with Lorenz's concept of primary aggression and innate release mechanism, and with the works of Magoun, Arnold, Allport, and Toynbee. The American Psychiatric Association's Committee on Leisure Time and Its Uses firmly believed leisure to be synonymous with receptiveness to experience *and* the relaxation from effort necessary to return on to this initial state of receptiveness.

I want to suggest that the young child's play is its initial fondling with leisure consciousness. It naturally engages in things that provide inner satisfaction, perhaps even at the expense of a little pain. The motivation is autonomous; the rewards are present-moment and felt as inward joy and pleasure. There is also the notion that even as adults we can play and leisure in earnest, for the joy of our effort/motivation flows from a receptivity to its intrinsic worth.

On the other hand, the concept of work has been characterized by a state of extrinsic motivation, effort, or worth. The locus of control for work is not within but without. It is not autonomous but is rather allonomous — a string of events leading toward a goal, probably symbolized by money, time off, and acquiring the symbols of the good life.

We might say, then, that leisure can be characterized by autonomous relaxing effort, certainly, a type of involvement that can include a kind of work and recreation that is pleasureful in and of itself.

Reason — Intuition

The consciousness of work-responsibility-dutifulness is also wrapped up in the pursuit of reason (what the work-market ideology calls "rational calculation" or the "matrix of logic"). There is a reasonable way to behave (and thus predictable), a logical way to think and do things, and a rational explanation for everything. One is also expected to be neat and orderly, conforming, and above all on time. A preoccupation with reason is what stifles creativity, loosening of ego boundaries, a sense of autonomous control of one's life-style. Instead, we find ourselves graded, judged, and evaluated according to some contrived criteria of behavior.

The intuitive dimension of consciousness is what allows us to step outside the bounds of a stifling present-moment. There becomes, as Jerome Bruner once said, something antic about creating, although the enterprise may be serious. He was talking about the combined function of the two modes of consciousness. During mental action/effort, our thinking is more serious, rational, deductive, analytical, and logical; we are more concerned with the existence of things within a time frame of work-responsibility-dutifulness to a task. During mental reception/relaxation, our thinking is more curious, light-headed (if not playful and childlike), nonrational, inductive, synthesizing, and analogical; we are more concerned with the essence of things.

The intuitive dimension of leisure consciousness must be considered, for there definitely is a commonality, whether we use terms such as the metaphoric mind, the dreaming mind, the receptive mind, the relaxed mind; or even the natural, poetic, figurative, ideographic, and passionate mind. The timelessness and receptiveness of a leisure state of mind is what allows us to create the pleasure in those experiences. We can invent a hero for ourselves; we can find delight in simple self-expression that is neither right or wrong, logical or conforming. We can fall in love with our passions and our sensualness; we can live for the anticipation and hopeful pleasure of a dream, fantasy, and real future happening. We can solve a puzzling problem while taking a relaxing shower or clinging to the cracks of a wall of granite. We can finish a painting even before it is started, or vicariously experience what it would be like to be the boss.

Finally, we can use the receptive, creative aspects of leisure consciousness and infuse them in the spirit of our work. Pleasant surroundings create productive working spirits; worker latitude allows people to monitor their own effort-relaxation cycles independent of time and machine; a sense of playfulness can loosen the grip of boredom. All this may not make our work entirely creative and leisurely, but it may make it feel less constraining.

Boundedness — Unboundedness

A consciousness given to work-responsibility-dutifulness, at the expense of any other consciousness, bounds us to time, reason, and effort seen as work. In short, our life's energies and rhythms become *focalized*. We are scheduled, routinized, hurried, harried, rushed. Even in chaos of time and emotions, we strive for order, conformity, reason, logic. Even some type of work, job, career, vocation centers our life's ambitions. At an early age we are asked, "What do you want to be when you grow up?" Both the institutions of education and family ask us to narrow our perspective of the world of work, in short, to "find our groove."

I meet people every day who describe their life in the context of an "8-to-5." Their consciousness of boundedness is pathetic, in which they submit to taking the solemn vow: "I take this work to be my wedded life." In spite of feeling totally enslaved to such a consciousness (and surely at the risk of otherwise experiencing terrifying guilt for not being so minded), there is also the lingering need to experience unconfining freedom, "To do what I want, to be what I want, to seek what I want," not to cast away responsibility, but to accept it on more unconstraining terms, where the impetus of motivation is autonomously controlled.

A consciousness of leisure is our greatest link with inner freedom or unboundedness. Perhaps this is because leisure, like nature, exists in such *diffusity* (seeking the diffuse and the gestalt of experiences is an inherent quality of the right or intuitive mode of consciousness). Simply speaking, there do not exist any norms for experiencing leisure. This has been one of the most penetrating dialect inquiries for philosophers for centuries. The diffuse nature of leisure is what gives it a dynamism that is in constant change and flux as we age, move from here to there, increase and decrease in ability, among many other factors. In life, we most often focus on one type of work and our life-style seems to be bound by it. What we experience as leisure — our recreational and play activities, and even our family, worship, or work activities — is polymorphically broad. We do not focus on one source for leisure, but instead seek it from a collage of interests, attitudes, and values. Leisure, then, emerges from a consciousness that seeks the pleasure within felt freedom. It is an attitude that says, "I have the say in what I want to experience." Perhaps this bit of insight is what led Emerson to remark that the soul is the color of its leisure thought.

Activity — Experience

When we focus on activity, we do just that and only that. It is like wearing blinders that keep us focused on what is explicitly and observably in front of us. We see, and we sense only what we see, and we make evaluations based upon that. The nature of the rational mode, and work-responsibility-dutifulness consciousness, is to view everything as activity occurring in time. For this reason, in a work-market society, activity becomes a virtue synonymous with busyness, and inactivity becomes associated with laziness, idleness, and unproductivity.

The beauty of the intuitive consciousness, and the wellspring of our leisure consciousness, is its sense of privacy tucked within experiences. We must understand that leisure cannot be viewed solely as an activity the way work is culturally viewed from its own public form of consciousness. An activity does not guarantee that we will feel leisure, be leisurely, or be leisure filled. Many of our fondest leisure experiences are tacit, inward, and made up of a gestalt of our pleasant feelings.

When we use terms such as leisure activity or leisure time, we must realize that we are doing so from the left-rational mode. We assign it dimensions inherent in our attitudes about work-responsibility-dutifulness, although we do not use terms such as work activity or work time (we simply say "work"). From the right-intuitive mode, leisure is an experience, and thus leisure experience is the more accurate form of expression. Experience can refer to both an outward stimulus in the form of activity *and/or* an inward stimulus in the form of just being: being in touch with, sensitive to, open to, receptive to, free to. This type of consciousness is why we can speak of the total experience we had with someone or something, even as we are aware that some aspects of the experience may have been frustrating or could have been different.

We are born with the ability to view the gestalt, or the whole, of our experiences at the same time we are able to focus on any particular aspect we wish. It may not be just the observable activity we are engaged in that accounts for the major source of pleasure in a leisure experience. Leisure can be anticipation and reflection, as well as a collage of receptiveness to a host of feelings and things that emerge from individual uniqueness. It is for this reason, for example, that some people climb mountains just to get to the top, while others do so as another stroke for their ego, and still others do so just to see the beauty along the way. Yet, we may label each person's activity as that of mountain climbing.

It is my opinion, after discussion with countless people, that we are constantly trying to seek the pleasures of experiencing more than what an activity may apparently be. We are constantly trying to transcend the mundaneness of time and reason, to constrain effort that is not autonomously derived. We are aware of the pleasures of what Csikszentmihalyi (1975) describes as the "flow experience" between the two modes of consciousness. We seek it in the meditative act of distance running or isolation tanks, in sexual expression or the sensualness of the preparation and eating of a fine meal, in the search and hope that a type of work is our calling. We seek it in leisure experiences even as we must unlearn that leisure is the activities we assign it to be, the time within which it must occur, and the price by which it must be bought.

Thus far I have attempted to pull together some concepts that may give credance to the idea that our beliefs about work-responsibility-dutifulness and leisure-pleasure-play stem both from the inherent characteristics of the brain and its two modes of consciousness and from cultural beliefs/myths. We cannot escape that our life-style preferences are heavily influenced by the work-market society in which we live. Today, we can forget that many languages lack a word for labor or work, or that the Greeks, Romans, and medieval Europeans did not distinguish between production and consumption and even lacked a word for consumer (Tiger, 1979; Toffler, 1980). The work-market society has redefined effort as work, and leisure as nonwork, even though the derivation of leisure can be traced to the Latin "licere," meaning "to be permitted to be," and to the Greek equivalent "schole," meaning "education of one's being." The Greeks, in viewing leisure as a state of mind, saw work, or "ascholia," as the absence of leisure. In other words, work was defined as a function of leisure, whereas today the opposite belief exists: leisure receives its worth as a reward from work.

In order to understand the contribution leisure makes to life satisfaction, we need to look at it in terms of the work-market society and the accompanying ideologies for both leisure and the work-market that exist. Such a discussion will allow us to better understand the concept of leisure well-being presented later and the subsequent role of leisure counseling in the work-market society.

Influence of Work-Market Ideology and Leisure Ideology on Life Satisfaction

Perhaps what is central to an understanding of the relationships between a work-market ideology and a leisure ideology is a familiarity with the role of an economic coordinating system in shaping leisure preferences.

First, an economic coordinating system orders power relationships and locates who shall make decisions. As the findings of Berelson (1964) suggest, in the market economy, public or subsidized channels account for less than one-quarter of the total amount of cultural presence. It is the private decision-makers who decide what shall be for the remaining three-quarters. What this says in regard to a leisure ideology is clear. What we do, prefer, and think about leisure is mainly predicted by private enterprise. In America, we talk about the Madison Avenue image in which an enterprising few govern the whims of the masses. Of course, the greatest persuasion process (Glasser, 1970) is mass media.

Second, an economic coordinating system finances and serves the leisure culture. In short, it structures the field of available choices, resources, and opportunities. It also maximizes the principle of substitutability, wherein values such as tastes, preferences, goods, services, and people are easily and frequently substituted or replaced for each other according to price, scarcity, obsolescence, and faddishness. Again, it is the mass media that continues to serve as the medium of persuasion, as it embarks upon what Glasser (1970) describes as "aducation," as opposed to education.

Third, the market economy shapes an ideology to justify its offerings. The work-market must develop a culture that not only affects the view toward leisure but also toward the quality of life of the culture itself. The work-market ideology, then, must create an image of the good life that can be reached.

There are two equations that seem to depict well the image of the good life. The first is offered by the economics authority Dr. Paul Samuelson: Happiness = Material Consumption/Desire. The implication is that as long as we continue to buy things we think we need, we will be happy. Furthermore, we believe that as long as we continue to work hard, we can assure ourselves that we can continue to buy those things we think we need to make us happy. This last premise leads directly to an equation I have found useful in understanding the work-market ideology and the leisure ideology: (Work = Money) = (Pleasure = Leisure). Here, work (called earning a living) merely provides the money in which to buy the pleasures of the good life. For most people, then, earning a living does not become pleasurable in and of itself (this is why so many people dislike their work and only see it as a "necessary evil to survive"), but rather the pleasure is sought independent of work and within the availables that money can buy within the market place. Of course, in this equation we should ask why work cannot be a source of pleasure, independent of the motivational power of money. For many people this would be an ideal, just as would be the hope that in work one can find leisure (notice, however, the bipolar extremes of these two concepts in the equation). The work-market society, however, has created the belief that it is not work that provides pleasure, but according to their proximity in the equation it is what money can provide for pleasure in the form of availables.

If we took money out of the equation, we would be very near to the mergence or flow between a work consciousness and a leisure consciousness: Work = Pleasure = Leisure. The research of Maslow of self-actualized people has found that this new equation holds the most truth for vocational-leisure enjoinment. He found that such people had some work they felt worthwhile and important. They found work a pleasure and a joy, and there was little distinction between a spirit of work and a spirit of leisure/play. In a sense, these people could not identify with earning a living. They were most in tune with earning pleasure and satisfaction.

We should keep the above equations in mind as we explore six assumptions that distinguish the two ideologies.

Ideological Assumption I: External vs. Internal Rewards/Satisfaction

The work-market ideology assumes that people are motivated primarily by external or extrinsic rewards, notably, pay, money, and time gifts. The recent research of Professor Locke (Locke, 1980) in industrial psychology at the University of Maryland supports this assumption. It was found that various monetary incentives lead to a median increase in productivity of 30%, more than double and triple traditional goal-setting and job enrichment approaches.

This assumption also supports the Work = Money part of our good life equation. In Maslovian terms, it might suggest that the work-market depends upon deficiency needs, whereas leisure may depend upon self-actualizing needs that emerge only after deficiency needs are satisfied. We can understand, then, the point of view of a leisure ideology: people may be, and at their best are, motivated by internal/intrinsic rewards and satisfaction.

Ideological Assumption II: Rational Calculation vs. Intuitive Function

Within the single goal of profit efficiency in production and of gratification maximization in consumption, the work-market ideology employs a calculated instrumental rationality to assess its success and correct for its errors. This rational "matrix of logic" can only make sense because in a work-market society people's values are fungible in money terms and are ultimately accounted for in terms of income and wealth for individuals and profits for private enterprise. This assumption naturally taints a view of the role of leisure in people's lives, for it assumes that the central limited purpose of leisure is to rest to improve the next day's work (the idea of production efficiency).

The leisure ideology, however, has no single measure of its success, and thus no comparable unit for measuring success in terms of life-style satisfaction. Leisure embodies an expressive function and an intuitive approach toward experiences. It may embrace challenge and stress, as well as rest and relaxation. It aims for self-fulfillment and pleasure, pleasant escape and diversion, achievement and pride, novelty and play, privacy and public display of ego. It moves one in hope toward a desired identity and prizes the emotions, ranging from transcending elation to cautionary guilt. All of these dimensions would surely irritate the most devout logician, statistician, or actuarian who attempted to narrow the leisure experience to a couple of tangibles.

On the other hand, a work-market ideology can rationally bid for the tangible observable elements that govern most people's lives: time and money (Benjamin Franklin said "Time is money," thus echoing productivity and efficiency). It can adjust its strategies according to the greater or lesser amounts of time and money people have, or would like to have.

Ideological Assumption III: Doing vs. Being and Becoming

The work-market ideology places a high value on doing, striving, achieving. Keeping busy and occupied, whether by working or consuming, is viewed as virtuous behavior. People, then, must always be on the go (a favorite theme in commericals ranging from soft drinks to cars, cologne, or deodorant and personal hygiene) and active. It is this assumption that sees mankind as dominant over nature and accounts for what Maslow (1969) speaks of as the active mode of experiencing.

The leisure ideology does *not* function, as might be expected in the light of a contrasting ideology, on the assumption of passivity or inaction (especially in the form of rest and relaxation) as a balance to doing. (I might add, however, that "aducation" — the use of media brainwashing — does in fact impart a strong image that leisure is loafing, resting, relaxing. This may be witnessed especially in clotheswear: the ubiquitous leisure suit; the separation of shoes for active sports from those for leisure, although the manufacturer never tells us just what those leisure shoes look like). Rather, there is the belief that man lives in harmony with nature and makes room for the receptive mode of consciousness. As Deci (1975) proposes, the individual controls his own fate through the learning and expression of competence, a feature of intrinsic satisfaction. In contrast to this assumption is the overriding belief of the work-market ideology that man must be driven and guided toward the illusion of the good life the market has created.

Ideological Assumption IV: Assigned Responsibility vs. Self-Motivation

The work-market ideology operates on the belief that people would chose not to work if given that choice. Of course, this would be catastrophic to all the other assumptions that form the basis of a work-market culture. Therefore, an image of the good life must constantly be dangled in front of people in the classic carrot-and-the-stick pose. The subliminal message becomes one of believing that work is a sacrifice or cost for wanting to obtain this good life. The only way to insure that people will continue to believe in this message is to impose carefully structured incentives, audits, and sanctions within work and responsibility. Responsibility to one's work (and ultimately to the market in the role of consumer) assures that the individual fits within a norm of behavior; that he moves within a set schedule, whether on or off the job; that she wears the type of clothes, speaks the type of language, eats the type of food, and seeks the types of pleasures as her peers; that he in fact conforms to modes of behavior that may be outside of his own.

The leisure ideology puts the impetus of responsibility for experiencing pleasure, for being and becoming, within the individual. It believes in the natural course of self-chosen, self-motivated activities. People constantly move toward pleasure in functioning and will seek not only a type of purposeful effort (work) but also a pleasant work-effort rhythm desired ideally without constraint of time, monetary, or other extrinsic incentives. This leisure ideology sees a natural need to structure activity/experiences, but not to police, require, or even measure or reward the yields of pleasure.

Ideological Assumption V: Productive Worth vs. Self-Worth

The work-market ideology sees the worth of man through his/her productivity. The leisure ideology lets people measure their own worth through pleasureful, self-fulfilling, self-growth experiences (whatever activities, work, education, family, recreation/play, or otherwise these experiences may engage. These are two critical assumptions to clarify.

The activities/experiences of leisure are essentially autotelic, not homotelic, which make up the motives of the work-market. Put in other words, the criteria for pleasure, fulfillment, and growth for the leisurer is essentially self-referential. The legitimacy for self-interest is certainly why 50 people engaged in an activity may be there for 50 different reasons, may experience individually a wide range of emotions from disgust, boredom, enjoyment, or ecstasy, and may leave with various personalized recollections.

The homotelic nature of the work-market, however, is designed for the growth and pleasure of mankind in general, not for the individual. Lane (1978) further clarifies this assumption: "While it is true that the market ideology licenses and legitimates self-interest, the rational behind that legitimation is the social good, indeed, not the wealth of the individual but the wealth of nations" (p. 172). The motive of the work-market society rides on the assumption that the other person, as well as the self, will gain from the availables offered. Sounding rather narcissistic, the leisure ideology may not consider another's benefits unless they contribute something to oneself. (This is perhaps why society could not survive the full quest of the leisure ideology.)

Ideological Assumption VI: Authority vs. Autonomy

When a person "works for the other guy," a sixth ideological assumption of the work-market society comes into effect. At the imposition of authority, the individual's innate autonomy is limited. It is this alienating aspect of work in a market economy that Marx wrote about. The person's time essentially is not his/her own, simply because by entering employment, the person puts him/herself at the disposal of what is good for the enterprise. What is good for enterprise is efficiency in production and output, where the worker's activities are directed, observed, evaluated, altered, and manipulated within some tolerable range under the auspices of management.

The leisure ideology strives to preserve an individual's sense of autonomy. The individual sets his/her own limits, challenges, and criteria for worth. He/she directs his/her own activity, depth of involvement, loosening of ego boundaries. The leisure ideology allows one to explore beyond his/her own limits, or to find sanctuary within simple or mediocre expressions. Although pursuit of leisure experiences may lead one closer to some desirable identity, as that identity may be defined and sold through the market media, it is the individual who acts as the final judge of an identity-worth. The leisurer can nibble with discretion as consumer of the market's ideals, or he/she can seek his/her own inner resourceful joys. Perhaps Lane (1978) best summarizes the inherent assumptive differences of these two ideologies: "The Work-Market tosses the individual into the water to learn to swim (self-reliance). The leisure culture permits him to wade into the water — if he chooses (self-development)" (p. 172).

Leisure: Functional and Definitional Dimensions

In reviewing the elements of consciousness and the effects of a work-market society, we are to a point of capsulating various functional and definitional dimensions of leisure. I have always been at variance in defining anything, especially leisure. Perhaps I am influenced by St. Augustine's comment on time: we know exactly what we mean by it until we try to define it. This seems to be the dilemma concerning leisure. Most definitions and characteristics bestowed upon leisure have an empirical sense about them that monitor a relationship not proper to the intuitive mind, but rather to the rational mind. Thus, leisure is described as unobligated time, time away from necessary duties, nonworking time, freedom from work, and even time for rest and relaxation. On the other hand, there is the strong need to view leisure in the normative sense: as an ideal toward which one should strive. It is my admission that this view is the most preferred in terms of clarifying the value and function of leisure in people's life-styles. For this reason, leisure may be likened to a personal philosophy one may have about pursuing aesthetic experiences, just as one may have convictions about love, happiness, satisfaction, or even work.

Indeed, the challenge for leisurologists, happyologists, leisure psychologists, sociologists, and anthropologists might be to reassess their traditionally rational observations about leisure and to impart functional dimensions independent yet inclusive of work-responsibility-dutifulness norms. These functions would seem to be most apparent in the qualities of the intuitive mind as it seeks a complementary flow with the rational mind.

I have come to identify leisure in the following manner (with two differently stated means to characterize its inherent qualities):

- Leisure is a stream of consciousness associated with self-determined aesthetic experiences that give one a sense of pleasure and fulfillment.
- Leisure is a desirable form of aesthetic participation for the individual — a self-determined pleasure and fulfillment that can occur in any activity/ experience — which is freely willed and hoped for.

As such, a leisure experience can be exhibited in a leisure mode of consciousness, which itself can be evident in three interrelated dimensions:

- Expositive or anticipatory dimension:
  This recognizes that leisure can be experienced simply in anticipation, preparation, daydreaming, fantasizing, expectation of some involvement, whether this involvement may be years or moments away.
- Thematic dimension:
  This depicts an actual activity involvement that is the source for experiencing, i.e. the swim for experiencing relaxation, the mountain climb for expe-

riencing eustress, etc.

- Repositive or reflective dimension:
  This recognizes that leisure can be experienced and sustained through memory, review, reflection of some involvement, whether it occurred years or just moments ago.

It is important to realize that these flowing, integrative dimensions of leisure consciousness are mutually dependent upon those qualities that make up the above "definitions" of leisure. The leisure experience, then, as a conditional, situational, motivational state of mind and being is characterized by —

1. a perceived sense of freedom;
2. a focus on what is desirable to experience;
3. a synergism of capability with opportunity and willingness;
4. self-determination;
5. hope;
6. autonomous aestheticness (what is good to express and experience for oneself).

Of course, what determines each individual's ability to express the above characteristics within any of the dimensions of leisure consciousness are at least three important factors:

1. Individual differences: Attitudes, beliefs, values, as well as physical, spiritual, mental-emotional, social factors,
2. The environmental, ecological, political, work-market set,
3. The importance of the theme (leisure experience) for the individual, as the drama is played out between the above two factors.

All of this would seem to say that leisure, as an integrative life experience, is basically "institutionally interstitial" (Ennis, 1968) and has what may be called multiple norms. Work can be very successfully separated from family, education, community, spirituality, as can any of these in turn be separated from each other in some mutually exclusive fashion. However, the concept and experience of leisure interweaves, permeates, even adds to and complements all these institutions. For this reason, leisure may be described in an absolute sense, or in relationship to the life activity associated with it at the time:

- work-leisure
- family-leisure
- recreational-leisure
- communal-leisure
- educational-leisure
- relaxing-leisure
- exercise, nutritional-leisure
- spiritual, meditational-leisure
- etc.

The suggestion that leisure is a powerfully integrative aspect of life probably does more harm than good in attempting to define it in empirical terms. Perhaps leisure is an integral part of what Bateson (1979) describes as the "pattern that connects." Therefore, it cannot be defined by what it supposedly *is* in itself, but rather by its relationship to what is aesthetic. In other words, the function of leisure rests not in a single activity but rather in the pattern of activities/experiences that instill in one a unity with what is aesthetic (self-determined pleasure and fulfillment). Recognizing the limited space to clarify what I believe are some relevant functions of leisure, I will simply offer the following list as a start:

- Leisure activities/experiences give one a heightened sense of, or movement toward, a desirable identity (Glasser, 1970).
- Leisure activities/experiences give one an increased feeling of optimism (it is good to think good thoughts, feel good feelings, do good things) (Tiger, 1979).
- Leisure activities/experiences have hedonic value.
- Leisure activities/experiences give one a heightened sense of self-expression and autonomous control (Martin, 1975; Csikszentmihalyi, 1975; Deci, 1975; Calder & Straw, 1975).
- Leisure activities/experiences offer opportunities for, but are not solely dependent on nor require, achievement learning, self-fulfillment, and self-development as standards by which to determine the value of leisure (Lane, 1978).
- Leisure activities/experiences offer a mix of challenge/striving, rest/relaxation, play/entertainment, socialization/aloneness, construction/distraction, among many other balancing involvements.
- Leisure activities/experiences allow one to explore the outer ranges of tolerance for novelty, complexity, unfamiliarity, stress, competence.
- Leisure activities/experiences insure one of a sense of privacy independent of socialization and otherwise public places and spaces.
- Leisure activities/experiences are compatible with the individual's conscience (however warped or virtuous it may be perceived by others) (Lane, 1978; Flugel, 1970).
- Leisure activities/experiences are chosen by the individual as something positive in themselves, and in which part or all of the individual's self-esteem may be committed to the involvement or its outcome.
- Leisure activities/experiences serve to tighten or loosen ego boundaries.
- Leisure activities/experiences allow an opportunity for varying levels of intimacy and satisfaction with others, oneself, or the environment.
- Leisure activities/experiences complement or compensate for other life involvements (especially work and family — see below).

That leisure exists within multiple norms and complements other life activities appears to be a major reason it is an important predictor of life satisfaction. Dubin (1956) found that for many people their leisure identities and leisure satisfactions had become central to their lives, and more important in these respects than their work. Campbell, Converse, and Rodgers (1976) similarly found that "nonworking activities" were more important than either work or family. In his report of a "New Breed of Americans," Yankelvich (1978) found that family and work have grown less important, and leisure more important. When compared as sources of satisfaction, only one of five (21%) stated work meant more to them than leisure. The majority (60%) said that while they enjoyed their work, it was not their major source of satisfaction. The other 19% could not even conceive of work as a minor source of satisfaction.

Although leisure is seen as a viable source of satisfaction, this does not mean that people are in and of themselves fully satisfied with their leisure. A U.S. Department of Commerce report (1976) found that only 58 of 100 people claim a "great deal" of satisfaction with their leisure, while the remaining 42 persons are almost split between feeling "only some" and "hardly any" satisfaction. Internationally speaking, even the Japanese government has found that over 65% of the citizenry are not satisfied with their leisure.

I have reason to believe that a blatant paradox exists in a work-market society that peddles leisure in terms of time, money, and goods; the paradox exists between the amounts of free time, money, and goods-for-pleasure people are led to believe makes up a leisure experience, and the degree of actual satisfaction they feel when leisuring or having leisured. It could very well be possible that people cannot recognize a leisure experience when they have one, or, the converse, that what they have been sold, through aducation and consumer-media hype, as to what constitutes sources for fun, enjoyment, leisure, really does not meet the deeper leisure satisfaction needs people feel. In other words, the leisure experienced is superficial, short-term, spotty — and so is the satisfaction.

The quality of one's leisure should be the primary determinant of satisfaction with leisure. For this reason, it is not enough to know *what* people try to do for leisure. It is not enough to provide counseling, guidance, or education toward potential opportunities to experience leisure. People need to know *what* the concept of leisure in their lives is all about. They need to know *why* and *what is it about* leisure that gives them vibrant satisfaction and pleasure, or conversely guilt, dis-ease, unsatisfaction. They need to know that their overall well-being is as integrally tied to their leisure as leisure is integrally tied to their well-being. They need to know that their own leisure well-being is an important means to determine how well they are assuming the responsibility to experience leisure and pleasure (what I like to call "pleisure") as the central source of life satisfaction that it has been identified to be.

LEISURE AND WELL-BEING

In spite of what appears to be rather nebulous intangible criteria by which to determine leisure satisfaction (especially by viewing leisure in the normative sense as presented above), there appears to be a developing concept that may serve well to foster sound theoretical roots for understanding people's leisure-style. The concept is that of well-being or wellness. In this section we will briefly discuss the concept of well-being and then suggest the concept of leisure well-being as means to measure people's degree of leisure consciousness, concluding by relating leisure well-being to a schema of life-style issues (borrowed from the life/work planning concepts of Bolles & Crystal) and to a suggested schema for outlining client concerns and self-care skills.

Well-Being

For most people, the quality of their life basically boils down to one issue: a sense of fulfillment (Werkmeister, 1967). When we speak about quality, we essentially step out of the traditional role of identifying *what* people do in pursuing a desirable identity, life-style, leisure-style, whatever. Instead, the focus is on the *why* and *what is it about* people's way of living that gives them vibrant satisfaction and enjoyment, or conversely, unsatisfaction, dis-ease, and discomfort.

The concept of well-being care (the more popular terms used are behavioral medicine, preventive health care, holistic health, holistic medicine, the new medicine) views the person as an integrative whole: the balance and harmony of the mind, body, and spiritual aspects of the individual with the environment, universe, others, and himself. The individual is viewed as not living in a static state; rather their well-being reflects how they see themselves as a growing, changing person.

How well and healthy a person is may be likened to viewing oneself as a human barometer that is always fluctuating between more integrative, positive levels of well-being and more segmented, negative levels of well-being. As such, the overall reading of well-being may be determined by assessing the degree of self-responsibility one assumes in five core areas (these core determinants are widely acknowledged in wellness literature, as well as in the Public Health Service's Forward Plan for 1978-1982, the enactment of Public Law 93-641, and Section 1513 of that law on the functions of Health Service Agencies):

- Fitness (physical, mental, social, spiritual)
- Stress control
- Nutritional awareness
- Environmental regard
- Self-responsibility

The quality of one's well-being — a barometer of sorts of the above determinants — is always acting in response to two universal factors:

- One's life-style (the *way* we live from moment to moment, inclusive of values, beliefs, attitudes)
- One's environment (*where* we live from moment to moment)

Stated as a simple formula:

Quality of Well-Being $=$ Quality of Life-style $+$ Quality of Environment
_(is dependent upon)

An obvious example of one aspect of well-being — stress control — may include the *way* we stay fit (an issue of life-style) to handle stress, in relationship to *where* (on the job, at home, in an emergency — in any case, an issue of environmental factors) that stress might be precipitated and occur.

It is generally agreed among well-being theorists and practitioners that each person must assume the self-responsibility to take care of him/herself. This is because each person basically has his/her own idea of what being well is.

However, it is also agreed that most persons do relatively poorly in such self-care responsibility and thus are not living as well or self-fulfilled as they report that they would like to be. Many persons could be classified as "worried well." This concept describes the majority of the population, who are actually in an early stage of illness, dis-ease, and discomfort (Tubesing, 1977). Even the American Medical Association pronounces that most people suffer from the "ills of affluence" and consequential self-indulgence and apathetic self-care. Perhaps it is the widespread occurrence of what can be termed "social iatrogenesis" — the dis-ease, discomfort, frustration, and ambivalence that makes people feel unable to cope or actively attend to their own well-being — that renders obsolete the traditional attitude that others, especially medical/psychological professionals, can keep one well.

The concept of self-responsibility for health and well-being — to "heal thyself" — then, is more than a flowery phrase. As a prosumer of helping services instead of the traditional consumer (who seems to only use the "helping care market" when low on wellness), self-care becomes a self-preservative mandate in one's quest for the hope of self-fulfillment in life.

Well-being as a helping concept attempts to relate to the individual on a nonpathological and definitely holistic human dimension. This is directly antithetical to the traditional medical/psychological practice of identifying and treating primarily the signs, symptoms, or disabilities associated with illness or disease. Vibrant wellness for the ability and condition level of the person, and not just the absence of illness and disease, is the goal of facilitators of well-being.

The processes used in well-being helping care acknowledge the failure of traditional delivery of health and educational services in providing the following for people:

• self-management skills
• risk-reduction skills
• behavioral humanism (care for *people* instead of the traditionally labelled diseases, cases, patients, diagnostic classifications, and so on)
• the fostering of an attitude of informed self-responsibility for one's health and well-being

Therefore, the term "prevention" is the central concept that ties together the processes used to allow people to take care of themselves. Secondary prevention involves the application of behavioral self-care procedures to enhance health and well-being and to prevent chronic disease, dis-ease, or disability *after* an important risk factor has been identified (such as obesity; poor cardiovascular fitness; stress-inducing environment; no "time" for leisure, relaxation, the family, etc.). Primary prevention refers to procedures to decrease the possibility of developing a risk factor. It involves giving the person enough knowledge, skills, and strategies to control the advent of any risks to desirable wellness.

In summary, well-being care essentially takes a person at any point on the scale in their life-style and gives them the awareness, knowledge, skills, resources, and strategies to take care of themselves. The principles around which this helping process is organized include the following:

1. *Holism* — there needs to be a balance and harmony within the physical, mental, social, spiritual aspects of a person's life-style, behavior, and environmental relationships.
2. *Self-responsibility* — a person has the capacity to determine his/her own level of well-being and to assume the basic responsibility to obtain or maintain it.
3. *Dis-ease, discomfort as message from within* — such messages always have a meaning first in terms of a person's inner states, then are likely to find display in overt behavior or conditions. In this sense, illness or discomfort or frustration are not necesarily bad, but rather are messages to gain information from one's chosen life-style and environment and to be used for creative growth.
4. *Provider as facilitator* — the traditional parent-child relationship of medicine, psychology, education is rejected in favor of an egalitarian one, where the client fosters an active attitude and role in learning experience/relationship with the facilitator (it is interesting to note that the word "doctor" itself derives from the Latin, *docere*, meaning "to teach"). The facilitator provides information, guidance, resources, and strategies for people to take care of themselves.
5. *Humanism* — interpersonal skills used such as intuition, caring, empathy, genuineness, inventiveness, honesty, are just as important for the facilitator as are his/her "tools of the trade."
6. *Life-style* — the way one lives in a chosen environment is a crucial factor in considering realistic and potential levels of well-being.

Without a doubt, the concept of well-being, and its corresponding and developing delivery of service (the proliferation of "wellness centers" throughout the western United States), seeks to give "power to the person" in form of prosumer autonomy, rather than to limit that power to traditional medical/health care practices and the penetrating influence of the market and media (what we may call market sovereignty). Regarding such "self-empowerment," Mahoney and Thoreson (1974) assert: "A person is really free who directs and guides his/her own actions. Looking ahead, we can predict that if more individuals could become more effective in their self-management skills, the need for professional helpers to deal with passive 'you-help-me' people might be sharply diminished" (p. 20).

Leisure Well-Being

As I have suggested earlier, the holism of leisure is not dependent upon knowing what a person does for leisure. Knowing interests can only hope to give a quantitative index of a person's leisure-style. How such involvements carry over into the optimistic pursuit of some desirable identity and fulfillment can only be left to conjecture at best. It is only by demanding a more qualitive inspection of a person's leisure-style that we may better understand how and why that person demonstrates effective responsibility and self-care for their leisure.

A search for the quality of people's leisure-style, then, would naturally seem to lead us to the concept of well-being, and in our particular case, the concept of leisure well-being. As an exhaustive search of the literature suggests (McDowell, 1976), we now know the positive impact high levels of leisure well-being have on a person's mental health (Gans, 1962; Brennecke & Amick, 1971; Martin, 1969; Gussen, 1967; Fromm, 1968; Havighurst & Feigenbaum, 1959; Havighurst, 1957; Brooks & Elliot, 1971; Kleiber, 1972; Neulinger, 1971; Moore, 1975; Spreitzer & Snyder, 1974), physical health, ability to handle stress, and ability to communicate and interact with others.

Unfortunately, we are not endowed with leisure interests, attitudes, and skills. As I have suggested, we are born with the capacity of leisure consciousness in which to experience the pleasure of leisure, but we must develop the types of responsibility (in integration with spontaneity) that can aid in obtaining and maintaining some desirable level of leisure well-being. For many people throughout their lives, the process of leisure fulfillment may be no more than flying by the seat of their pants. Such people may appear to be more the rule than the exception, simply because the influence of the work-market society engrains their concepts of leisure as a mirror image of work: They fill their so-called leisure time with obligations and tasks and "have-to's" that attitudinally resemble work. Frequently they are busy, busy, busy, rushing with a kind of hurry sickness to do this or that, to achieve, and to consume with almost blind obsession and compulsion (the psychiatric term "freizeitsuchtigkeit" describes this "free-time sickness and mania"). Many people assume that to leisure well means to store up the time and money, and these escape with both. In short, such people run their leisure by the clock and the dollar, just as they do their work.

There is some reason to believe that such people, in spite of perhaps a self-described joyous or masochistic style of living and leisuring, are not really as well as they lead others to believe. Whether leisure takes on "kamikaze" or "slothen" proportions for the individual may not seem to be the rightful concern of helping professionals. However, it should be considered whether people's involvements really do meet some inner felt needs, really do fit life-style priorities, and are deeply satisfying. Only then can we be sure that within leisure lies some potion that aids the deterministic quest for fulfillment.

Leisure well-being very simply is a measure of how well prepared we are to assume and maintain responsibility for an aesthetic, enjoyable, satisfying, healthful, and dynamic leisure-style. One's leisure well-being can also be

By developing and maintaining the proper skills, knowledge, resources, and self-responsibility in each of the four aspects of leisure well-being, one can be as well in one's leisure-style as one wants to be.

I. *COPING* with interruptive behaviors in leisure

i.e.

Boredom	Excuses	Chronic TV, Sleep
Compulsiveness	Guilt	Drink, Drugs, Spending
Unsureness	Obligation	"I Can't" Syndrome
Flightiness	Un-motivation	Unrealistic Planning
	Etc.	

II. *AWARENESS-UNDERSTANDING* of the impact of leisure upon one's life-style

A. INFLUENCE OF WORK, DUTIFULNESS, RESPONSIBILITY
B. ABILITY TO LEISURE (influence of attitudes related to sex stereotypes, aging, dying, retirement, disability and object loss, the way one was raised, and views toward money, time, health, age, locale, wellness, etc.
C. VALUE OF LEISURE (the understanding of leisure's importance in one's life-style, and why one does what they do as leisure)

III. *KNOWLEDGE* of the Breadth and Balance in —

A. LEISURE INTERESTS/DESIRES
B. RESOURCEFULNESS (both personal and community; and one's ability to plan time, money, and energies for leisure)
C. FITNESS AND WELLNESS (the role and effect of various leisure involvements on total health and well-being) including nutrition, stress control, physical conditioning, environmental regard

IV. *ASSERTION* in making time and right attitudes for leisuring

A. ASSERTING ONE'S RIGHT TO LEISURE
B. ASSERTING THE 7 LEISURE ASSERTIVE RIGHTS in a guilt-free leisure-style
    % The Right to Do Nothing
    % The Right to Procrastinate
    % The Right to Be Uncertain
    % The Right to Be Alone
    % The Right to Be Playful
    % The Right for Self-Expression
    % The Right to Be Childlike

Figure 1-1. The four aspects of *leisure well-being*.

viewed as a barometer of one's life-style and environment, the breadth and balance within that life-style and environment, and the effective self-care processes that allow leisure well-being to be obtained and maintained at desirable levels of vibrancy.

It has only been through the valued experience of interfacing with many hundreds of people's leisure concerns and joys, and through the subsequent research and theoretical formulation for the past decade, that I have come to believe that one's leisure well-being consists of four components: coping; awareness-understanding; knowledge; assertion. When we are speaking of leisure well-being, then, we are addressing ourselves to the level at which people are taking self-care and responsibility in these four areas. Figure 1-1 depicts in more detail the essential concerns within each component.

At the risk of being redundant, I would like to re-emphasize the holistic nature of the leisure experience, as depicted in these determinants of leisure well-being. It is not enough, for example, to know one's interests/desires (just one dimension of knowledge), because this may not tell me enough about that person's ability to *assert* responsibility for engaging in these interests, or even if they are aware that their attitudes toward work or achievement have influenced to some degree those involvements/desires.

I believe that, as a theoretical concept, leisure well-being has enough substance and tangibility to be worthy of further investigation and research. As such, it may also provide the foundation upon which to develop sound counseling, educational, and other helping approaches and methodolgies.

A Schema for Understanding Leisure-Style/Life-Style Issues, Self-Care Skills, and Client Concerns

Clearly, the major task in developing and maintaining a unique leisure-style and life-style appears to be one of finding the right balance between one's beliefs, actual involvements, and any intervening variables, factors, or forces (such as money, time, climate, geography, health, etc.). It is not likely, however, that people think of their leisure-style as a systematic interplay of factors until they are clearly confronted with difficulties. This last point is evident in those situations in which a rather unexpected event (loss of job, divorce, loss of spouse, disability, etc.) suddenly presents the individual with a need to adjust and adapt their leisure-style/life-style.

The work of Dr. Richard Bolles and Dr. John Crystal in the concept of life/work planning adds yet another dimension to the concepts of leisure consciousness and leisure well-being. Bolles (1978) offers a pyramid of life issues that people must confront consistently and perhaps even daily in their activities and decisions:

I would like to address this hierarchy of life-style issues within the concept of one's leisure (a point Bolles admittingly hedged on doing in his insightful book *The Three Boxes of Life*).

Bolles likens a person's sudden confrontation with life-style issues to that of a fantasy in which one goes to bed in his/her familiar room, but awakens the next morning having been transported, self and bed, into the middle of some mysterious jungle. Bolles continues:

> Now, what kinds of issues, perplexities, or problems do you have to work through? Well, the first issue — or family of issues — is one which we might title *What's Happening*? You know, the kind of questions that would naturally occur to you, right off the bat: Where am I? How did I get here? What on earth is happening? Is this truly a jungle? What kind of jungle is it? Are there dangerous beasts or people here? What kind of food or drink is available? And so forth. Your absolute first need would be to settle this question What's Happening? — or at least to get a kind of temporary "fix" on it. Until that happens, the question would preoccupy your attention, and you would be pretty well immobilized, and thus prevented from doing anything else. (p. 11)

As a life-style issue, then, "What's Happening?" becomes the first matter of business in sorting out the way we live, where we live, and the role of intervening forces. With respect to leisure, it may be accurate to say that many people do not know What's Happening. Within the free time jungle created by the work-market society, they may not know what leisure is really all about independent of escape, hurried-harriedness, frantic consuming, or boredom. The quest may be for activities we might identify as recreation, play, pleasant work, etc. but such involvements may not really allow one to inwardly touch and feel the leisure experience.

To continue with Bolles' treatise on life-style issues, he suggests that when people have, at least for the time being, gotten enough of an answer to satisfy themselves about What's Happening, they would then be able to turn their attention to the next issue — *Survival*. Within the fantasy jungle, a person would begin raising questions concerning physical survival, emotional survival, spiritual survival, even social, financial, or creative survival among perhaps others.

Again, to draw an analogy to our leisure (or the "free-time jungle"), the issue of survival seems to center around two questions:

1. How am I going to make it in leisure?
2. What's there to do?

These two questions tell us that many people must still learn, develop, and then maintain the necessary skills, knowledge, and resourcefulness to survive in leisure. Many such people are institutionalized; many are being normalized and mainstreamed within the community. Many are workaholics and busyholics who know they could not survive successfully within the leisure jungle because they never could figure out just what leisure is all about (the What's Happening? issue). Many are young children in need of leisure education; many are people seeking mid-career changes.

Only when we can be assured (1) of knowing what things are all about and (2) that we have the types of skills, knowledge, and resourcefulness to survive in the jungle of life, can we narrow the scope of our life down to what *really* is important to us. Bolles identifies this next life-style issue as *meaning and mission*, and also characterizes the variance that exists between people's unique meaning and mission:

- Some people "fly by the seat of their pants," taking in their life-style jungle day-to-day, no more, no less.
- Other people decide that it is not enough to just live and keep busy day-to-day, so they determine what kinds of things they really enjoy, and go for it.
- Still, other people (and a more narrow group) say, "It is not enough to just enjoy myself; I want to derive some meaning to my life through the things I do."
- Finally, there are those few people who characteristically possess an impassioned drive toward some ultimate goal, mission, or calling in their life.

Again, we can make an analogy of meaning and mission to one's leisure. Meaning and mission depicts direction, in short, goals, intentions, values, objectives, ambitions, targets. It can be expected, then, that there will be many people of all ages, abilities, and kind who may be lacking in some strongly identified direction in their leisure-style.

It is not enough, however, to simply identify or solve the question of meaning and mission in one's life-style jungle. There should spring out a need and desire to improve the way in which we are working toward our goals and intentions, which is the final life-style issue — *effectiveness*. This is the question of, "Am I pre-occupying myself with the sorts of activities that I really want to be doing (as opposed perhaps to ought to be doing)? If so, am I doing these things in the most effective and efficient manner possible for me?" Effectiveness is a purposeful form of self-directed questioning and clarifying of what is really important in life, and the ways and means to get there.

Quite often, people fail to take the final step to sort out their effectiveness in pursuing a desired leisure style and leisure experiences. Often, the result is a sort of flightiness characterized by a wide array of unclear or unfinished leisure goals and pursuits, or on the other hand, a type of apathy that not only permeates leisure but also other areas of life (especially family and work spheres).

If we turn our attention now to Figure 1-2, we will see the pyramidal relationship between Bolles' life-style issues and leisure. I would also like to draw attention to the "well-being self-care processes" depicted to the right and to clarify the relationship to the idea of self-responsibility.

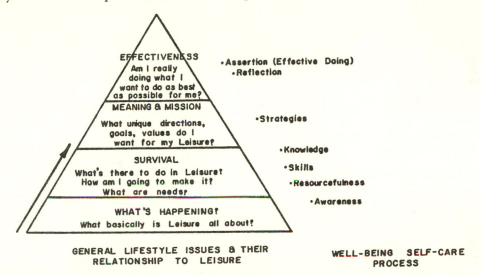

Figure 1-2. Relationship of leisure to life-style issues and well-being self-care. (Adapted from R.N. Bolles, *The Three Boxes of Life*, 1978, Three Speed Press, Berkeley.)

We learned earlier that effective levels of well-being are directly related to the degree of responsibility one wishes to assume for one's self to manage oneself. Free will admittingly is a rather nebulous deterministic inner concept when considering this responsibility. Therefore, when we speak about self-care we are talking about a process that entails seven essential and interrelated steps:

The Self-Care Process

1. Awareness
2. Knowledge
3. Skills
4. Resourcefulness
5. Strategies
6. Assertion (actually doing)
7. Reflection

In respect to life-style/leisure-style issues, the following relationships can be drawn:

- When we ask What's Happening? we are responding to our initial *awareness* of the object of inquiry. We may not know how to deal with the subject of our awareness (for example boredom, guilt, poor cardiovascular fitness, or the need for more time) until we consider the issue of survival.
- When we ask "What are my needs?" (in order to survive in some respect socially, physically, etc.), we realize they are really dependent upon adequate *knowledge, skills,* and *resourcefulness* in obtaining and maintaining them.
- When we define our needs in respect to some direction (based upon preferred goals, objectives, intentions, values), some meaning and mission, then we focus our attention upon those selected *strategies* in which to carry out our knowledge, skills, and resourcefulness.
- Finally, the effectiveness of our direction can only be determined through actual *assertion* and ultimately *reflection* about the direction pursued. Only at this point can one determine what parts of the self-care process may need to be returned in order to assume further responsibility.

Within a helping process, it becomes important to determine where a person may in fact be "stuck" regarding the above four life-style/leisure-style issues and their own self-care ability. Only then can the role of the facilitator become more clear.

For the counselor-educator, the concerns of the individual surrounding life-style/leisure-style and self-care responsibility may be viewed from several perspectives:

- First, a person is always making decisions based upon informed CHOICES and preferences — what *resources* to use, which *skills* to develop or use in a particular situation, what *knowledge* is important to acquire or use, which *strategies* are likely to be most effective, what ways are the best to behave, think, and feel.
- Second, a person is also always desiring to CHANGE aspects of themselves in relationship to their daily activities — the decisions they make, the feelings or thoughts they have or express, their relationships with others, their skills, knowledge, resourcefulness, the way they use strategies, and so on.
- Third, every person may be viewed in any involvement as always being in a state of BUILDING COMPETENCIES (and maintaining them) around which to assert themselves, carry out skills, knowledge, resourcefulness, relate to others, and achieve a feeling of self-worth and fulfillment.
- Fourth, at times a person may express the need to REDUCE CONFUSION they may have about themselves or others, if only to ensure some order in their life.

The pioneering work of Leona Tyler and her associates has led to the identification of the above concerns that an individual may have (and ultimately bring to counseling) as the "Four C's": Concerns about Choice; Concerns about Change; Concerns about Competency Building; Concerns about Confusion Reduction (Gilmore, 1973). This simplistic typology recognizes that regardless of which level of life-style issues or the self-care process people may be, they may be faced with one or more concerns affecting their ability to assume further responsibility for their life. Figure 1-3 briefly outlines these four general areas of concerns.

I. *CHOICE* (concerned with)

% Information Sources — Knowing/learning what is out there, how to get to it and use it
% Prioritizing and Valuing Choices/Decisions — Knowing what is important to value
% Knowing Alternatives and Consequences and Risks of Choices

II. *CHANGE* (concerned with)
% Interpersonal Communication/Relationships
% Life-style Direction and Thrust
% Effective Coping Skills and Problem Dealing
% Understanding Attitudes, Needs, Values, Beliefs, etc.

III. *COMPETENCY-BUILDING* (concerned with)

% Development of Skills, Knowledge, Resourcefulness
% Effective use of Skills, Knowledge, Resources
% Ability to Relate to Others and One's Environment

IV. *CONFUSION REDUCTION* (concerned with)

% Intensive Personality Reorganization
% Short-term Crisis Intervention
% Other- and Self-Preservation (Regarding health, welfare, safety, etc.)

Figure 1-3. Four general areas of client concerns. (Adapted from S. Gilmore, *The Counselor in Training*, 1973, Appleton-Century-Crofts, Englewood Cliffs, N.J.)

It is my opinion that, no matter what the specific topic of counseling, whether it be vocational, marital, sex, nutrition and fitness, or even leisure, it is important that the helper cue in on which area(s) of concern the person is presenting. With specific reference to leisure and the concept of leisure counseling, a knowledge of these four areas of concerns may leave us with the following assumptions upon which to offer help:

1. Clients with primarily *choice* concerns about their leisure-style (refer to Fig. 1-3 for possible dimensions involving choice) may benefit best by appropriate helping processes involving resource guidance.
2. Clients with primarily *change* concerns about leisure behavior and leisure-

style direction may benefit best from approaches that focus on life-style awareness and behavior change.

3. Clients with primarily *competency building* needs about leisure skills, knowledge, and resourcefulness may benefit best from educational and skills development processes.

4. Clients with need for *confusion reduction* (generally apparent in severe behavior and emotional disorientation) may *not* be responsive at all to any interventions or help with their leisure behavior.

From the above we can conclude that, where the person's leisure well-being is concerned, much of the helping process is generated around leisure concerns of choice, change, and/or competency building, as influenced by where the person stands in terms of their self-care ability. Two examples may clarify this last point. First, before embarking on helping the client in matters of *choice* of appropriate leisure involvements, the helper should understand that if the client has little or no personal/community *resourcefulness* (an issue of survival in the leisure jungle), then any *knowledge* of leisure interests may be useless. In a second example, if the helper inadvertently assumes that the client only needs help with choice matters when in fact behavior change or skills development concerns are more immediate, then he may actually be doing more harm than good to the client.

It is not without accident that the pyramid of life and leisure issues, the well-being self-care process, and the four areas of client concerns fit well into a schema that integrates with the present knowledge of specific leisure concerns people may have, and the subsequent leisure counseling process(es). I have attempted to depict the relationship of all these dimensions in Figure 1-4. The re-

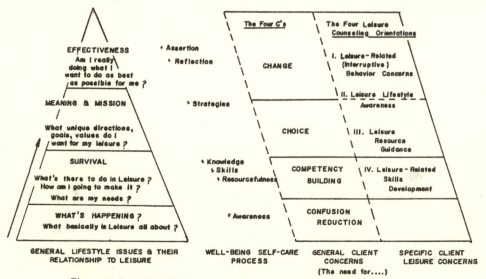

Figure 1-4. A simplistic schema for understanding client concerns.

mainder of this chapter will be devoted to the concept of leisure counseling and its apparent four orientations.

LEISURE COUNSELING

An objective for the counselor/helper of people's leisure concerns follows:

> The facilitation of an individual (or group) toward effective self-responsibility in obtaining or maintaining desired levels of well-being in his/her (their) life-style.

Within this statement we can basically deduce the following:

- First, desired level of leisure well-being is the responsibility of the client.
- Second, the counselor/helper is expected to use an appropriate methodology within his/her helping skills *and* knowledge of the concept of leisure.
- Third, the counselor/helper is assumed to be operating from some theoretical base about the nature of man, behavioral change, and counseling.

It is the second and third dimensions in the counseling process above that I want to address in this section.

In my original analysis of the literature on leisure counseling in the mid-1970s (see McDowell, 1975, 1976, 1977a, 1977b), it was necessary to devise some sort of typology to make sense of the many directions practitioners and armchair theorists were taking. It became clear that leisure counseling was being offered under several pretenses, each of which demanded the helper to "orient" to the various leisure needs of the client, and then to muster-up some facilitative strategy. The result of my research indicated that leisure counseling could be characterized according to four orientations. These four orientations can be depicted below in relationship to the general focus of concerns (see also the right-hand of Fig. 1-4):

Leisure Counseling Orientation	*General Focus of Concern*
I. Leisure-Related (Interruptive)	Primarily Change
II. Leisure Life-style Awareness	Primarily Change-Choice
III. Leisure Resource Guidance	Primarily Choice
IV. Leisure-Related Skills Concerns	Primarily Competency-Building

In a more specific analysis and comparison of typical client concerns in each of the above areas (McDowell, 1979) I would like to refer you to Figures 1-5 and 1-6. As may be evident and expected, the concept of leisure and the concerns people may have about this important area of their lives are comprehensive and demanding. Furthermore, it would seem paramount that if any effective intervention on behalf of any helpers is offered, it would need to stem from a purposeful conceptual and facilitative base.

Actually, the facilitative direction and methodology used in leisure counsel-

L. C.
ORIENTATION

I BEHAVIORAL	• NEED TO DEVELOP EFFECTIVE COPING SKILLS AND PROBLEM SOLVING ABILITY TO DEAL WITH CHRONIC OR EXCESSIVELY EXPRESSED LEISURE-RELATED BEHAVIOR CONCERNS, SUCH AS: guilt, boredom, obligation, social isolation, unsureness, procrastination, obsessiveness, impatience, nervousness, lack of assertiveness, flightiness, anxiety, low frustration tolerance, unrealistic "ideal" formulation, escape involvements such as chronic TV watching, sleeping, drinking, buying, etc.
II LIFESTYLE AWARENESS	• NEED TO UNDERSTAND RELATIONSHIP BETWEEN LEISURE AND OTHER LIFESTYLE CONCEPTS (Vocation, Family, Education, Spirituality, Community) • NEED TO UNDERSTAND AGING AND SOCIAL PROCESSES AND EFFECTS ON LEISURE/LIFESTYLE • NEED TO UNDERSTAND ATTITUDES, BELIEFS, VALUES, AND IDENTIFY PERCEPTION ABOUT LEISURESTYLE • NEED TO CONCEPTUALIZE AND IDENTIFY WITH PERSONAL LEISURE/LIFESTYLE NEEDS • NEED TO MAKE LIFESTYLE ADJUSTMENTS BASED UPON PERCEIVED FELT DIFFICULTIES (retirement, career change, object loss, marriage or divorce, etc.)
III RESOURCE GUIDANCE	• NEED TO KNOW LEISURE INTERESTS (past, present, desired) • NEED TO KNOW WHAT TO DO WITH FREETIME • NEED TO KNOW WHERE TO ENGAGE IN RECREATIONAL OPPORTUNITIES • NEED TO KNOW WHEN OPPORTUNITIES ARE AVAILABLE • NEED TO KNOW COST, EQUIPMENT, AVAILABILITY • NEED TO KNOW COMMUNITY/PERSONAL RESOURCES

IV
SKILLS DEVELOPMENT
	• LACK OF, OR NEED FOR REMEDIATION OF, SKILLS IN:
	  • APPROPRIATE SOCIAL BEHAVIOR, GROOMING, ASSERTIVENESS
	  • ACTIVITY ANALYSIS (effects of certain types on physical wellness)
	  • TIME MANAGEMENT, BUDGETING, PLANNING
	  • EFFECTIVE USE OF COMMUNICATION SYSTEMS AND TRANSPORTATION
	  • COORDINATED MOTOR MOVEMENT
	  • GENERALLY ACCEPTED LIFETIME RECREATION EXPERIENCES AND CONCEPTS AND ACTIVITIES

Figure 1-5. Comparision of typical client concerns.

ing to date has been perhaps needlessly broad, if not flighty. The field is inundated with "cookbook" approaches with little or no understanding of the theoretical ingredients indicative of the development of sound counseling processes. Leisure counseling has been depicted in several ways: from systems approaches to humanistic existentialism; from activity selection to therapy; from a focus on affective dimensions to a focus on cognitive or behavioral dimensions or some combination thereof; and from consulting to lecturing within defined pedagogical processes.

The systems approaches seem the most vague in terms of theoretical ideology, yet have received wide support (Gunn, 1977; Hayes, 1977; Burk [in McDowell, 1976]; Mundy, 1976; Joswiak, 1975). Humanistic leisure counseling processes, however, have also drawn their array of supporters. Gunn (1976) has utilized Gestalt therapy. Gunn (1977) and Ryan (1977) have explored the use of assertive training. Montagnes (1977) reports use of reality therapy. Rule

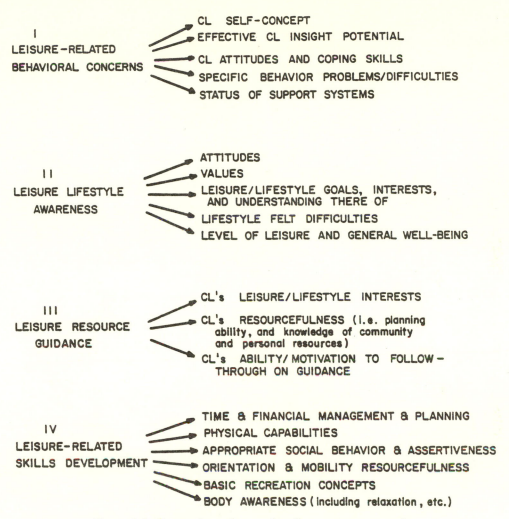

Figure 1-6. Comparison of counselor-client assessment needs.

and Stewart (1977) have promoted Adlerian processes. Gunn (1976, 1978) has extensively explored the use of transactional analysis. Many professionals have developed the use of values clarification principles (McDowell, 1976; Woodburn, 1978; Pellett-Johnson & Zoerink, 1977; Connolly, 1977; Gunn, 1977; Davis, 1976; McLellan, 1977). In another distinct, yet apparently theoretically unfounded, dimension, activity selection and guidance approaches have found their share of proponents (Overs, 1974; Wilson et al., 1975).

Clearly, the quandry that presently exists in leisure counseling is not so much which facilitative methodology is useful in approaching people's leisure concerns, but rather upon what theoretical bases any methodology can unify itself. This inquiry would naturally lead us into depicting the relationship between counseling theory and practice. Such a relationship, as suggested by

Hansen, Stevic, and Warner (1972), might consider the following levels:

> Level I — General theories of human development and personality (most abstract)
> Level II — Theories of behavior change
> Level III — Theories of counseling
> Level IV — Counseling practice (most concrete)

At present, leisure counseling may be most guilty of being attracted to the icing that counseling practice offers atop this predominantly theoretical cake. Although actual counseling practice entails only a fractional component or level of overall counseling methodology, today's "leisure counselor's" have become mostly attracted to the "sweetness" of techniques at the expense of questioning their own assumptive base upon which to offer any techniques at all.

I have spent almost a decade now "playing around" with the four various leisure counseling orientations — finding one particularly more useful than another with a particular client, or finding the need to integrate two or more into an effective helping process. Early in my practice, although my inner assumptive base about the nature of man never changed, when I focused with a particular orientation it received an added dimension about man's nature and the helping process apparently helpful to effectuate change. Admittingly, in the past few years, the concept of leisure well-being has even more dramatically clarified my own assumptive base upon which to offer help, as has the refreshing concepts of a leisure consciousness.

It might be useful to share, from my knowledge of the use of these four leisure counseling orientations among practitioners and theorists, some purely intuitive perceptions about their theoretical foundations. Figure 1-7 identifies these theoretical notions within a suggested matrix. I will simply expand on each orientation below.

Leisure-Related (Interruptive) Behavior Concerns

It seems apparent that this orientation derives from learning theory perspective of man. Four essential characteristics seem obvious:

1. Man's personality is determined largely by his interaction with the environment (social and physical). Viewed as somewhat reactive in nature, man relates to stimuli as they are presented to him and thus forms patterns of behavior and personality.
2. The individual learns through experience that certain situations will present certain satisfiers and dis-satisfiers. Depending on how the individual perceives their importance, he/she will adopt a framework of goal direction toward such satisfiers and dis-satisfiers.
3. Through experience, the individual develops different patterns of needs and motives, which lead to different patterns of behavior (see Rotter, 1964).
4. Individual differences develop because individuals perceived a specific situ-

ation differently in relationship to their needs hierarchy.

The basis for the structure of a person's behavior, then, can be seen in a learned pattern of responses to environmental stimuli. The behavior patterns develop from early childhood in large part by the kinds of reinforcements the individual receives. We can expect, then, that maladaptive behavior is different from normal behavior, not in the manner in which it was learned but only to the degree that the behavior is typical or maladaptive to observing others or to the person himself.

The implications to leisure seem obvious. We might suggest that just as he may learn the value of work, leisure, play, and other aspects of life, so the individual also learns various coping means to relate to these entities. The consequences of a work-market society, with the penetrating influence of a work-responsibility-dutifulness ideology and consciousness, affects leisure well-being and especially the ability to *cope* with dimensions such as guilt, obligation, boredom and the like. The goal of counseling, then, must be to help the individual resolve the concern(s) unique to his/her situation and to develop heuristic strategies useful in obtaining and maintaining desired levels of leisure well-being.

Leisure Life-Style Awareness

This orientation appears to adopt a view of man from the position of self-theorists. The conscious and thoughtful process that is man's becoming is perceived to be an awareness-seeking one. Consequently, one's lifelong search is to understand the meaning of various life experiences such as aging, social relationships, work, play, family, leisure, and so on. Only then do personally unique life-styles develop that reflect some understanding or lack of understanding of the perceived interrelationships of life-style components.

Man is viewed as a being in the process of becoming, a being that is basically good and with the rational potential for controlling and changing his own behavior and destiny. The holistic dimension of this orientation assumes that man is always actively involving himself in introspective measures of his relationship with life-style issues. As such, leisure well-being is not some isolated concept, but it is intricately connected to family, education, vocation, community, and one's sense of spirituality.

This orientation also best depicts man's movement toward the ultimate goal of self-fulfillment. He is seen as capable of evaluating his own life-style and then acting accordingly in some derived optimistic sense. Unfortunately, such idealistic optimism does not assure that the self-fulfilling drive is without difficulties. For this reason, awareness processes focus on clarifying dis-eases, discomforts, frustrations, myths and misbeliefs, and questions people may have about their leisure and its role in their life-style. The methodology is clearly preventive and educative as it attempts to elicit self-insight about one's feelings,

Levels of Counseling Theory-to-Practice Development

LEISURE COUNSELING ORIENTATION		
I **Leisure-Related Behavioral Problems**	Both normal & maladaptive behaviors are learned by an individual through his interaction with his environment.	Man learns new and appropriate behaviors as these behaviors are deemed acceptable to self and significant others.	Development of heuristic problem-solving abilities can allow individual to rationally interact or to cope with his/her environment.
II **Leisure Life-style Awareness**	Man is being in the process of becoming.	Man seeks to understand the meaning of various life experiences such as leisure, work, play, aging, social relationships, etc.	Self-fulfilling-actualizing life-style can be developed based upon providing learning opportunities for understanding the interrelationships of life-style components.
III **Leisure Resource Guidance**	Leisure activity involvement results from man always steering his efforts in the right direction, morally right for himself and society.	Man will seek leisure activity as form of aesthetic participation for his well-being.	Demand for leisure resource consumption exists, and proper guidance can help the client to fulfill desired interests.

Levels of Counseling Theory-to-Practice Development (continued)

IV Leisure skills Development	Individual responsibility must be assumed for structuring and pursuing leisure experiences/activities.	Man uses adaptive skills to successfully pursue varying leisure interests.	Development of leisure-related skills can allow the client to plan, initiate, and evaluate enjoyable leisure pursuits.
	Level I General Theory of Human Development and Personality	Level II Theory of Behavioral Change	Level III Theory of Counseling

Figure 1-7. A suggested matrix for integrating leisure counseling practice with theory.

knowledge, skills, strategies, and effectiveness in caring for leisure-style needs. The major helping assumption is that the person has the capacity and motivation to gain the necessary awareness to adjust his/her leisure-style accordingly. He/she is the actor in the life-style/leisure-style drama and therefore assumes an active role in any helping processes.

Leisure Resource Guidance

Glasser (1970, 1976) suggests a somewhat distorted, romantic view of natural man in this orientation. This view is primarily concerned with the what, where, and right directions for man to pursue his desires. Accordingly, it suggests that man's endowment of abilities and motivations, if allowed free play, will infallibly guide him toward fulfillment. This, of course, assumes that man will not depart from an original natural condition — a condition of goodness and happiness, which infers that man is happy because he is good. In short, it is man's understanding of his inner nature that drives him toward his desires.

It should be pointed out that the basic premise of this romantic position would appear to have total justification if it were not for the conditions and demands of modern industrial society; thus enters the distortion of natural man by the superimposed demands of an inner mechanized being who is controlled by major mechanized messages or commands that permeate today's work-market society. In the first part of this chapter, we explored an array of ideological assumptions and the influence of mass media in creating what I consider to be this "human robot." For such a human robot (who, in spite of inner feelings, actually seems most regulated by the outer commands of the good life), behavior erroneously equates happiness with *what* is good to have or do, and not with *why* it is good to have or do in the first place.

This orientation, therefore, would seem to address the uncritical consumer role of people in their pursuit of leisure experiences and products. For this reason, I suggest that leisure resoure guidance should align itself with the demand-and-supply school of leisure thought (in other words, the empirical position). The theoretical premise upon which to base counseling and guidance appears to be this: A demand exists to fill free time and society should arrange to meet the demand.

Admittingly, the theoretical stance of this orientation is simplistic, but it is valid. It acknowledges leisure as a residual life activity in which the person makes leisure choices from criteria:

1. The extent to which the activities are approved by others, and the indications, as the individual interprets them, of what society expects of him in terms of an approved identity.
2. A selection of those leisure activities that will confirm and enhance, to himself, the perception the individual has of a desired identity.

By residual life activity, we may assume that the client and/or helper view leisure within the narrow perspective of simply something used to fill a time frame need, and not as something intricately connected to other aspects of life (such as family, vocation, community, education, etc.) and well-being. In short, then, the objective of leisure resource guidance is to guide the individual into consumptive states of leisure satisfaction. It its purist form, the processes used may be like a yellow pages directory, in which the counselor merely plugs the individual-consumer into activity resources with minimal concern about possible affective sources of the original demand for help, or the anxieties associated with it. In terms of leisure well-being, the counselor and client may be more concerned with knowledge aspects of interests and resourcefulness. Little need is assumed to exist in examining coping or awareness-understanding dimensions.

Leisure-Related Skills Development

This fourth leisure counseling orientation may be suggested to view man's nature as basically deterministic, in which skills determine concomitant behavior or action. From this perspective, the degree to which man adapts to the environment is closely related to the types and levels of his adaptive skills. Each person, then, has a right to be exposed to opportunities to develop, rehearse, perfect, and re-learn skills for living and leisuring. Only then can responsibility be expected to be assumed by the individual for identifying desirable life directions and leisure experiences.

I have discussed what I consider to be merely intuitive ideas about the theoretical stance the four leisure counseling orientations appear to assume. With more practical implications an obvious concern as well, I offer in Figures 1-8 and 1-9, respectively, a comparison among the orientations of suggested counselor facilitating focus and apparent counseling resources needed. Indeed, the challenge among theorists and practitioners would be to meld the innovative ideas of leisure consciousness, leisure well-being, and leisure counseling with the salient features of more traditional theories and methodologies of counseling and psychology, without destroying the salient and beautiful dimensions of leisure itself. For this reason, perhaps the greater demand for counseling professionals is to get in touch with the penetrating effect leisure has on their own philosophy of life. Only then can empathic concern be shown for a person who presents leisure concerns of their own.

CONCLUSION

There is the risk of viewing leisure in the ethereal: as some all-encompassing ideal that, like self-actualization, is difficult to conceive and explain, and even more difficult to experience. Indeed, it is difficult to imagine that the baseball fan with a hotdog in one hand and a beer in the other sees

I **BEHAVIORAL**	• Close, interpersonal, empathic relationship with CL • Active role in formulating problem / goal descriptions and problem-solving principles • Clarifying / restructuring role in communicating with CL • Supportive and confrontive • Use of appropriate facilitative methodology
II **LIFESTYLE** **AWARENESS**	• Active role in initial individual/group facilitation of subject/topic/discussion • Clarifying role, both supportive and confrontive, in non-evaluative framework • Initiating role in experimental, awareness-raising, and practical self-help leisure learning exercises • Andragogical posture
III **RESOURCE** **GUIDANCE**	• Active role in leisure interest exploration • Active role in leisure interest planning • Active role in assessment and dissemination of leisure opportunities in community • Active role in referral processes and inter-agency coordination & follow-up
IV **SKILLS** **DEVELOPMENT**	• Active role in identifying key developmental/normalizing concerns of CL; Prioritizing concerns; And identifying goal attainment criteria • Active role in establishing effective processes which will provide realistic and normalizing movement toward alleviation of concerns • Supportive/confrontive role in evaluating CL's development • Continued awareness of appropriate inclusion of other leisure counseling orientations

ISSUES

1) Note additive effect of counselor facilitating roles as orientations merge and synergize!!

2) Does counselor facilitating focus = Trained skills needed?

Figure 1-8. Comparison of counselor facilitating focus.

I BEHAVIORAL	• THIS IS A HIGHLY VERBAL-ORIENTED ORIENTATION, AND THUS REQUIRES WELL-DEVELOPED LISTENING AND HELPER FACILITATIVE SKILLS/TECHNIQUES • COUNSELOR ACCESS TO MATERIALS AND METHODOLOGY IN OTHER L.C. ORIENTATIONS, IF ANY INTEGRATION OF ORIENTATIONS IS DEEMED NECESSARY AND APPROPRIATE
II LIFESTYLE AWARENESS	• COMPREHENSIVE NUMBERS OF FACILITATIVE "HERE-AND-NOW" CLARIFICATION EXERCISES • COMPREHENSIVE NUMBERS OF SELF-HELP MATERIALS, BOTH PAPER AND VERBAL-THOUGHT ORIENTED • COUNSELOR WRITTEN METHODOLOGY (purpose, objectives, etc.) FOR A COHESIVE NUMBER OF LEISURE/LIFESTYLE TOPIC AND DISCUSSION AREAS
III RESOURCE GUIDANCE	• VARIOUS TYPES AND STYLES OF INTEREST SURVEYS • INTERVIEW FORMS • REFERRAL FORMS • LEISURE INTEREST PROFILE SHEETS • COMMUNITY LEISURE RESOURCE FILE; GENERAL LEISURE ACTIVITY EXPLORATION FILE AND MATERIALS; ACCESS TO LEISURE RESOURCE INFORMATION
IV SKILLS DEVELOPMENT	• COMPREHENSIVE NUMBER OF LEISURE-RELATED SKILLS ASSESSMENT AND EVALUATION METHODOLOGY • FILE OF, OR ACCESS TO EFFECTIVE RESOURCES IN COMMUNITY WHICH ALLOW APPROPRIATE INTEGRATION OF CL WITH OPPORTUNITIES TO PRACTICE SKILLS • KNOWLEDGE OF EFFECTIVE PROCESSES/ACTIVITIES BY WHICH SKILLS CAN BE OBTAINED, REHEARSED, ETC.

ISSUES

1) NOTE COMPLEXITY OF SERVICE DELIVERY AS ORIENTATIONS MERGE

2) THE MORE VARIED THE CLIENTELE, THE MORE BREADTH OF RESOURCES AND STAFF-TRAINED SKILLS NEEDED (assuming merging of L.C. orientations)

Figure 1-9. Comparison of counseling resources needed.

leisure from the point of view of a type of consciousness or even from a level of well-being. Leisure for the masses is what the mass media sells it to be; it is what religious dogma degrades it to be; it is what the work-market society rewards it to be. All this may be a far cry from the self-fulfilling concept of leisure that I have presented in this chapter.

Again, the challenge for professional helpers is to determine how we, as a consort of theorists and practitioners, wish to view leisure. Even as we live in a culture dictated by time, money, work, consumptive commands, and "aducation," we carry within us a birthright link with an intuitive, metaphoric consciousness. We can decide to link leisure with this type of consciousness or to marry it to the belief of what is rational to want (i.e., to want more time, more money, less work but more responsibility, more things, more love, and so on). In any case, we must realize that the dilemma for the individual rests between his/her will for aesthetic pleasure and his/her will for reason. The challenge is to find the balance between them.

I am immediately suspect of those who call themselves leisure counselors. I just don't believe that we really know enough yet about the concept of leisure to qualify to help others. We can lend a genuine, empathic ear, but for some reason listening to the leisure concerns of others always cues us in to our own puzzling concerns about leisure. We can learn as we go along, but that would be the same route psychology and biology had followed until recently: viewing the mind without a brain, and the brain without a mind. I believe that the psychocultural and psychobiological implications for the study of leisure may give us some deeply needed and rooted concepts upon which to develop a science of leisure, and an art of addressing people's leisure concerns. There could be a definite link between the neurochemical transmission of feelings of well-being, pleasure, and self-will and the leisure experience. I would personally not want to rule out the innovative new ground and possible dimensions from which to view leisure. It would confirm my notion and belief that leisure is indeed an inner experience linked to our innate inner resources, and need not be subjected to, nor receive its entire worth from, our ideas about work, time, money, and consumption of the good life.

REFERENCES

Bateson, G. *Mind and nature, a necessary unity*. New York: Bantam Books, Inc., 1979.

Berelson, B. In the presence of culture. *Public Opinion Quarterly*, 1964, *28*, 1-12.

Bolles, R.N. *The three boxes of life*. Berkeley: Three Speed Press, 1978.

Brennecke, J.H., & Amick, R.G. *The struggle of significance*. Beverly Hills, CA: Glencoe Press, 1971.

Brooks, J.B., & Elliot, D.M. Prediction of psychological adjustment at age thirty from leisure time activities and satisfactions. *Human Development*, 1971, *14*, 51-61.

Bruner, J.S. *On knowing: Essays for the left hand*. New York: Atheneum, 1973.

Burk, G. A community-based model for the delivery of leisure counseling services to special populations. In C. F. McDowell, Jr., *Leisure counseling: selected lifestyle processes.* University of Oregon: Center of Leisure Studies, 1976.

Calder, B.J., & Straw, B.M. Self-perception in intrinsic and extrinsic motivation. *Journal of Personality and Social Psychology*, 1975, *31*, 599-605.

Campbell, A., Converse, P., & Rodgers, W.L. *The quality of American life.* New York: Russell Sage Foundation, 1976.

Connolly, M.L. Leisure counseling: A values clarification and assertive training approach. In A. Epperson, P.A. Witt, & G. Hitzhusen (Eds.), *Leisure counseling: An aspect of leisure education.* Springfield, Il: Charles C Thomas, Publisher, 1977.

Csikszentmihalyi, M. *Beyond boredom and anxiety.* San Francisco: Josey -Bass, 1975.

Davis, J. Valuing: A requisite for education for leisure. Leisure Today supplement to *Journal of Physical Education and Recreation*, 1976, March, 30-31.

Deci, E.L. *Intrinsic motivation.* New York: Plenum, 1975.

Dubin, R. Industrial workers' worlds: A study of central life interests of industrial workers. *Social Problems*, 1956, *3*, 131-142.

Ennis, P.H. The definition of leisure. In E.B. Sheldon & W.E. Moore (Eds.) *Indicators of social change.* New York: The Russell Sage Foundation, 1968.

Flugel, J.C. *Man, morals and society.* New York: International University Press, 1970.

Fromm, E. *Escape from freedom.* New York: Holt, Rinehart, and Winston, 1968.

Gans, H.J. Outdoor recreation and mental health. In *Trends in American living and outdoor recreation* (Volume 22 of the Report of the Outdoor Recreation Resources Review Commission). Washington, D.C.: U.S. Government Printing Office, 1962.

Gilmore, S. *The counselor in training.* Englewood Cliffs, N.J.: Appleton-Century-Crofts (Prentice-Hall), 1973.

Glasser, R. *Leisure: Penalty or prize?* London: Macmillan, 1970.

Glasser, R. Leisure policy, identity and work. In J.T. Haworth & M.A. Smith (Eds.), *Work and leisure.* Princeton, N.J.: Princeton Book Co., 1976.

Goleman, D., & Davidson, R.J. (Eds.) *Consciousness: Brain, states of awareness, and mysticism.* New York: Harper & Row, 1979.

Gunn, S.L. Leisure counseling: An analysis of play behavior and attitudes using transactional analysis and gestalt awareness. In G. Hitzhusen & G. Robb (Eds.), *Expanding horizons in therapeutic recreation III.* Columbia, Missouri: Department of Recreation and Park Administration, Technical Education Services, 1975.

Gunn, S.L., & Peterson, C. Removing blocks to play behavior: A gestalt approach to leisure counseling. *Leisurability*, 1976, *4*, 27 + .

Gunn, S.L. Leisure counseling using techniques of assertive training and values clarification. In G. Hitzhusen (Ed.), *Expanding horizons in therapeutic recreation IV.* Columbia, Mo.: Department of Recreation and Park Administration, Technical Education Services, 1977.

Gunn, S.L. A systems approach to leisure counseling. Leisure Today supplement to *Journal of Physical Education and Recreation*, 1977, April, 8-11.

Gunn, S.L. Structural analyses of play behavior: Pathological implications. In G. Hitzhusen (Ed.), *Expanding horizons in therapeutic recreation V.* Columbia, Mo.: Department of Recreation and Park Administration, Technical Education Services, 1978.

Gussen, J. The psychodynamics of leisure. In P.A. Martin (Ed.), *Leisure and mental health: A psychiatric point of view.* Washington, D.C.: American Psychological Association, May, 1967.

Hansen, J.C., Stevic, R.R., & Warner, R.W. *Counseling: Theory and process.* Boston: Allyn and Bacon, 1972.

Havighurst, R.J. The leisure activities of the middle-aged. *American Journal of Sociology,* 1959, *64*, 396-404.

Hayes, G. Leisure education and recreation counseling. In D.M. Comptom & J.E. Goldstein (Eds.), *Perspectives of leisure counseling.* Arlington, Va.: National Recreation and Park Association, 1977.

Joswiak, K. *Leisure counseling program material for the developmentally disabled.* Washington, D.C.: Hawkins & Associates, 1975.

Kleiber, D. *Free time and sense of competence in college students.* Unpublished doctoral dissertation. University of Texas at Austin, 1972.

Lane, R.E. The regulation of experience: Leisure in a market society. *Social Science Information,* 1978, *2,* 147-184.

Levy-Agresti, J., & Sperry, R. Differential perceptual capacities in major and minor hemispheres. *Proceedings of the National Academy of Sciences,* 1968, *61,* 11-16.

Locke, E. A simple solution to job motivation and more money. *Psychology Today,* 1980, *13(12),* p. 16.

Mahoney, M., & Thoreson, C. *Self-control: Power to the person.* Monterey, Ca.: Brooks/Cole, 1974.

Martin, A.R. Idle hands and giddy minds. *American Journal of Psychoanalysis,* 1969, *2,* 147-156.

Martin, A.R. Leisure and our inner resources. *Parks and Recreation,* 1975, *March,* 1a-16a.

Maslow, A.H. *The psychology of science.* Chicago: Regnery, 1969.

McDowell, C.F. Leisure counseling: Review of emerging concepts and orientations. *Journal of Leisurability,* 1975, *2(4),* 19-26.

McDowell, C.F. Leisure counseling: Professional considerations for therapeutic creation. *Journal of Physical Education and Recreation,* 1976, *47(1),* 26-27.

McDowell, C.F. Integrating theory and practice in leisure counselng. Leisure Today supplement to *Journal of Physical Education and Recreation,* 1977, *April,* 27-30.

McDowell, C.F. *Leisure counseling: Selected lifestyle processes.* University of Oregon, Eugene: Center of Leisure Studies, 1976.

McDowell, C.F. Analysis of leisure counseling models and integrative possibilities. In D.M. Comptom & J.E. Goldstein (Eds.), *Perspectives of leisure counseling.* Arlington, Va.: National Recreation and Parks Association, 1977.

McDowell, C.F. *Leisure counseling issues: Reviews, overviews and previews.* Speech at the National Leisure Counseling Forum, Oglebay Park, Wheeling, West Virginia, 1979.

McDowell, C.F. Leisure well-being: A counseling mandate? *Leisure Information Newsletter,* 1979, *6(1),* 6-8.

McLellan, R. Valuing: A necessary phase of leisure counseling. Leisure Today supplement to *Journal of Physical Education and Recreation,* 1977, April, 31-32.

Montagnes, J.M. Reality therapy approaches to leisure counseling. In A. Epperson, P.A. Witt, & G. Hitzhusen (Eds.), *Leisure counseling: An aspect of leisure education.* Springfield, Il.: Charles C Thomas, 1977.

Moore, J.E. *The relationship between self-actualization and leisure attitudes.* Unpublished doctoral dissertation, Oregon State University, 1975.

Mundy, J. Leisure education: A conceptualization and program design. Leisure Today supplement to *Journal of Physical Education and Recreation,* 1976, March, 17-19.

Neulinger, J., & Breit, M. Attitude dimensions of leisure: A replication study. *Journal of Leisure Research,* 1971, *3(2),* 108-115.

Ornstein, R. *Psychology of consciousness.* New York: Viking, 1972.

Overs, R.P., Taylor, S., & Adkins, C. *Avocational counseling in Milwaukee* (Final Report, No. 5D). Milwaukee: Curative Workshop of Milwaukee, May, 1974.

Pellett-Johnson, L., & Zoerink, D.A. The development and implementation of a leisure counseling program with female psychiatric patients based on value clarifcation techniques. In A. Epperson, P.A. Witt, & Hitzhusen (Eds.) *Leisure counseling: An aspect of leisure education.* Springfield, Il.: Charles C Thomas, 1977.

Rotter, J.B. *Clinical psychology.* Englewood Cliffs, N.J.: Prentice-Hall, 1964.

Rule, W., & Stewart, M. Enhancing leisure counseling using an Adlerian technique. *Therapeutic Recreation Journal,* 1977, *11,* 87-93.

Ryan, K.A. Assertive therapy: An applied approach for use in leisure counseling. *Leisurability,* 1977, *4,* 7-13.

Samples, B. *The metaphoric mind.* Reading, Mass.: Addison-Wesley, 1976.

Spreitzer, E.A., & Snyder, E.E. Work orientation meaning of leisure and mental health. *Journal of Leisure Research,* 1975, *6(3),* 207-219.

Tiger, L. *Optimism: The biology of hope.* New York: Simon & Schuster, 1979.

Toffler, A. *The third wave.* New York: William Morrow, 1980.

Tubesing, D.A. & Holinger, P.C. The holistic health care project. *Medical Care,* 1977, *15,* 217-227.

U.S. Department of Commerce Report: *Social Indicators, 1976.* Washington, D.C.: Superintendent of Documents, December, 1977.

Werkmeister, W.H. *Man and his values.* Nebraska: University of Nebraska Press, 1967.

Wilson, G.T., Mirenda, J.J., & Rutkowski, B.A. Milwaukee leisure counseling model. *Journal of Leisurability, 2,* 1975, 11-17.

Woodburn, B., & Cherry, C. *Leisure: A resource of educators.* Ministry of Culture and Recreation, Ontario, Canada, 1978.

Yankelvich, J. Special report on work in America. *Psychology Today,* May, 1978.

Chapter 2

TOWARD A COGNITIVE DEVELOPMENTAL THEORY OF LEISURE AND WORK

DONALD H. BLOCHER AND ROBIN SIEGAL

ONE of the central thrusts that has served to differentiate counseling psychology from other helping professions and psychological specialities has clearly been its concern with the problem of understanding career-relevant behavior in its broadest and fullest sense. Historically, the expansion and elaboration of this concern has punctuated the development of the field. The past quarter century has seen an inexorable movement away from theories and research directed towards relatively simple and easily specifiable problems of vocational choice, persistence, and satisfaction, and towards much more global and diffuse concepts of career patterns and career developments.

Undoubtedly, this trend has yielded some benefits for both practice and science. It has tended to move vocational behavior closer to the context to total human experience and to make vocational counseling interventions and strategies somewhat less arbitrary and artificial. As our conceptual foci have expanded, we have tended to lose specificity and indeed at times real intellectual contact with the phenomena that we set out to study. We are relatively unclear about what constitutes a psychology of careers. We seem to embrace a very wide spectrum of activity within the rubric of career development.

This book is perhaps a case in point. We set out to examine the activity called "leisure counseling." Presumably, "leisure" refers to that time in which the individual is not engaged in work. Yet, that distinction hardly seems to be one that can dignify the process of psychological counseling beyond a trivial and almost ludicrous level of importance. Clearly, we are not seeking an approach to psychological helping aimed at assisting clients to choose between an evening of bridge or backgammon, or beach-combing vs. bird-watching.

Instead, as we examine the problem associated with "leisure counseling" we obviously sense the presence of the same kind of unities that we seek to understand in a vocational psychology. Human beings are purposive organisms. They actively reach out to organize information about their environment. They seek to find meaning in their interaction with the world.

In a career psychology, we do not really seek or expect to predict or control the specific choices or behaviors that define a career in a totally external sense. We doubt that a single reader of this chapter could, for example, create a fully

---

This chapter is based on an article of the same title that originally appeared in *The Counseling Psychologist*, 1981, *9*(3).

plausible or satisfying *psychological* explanation of his or her path to the present life situation.

For all of us, the overriding social, economic, cultural, and political events of a fantastically complex and interdependent world move our lives with tremendous force. Wars, recessions, social revolutions, and technological breakthroughs all have dramatic effects on where we go career-wise and how we get there.

The unities and regularities that we seek to understand in a psychology of *either* work or leisure reside heavily, then, in how individuals perceive and process information *about* these dynamic events that shape the external configurations in their lives.

We maintain that a psychology of leisure and work is inevitably a *cognitive* psychology. Indeed, one of the best reasons for studying the use of leisure may be precisely because it will cast additional light on the psychology of work. If we can understand how people process information about, and make choices with regard to, that portion of their lives that is most amenable to individual control, we may learn more about their ways of construing those more externally contrained aspects of their experience that we call work.

Work-Leisure Relationships

Leisure activities have meaning to individuals. They serve purposes, meet needs, and advance goals in ways not utterly different from vocational activities. We can look at the purposes of leisure and their relationships to vocational activities in at least three psychologically relevant ways.

The first we can term *complementary*. In this "work-leisure style" close relationships exist between the two sets of activities. These relationships tend to locate in three major areas. The activities may tend to be of a similar nature in terms of the intrinsic interests or satisfactions involved. The librarian may spend leisure time writing novels, the auto mechanic may restore antique cars, the school teacher may lead a Scout Troop. In this type of complementary work-leisure style we might expect, for example, that casting the two sets of activities into a Holland typology would locate them in identical or adjacent cells.

A second subtype of work-leisure complementarity involves interaction in terms of personal relationships or associations. Complementarity exists in terms of the individuals with whom we perform the activities. In such work-leisure patterns the "people at the office" drink together on Friday evening, play golf together Saturday morning, and go to concerts together on Sunday nights. The leisure activities are in many ways extensions of relationship patterns that originate around work.

A final complementary subtype involves the physical and social framework within which work and leisure relate. Often membership in the same profession, occupation, or large institutional group heavily influences leisure activities. Opportunities for travel and recreation may arise out of business trips, conventions, or special facilities available through membership or position in a work setting or organization. The airline stewardess vacations in Hawaii because she can travel cheaply, the executive joins the country club because his membership is paid, the physician organizes his vacation around the tax deductible trip to the A.M.A. Convention.

Complementarity, then, is one powerful and psychologically relevant type of interaction between work and leisure activities. Many times these interactions are formalized in the general role expectations associated with a job. Such role expectations and the demands for comformity that accompany them may be sources of satisfaction or discomfort for an individual. This pattern is similar to that which Allen (1980) calls "fusion."

The second psychologically relevant pattern of work-leisure interaction may be termed *supplemental*. In this pattern, leisure activities may be chosen for their contribution to a rounding out of experiences to help establish a generally fulfilling life-style. In this work-leisure pattern, sharp contrasts between work and leisure in terms of types of activities, personal associations, and physical or social settings may be evident. The purpose and meaning of leisure in this style is the filling out or balancing of fulfillments and satisfactions. The professor who deals daily in abstract ideas may join a glee club or chorus, the accountant may climb the highest mountain or race sports cars. The relationships between work and leisure is essentially *supplementary*. The opportunity to engage in supplementary activities may be vitally important to the overall health and happiness of the individual. This pattern is similar to that which Parker (1971) termed "opposition."

The third relevant type of interaction between work and leisure can be called *compensatory*. In one sense it is really an extension and exaggeration of the supplemental patterns described above. Compensatory interactions are defined by the use of leisure activities to escape or alleviate stresses or tensions that build in work or family life. Sometimes these patterns have a driven or compulsive quality and sometimes they involve self-defeating or debilitating consequences. Various forms of substance abuse such as excessive drinking, overeating, or drug use may represent compensatory activities and may be enmeshed in specific leisure patterns or activities. Excessive gambling, sexual promiscuity, chronic reckless driving, or petty criminal activity may also be compensatory.

Not all compensatory activities are necessarily undesirable. Life almost inevitably brings with it sources of chronic stress that are very difficult to control. Compensatory activities that involve fantasy, excitement, increased relaxation, or heightened self-awareness may provide legitimate and badly needed escapes from chronic stress and tension. Often they need to be carefully planned and controlled to avoid negative long- or short-term consequences.

The major point that we make here is that leisure and work are closely related *psychological* phenomena. We believe, with Katz (1973) and Wrenn (1974), that a full blown "career psychology" must be able to investigate these interactions. We believe further that a counseling profession committed to the enhancement of optimal human development within individual life-styles characterized by health, happiness, and social involvement must help people plan and actualize their lives within patterns of activity that are familiarly termed work and leisure.

We are not attempting to make distinctions or coin new definitions for the terms work and leisure. The difficulties with such definitions that are so ably described in the companion chapters in this book seem to constitute a semantic swamp that we prefer to avoid. We believe it is possible to preserve the standard, time-honored dictionary definitions of work and leisure while examining their *psychological* relationships. The concept of centrality of work or leisure within a given life-style seems a useful one to describe individual differences in commitment (Blocher, 1973). The degree of centrality in involvement and commitment of an individual to activities labeled work or leisure is psychologically relevant.

In succeeding pages we will examine and critique theories and approaches to career counseling and career development in the belief that concepts of work and leisure are inextricably linked within them. When we treat them as companion concepts we do so quite deliberately and consciously, in the same vein that Katz (1973) combines them in the concept of career guidance.

Let us begin then to move toward an approach to studying work and leisure with a brief examination of the field of cognitive development.

Emergence of Constructivist Models in Psychology

The idea that people's life decisions are influenced by the manner in which their thinking is structured is compatible with the constructivist approaches that are emerging in many areas of psychology. The constructivist explanation of personality essentially proposes that people should be viewed as holistic information processors and creators of cognitive structures through which stimuli are interpreted and evaluated. Responses to these stimuli are mediated by these structures and are not determined solely by the external stimulus events.

The constructivist perspective originated in cognitive-developmental psychology. Theories such as those of Piaget (1965), Fohlberg (1969), Loevinger (1976), and Harvey, Hunt, and Schroder (1961) are based on an assumption: as a result of people's information processing activities, they move through a series of well-defined developmental stages. These stages are distinguished from each other by the kinds of cognitive schemas that are used. Generally, higher stages of cognitive development are characterized by increasing levels of differentiation, hierarchial organization, and complexity and by decreasing levels of egocentricity and stereotype in those schemas. The stages, then, are attempts to categorize distinct patterns of information processing activity.

Cognitive development is assumed to be motivated by an inherent drive to improve predictability and control (Kelly, 1955) and reduce uncertainty (Klahr, 1976). Creation of higher stages of thinking occurs when individuals perceive that present stages of thought are less able to accurately explain and predict environmental events than is a more complex and differentiated conceptual system. Information perceived to be somewhat discrepant from present cognitive structure acts as a stimulus to motivate further integration and cognitive development (Hunt, 1971). Further, novel information has been demonstrated to motivate exploratory behavior (Lester, 1969) and presumably is a source of satisfaction.

Constructivist Trends in Psychotherapy

A constructivist orientation has also been explicitly postulated in other areas of cognitive psychology. Theoretical frameworks to cognitive therapies have been developed by researchers such as Kelly (1955), Ellis (1962), and Beck (1976). They are derived from the philosophical tradition of Kant and Plato. A basic assumption is that therapeutic change depends on restructuring cognitions within the phenomenological field of the client. Change in feelings and behaviors then follows. In addition, new behaviors observed or attempted by the client serve as sources of information to create new meaning and action plans that are verified in the process of implementation. Clearly, the focus of theory and treatment is on human information-processing activity.

While the idea that people use structurally differentiated frameworks to abstract and organize meaning developed out of developmental and cognitive psychology, there has been increasing empirical support for, and adoption of, constructivist conceptualizations in other areas of psychology.

In social psychology, both psychological consistency theory (Festinger, 1957; Heider, 1958) and attribution theory (Kelley, 1971a; Bandura, 1977) are compatible with constructivist approaches. Festinger and Heider postulated that people are characterized by their desire to keep incoming information organized in a meaningful and consistent manner. Inconsistent information threatens existing organization and plans for action, and thus serves as a source of anxiety. However, in order to bring about change in personality and behavior, it is seen as necessary to introduce optimally discrepant information in order to induce the need to reorganize cognitive structures in the direction of greater accuracy and differentiation. In therapy it is often of fundamental importance to help people alter their attributions about life situations in the direction of greater perceived self-control and responsibility (Kelley, 1971a). Bandura's emphasis on the crucial importance of improving perceived self-efficacy in the therapeutic change process is based on ideas about the motivational consequences of greater self-attribution of internalized control. In short, social learning approaches, like the constructivist approach, are heavily based upon the idea of inducing behavior change through altering perceptions of self-efficacy and responsibility.

Changes in Modern Behavior Theory

Murray and Jacobsen (1978) point out that conceptions of classical and operant conditioning have encountered research data inexplicable purely in terms of traditional conditioning theory. Again, this has led to conceptual changes in the constructivist direction. After reviewing the conditioning literature, Murray and Jacobsen conclude that since learning can occur without overt responding and since motivational and situational factors are clearly important, an information processing explanation of human behavior change is better than one based solely on neural connections. Similarly, McGuigan and Lumsden (1973) point out that conditioning depends on a number of personal, social, and cognitive factors. More specifically, Murray and Jacobsen suggest three active cognitive processes that provide a more satisfactory explanation of behavior change:

a. expectation of favorable outcome (Lick & Bootzin, 1975)
b. change in perceived self-efficacy (Bandura, 1977)
c. the development of active coping strategies and techniques (Goldfried & Goldried, 1976: Meichenbaum, 1974).

Again, these cognitive processes are congruent with the view of personality as an organized pattern of constructed cognitive schemas and attributions that result from interaction with the environment. Change in personality results from introducing discrepant information, thus enabling different perceptions of alternatives and, in turn, strengthening and supporting new cognitions with new and more effective behaviors.

Extension of Constructivist Conceptualization to Career Theory

Within the last ten years, the idea that cognitive structures ordered along a developmental continuum are at least one significant factor in career decision making has begun to attract recognition. This recognition has come particularly from Bodden (1970), Bodden and Klein (1972), Winer, Cesari, Haase, and Bodden (1979), Jepsen (1974, 1979), and Knefelkamp and Slepitza (1976). However, in terms of a comprehensive stage theory of careers based on cognitive-development principles, we still do not have a fully satisfying and usable model.

Bodden (1970) took as a starting point the cognitive-developmental principle that as people develop, their cognitive structures tend to be characterized by greater complexity. The cognitively complex individual is believed to have a greater number of constructs or meaning categories available for processing stimulus information input than do cognitively simple individuals (Bieri, 1955). Bodden further hypothesized that if cognitively complex persons are able to make discriminations among stimulus information input, and as a result have a more flexible response repertory, then cognitively complex individuals should be more likely to make appropriate career decisions than cognitively simple individuals (Bodden, 1975). Appropriate vocational choice was defined as (a) agreement between intellectual ability and the level of occupational choice and (b) congruence between personality style and vocational environment according to Holland's model. Cognitive complexity was measured by the Bieri Repertory Test. The results indicated a moderate but significant relationship between cognitive complexity and the choosing of an occupation in which the environment was compatible with the subjects' personal coping style. This finding was replicated by Bodden and Klein (1972), who found a significant positive correlation. A second finding in the Bodden and Klein (1972) study was that "cognitive complexity operates independently of personality style in vocational choice" (p. 256) as assessed by, respectively, Bieri's Rep Test and Holland's Vocational Preference Inventory.

Winer, Cesari, Haase, and Bodden (1979) hypothesized further that if cognitively differentiated individuals are likely to choose an occupation congruent with their measured vocational preference, then cognitive complexity as measured by the Bieri Reperatory Test and the Bodden Cognitive Differentiation Grid should be positively associated with the cognitive variables included in the Crites model, which are measured by CMI-Competence Test. The scales comprising the CMI-Competence Test are (a) self appraisal; (b) occupational information; (c) goal selection; (d) planning; and (e) problem solving. The results were consistent with the prediction that greater cognitive complexity is associated with higher scores on the cognitive scales of the CMI-Competence Test.

The basic thrust of this research is that cognitive complexity is directly related to career choice "appropriateness" or degree of congruence in what Holland terms personal-environmental match. Cognitive developmental theory does, indeed, suggest that higher cognitive stages are more highly differentiated and does allow information to be used to evaluate more precisely and completely personal and environmental characteristics.

Jepsen (1974, 1979) has also worked from the assumption that career development "is one aspect of general human development" (1974, p.124) and that the postulates of cognitive developmental theory should also be relevant for career development research. In particular, Jepsen investigated the requirements of the cognitive developmental use of the stage concept. The first assumption he investigated was the idea that "stages imply distinct or qualitative differences in modes of thinking or of solving the same problems at different ages" (1974, p. 126). Influenced by Martin Katz (1973) and Thomas Green (1958), Jepsen concluded that Piaget's "problems" or central human task might be more simply defined as the process of searching for logical truth. The quest for logical truth provides the energy and momentum that pushes individuals toward higher and higher levels of cognitive development. Similarly, the phenomenon of moral judgment investigated by Kohlberg and his associates may be viewed as impelled by a search for the basis of moral action. This search again moves individuals along paths of increasing levels of development.

The essential human quest involved in career development was seen by Jepsen as the search for activity that offers personal *potency* and *meaning*. Here, then, is one of the sources of unity that seems able to tie career development to the mainstream of cognitive developmental psychology. If, indeed, human beings are intrinsically driven to seek work or other structured activity (leisure) that has personal meaning and potency, then as career psychologists we may expect to find orderly systematic patterns of cognitive growth related to career thinking and career decisions. Such a formulation seems to be particularly relevant to leisure choices and their related motivations.

Jepsen has further attempted to tie in other cognitive developmental principles including the identification of invariant sequences and the requirement that these sequential modes form an integrated whole so that each stage can represent an integrated revised structure. Each stage thus provides separate sets of rules for responding to or coping with the control problems, in this case the quest for potent and personal meaning in work or leisure.

Jepsen's work is a laudable and encouraging beginning, but at this point can be viewed as only a beginning. Most of the evidence tying vocational behavior to a solid cognitive developmental theoretical framework remains sketchy and tentative. While Jepsen's effort to link decision-making models to cognitive stages is promising, it does not relate well with the more traditional lines of research on vocational decision-making that treats decision-making as involving sets of discrete skills easily taught as separate entities (Crites, 1970). The notion of decision-making models as highly integrated and interrelated sets of rules for information processing needs much further research.

At this point, however, we must pause to examine the impact of these promising, if rudimentary, attempts to move career development closer to the mainstream of cognitive developmental psychology. As we remarked earlier, the crucial feature is the identification of a central human task or concern that moves and motivates individuals along a path of ascending levels of cognitive development. This crucial feature must be identified in terms of those activities that we classify as work or leisure.

If we are to tie career (that is, work and leisure) development to general cognitive development we must posit some central, unifying motivation such as the search for potency and personal meaning. Without this unity and the regularities that flow from it, the field of career development will continue to rest on a sloppily constructed foundation of convenient catchwords having no visible means of intellectual support.

We cannot think of leisure without thinking of work. The very dichotomy of work and leisure represents a rather low level construct derived from our economic and social history. When work is viewed as a product of original sin — a curse visited upon men and women as an act of retribution — leisure has a clear but limited meaning. Men and women earn their bread by the sweat of their brows and then are permitted to rest their bodies in order to resume their punishing and intrinsically unrewarding efforts. While this is, in a sense, a primitive and cognitively simple way of viewing both work and leisure, it is probably closer to the experience of many people in our industrial society than most vocational counselors care to admit. The point is that such a view severely limits the *psychological* factors involved in both vocational and leisure orientated behavior.

If leisure can only represent a temporary, albeit distracting, escape from the "curse of Adam," can we really expect to provide a psychologically relevant form of leisure counseling? Indeed, little need would seem to exist for such a service. Contemporary television, spectator sports, and other mass entertainment media seem to capture almost perfectly the spirit of simplistic definition of leisure described above. Leisure is simply the few hours of boob tube time that intervene between escape from work and release through sleep. This dismal picture is, of course, merely a product of a particular way of thinking about human existence in such limited either-or terms.

Instead, of course, it is possible to view work as a set of relatively structured and continuing activities in the life of an individual that provide opportunities for both extrinsic material rewards and intrinsic psychological satisfactions. It is also possible to differentiate among different individual life-styles in terms of centrality of either work or leisure. It is the latter view, of course, that makes viable a psychology of career development and a psychologically oriented career counseling enterprise.

Parallel to this view of work is a concept of leisure not merely as an escape from work but as a set of somewhat less externally structured and more personally controlled activities that are pursued primarily for the intrinsic and largely psychological satisfactions derived from them.

It seems clear, from the latter set of definitions, that work and leisure need not be construed solely as dichotomous or mutually exclusive. For the fortunate few, at least, work and leisure might well merge into an experientially indistinguishable collage of individual activities and commitments. This is the extreme end of the complementary work-leisure style.

Viewed in this way, work and leisure are sets of companion activities that share similar, but distinguishable, motivations and consequences. Both work and leisure may contribute to individual development and well-being. Both may also provide significant social contributions. Ideally, work and leisure combine to elaborate a life-style that supports the health, continued intellectual development, and psychological well-being of the individual, and the enhancement of the society of which that individual is a valued part.

The view stated above is clearly an ideal, but of course one that can only be aspired to or realized if conceptualized. Lest we be accused of being Pollyannas, it may be pertinent to review some evidence to indicate some approximation of the concepts of work and leisure described above is indeed increasingly a part of contemporary culture.

One of the striking facts of the past forty years of American economic life is that there has been no decrease in the length of the working day or working week of the average American industrial worker. After decades in which a demand for shorter working hours and work weeks was a primary goal of workers, the forty hour week has remained a basic standard for nearly one-half century. It appears that the eight hour day, roughly half of one's working hours structured in work over a five day week, has been accepted as a basic norm of contemporary life.

In those occupations where the working week has, for a variety of reasons, shrunk below the forty hour standard, one very frequently finds the "moonlighting" or second job phenomenon. Even with the forty hour week, the tremendous expansion of activities like the "do-it-yourself" home improvement craze, the ubiquitous self-improvement courses, and myriad hobby and craft activities give ample observational data to support the premise that leisure and work are viewed in very similar ways by large segments of the population. It seems clear that Americans, at least, do not have an insatiable thirst for increased leisure, if that leisure is viewed solely as escape from useful endeavor.

In terms of more systematic and convincing psychological data to bear upon this subject, the work of Richard de Charms (1968) and his associates seems compelling. In a variety of laboratory studies, de Charms has shown the ways in which a worker perceives an activity, particularly in terms of autonomy and control over his own performance, is a much stronger motivational factor in sustaining a continued high level of productivity than is the presence of extrinsically manipulated incentives or rewards. Indeed, an impressive body of evidence exists to support the view that the manipulation of extrinsic rewards, either material or psychological, may in fact depress performance in very powerful ways (Levine & Fasnact, 1974). Notz (1975) has also reported evidence for this same phenomenon in field studies of worker performance in a variety of industrial settings. Robert White's (1959) venerable theory of effectance motivation or competencies seems very much alive and well in contemporary American life. At this point it is interesting to note the etymology of the word leisure. As Beck (1975) notes, "leisure" descends from the Latin *Licere*, meaning "to be permitted." The notion of freedom and autonomy is clearly rooted in the word leisure itself.

What emerges for us from this evidence is renewed support for the hypothesis that human beings are similarly motivated in activities termed either work or leisure. A basic human motive seems to exist around activities that produce effects on the environment that can be interpreted as proofs of the individual's own freedom, autonomy, power, and control over his own destiny. The phenomenon can be roughly translated as a search for personal meaning and potency. This basic drive, then, seems part of the overall motivational pattern that sustains progress toward higher and higher levels of cognitive growth and development in many human beings.

Along with the evidence, however, we must acknowledge that changes are occurring in perceptions of both work and leisure. Dubin (1973) found that industrial workers reported that work was not a central life interest for them. Wilensky (1960), Godby and Parker (1976), and Kando and Summer (1971) all argue that workers are becoming more and more alienated from work. The centrality of work as an organizing force in individual lives is apparently declining. Leisure may indeed be in the process of replacing it.

For leisure as a distant component of career development to be viewed as psychologically relevant, and for a psychological speciality called leisure counseling to justify its existence, we must tie it to a comprehensive view of human needs and motivations. In a sense, we attempted this in relating concepts of work and leisure within the overall rubric of career. We need to pursue the matter further, however.

Implications of a Cognitive Development Theory of Leisure and Work

What now are the implications of this view for the theory and practice of career (work and leisure) counseling? Let us first examine the question of development of a basic theory.

A prevailing view of the basic enterprise of science is that it involves the process of creating theoretical frames of reference of nomological networks (Cronbach & Mehl, 1955) that can be verified, refined, and elaborated through empirical research. When existing theories fail to be supported by research or fail to generate relevant research, the basic structure of the theory must be altered. This process of restructuring is termed a paradigm shift (Kuhn, 1962).

It must be clear by now that we believe that the field of career development is in urgent need of such a shift. We believe that existing theories have failed to generate converging lines of research evidence about important areas of work or leisure behaviors. Some aspects of existing theories seem to ignore the salient evidence provided by recent research in general personality development. They tend to omit from their perspectives the view of human beings as active seekers and creators of new cognitive structures born out of the search for order, meaning, and potency.

We believe that it is now possible to define at least some of the criteria on which we can base this desperately needed paradigm shift. Four such basic criteria can be delineated and the shortcomings of existing theories can be identified in regard to them. These four criteria follow:

1. A clear statement must be made about the causality involved in career and leisure behavior.
2. An integrated explanation must be attempted to account for differential behavior, that is, individual differences.
3. The impact of environmental opportunities, restrictions, and limitations must be considered.

4. Integration and utilization of findings in modern cognitive developmental, social, and behavioral psychology must be attempted.

Let us examine each of these criteria briefly in terms of our major existing career development theoretical frameworks.

Present Theories of Career Behavior

Two main traditions for understanding career behavior are the developmental view (Super, 1974; Crites, 1974a; Levinson, Darrow, Klein, Levinson, & McKee, 1974) and the differential view (Williamson, 1972; Lofquist & Davis, 1969; Holland & Gottfredson, 1976). A third more recent approach can be termed the social learning approach and has been espoused by Krumboltz (1976) and Thoreson and Ewart (1976). Theories of career behavior developed in the near future are likely to be grist from the same mills.

Traditional Developmental Models of Career

The main assumption of the traditional developmental view is that careers can best be understood by documenting how career behavior changes over time in a normative sense (e.g., Binet) and/or determining what factors are critical in enabling such changes to take place (e.g., developmental tasks: Havighurst, 1964; Erikson, 1968). The process generally presented consists of invariant stages defined by normative behaviors, given the presence and successful resolution of critical tasks and experiences.

Super's vocational theory accounts for a sizable (17%) portion of career decision research activity (Mitchell, Jones, & Krumboltz, 1975) and is an example of a traditional career developmental theory. According to Super (1957), the process of career development is emphasis on the normative behaviors and developmental tasks, and toward the assumption of a set of developing cognitive structures. However, there is little clear elaboration of self-concepts as qualitatively different, hierarchially organized, cognitive structures. Also, there is a lack of specification of the interaction between self-concept and normative behaviors and developmental tasks. This precludes classifying Super's theory as a true cognitive stage theory. His focus is still heavily on normative behaviors and tasks.

Another career theorist working within the traditional developmental approach is Crites (1974, 1976). Crites (1974) suggests that vocational maturity is the combination of several dimensions. These dimensions, such as consistency of vocational choice, realism of vocational choice, competencies for vocational choice, and attitudes in vocational choice are subject to maturational processes. In turn, these dimensions are comprised of various specific variables. It is hypothesized that these dimensions and variables are moderately intercorrelated.

Let us now examine these traditional developmental models in terms of the four criteria described earlier.

The Nature of Causality

A first criterion that can be applied to both Super's and Crites' theories concerns the adequacy of attention to the nature of causality of behavior. These models neither logically nor empirically demonstrate that the supposed events occur in the suggested order. Hunt (1967) observed that because self and occupational concepts are significantly related does not prove that self-concept determines occupational choice. The self-perception research of Bem (1972) suggests that percepts of self may be consequent to actions, not antecedent to them. One can ask whether vocational maturity makes possible vocational behaviors characterized by consistency, realism and competency or whether such behaviors themselves lead to a more complex set of cognitive attitudinal changes conveniently called vocational maturity. The relationship between these constructs, at any rate, is not completely clear.

Integration of Cognitive Developmental and Differential Career Behavior Formulations

A second criticism of the traditional developmental approach to careers is also a criticism of the cognitive developmental approach. A classification scheme based solely on either structural or normative changes is not adequate to account for individual differences in specific vocational content. Blasi (1976) notes that "a purely formal notion of structure such as Piaget's logical operationalism, with its focus on external relations, does not suffice for the understanding of contents and internal constituents" (p. 53). Similarly, Holland (1976) suggests that in formal terms, theories of personality, interests, or decision making require a classification system to describe and organize what we know about both people and environments. Also needed are some speculations to explain behavior change and personal development. Theories and speculations about career choice, career patterns, and career adjustment are generally much more useful for only one of these purposes. In other words, Blasi and Holland are assuming two distinct ways in which people differ, and they suggest that both are necessary to a comprehensive theory. In the first, people differ along a developmental dimension, composed of normative behavior tasks and/or cognitive structural changes. The second involves variations in content or the directionality of development. Why, given the same degree of development, do people have diverse interests, preferences, and desires (content differences)? In all areas of development, but most particularly in leisure and work, it seems necessary to deal with both kinds of differences. Indeed the concepts of complementarity or supplementarity require such schemas.

Another logical question regards the sources of individual directionality. It is possible to postulate several sources of individual differences, including very general inherent dispositions and the characteristics of past and present social, physical, and economic environments. This argument becomes more clear if we take an information processing analogy. Given a system that is programmed to analyze incoming information in accordance with specified rules, the eventual output will depend on the nature of the specific information that is abstracted from the surrounding environment. The same rules applied to different content results in different outcomes, including eventual changes in the nature of the rules themselves.

This distinction between structural changes in thought and individual differences in content is insufficiently acknowledged and provided for in either current cognitive-developmental or traditional career theory. Holland (1976) is one of the writers who recognizes that both types of differences exist and should be accounted for in a comprehensive theory of career development. For example, "the vocational developmental people need to create or acquire a compatible classification scheme to use with their developmental speculations; and vocational speculations with strong classificatory virtues need to acquire, revise, or strengthen their developmental speculations" (Holland, 1976, p. 15). In short, the criticism being made here of developmental approach to understanding career and leisure is that inadequate attempts have been made to classify or explain directional or content differences.

Effects of Environmental Limitations

To be complete, a theory of career (work and leisure) behavior should address the influence of environmental forces. Models of career behavior that emphasize career developmental norms and tasks (e.g., Super and Crites) inadequently account for the significance of environmental variability. In such models, appropriate developmental behaviors and tasks tend to be general correlates of typical middle class career decision making, selection, and performance. How these behaviors might be affected by differing environments of either short or long duration is not adquately considered. Social, educational, and economic differences in opportunity are inevitably profound influences on leisure choices. The basic processes of socialization and acculturation are powerful determinants of leisure choice opportunities. Indeed, the most striking consequences of what is called a "liberal education" are the opportunities generated for leisure choices in areas of intellectual and aesthetic pursuits.

Proper Understanding and Utilization of
Cognitive Developmental Theory and Research

An even more fundamental problem is that career development theorists espouse a developmental orientation to career behavior and have advocated the importance of such a position. However, they seem to have made little use of the conceptualizations or the research generated by the cognitive developmental paradigm. Instead, they refer to development only in the sense of sequential normative behaviors and tasks. This is a very different meaning for development than the cognitive developmental conceptualization of increasingly complex, qualitatively different, cognitive structures (stages). A cognitive conceptualization of development together with differential or content differences offer promise for more comprehensively studying career behavior than do theories focusing on developmental norms only.

Super hypothesizes that vocational development leading to congruent career choice stems from an interaction of a self-concept and the demands of the work world resulting in a sequence of analagous life-stages. However, the resultant normative behaviors are differentiated only in terms of location on typical career sequences, and little recognition is given to the kind of qualitatively different, increasingly complex, hierarchically organized systems of constructs or modes of thinking concerning career development that are important to the cognitive developmental approach.

Crites proposes a constructivist, developmental approach to careers that he characterizes by hierachical organization and increasing differentiation (Crites, 1974). However, it seems questionable whether he has really been able to maintain and elaborate this kind of developmental outlook. Holland (1976) notes that "when you look closely at the proposed model, it has a marked resemblance to the old trait-and-factor model" (p.13). We agree. The amount of explicit developmental and logical relationships among the factors is not sufficient to relate them to a constructivist or cognitive developmental theory. Instead, the theory identified bits and pieces of vocational behaviors normative for various ages. It is not a truly holistic picture of the various modes of thinking people utilize to understand and make career decisions.

Further, Crites (1976) suggests that the most advantageous sequence for career decision making is information gathering (self and work), goal selection, planning, and problem solving. He adds that presumably a client not only passes through these stages, as needed, in career counseling but also that he learns them as a modus operandi for decision making in the future. This conception of decision making as a skill to be learned is advocated by Crites and would seem to be acceptable to Super. It is also emphasized as a goal by Krumboltz (1976) and Thoreson and Ewart (1976). However, if decision making is viewed solely as a set of discrete skills, much is overlooked that is crucial from a cognitive developmental perspective.

Crites' decision-making procedures can be viewed as analogous to the developmental processes of assimilation (information gathering), accommodation (goal selection and planning), and equilibration (problem solving). Perhaps these procedures can be facilitated in specific content areas such as vocational or leisure decision making, but the essential questions stemming from a cognitive developmental approach are not asked if one keeps to a view of decision making as an isolated skill. More importantly, a comprehensive theory needs to address modes of thinking used in attempting to understand and make career decisions. According to cognitive developmental theory, different modes of increasingly differentiated and hierarchically organized thinking are sequential in their development, if not always in usage (Rest, 1974; Piaget, 1965; Loevinger, 1970, 1976; Klahr, 1976; Selman, 1976). Modes of thinking determine the frame of reference used to gather information and the methods used to evaluate goals. To discuss decision-making procedures without reference to broader cognitive developmental mode of thinking, or stage, seems to ignore very significant data.

Holland's Differential Mode of Career Behavior

The second major tradition in understanding career behavior has been the differential approach. The most modern, empirically supported, and influential version of this approach, John Holland's typology, must be considered.

Holland (1973) postulates six vocational types of clusterings of vocational preference that are seen to endure as personality traits, or what has been referred to here as content or directionality differences. These are the realistic, investigative, artistic, social, enterprising, and conventional types. Holland depicts these six types as forming the corners of a hexagon. In moving about the perimeter one passes from realistic to investigative, artistic, social, enterprising, and convention (again adjacent to realistic). Holland suggests that closeness on the hexagon is indicative of consistency of preferences. By way of illustration Thoreson and Ewart (1976) note that "in this scheme, a person would find it somewhat easier to reconcile interests in the Investigative domain with a Realistic preference than with an interest in work that fails in the Enterprising category" (p. 31). This typology seems to be just as relevant to the world of work. It clearly classifies activities in terms of the types of interests and satisfactions that are offered. Indeed, if the Holland types are really basic personality types, we would have to expect that they would have leisure choice correlates.

The Nature of Causality

Holland's theory does not adequately deal with the questions of causality. An early criticism of Holland's typology was that he neglected to specify how types developed or changed (Osipow, 1973). It was unclear whether types were a result of environmental variables or functioned largely independently of the environment. More recently, Holland and his colleagues (Holland, 1973; Holland & Gottfredson, 1976) advocated a social learning model for the acquisition of types. They stated, "people grow up to resemble one type or another because parents, schools and neighborhoods serve as environments which reinforce some behaviors more than others and provide different models of suitable behavior . . . This experience contributes to the development of a characteristic, typological disposition, which, in turn, leads to a characteristic cluster of personal traits" (Holland & Gottfredson, 1976, p. 21).

As with the career developmental theories of Super and Crites, it does not necessarily follow that events occur in the order specified. Although typologies may function as predictive devices, it is not necessary that their causes be attributed totally or directly to the environment. The way in which individuals process, organize, and make use of contingencies existing in the environment might be considered to be as important as the contingencies alone. People of various developmental stages are likely to process the same perceived contingencies, and even the same information, in different ways. Individuals in the same environment functioning at different stages of thinking are likely to come to different conclusions. Even though Holland's typologies have predicative value, causality is not necessarily restricted to the external environment.

Integration of Cognitive Developmental and Differential Career Behavior Formulations

A second issue regarding Holland's typology again concerns the usefulness of emphasizing a developmental versus a differential point of view. We saw earlier that Holland suggests it is necessary to understand both aspects of career behavior. Accordingly, in 1973 he enlarged his vocational typology by incorporating a social learning theory paradigm in order to explain type acquisition, development, and change. Still, Holland and Gottfredson (1976) feel that at present a "typology of persons and environments is more useful than any life stage strategies for coping with career problems . . . they [the life strategies] usually treat people with a single type, differing only in stage development, so they fail to deal adequately with the diversity of human personality" (p. 23). Holland is right, we concede, if he limits his understanding of development to confrontation with characteristic environmental contingencies (developmental tasks). However, as we saw, there is more to developmental theory than task theory. A view based on the sequential creation of hierarchically organized modes of thinking seems to present a way of understanding careers and leisure patterns that effectively integrates developmental with differential formulations.

Effects of Environmental Limitations

A third issue regarding Holland's theory is whether it adequately accounts for the full impact of the environment. Construing environmental influence solely in terms of the formation of typologies is probably insufficient. Other factors — such as economic conditions, prejudice, power hierarchies, personality conflicts, and other problems — clearly serve as strong influences on work or leisure selection and satisfaction. The ways in which people process information about these factors in their lives is also crucial. This issue is acknowledged but not dealt with by Holland and Gottfredson (1976). They state "many important personal and environmental contingencies may be outside the scope of the typology" (p. 27). Thoreson and Ewart (1976) also point out that "in recent years personality research studies of aptitudes have seen a growing recognition among investigators that assessment techniques must take account of considerable situational variability in what people think, feel and do" (p. 34). Insel and Moos (1974) suggest that characteristics of persons such as interests are not expressed in identical ways over time and across situations. Logically, a comprehensive vocational and leisure (that is, career) theory should allow for situational variability in individual preferences.

Proper Understanding and Utilization of Cognitive Developmental Theory and Research

Holland's recent developmental formulations are based on a view of the environment as the major source of change (Holland & Gottredson, 1976). Development is defined in terms of environmental differences rather than normative behavior, tasks, or cognitive stage. This model places major responsibility for developmental change directly within the environment rather than on interaction with the environment. The former view is not compatible with the cognitive developmental model of an active information processing and interactionist view of people and environments.

Social Learning Approaches to Career Behavior

The explanation of career behavior on which Holland based his developmental formulations is derived from social learning theory. According to Krumboltz (1976), one of the primary proponents of a social learning explanation of career behavior:

> The social learning theory of career selections was designated as a first step toward understanding more precisely what specific kinds of learning experiences contribute to the development of occupational preferences. It posits certain environmental and cultural events that facilitate or inhibit the reinforcing and punishing consequences which contribute to various occupational preferences. It was designed to make more explicit how certain skills in decision making and other task approach skills are developed as a result of the interaction of genetic endowment and learning experiences in a cultural context. It was also designed to explain how specific occupational entry behaviors result from the interaction of skills and preferences generated in the past with current cultural, social and economic forces. (p. 17)

In short, vocational behavior is seen to result from an interaction of genetic endowment, preferences, and skills learned as a result of environmental contingencies and from present environmental limitations. The theory does not directly address the leisure component of a career psychology. We see little reason to assume that a social learning approach that adequately explains vocational choices and preferences would not equally account for choice and preferences in the leisure area. Certainly, patterns of social reinforcement pertain to leisure activities. Areas of leisure such as sports, music, and art are striking examples of activities in which skills and talents are socially reinforced in very systematic and comprehensive ways.

Nature of Causality

A social learning point of view offers a potential resolution to some of the problems inherent in other theories. For example, the causality of career change is attributed to contingencies existing in the environment. As noted in the discussion earlier, it is not logically necessary that preferences and skills are *solely* a consequence of these contingencies. It can be argued that the cognitive processing, evaluation, and organization of these contingencies varies according to cognitive stages, thus giving the individual processing level and ability considerable antecedent responsibility for the development of preference and skills. However, the social learning formulations of Krumboltz, or Holland, seem to offer a more explicit and persuasive causality argument than those of earlier theories.

Integration of Cognitive Developmental and Differential Career Behavior Formulations

Both developmental and differential aspects of vocational behavior can be accounted for using a social learning theory perspective. Krumboltz (1976) sees social learning as offering primarily an environmental explanation for the development of career behavior. The focus of developmental change is directly on interaction with the environment rather than on normative behavior, tasks, or cognitive change. Holland properly realizes that this social learning principle can also serve as the basis for a classification scheme. As noted earlier, Holland and Gottfredson (1976) state that "reinforcement . . . experiences contribute to the development of a characteristic, typological disposition, which in turn, leads to a characteristic cluster of personal traits" (p. 21). It seems possible that both developmental and differential aspects of behavior could be dealt with in a social learning approach.

Effects of Environmental Limitations

A social learning perspective also makes some provision for the powerful limitations on vocational and leisure behavior imposed by cultural, social, and economic environments. Traditional developmental theories make little mention of these factors. Holland, as noted, fails to account for their power beyond their probable effects in creating his six characteristic types of environments. Any comprehensive theory of vocational and leisure behavior should attend carefully to these forces if we are to have theories useful in working with the full range of people in our pluralistic society.

Proper Understanding and Utilization of Cognitive Developmental Theory and Research

Career social learning theory tends to limit itself to a basic model of people as passive reactors to environmental contingencies, rather than to view human beings as active information processors and creators of conceptual schemas. This is our primary criticism of this approach to career theory. A wealth of evidence from social psychology (Bandura, 1977), cognitive behavioral psychological (Mahoney & Arnkoff, 1978; Meichenbaum, 1974; Beck, 1976) and developmental psychology (Piaget, 1965; Kohlberg, 1969; Rest, 1974) suggests that reactive formulations of many are insufficient.

As a result of this passive model of man, one of the primary interventions devised by career social learning theorists is the teaching of decision making as a relatively simple and discreet skill. Krumboltz (1976) states, "the goal of counseling is not seen as merely identifying an occupational label as a goal, but helping clients realize that this particular career decision is one of hundreds of decisions that will be required in the future and that there are some logical steps that one can take in order to improve the likelihood that the resulting decisions will be more satisfactory" (p. 18). As we discussed earlier, this goal is somewhat different from that which might be advocated in a cognitive developmental approach. The latter position would suggest that the decision-making process is inherent in development and is analogous to the cognitive processes of assimilation (information gathering), accommodation (goal selection and planning), and equilibration (problem solving). When one deals with the leisure-choice component of career decision making, particularly, very broad questions of how the client construes the very complex and often ambiguous opportunties available make mechanical models of problem solving and decision making minimally useful. While these processes may be useful at particular stages of the counseling process, it is important to help a client see clearly the general style of thinking or general frame of reference that he/she is using to formulate and evaluate alternatives. The assumption is that a clear understanding of one's own cognitive style and available options facilitates the process of making realistic decisions as much as practice in using a decision-making formula.

A step in this direction is made by Thoreson and Ewart (1976). While anchored largely within a social learning perspective, they argued for the importance of attending to client's cognitive processes in career counseling. Specifically, they advocate teaching self-control skills, defining self-control "as learnable cognitive processes that a person uses to develop controlling actions which, in turn, function to alter factors influencing behavior. Further, self-control should be viewed as a series of specific, cognitively-mediated actions that a person uses to regulate and alter situations, including the cognitive commitment that the desired change takes place" (p. 37). They clearly advocate exploring beliefs and attributions prior to restructuring environments.

We have some questions whether Thoreson and Ewart fully emphasize the essential importance of self and career attributions, beliefs, and anticipation. Rather than attending to the developmental nature of cognitions, these writers view cognitions primarily as "irrational beliefs and distorted stereotypes of themselves and career areas that must be altered . . . as one step in creating commitment" (Thoreson & Ewart, 1976, p. 37). Further, once commitment is secured, true change is thought to be best brought about by observing behavior, restructuring environments, and assessing and changing current reinforcement contingencies. While Thoreson and Ewart advocate a goal of self-control, and state that self-control is cognitively mediated, their procedural emphasis is on environmental observation and restructuring with minimal explicit attention to cognitive changes (i.e., changes in beliefs, attributions, and ways of organizing information).

Characteristics of a New Paradigm for Career and Leisure Counseling

We believe that a new theoretical framework must be developed to underpin the practice of career counseling. That framework must be compatible with recent research in personality development, social psychology, and cognitive developmental psychology. It must also be compatible with the approaches to counseling and psychotherapy that are termed cognitive behavioral and that are now in the process of providing a major paradigm shift to those areas of helping.

This new paradgim can and should incorporate major features of traditional developmental, differential, and social learning theories of career development. It must elaborate much more fully, however, significant aspects of these approaches and, most importantly, articulate many of the missing interrelationships among constructs. We believe the broad outlines of such a theoretical framework is suggested in the following set of postulates and corollaries:

POSTULATE: Human beings are active stimulus-seeking, information processing organisms. They seek to establish logical order, consistency, and predictability in their stimulus world.

WORK AND LEISURE COROLLARY: In regard to those structured and continuing activities that we term work and leisure, human beings seek to construe information and act upon the environment to produce effects that give proof of personal power, autonomy, and efficacy.

POSTULATE: Human begins are motivated to develop when presented with information somewhat discrepant from or incomprehensible within existing schemas. Such discrepant information will be perceived as arousing and even pleasing when the inconsistency is within an optimal range.

WORK AND LEISURE COROLLARY: In work and leisure, humans are motivated to integrate discrepant information and will reorganize cognitive structures in order to do so. In work, optimally discrepant information may be perceived as stimulating. In leisure, novel constructs may be perceived as pleasurable since novel experiences are more directly controllable and the risks are less. This search for novelty may be a major factor in leisure choices.

POSTULATE: The interaction between human beings and environments through which basic motivations are exercised leads to the formation of cognitive structures through which events are construed, interpreted, and evaluated. These structures are significant mediators between external stimuli and individual behaviors.

WORK AND LEISURE COROLLARY: The primary source of order and regularity in human beings with regard to work and leisure are related to the cognitive structures that are used to process information regarding them. The relationship between cognition and performance or behavior may be relatively stronger in leisure activities than in work due to less constriction of environmental opportunities and psychological risk levels.

POSTULATE: Human cognitive activities vary on at least two essential dimensions. One dimension, *structure*, refers to characteristics such as differentiation, complexity, hierarchial ordering, and integration of diverse elements. A second, *content*, refers to representations or ways of categorizing the objects of cognition, that is, stimulus situations or events.

WORK AND LEISURE COROLLARY: Adequate explanations of individuals' cognitions with respect to work and leisure must include both *structual* and *content* variables.

POSTULATE: Individual human beings vary widely in cognitive level of development. Sequences of growth characterized by similarities in use of rules may be identified as stages and have been shown to have explanatory and predictive utility.

WORK AND LEISURE COROLLARY: Cognitive patterns such as decision-making models used in making choices or plans for work and leisure should specify sources of individual variation in information processing activity. The ways in which individuals differentiate among factors, integrate diverse information, or establish value hierarchies should be specified.

POSTULATE: Psychological intervention should involve, first, thorough understanding of the nature of present conceptual systems and, second, the presentation of optimally discrepant or novel information through a variety of media in order to facilitate development and the resulting experience of increased predictability, freedom, and control.

WORK AND LEISURE COROLLARY: In vocational or leisure counseling, attention should focus on structural and content alternative concepts related to decision making. In leisure counseling, attention should be given to leisure as an opportunity to explore, with less constraint, novel interests and conceptualizations. Tentative hypotheses that are verified in leisure might then be integrated to play an important role in work or other life areas. Concepts of the relative centrality of work and leisure within a total "career life-style" should be a major focus of career counseling.

Implications for Counseling

We see leisure counseling as a parallel and companion activity to vocational counseling. These two services, in our view, combine to assist clients in building life-styles that support optimal levels of individual growth and development, personal health and satisfaction, and social contribution. Essentially, the two elements of work and leisure combine to generate the concept of career.

Since leisure time is, by definition, under the control of the individual, it is particularly important to help people utilize leisure activities to enrich their total pattern of interaction with the environment. One of the authors has elaborated elsewhere an ecological model for enhancing life-long development (Blocher, 1974). This model postulates several characteristic patterns of person-environment interaction that support continued personal growth.

As counselors work with clients, the presence or absence of these kinds of interactions can be examined in order to set goals for optimal interactions.

Involvement

Involvement is a pattern that is characterized by the placing at risk of significant material or psychological values. Life without involvement is boring and stultifying. When levels of involvement in work or family life are very low, individuals may seek very highly involving leisure activities. The parachute jumper, race driver, or mountain climber are examples. Leisure-oriented career counseling may help an individual set optimal levels of involvement in his/her life-style.

Challenge

A second pattern of interaction involves the discrepancy between an individual's present performance and an expected or possible performance. Individuals with high needs for challenge often seek out activities that offer opportunities for progressive mastery or very high levels of accomplishment. Many athletic, musical, or artistic activities are of this nature, as are very complex games or intellectual pursuits. Extremely high levels of challenge in all areas of life may impose high levels of physical or psychological stress. Again, leisure counseling can help clients find acceptable levels of challenge in their overall life-styles.

Support

Support involves participation in a network of warm, empathetic, and caring relationships. For some clients the major opportunities for such supporting relationships may come through leisure activities. Clubs, teams, and volunteer groups, for example, offer opportunities for support. Again, optimal levels are the key. For some clients, ample support may already exist in work or family life.

Structure

Structure involves a clear sense of direction and purpose in regard to goal attainment. Some individuals with high needs for achievement may be in work situations that are characterized by great ambiguity and high levels of abstraction. Highly structured activities in art or craft areas, or within clearly defined rules sets, may give additional structure. Cognitive growth may reduce the need for structure and open up new opportunities of satisfying leisure activities.

Feedback

Feedback is the name given to a pattern of person-environment interaction in which clear, continuous, and immediate information is available about the quality of performance. In many life situations, such information is delayed or unavailable. Many leisure activities are attractive because of their feedback properties. The "hit or miss," "win or lose," "work or fail" ingredient is satisfying to the performer who seeks feedback. Positive feedback about self may enhance self-esteem and may be an important source of psychological growth derived from leisure activities.

Application

Application involves the practical tryout and demonstration of skills and understanding. People who operate at high levels of abstraction and ambiguity in other life areas may find practical applications particularly attractive. The engineer who builds experimental aircraft, the dance teacher who performs, the critic who writes poetry, all engage in application activities. Leisure activities may provide opportunities for application that can reduce sources of chronic dissatisfaction or stress in people who deal with high levels of ambiguity and abstraction.

Integration

The final pattern of interaction, integration, involves opportunity to reflect, introspect, and organize views of life or personal experiences. Privacy, solitude, peace, and quiet are aspects of this pattern. People who experience rapid change in many phases of their lives may particularly yearn for integrative experiences. Reading, simple dialogues with significant others, or outdoor activities such as camping or hiking may afford these kinds of activity.

The patterns described above, we believe, provide a psychological framework for understanding the role of leisure in a healthy, growth-oriented life-style. It is crucial in a developmental psychology of work and leisure to understand that the role and perception of leisure activity may change as cognitive structures change. As individuals move into higher cognitive levels, the meaning of leisure activities may change. Competitive activities that once were exciting may, for example, seem childish and trivial. As individuals enter new cognitive levels they may need to reassess their use of leisure and the consequences of their changing interests of significant personal relationships.

Generally, as people grow cognitively they are attracted to stimuli that involve higher and higher degrees of *novelty, complexity, ambiguity,* and *abstraction*. The interaction with such stimuli, as we have seen, in turn enhances further development. Leisure, along with work, is a vital part of the growth process. We need theoretical frameworks to support leisure-oriented career counseling that can help explicate and enlighten our professional practices.

In summary we are suggesting that the field of career counseling and development requires a major paradigm shift if it is to remain an intellectually and scientifically viable enterprise. This shift can draw upon elements contained in contemporary theories of career development but must go well beyond them. New theories should explain both leisure and vocational behavior and their interrelationships. They must deal with cognitive processes involving both structure and content. They must focus on the overall interaction between the individual and the environment, not merely on the reinforcement contingencies in the environment. They must also provide hypotheses and explanations that are relevant to the lives of the full range of people in our pluralistic society.

It is fitting that our interest in leisure from a psychological standpoint should help us point the way toward this paradigm shift. It is in leisure activities that men and women have the greatest opportunities to manifest themselves as practical, stimulus-seeking, information-processors. Leisure in its generic concept of freedom puts us in touch with an essence of human development that we have too long ignored.

When we, as psychologists, sensitize ourselves to the human zest of novelty, joy in play, and hunger for new understanding and experience that is rooted in what we prosaically call "leisure," we may learn much more about those activities that define human experience. Leisure is not a trivial or superficial fringe area of human functioning. It can represent the fullest expression and development of our drive toward freedom, fulfillment, and actualization.

REFERENCES

Allen, L.R. Leisure and its relationship to work and career guidance. *Vocational Guidance Quarterly*, 1980, *28*(3), 257-262.

Bandura, A. Self-efficacy: Towards a unifying theory of behavioral change. *Psychological Review*, 1977, *84*, 191-215.

Beck, A.T. *Cognitive therapy and emotional disorders*. New York: International Universities Press, 1976.

Beck, C.E. The roots of leisure. *Counseling and Values*, 1975, *20*, 3-4.

Bem, D. Self-perception theory. In L. Berkowitz (Ed.), *Advances in experimental social psychology*, Vol. 6. New York: Academic Press, 1972.

Blasi, A. Concept of development in personality theory. In J. Loevinger, *Ego-development: Conceptions and theories*. San Francisco: Jossey-Bass Publishers, 1976.

Blocher, D.H. Toward an ecology of student development. *Personal and Guidance Journal*, 1974, *52*(6), 360-369.

Blocher, D.H. Social change and the future of vocational guidance. In H. Borow (Ed.) *Career guidance for a new age*. Boston: Houghton-Mifflin, 1973.

Bodden, J.L. Cognitive complexity as a factor in appropriate vocational choice. *Journal of Counseling Psychology*, 1970, *17*, 364-368.

Bodden, J.L. & Klein, A. Cognitive complexity and appropriate vocational choice: Another look. *Journal of Counseling Psychology*, 1972, *19*(3), 257-258.

Cronbach, L.S. & Meehl, P.E. Construct validity in psychologial tests. *Psychological Bulletin*, 1955, *52*, 281-302.

Crites, J.O. Career development processes: A model of vocational maturity. In E.L. Herr (Ed.), *Vocational guidance and human development*. Boston: Houghton-Mifflin Company, 1974.

Crites, J.O. Career counseling: A comprehensive approach. *The Counseling Psychologist*, 1976, *6*(3), 2-12.

DeCharms, R. *Personal causation: The internal affective determinants of behavior*. New York: Academic Press, 1968.

Dubin, R. Industrial worker's worlds: A study of the central life interests of industrial workers. In E. Smigle (Ed.), *Work and leisure*. New Haven, Conn.: College and University Press, 1962.

Ellis, A. *Reason and emotion in psychotherapy*. New York: Stuart, 1962.

Erikson, E.H. *Identity: Youth crisis*. New York: W.W. Norton and Company, 1968.

Festinger, L. *A theory of cognitive dissonance*. Evanston, Il.: Row, Peterson, 1959.

Goldfried, N.R., & Goldfried, A.P. Cognitive change methods. In F.H. Kanfer & A.P. Goldstein (Eds.), *Helping people change*. New York: Pergamon Press, 1976.

Green, T.F. *Work, leisure and the American schools*. New York: Random House, 1968.

Harvey, O.J., Hunt, D.E., & Schroder, H.M. *Conceptual systems and personality organization*. New York: Wiley, 1961.

Havighurst, R.J. Youth in exploration and man emergent. In H. Borrow (Ed.), *Man in a world at work*. Boston: Houghton-Mifflin, 1964.

Heider, F. *The psychology of interpersonal relations*. New York: Wiley, 1958.

Helms, S.T. & Williams, G.D. *An experimental study of the reactions of high school students to simulated jobs*. (Research Report No. 161). Baltimore: Center for Social Organization of Schools. John Hopkins University, 1973. ERIC document Reproduction Service No. ED 087-882.

Holland, J.L. *Making vocational choices: A theory of careers*. Englewood Cliffs, N.J.: Prentice Hall, 1973.

Holland, J.L. A new synthesis for an old method and a new analysis of some old phenomena. *The Counseling Psychologist*, 1976, *6*(3), 12-15.

Holland, J.L., & Gottfredson, G.D. Using a typology of persons and environments to explain careers: Some extensions and clarification. *The Counseling Psychologist*, 1976, *6*(3), 20-29.

Hughes, H.M., Jr. Vocational choice, level and consistency: An investigation of Holland's theory in an employed sample. *Journal of Vocational Behavior*, 1972, *2*(4), 377-388.

Hunt, J.McV. Intrinsic motivation: Information and circumstance. In H.M. Shroder & P. Suefeld (Eds.), *Personality theory and information processing*. New York: The Ronald Press Company, 1971.

Hunt, R.A. Self and other semantic concepts in relation to choice of a vocation. *Journal of Ap-

plied Psychology, 1967, *51*, 242-246.

Insel, P.M. & Moos, R.H. Psychological environments: Expanding the scope of human ecology. *American Psychologist*, 1974, *29*, 179-188.

Jepsen, D.A. The stage construct in career development. *Counseling and Values*, 1974, *18*(2), 124-131.

Jepsen, D.A. *Assessing career decision processes as developmental change*. Paper presented at American Personnel and Guidance Association Convention, Las Vegas, April, 1979.

Kando, I.M. & Summer, W.C. Impact of works of leisure. *Pacific Sociological Review*, 1971, *14*, 310-327.

Katz, M. The name and nature of vocational guidance. In H. Borow (Ed.), *Career guidance for a new age*. Boston: Houghton-Mifflin, 1973.

Kelley, H.H. Attribution in social interaction. In E.E. Jones, D.E. Kanouse, H.H. Kelley, R.R. Hisbett, S. Valins, & B. Weiner, (Eds.), *Attribution: Perceiving the causes of behavior*. Morristown, N.J.: General Learning Press, 1971.

Klahr, D., & Wallace, J.G. *Cognitive development: An information-processing view*. Hillsdale, N.J.: Laurence Erlbaum Associates, 1976.

Knefelkamp, L., & Slepitza, R. A cognitive-developmental model of career development — An adaption of the Perry scheme. *The Counseling Psychologist*, 1976, *6*(3), 53-59.

Kohlberg, L. Stage and sequence: The cognitive-developmental approach to socialization. In D. Goslin (Ed.), *Handbook of socialization theory and research*. New York: Rand-McNally, 1969.

Krumboltz, J.D. A social learning theory of career decision making. In A.N. Mitchell, G.B. Jones, & J.D. Krumboltz (Eds.), *A social learning theory of career decision making*. Final report, Contract No. NIE-C-74-0134, Palo Alto, Calif: American Institute for Research, 1975, 13-29.

Krumboltz, J.D. This Chevrolet can't float or fly. *The Counseling Psychologist*, 1976, *6*(3), 17-19.

Kuhn, T.S. *The structure of scientific revolutions*. Chicago: University of Chicago Press, 1962.

Lester, D. *Explorations in exploration: Stimulation seeking*. New York: Van Nostrand Reinhold Company, 1969.

Levine, F.M. & Fasnact, G. Token rewards may lead to token learning. *American Psychologist, 1974, 20*(11), 816-820.

Levinson, D.J., Darrow, L., Klein, E., Levinson, M., & McKee, B. The psychological development of men in early adulthood and midlife transition. In D.F. Ricks, A. Thomas, & M. Roff (Eds.), *Life history research in psychopathology*, Vol. 3. Minneapolis: University of Minnesota Press, 1974.

Lick, J., & Bootzin, R. Expectancy factors in the treatment of fear: Methodological and theoretical issues. *Psychological Bulletin*, 1975, *83*, 917-931.

Loevinger, J. *Ego development*. San Francisco: Jossey-Bass Publishers, 1976.

Lofquist, L.H. & Davis R.V. *Adjustment to work*. New York: Appleton-Century-Crofts, 1969.

Mahoney, M.J. & Arnhoff, D. Cognitive and self control therapies. In S.L. Garfield & A.E. Bergin (Eds.), *Handbook of Psychotherapy and behavioral change* (2nd ed.). New York: John Wiley and Sons, 1978.

Meichenbaum, D. *Cognitive behavior modification*. Morriston, N.J.: General Learning Press, 1974.

Mitchell, A.M., Jones, G.B., & Krumboltz, J.D. (Eds.) Final Report No. NIE-C-74-0134. *A social learning theory of career decision making*. Palo Alto, Ca. American Institute of Research, 1975.

Notz, W.W. Work motivation and the negative effects of extrinsic rewards: A review with implications for theory and practice, *American Psychologist*, 1975, *30*(9), 884-891.

Osipow, S.H. *Theories of career development*. New York: Appleton-Century-Crofts, 1973.

Piaget, J. *The moral judgment of the child* (M. Gabian, trans.) New York: The Free Press, 1965. (Originally published 1932.)

Rest, J.R. The cognitive-development approach to morality: The state of the art. *Counseling and Values*, 1974, *18*, 64-78.

Selman, R.L. A structural-developmental model of social cognition: Implications for intervention research. *The Counseling Psychologist*, 1977, *6*(4), 3-6.

Super, D. *The psychology of careers: An introduction of vocational development*. New York: Harper and Bolners, 1957.

Super, D.E. Vocational maturity theory. In D.E. Super (Eds.), *Measuring vocational maturity for counseling*. Washington, D.C.: American Personnel and Guidance Association, 1974.

Super, D., & Overstreet, P. *The vocational maturity of ninth grade boys*. New York: Bureau of Publications, Columbia University, 1960.

Thoresen, C.E., & Ewart, C.K. Behavioral self-control: Some clinical concerns. *The Counseling Psychologist*, 1976, *6*(3), 29-43.

White, R. Motivation reconsidered: The concept of competence. *Psychological Review*, 1959, *66*, 297-333.

Parker, S. *The future of work and leisure*. New York: Praeger, 1971.

Wiggins, J.D. The relations of job satisfaction to vocational preferences among teachers of the educable mentally retarded. *Journal of Vocational Behavior*, 1976, *8*, 13-18.

Williamson, E.G. Trait-factor theory and individual differences. In B. Stefflre & W.H. Grant (Eds.), *Theories of Counseling* (2nd ed.). New York: McGraw-Hill, 1972.

Wilensky, H.L. Work, careers and social integration. *International Social Science Journal*, 1960, *12*, 543-560.

Winer, J.L. Cesari, J., Haase, R.F., & Bodden, J.L. Cognitive complexity and career maturity among college students. *Journal of Vocational Behavior*, 1979, *15*, 1 86-192.

Wrenn, C.G. Hopes and realizations, past and present. *Vocational Guidance Quarterly*, 1974, *22*, 256-262.

Chapter 3

LEISURE COUNSELING MODELS

HOWARD E.A. TINSLEY AND DIANE J. TINSLEY

ALTHOUGH the importance of leisure has been recognized since antiquity (Berlyne, 1968), it is only during the last decade that social scientists have begun to stress the important influence of leisure on the mental health and life satisfaction of the individual (e.g., Brooks & Elliott, 1971; Iso-Ahola, 1980; Kaplan, 1975; Mendel, 1971; Neulinger, 1974; Oberle, 1971; Skinner, 1971; Tinsley, 1978). These scholars believe that to gain a sense of personal stability and continuity, many persons will become increasingly dependent upon the extent to which they use their leisure to fulfill their needs. Ideally, individuals should be able to use their leisure to raise self-esteem, increase life satisfactions, and facilitate self-actualization. Although some individuals are no doubt able to gain these benefits independently through creative use of their leisure, others may need to turn to qualified professionals for assistance.

Over the past few years several pilot programs in leisure counseling have been developed and a number of books and manuals have been written on the topic (e.g., Edwards & Bloland, 1980; Epperson, Witt, & Hitzhusen, 1977; Gunn, 1977; Overs, Taylor, Cassell, & Chernov, 1977). Two important contributions of these earlier efforts are (1) their pioneering work in sensitizing the recreation and counseling professions to the important contributions that leisure counseling can make and (2) their emphasis on detailed knowledge of leisure activities and the role these activities can play in the individual's life. From our perspective as counseling psychologists, however, most leisure counseling models have serious limitations, including (1) a narrow focus on leisure activity choice, (2) an emphasis on dealing exclusively with leisure concerns and referring clients elsewhere for help with other concerns, and (3) a failure to recognize the importance of formal training in communication and intervention skills for leisure counselors.

Despite the previous activity, therefore, no coherent field of leisure counseling currently exists. Rather, our review reveals a growing awareness of the importance of leisure in the life of the individual and an increasingly held conviction that there *should be* a field of leisure counseling. In order to illustrate the current status of leisure counseling and the areas of development needed, this chapter will review a representative sample of leisure counseling programs and briefly outline a holistic model of leisure counseling that we

This Chapter is based on an article of the same title that originally appeared in *The Counseling Psychologist*, 1981, *9*(3).

believe deals directly with the three shortcomings mentioned above.

Patterson (1974) has suggested a continuum of psychological helping relationships that is useful in reviewing leisure counseling programs. According to Patterson, helping relationships vary from those that are primarily information giving in nature to those that involve counseling (see Fig. 3-1). In our chapter, information-giving relationships are defined as helping relationships in which the emphasis is primarily on attaining new information in a cognitive manner. The focus of the relationship is quite specific. Although some concern may be expressed for establishing a good interpersonal relationship, the relationship is clearly of secondary importance. Counseling relationships may also be concerned with the attainment of new

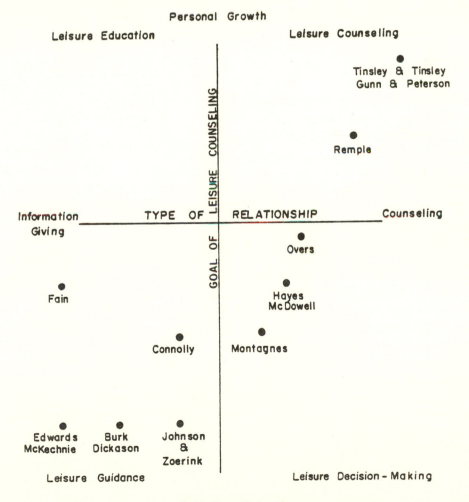

Figure 3-1. Classification of leisure counseling models by type of relationship and goal of leisure counseling.

information, and highly cognitive techniques may be used during the counseling process. The distinction is that although the presenting complaint may be very specific, the initial focus of the counseling interaction will be quite general and the establishment of a therapeutic relationship will be regarded as of primary importance, regardless of the intervention techniques to be used.

A second continuum that is helpful in distinguishing among the counseling models to be reviewed concerns the goals of counseling. It may be logical to assume that the developer of each leisure counseling model had some theory about how counseling based on his/her model would contribute to the personal growth of the individual. Nevertheless, the presently existing models vary markedly in this respect. At one extreme, some models of leisure counseling seem to focus very narrowly and theoretically on helping the client decide which leisure activity to pursue. At the other extreme, some models have the more general goal of facilitating the client's personal growth.

Figure 3-1 illustrates the relative position of the various leisure counseling programs as we have evaluated them. In many instances the proposed leisure counseling models have been only briefly sketched out by their developers or combined with descriptions of leisure education services. In other instances the issue of how leisure counseling contributes to personal growth has not been clearly addressed. Consequently, we consider the placement of the programs on the continua as only approximate. Given the information currently available, we are more confident in the placement of the programs in relation to each other and in the placement of the programs in the four quadrants than in the absolute placement of the programs within quadrants.

Leisure Guidance

We are in agreement with McDowell (1976, 1977) that leisure counseling models that rely primarily on information-giving techniques and are primarily intended to help the client choose an appropriate leisure activity are basically leisure guidance models. To our knowledge, seven leisure guidance models have been proposed (see Fig. 3-1).

Edwards (1977a, 1977b) and Edwards and Bloland (1980) have described a program consisting of 11 types of leisure counseling services. Five of the services are offered to individuals and differ primarily in terms of the number of sessions (one or two), the number of clients (one, two, or four), and the amount of testing performed (none, one, or multiple tests). The six group counseling services essentially differ along the same dimensions and vary from a single speech by a counselor to workshops of varying lengths. Regardless of the type of service offered, the focus is on helping individuals "select the most satisfying and practical leisure activities for their present lives" (Edwards, 1977a, p. 1). According to Edwards (1977b), this is a distinguishing feature of leisure counseling. In contrast to "therapeutic" counseling, "leisure counseling . . . gives the clients what they come for, not what a counselor thinks they need"

(Edwards, 1977b, p. 41). This is accomplished through an interview in which individual's interests are assessed and the individual is referred to an activity or group of activities. The focus of the interview is on the counselor's gathering factual information. For this purpose, Edwards had developed the Constructive Leisure Interview Sheet, which is a highly structured interview. Factual data (e.g., name, address, marital status), biographical data (e.g., educational history, academic major), and information about professional occupation, motivation (i.e., why seeking leisure counseling), past and current leisure activities, practical considerations (e.g., physical limitations, monetary considerations), leisure activity preferences, and personal skills is obtained through the structured interview procedure. When testing is performed, the interview is used "to supplement and reinforce the testing" (Edwards, 1977a, p. 17).

Once the counselor has obtained the necessary information, the counselor needs to study the collected information, decide "which interests the person really likes," select leisure activities that "stem from the interests" and specify ways and places in which the individual can participate in these activities (Edwards, 1977a, p. 49). The primary responsibility for increased knowledge and decision-making seems to belong to the counselor.

Edwards' emphasis on information collecting and giving is also apparent in the aspects of counseling she de-emphasizes. For example, Edwards argued that previous experience in testing, counseling, and referral is not essential since these skills can be learned as one practices the ingredients of her manual. Furthermore, formal training in psychology is not mandatory. Although the interview does not allow time for considering personality traits, this is not necessary since "Clients will consciously or unconsciously tell you all you need to know, as you go along" (Edwards, 1977a, p. 27).

Several scholars have previously reviewed Edwards' work. Osipow concluded that Edwards' first (1975) edition contain "little . . . that would help provide psychologically sophisticated leisure counseling, and the book has the danger of getting unsophisticated people involved in providing counseling services" (Osipow, 1977, p. 157). Barrett (1980) reviewed the second (1977) edition of this book and wrote "Apparently, the need for leisure counseling manuals, of whatever quality, is great. In any event . . . most of Osipow's original criticisms seem applicable once again" (Barrett, 1980, pp. 92-93). Dustin also reviewed Edwards' second edition and concluded that her book "offer[s] little to practicing counselors" (Dustin, 1978, p. 650).

Although less information is available about them, two additional systems of leisure guidance that do not focus on relationship variables deserve mention at this point. The first is that of McKechnie (1974) who developed the Leisure Activities Blank, which may be administered to the individual to determine the leisure activities best suited to the individual's personal needs. Since McKechnie stated that the counselor cannot assume the client knows what activities are best for him, he has focused his attention on the development of assessment techniques he believes will be able to provide the most accurate prediction of satisfying leisure choices. The second is that of Fain (1973; see Fig. 3-1) who, in contrast to McKechnie, has emphasized that the assessment that precedes decision making should focus on the individual and his/her attitudes rather than on the leisure activities. Finally, in contrast to both Edwards (1977a) and McKechnie (1974) who stated that the goal of leisure counseling is leisure activity selection, Fain wrote that the primary aim of leisure counseling is increased independence of the client.

Burk (1975) has discussed the nature of the counseling process in more detail than Edwards and was rated by us to be further toward the counseling end of the continuum than the Edwards, McKechnie, and Fain models (see Fig. 3-1). Burk indicated that after referral, the counselor should discuss with the client his/her leisure concerns, identify the client's leisure problems, administer tests to determine the client's leisure interests, and identify specific leisure activities for the client to pursue. The counselor and client should then work together to establish mutually agreeable behavioral objectives and performance criteria for each objective. Next, the counselor should provide information that will assist the client in implementing the leisure plans. After a suitable follow-up period during which the counselor may need to provide further assistance, the counselor should evaluate the leisure counseling outcome. If additional leisure services are not needed, leisure counseling is terminated.

Dickason (1972), like the other developers of leisure guidance models, indicated the goal and focus of leisure counseling as providing the information the clients needs to make a leisure activity choice. He did, however, note the importance of rapport between the counselor and client. Moreover, he suggested that the counselor should sometimes enlist family support to help the client achieve the goals of leisure counseling. In order to encourage external support, he believed that an educational program geared to these friends and/or relatives may sometimes be required. On the basis of all evidence available to us, we rated Dickason's model to be approximately equal to Burk's model in terms of its emphasis on the counseling relationship.

Johnson and Zoerink (1977) have advocated the use of values clarification techniques as one method for helping individuals learn about themselves. Johnson and Zoerink believe values are important determinants of a person's life-style and have implications for how he/she will be most happy in spending his/her leisure time. Despite their advocacy of a wider range of counseling techniques and some consideration of relationship variables, however, Johnson and Zoerink have stated the primary goal of leisure counseling as helping the individual identify leisure activity that will meet their interests.

Connolly (1977; see Fig. 3-1) suggested the use of values clarification and assertive training techniques in leisure counseling. Although the ultimate goal as written is still the selection of an appropriate leisure activity, the first step is the discovery of self-knowledge through values clarification activities. In addition, Connolly has specifically criticized the limited view of leisure counseling as consisting of an expert picking activities for clients. In this respect, then,

Connolly seems to have conceptualized the goals of leisure counseling more broadly than any of the authors previously reviewed and acknowledges that both the client and counselor have certain responsibilities for working together within a counseling relationship. Once the client is aware of his/her values and the implications these values have for the choice of leisure activities, the client can make a leisure activity choice while retaining the power and responsibility for making his/her own decisions. Following the attainment of self-knowledge, Connolly (1977) also advocated the development of skills that will facilitate the client's attainment of what is valued. To accomplish this, assertion training was recommended to "give the client behavioral practice in acquiring those new leisure pursuits he/she desires" (Connolly, 1977, p. 201).

Several reports of the application of leisure guidance approaches are available in the literature. Leisure guidance approaches have been used with public offenders (Brayshaw, 1974), college students (Epperson & Jenison, 1977), psychiatric patients (Hoffman & Ely, 1973), the general public (Edwards, 1977a), and the developmentally disabled (Joswiak, 1977).

Leisure Decision Making

We have given the label "leisure decision making" to four models (see Fig. 3-1). The main focus of each of these approaches is still on helping the client obtain the information necessary to make an appropriate choice of leisure activities. Unlike the leisure guidance models, however, these approaches offer some hint that the goals of leisure counseling must be conceptualized more broadly and/or that the affective qualities of the relationship are important. Consequently, we believe these models indicate a greater awareness of the psychological complexity of the decision-making process, as described by Harren (1979) and Miller and Tiedman (1972).

Montagnes (1976) has discussed a reality therapy approach to leisure counseling. Going beyond mere information giving, he advocated the counselor become involved by interacting with the client in a knowing, caring way (i.e., treating the client as a unique individual). He also indicated that it is important that the counselor let the client learn something about the counselor's likes and dislikes. Although Montagnes does not identify this as self-disclosure per se, he does seem to advocate the use of the affective variables within the relationship to influence counseling outcomes. Also implied in Montagnes' model is the idea that the counselor should help the client to increase his/her self-knowledge. The primary focus, however, is still on the client's gaining self-knowledge in order to make an appropriate leisure activity choice.

The leisure decision-making approaches of Haynes and McDowell include additional elements not evident in Montagnes' model. Although these programs also focus on providing information so that individuals may make the most appropriate leisure choice, we think these approaches represent a somewhat more flexible, sophisticated model of leisure decision making.

Hayes's (1977a, 1977b) model resulted from his work in a program designed to help retarded individuals adjust to community living. He noted that many retarded persons fail in their attempts to adjust to community living as a result of inappropriate use of their leisure time. The core of Hayes's model is a "Leisure Education and Recreation Counseling Service," which is intended to (1) involve the individual in appropriate leisure activities, (2) involve the individual in total community living, and (3) facilitate development of positive feelings toward self and towards community living. Prior to the initiation of the educational service, however, the counselor is expected to establish rapport with the client, to establish lines of communication, and to establish a casual atmosphere. During the leisure education service, the focus is on helping the individual select and participate in appropriate activities and develop the necessary skills. Even during this phase, the counselor is expected to continue to facilitate client expressions of feelings, emotions, and attitudes and to help the client develop a positive self-concept. Although the leisure education aspects of the model are not a direct focus of this chapter, information about the overall philosophy was used to provide the basis for classification within the leisure decision-making models (see Fig. 3-1)

McDowell (1976) has proposed a leisure decision-making approach that uses rational problem-solving and decision-making techniques techniques to facilitate "interpretative, affective, and/or behavioral changes" (p. 9) in the client. The ultimate goal is to help the client develop the "independent responsibility of choosing and making wise decisions as to his leisure involvement" (McDowell, 1976, p. 5). Clients needing help with any problem "more demanding than mere leisure satisfaction" (McDowell, 1976, p. 68) should be referred to another professional.

McDowell (1976) stated that the leisure decision-making counselor should be a competent counselor and regarded an effective counselor-client relationship as essential to the counseling process. In order to accomplish this, the counselor must possess effective interpersonal and facilitative skills. In addition, he indicated that the counselor must be knowledgeable about the nature of the leisure experience (e.g., the impact of leisure on man, contemporary leisure problems), the diagnosis and treatment of problems related to the client's physical, mental and social health, and the locally available leisure resources.

McDowell (1976) has outlined a nine-stage leisure counseling process. In the precounseling evaluation, a diagnostic interview and/or testing is (are) completed to assess such things as the client's leisure interests, self-concept, and attitudes. An outline of the counseling program is also provided. Counseling begins with identification of the client goals for counseling. The case studies illustrating this process focused very specifically on goal identification (e.g., "Counselor: What general problems do you find associated with your free time?" McDowell, 1976, p. 59). Next, the counselor attempts to identify the underlying needs that would be met by achieving each goal before moving to the identification of the specific, behaviorally observable performance criteria for the satisfaction of each goal.

During McDowell's fourth stage of counseling, the counselor identifies any possible barriers or obstacles to the attainment of each leisure goal and works out strategies for dealing with each barrier. The counselor and client then identify leisure alternatives relevant to each goal, perhaps through use of a leisure interest profile. Information is collected, shared, and used in planning of a course of action. The client then begins to participate in the activities selected, but the counseling relationship is maintained during the period of initial adjustment. Termination occurs after the adjustment period, but McDowell (1976) recommends a follow-up evaluation at a suitable interval.

Application of the approaches described above is not yet well documented in the literature. Similar but less well described programs have been used with adult psychiatric and alcoholic patients (Hitzhusen, 1973), adolescents (Hitzhusen, 1972), and institutionalized elderly persons (Stensrud, 1977).

The most extensively applied and most thoroughly evaluated leisure counseling model reported in the literature to date is that developed by Overs and his associates (Magulski, Faull, & Rutkowski, 1977; Overs et al., 1974; Overs, Taylor, Cassell, & Chernov, 1977; Wilson, Mirenda, & Rutkowski, 1975). According to our ratings, this model differs from the previously discussed leisure decision-making approaches in its overall flexibility in conceptualizing the goals of leisure counseling, its focus on the total individual, and its attention to the counseling relationship (see Fig. 3-1). Overs et al. (1974) indicated that problems associated with making leisure choice may involve lack of knowledge about self, avocations, or community resources; choice anxiety; or problems with one's avocational self-concept. Consequently, the program heavily emphasized the development and application of psychometric techniques. The information gained through testing is believed to be directly relevant to the perceived causes of leisure difficulties. It is not surprising, therefore, that five avocational choice instruments and the Milwaukee Avocational Satisfaction Questionnaire were developed by Overs et al. (1974) as part of their leisure counseling project.

Another contribution of Overs and his associates is the wealth of detail provided on the 122 handicapped clients (Overs et al., 1974) and 97 elderly clients (Overs, Taylor, Cassell, & Chernov, 1977) who received leisure counseling. Overs et al. (1974) reported, for example, that clients were seen for an average of 2.85 interviews and had an average of 2.84 telephone contacts with the center. In addition, the average client had 3.61 contacts with collateral personnel.

In most respects, the 1974 approach was a leisure guidance model. The core elements followed the trait-and-factor paradigm with (1) learning about the individual, (2) learning about the environment, (3) studying the relationship between the characteristics of the individual and the environment, and (4) recommending suitable leisure activities. In form, the 1974 approach was reminiscent of early career counseling approaches. The service usually began with a telephone call or interview. Individuals judged to need primarily career or personal counseling were referred to other counseling agencies. The service usually included testing and the use of printed information on leisure activities, may have included referral to persons knowledgable about selected leisure activities, and ended with the client making tentative leisure activity choices. Extensive follow-up of the clients was performed.

This information-giving approach to counseling was subsequently modified by the Milwaukee team. Although retaining a heavy emphasis on the use of tests in information gathering, the authors reported that "A large share of our counseling so far has been devoted to personal adjustment counseling (psychological counseling), rather than to avocational choice decision-making counseling. Although still within the leisure focus, clients had to work through problems of life adjustment before they were ready to embark on avocational choice decision making" (Overs, Taylor, & Adkins, 1977, p. 44). Clients obviously needing psychotherapy were still referred to another service facility whenever possible, but many such clients were retained in leisure counseling because of the unavailability of services or the clients' unwillingness to accept such services. Close review of the case studies provided by Overs, Taylor, Cassell, and Chernov (1977) revealed a variety of personal and emotional problems on the part of clients, the most common of which were depression and stress at life adjustment concerns. Moreover, the case histories revealed that attention was given to the relationship between the counselor and client, and numerous examples of the counselor establishing the facilitative conditions were evident. Unfortunately, evaluation of the effectiveness of this service focused on leisure participation and satisfaction, a rather narrow focus given the above observations.

Leisure Counseling

We are aware of three models (see Fig. 3-1) that clearly emphasize the following aspects, which we believe essential in an optimal approach to leisure counseling:

1. Focus on the total individual, not just the individual as a problem in leisure choice,
2. Emphasis on the establishment of counseling relationship embodying the facilitative conditions, and
3. Conceptualization of the goal of leisure counseling as contributing to the self-actualization of the individual.

Although he has not outlined a leisure counseling model, Neulinger's (1976, 1977) papers outlining the necessary elements of a leisure counseling model are largely in agreement with us on these points.

The model reported by Remple (1977) grew out of her work with the Ontario Ministry of Community and Social Services and the Etobicoke Parks and Recreation Services. Central to her model are these clearly stated beliefs:

1. Leisure is a state of being, a life-enriching experience that broadens and refines perception of self. Leisure must be defined on an individual basis as a state of mind in which the individual pursues whatever interests him/her, even though he/she may be working at gainful employment.
2. Leisure counseling is a process whereby individuals are helped to achieve a state of leisure.
3. Leisure education should be an integral part of the normal learning process.

Remple (1977) assumes that each individual possesses the potential to become a self-fulfilling person, that each individual is responsible for the development of his/her own potential, but that a variety of barriers operate to prevent people from developing this potential. Some of the barriers she identified include lack of knowledge, passivity, inertia, desire for perfection, inadequate social development, and lack of financial resources.

According to Remple (1977), the task of the leisure counselor is to help the individual identify and remove these barriers, which will free the individual so that personal growth may once again occur. To achieve this end, a Rogerian approach is advocated in which the counselor is expected to be empathic, to be congruent, and to have positive regard. The counseling process begins with the counselor encouraging the client to talk about him/herself. Often the counselor must help the client go beyond the superficial level of interaction to express "buried" feelings. Through this process, the counselor and client identify the client's leisure needs. When this is accomplished, an assessment of the client's past experiences, skill level, and past interests is made. The counselor and client then consult the leisure information file to choose an appropriate group or activity. Remple (1977) presented three case studies to illustrate the process, which was used with 20 clients.

In a collaborative effort, Gunn and Peterson have developed an approach to leisure counseling based on transactional analysis, Gestalt awareness, and systems theory, embedded in a therapeutic recreation context. Although leaning heavily on the use of jargon and "interpretation," Gunn's (1976, 1978) initial statements did provide an analysis of psychological dynamics of play behavior in the individual. From the Gestalt viewpoint, Gunn noted, a well-integrated person is one in whom need-fulfillment is going on continuously. Gestalt therapy, therefore, focuses on identification of ways in which clients prevent themselves from getting their needs met. Five factors that serve as blocks to healthy expression of play behavior are (1) inhibiting authority messages, (2) conflicting authority messages, (3) highly structured or organized games, (4) religious ideology that perceives play as idleness and, therefore, as evil and, (5) parental attitudes and values regarding appropriate sex role and competitive behaviors. Gunn (1976) stressed the importance of helping individuals to satisfy their needs more flexibly and completely by (1) becoming aware of their existing behavior and attitudes, (2) evaluating their time usage, and (3) changing their leisure attitudes and behavior in ways that are more consistent with self-expression and growth.

Expanding upon this line of thought, Peterson and Gunn (1977) more clearly conceptualized leisure as a state of mind in which the individual has maximum freedom for self-regulation and the potential for self-actualization. Although not a panacea, they indicated that "A [leisure] counseling approach which focuses on removing blocks to play behavior may well contribute to developing lasting feelings of significance and self-worth" (p. 30).

An even broader theoretical perspective is apparent in the writings of Peterson (1976), Gunn (1977), and Gunn and Peterson (1978). Within a biopsychosocial systems aproach to therapeutic recreation program designs, Gunn and Peterson (1978) classified services as rehabilitation, education, or recreation. Leisure counseling is viewed as a component of leisure education that promotes "self-awareness; awareness of leisure attitudes, values and feelings; and the development of decision-making and problem solving skills related to leisure participation" (p. 214). The six components of the leisure counseling process are assessment, goal determination, program planning, program implementation, evaluation, and postprogramming. A review of the sample questions suggested for use in assessment revealed a broad-based approach to information gathering intended to help clients clarify their perceptions of their problems, needs interests, and expectancies, rather than a narrow focus on leisure activity selection. Moreover, the authors noted that the process of obtaining information can promote the establishment of a therapeutic relationship and can promote the sharing of responsibility and goal setting.

Although closely allied with the Gestalt viewpoint, Gunn (1977) acknowledges that the leisure counselor may adopt many possible counseling styles and Gunn and Peterson (1978) apply a variety of theoretical approaches (e.g., Gestalt, client centered, behavioral, transactional analysis) to the conceptualization of leisure counseling. Given the theoretical position chosen for an individual client, the individualized goals may vary considerably. Usually, however, the goals adopted in leisure counseling have behavioral and attitudinal components and are related to the personal growth and development of the client rather than to a limited focus on leisure activity selection. Relationship factors are also deemed an important aspect throughout the counseling process. Moreover, Gunn and Peterson (1978) have noted that, "Regardless of the degree of complexity inherent in the counseling relationship, specific training in counseling is clearly necessary in order to effect positive behavioral changes" (p. 205).

Although the leisure counseling model we advocate (Tinsley & Tinsley, in press) builds upon previous work in the area, it differs markedly from any previously published. Influential in shaping this model have been our adoption of Maslow's (1970) theory of motivation as a conceptual basis, our ideas regarding the impact of leisure on the individual, our belief that the leisure counselor must be a generalist rather than a specialist, and our practitioner experiences

(Tinsley, 1977a, 1977b; Lindrud, 1977a, 1977b).

The paradigm we propose reflects our definition of leisure counseling as a process during which a client and a counselor work together to clarify and diagnose the client's concerns, to identify mutually agreed upon long- and short-term goals for counseling, and to develop and implement a treatment plan to achieve these goals. Like other forms of counseling, the focus of leisure counseling varies across time according to the needs of the client. The feature that differentiates leisure counseling from other forms of counseling, however, is that leisure counseling focuses in some substantial way on the client's leisure as it relates to his/her self-actualization.

The model we advocate differs from most other leisure counseling models in the attention given to the total counseling context in which the client's concerns are explored. In contrast to leisure counseling models that regard the first (and sometimes only) interview as an intense information-gathering session, we advocate a more unstructured approach. We believe that the first goal for the initial interview is that the leisure counselor begin to establish a warm, trusting relationship with the client. In this regard, the following four counselor behaviors or expressions of attitudes need to be communicated to the client from the beginning of the first leisure counseling session.

EMPATHY: The ability of the leisure counselor to understand the client's affective experience and to communicate that understanding to the client.

GENUINENESS: The condition achieved when the leisure counselor's words and behaviors are congruent with his/her inner feelings and beliefs.

RESPECT: Involves communication to the client of the leisure counselor's sincere belief that the client possesses the inherent qualities necessary to succeed in life, and that each person has the right to make his/her own decisions.

POTENCY: The communication of a dynamic, involved, charismatic, in-charge-of-self attitude to the client (Small, 1974).

Two additional goals for the initial interview are to clarify the client's expectations for leisure counseling and for the leisure counselor's role, and to begin exploring the nature of the client's problem. Most leisure counseling models proposed to date, as discussed above, assume the client's problems to be one of choosing a leisure activity. It is our experience, however, that client's concerns are usually more complex. Even in instances in which the client's presenting surface concern is clearly stated as a problem of leisure choice (e.g., "I want to find some new activities to do in my leisure time"), the client is frequently experiencing other problems and conflicts at a deeper meaning level (e.g., "I am bored and lonely because I don't have any friends and don't know how to make friends"). If the leisure counselor is too quick in narrowing his/her focus to the initially presented concern, the client most likely will not have an opportunity to experience a more thorough therapeutic relationship.

We recommend, therefore, that the leisure counselor resist the temptation to narrow the focus too quickly. We believe it is important for the leisure counselor to understand the full extent of the client's concern and to communicate that understanding to the client. In gaining this understanding, it will be necessary for the leisure counselor to assess the client's degree of psychological integration or intactness, to be on the alert for signs of anxiety, depression, or nonverbalized conflicts, and to assess the client's developmental progress. If the client's primary need is for help with a decision, all that will be lost is a little time. If the client has additional concerns he/she has not initially verbalized, an opportunity for significant personal growth may be gained.

As the counselor and client gain a more comprehensive understanding of the client's concerns, four additional aspects of the therapeutic relationship (i.e., concreteness, confrontation, immediacy, and self-disclosure) will become more essential to facilitate client self-awareness, understanding, and development (Small, 1974). These counselor behaviors, however, have much greater potential for frightening or intimidating the client than the previously described attending behaviors and attitudes. Appropriate pacing and timing is important so that the development of a quality helping relationship will not be hindered to the extent that the client prematurely terminates leisure counseling. Consequently, the leisure counselor should initiate these behaviors gradually when he/she believes the therapeutic relationship has developed to the point where it can be sustained in the face of the stress that will result.

The leisure counseling process, therefore, begins with the establishment of a therapeutic counseling relationship and the exploration of the client's problem. In practice, the client and leisure counselor need to state as clearly as possible their mutually agreed upon goals for leisure counseling and develop a plan for accomplishing and revising them as appropriate during the leisure counseling process. Some clients are basically well adjusted but need help in learning to make better decisions regarding their present situation and/or plans for the future. Other clients may need help in making changes in their attitudes or behaviors. Still other individuals may experience confusion in their efforts to live a secure, satisfactory, pleasureable life. Such individuals may be confused about prioritizing their problems and whether these problems arise from internal perceptual conflicts and external constraints. As the client's problems become more clear, the client and leisure counselor can establish specific goals for counseling and develop plans for accomplishing those goals. The goals of counseling can be modified as counseling continues.

When the counselor and client are both clear that the goals of leisure counseling have been accomplished, the counseling relationship is terminated. Sensitive awareness to and working through termination issues can be as critical to the future personal growth of the client as the other choices and changes made during the earlier phases of leisure counseling. Finally, we recommend followup of clients so the leisure counselor may gain additional information to continue to improve his/her counseling. Follow-up also provides an opportunity to let former clients know that they can seek additional contact as they determine appropriate.

We are aware that the model we have outlined requires that, to be effective, the leisure counselor must be able to counsel people with a range of concerns that are often complex and interrelated. We believe that the effective leisure counselor must be a generalist who understands and values the manner in which the creative use of leisure contributes to the self-awareness, life satisfaction, mental health, and personal growth of the individual. He/she should have a broad knowledge of the psychology of leisure and of the theories and research concerning human development and counseling. In addition, his/her training must include a solid grounding in the communication and intervention skills. Finally, the effective leisure counselor must be able to monitor clients' progress toward counseling goals in order to evaluate the effectiveness of counseling.

Summary

Two tendencies are discernable in the leisure counseling approaches reviewed. First, most of the approaches have been primarily information-giving in nature and have focused on helping clients select leisure activities in which to participate. Second, several writers have advocated the use of some technique (e.g., values clarification, assertion training) in leisure counseling without relating the application of this technique to any comprehensive theory of counseling. The amount of bootstrapping occurring in leisure counseling may be interpreted as an indication that there are clients needing leisure counseling services and professionals who are attempting to respond to this need. These tendencies also document the need for increased attention to the theoretical underpinnings of leisure counseling.

Although many of the efforts reviewed herein have provided services to clients having immediate needs, we believe most have contributed little to the conceptual development of leisure counseling. In our opinion, the advancement of our collective thinking about leisure counseling requires that researchers, theoreticians, and practitioners address the following questions in a systematic manner:

1. What is the nature of leisure?
2. What leisure counseling goals are appropriate under what conditions for which individuals?
3. What are the psychological processes involved in achieving these goals?
4. What counseling interventions can be used to influence the relevant psychological processes in such a way that the desired counseling goals will be effectively achieved?

The models of Gunn and Peterson (1978), McDowell (1976), Overs, Taylor, and Adkins (1977), Remple (1977), and Tinsley and Tinsley (in press), in particular, seem to us to provide the type of context necessary for a systematic approach to these questions. We encourage the further development and refinement of models such as these.

REFERENCES

Barrett, T.C. Review of P.B. Edwards' *Leisure counseling techniques* (2nd ed.) *Journal of Leisure Research*, 92-93.

Berlyne, D.E. Laughter, humor and play. In G. Lindzey & E. Aronson (Eds.), *The handbook of social psychology* (2nd ed.). Reading, Ma.: Addison-Wesley Pub. Co., 1968, vol. 3, pp. 775-852.

Brayshaw, R.D. Leisure counseling in corrections. *Journal of Leisurability*, 1974, *1*, 10-14.

Brooks, J.B., & Elliott, D.M. Prediction of psychological adjustment at age thirty from leisure time actitivies and satisfactions in childhood. *Human Development*, 1971, *14*, 51-61.

Burk, G. *A community-based model for the delivery of leisure counseling services to special populations.* Unpublished Master's Project, 1975. (C.F. McDowell, Jr. *Leisure counseling: Selected lifestyle processes.* Eugene, Or.: Center for Leisure Studies, 1976.)

Connolly, M.L. Leisure counseling: A values clarification and assertive training approach. In A. Epperson, P.A. Witt, & G. Hitzhusen (Eds.) *Leisure counseling: An aspect of leisure education.* Springfield, Il.: Charles C Thomas, 1977.

Dickason, J.G. Approaches and techniques of recreation counseling. *Therapeutic Recreation Journal*, 1972, *6*, 74-78.

Dustin, R. Review of P.B. Edwards' *Leisure counseling techniques: Individual and group counseling step-by-step* (2nd ed). *Personal and Guidance Journal*, 1978, *56*, 650.

Edwards, P.B. *Leisure counseling techniques: Individual and group counseling step-by-step.* Los Angeles: University Publishers, 1975.

Edwards, P.B. *Leisure counseling techniques: Individual and group counseling step-by-step* (2nd ed.). Los Angeles: University Publishers, 1977. (a)

Edwards, P.B. Practice makes perfect leisure counseling. *Journal of Physical Education and Recreation*, 1977, *48*(4), 40-42. (b)

Edwards, P.B. & Bloland, P.A. Leisure counseling and consultation. *The Personnel and Guidance Journal*, 1980, *58*, 435-440.

Epperson, A., & Jenison, K.N. Leisure counseling in the university setting. In A. Epperson, P.A. Witt, & G. Hitzhusen (Eds.), *Leisure counseling: An aspect of leisure education.* Springfield, Il.: Charles C Thomas, 1977.

Epperson, A., Witt, P.A. & Hitzhusen, C. *Leisure counseling: An aspect of leisure education.* Springfield, Il: Charles C Thomas, 1977.

Fain, G. Leisure counseling: Translating needs into action. *Therapeutic Recreation Journal*, 1973, *7*, 4-9.

Gunn, S.L. Leisure counseling: An analysis of play behavior and attitudes using transactional analysis and Gestalt awareness. In G. Rob & G. Hitzhusen (Eds.), *Expanding horizons in therapeutic recreation III.* Columbia, Mo.: University of Missouri Press, 1976.

Gunn, S.L. A systems approach to leisure counseling. *Journal of Physical Education and Recreation*, 1977, *48*(4), 32-35.

Gunn, S.L. Structural analysis of play behavior: Pathological implications. In D.J. Brademas, *New thoughts on leisure.* Champaign, Il.: University of Illinois, 1978.

Gunn, S.L., & Peterson, C.A. *Therapeutic recreation program design: Principles and procedures.* Englewood Cliffs, N.J.: Prentice-Hall, Inc., 1978.

Harren, V.A. A model of career decision making for college students. *Journal of Vocational Behavior*, 1979, *14*, 119-133.

Hayes, G.A. Leisure education and recreation counseling. In A. Epperson, P.A. Witt, & G. Hitzhusen (Eds.), *Leisure counseling: An aspect of leisure education*: Springfield, Il.: Charles C

Thomas, 1977. (a)

Hayes, G.A. Professional preparation and leisure counseling. *Journal of Physical Education and Recreation*, 1977, *48*(4), 36-38. (b)

Hitzhusen, G. Youth recreation counseling — A necessity in therapeutic recreation. *Therapeutic Recreation Journal*, 1972, *6*, 78-82.

Hitzhusen, G. Recreation and leisure counseling for adult psychiatric and alcoholic patients. *Therapeutic Recreation Journal*, 1973, *7*, 16-22.

Hoffman, C.A., & Ely, B.D. Providing recreation counseling in a psychiatric hospital: A vital link. *Therapeutic Recreation Journal*, 1973, *7*, 3-7.

Iso-Ahola, S.E. *The social psychology of leisure and recreation*. Dubuque, Ia.: W.C. Brown, 1980.

Johnson, L.P. & Zoerink, D.A. The development and implementation of a leisure counseling program with female psychiatric patients based on value clarification techniques. In A. Epperson, P.A. Witt, & G. Hitzhusen (Eds.), *Leisure counseling: An aspect of leisure education*. Springfield, Il.: Charles C Thomas.

Joswiak, K.F. Providing leisure counseling services to the developmentally disabled. In A. Epperson, P.A. Witt, & G. Hitzhusen (Eds.), *Leisure counseling: An aspect of leisure education*. Springfield, Il.: Charles C Thomas, 1977.

Kaplan, M. *Leisure: Theory and policy*. New York: John Wiley & Sons, 1975.

Lindrud, D.A. A career/life planning approach to leisure counseling. In D.J. Tinsley (chair), *Career planning and placement: Priorities for the future*. Symposium presented at the meeting of the American College Personnel Association, Denver, 1977. (a)

Lindrud, D.A. *Quality of living. A workshop enhancing self-actualization through the enrichment of work and leisure*. Workshop presented at the meeting of the American College of Personnel Association, Denver, 1977. (b).

Magulski, M., Faull, V.H., & Rutkowski, B. The Milwaukee leisure counseling model. *Journal of Physical Education and Recreation*, 1977, *48*(4), 49-50.

Maslow, A.H. *Motivation and personality* (2nd ed.) New York: Harper & Row, 1970.

McDowell, C.F., Jr. *Leisure counseling: Selected lifestyle processes*. Eugene, Or.: Center for Leisure Studies, 1976.

McDowell, C.F., Jr. Integrating theory and practice in leisure counseling. *Journal of Physical Education and Recreation*, 1977, *48*(4) 51-54.

McKechnie, G.E. The psychological structure of leisure: Past behavior. *Journal of Leisure Research*, 1974, *6*, 27-45.

Mendel, W. Leisure: A problem for preventive psychiatry. *American Journal of Psychiatry*, 1971, *127*, 125-127.

Miller, A.L., & Tiedeman, D.V. Decision making for the seventies: The cubing of the Tiedeman paradigm and its application in career education. *Focus on Guidance*, 1972, *5*, 1-16.

Montagnes, J.A. Reality therapy approach to leisure counseling. *Journal of Leisurability*, 1976, *3*, 37-45.

Neulinger, J. *The psychology of leisure*. Springfield, Il.: Charles C Thomas, 1974.

Neulinger, J. The need for and the implications of a psychological conception of leisure. *The Ontario Psychologist*, 1976, *8*, 13-20.

Neulinger, J. Leisure counseling: A plea for complexity. *Journal of Physical Education and Recreation*, 1977, *48*(4), 27-28.

Oberle, J.B. Life satisfaction and the alienated worker. *Rehabilitation Research and Practice Review*, 1971, *2*, 37-48.

Osipow, S.H. Review of P.B. Edwards' *Leisure counseling techniques. Journal of Leisure Research*, 1977, *9*, 155-157.

Overs, R.P., Taylor, S., & Adkins, C. *Avocational counseling in Milwaukee*. Milwaukee: Curative Workshop of Milwaukee, 1974.

Overs, R.P., Taylor, S., & Adkins, C. Avocational counseling for the elderly. *Journal of Physical*

Education and Recreation, 1977, *48*(4), 44-45.

Overs, R.P., Taylor, S., Cassell, E., & Chernov, M. *Avocational counseling for the elderly*. Sussex, Wi.: Avocational Counseling Research, Inc., 1977.

Patterson, C.H. *Relationship counseling and psychotherapy*. New York: Harper & Row, 1974.

Peterson, C.A. *A systems approach to therapeutic recreation program planning*. Champaign, Il.: Stipes Publishing Co., 1976.

Peterson, C.A., & Gunn, S.L. Leisure counseling: An aspect of leisure education. *Journal of Physical Education and Recreation*, 1977, *48* (4), 29-30.

Remple, J. A community-based "experiment" in leisure counseling. In A. Epperson, P.A. Witt, & G. Hitzhusen (Eds.), *Leisure counseling: An aspect of leisure education*. Springfield, Il.: Charles C Thomas, 1977.

Skinner, B.F. *Beyond freedom and dignity*. New York: Alfred Knopf, 1971.

Small, J. *Becoming naturally therapeutic: A handbook on the art of counseling, with specific applications to alcoholism counselors*. Austin, Texas: Texas Commission on Alcoholism, 1974.

Stensrud, C. Helping meet the needs of institutionalized aged people. *Journal of Physical Education and Recreation*, 1977, *48*(4), 46-48.

Tinsley, D.J. (chair) *Career planning and placement: Priorities for the future*. Symposium presented at the meeting of the American College Personnel Association, Denver, 1977a.

Tinsley, D.J. (chair) *Quality of living. A workshop enhancing self-actualization through the enrichment of work and leisure*. Workshop presented at the meeting of the American College Personnel Association, Denver, 1977b.

Tinsley, H.E.A. The ubiquitous question of why. In D.J. Brademas, *New Thoughts on Leisure*. Champaign, Il.: University of Illinois, 1978.

Tinsley, H.E.A. & Tinsley, D.J. A holistic model of leisure counseling. *Journal of Leisure Research*, in press.

Wilson, G.T., Miranda, J.J., & Rutkowski, B.A. Milwaukee leisure counseling model. *Journal of Leisurability*, 1975, *2*, 11-17.

Chapter 4

SOCIAL PSYCHOLOGICAL FOUNDATIONS OF LEISURE AND RESULTANT IMPLICATIONS FOR LEISURE COUNSELING

Seppo E. Iso-Ahola

IT is interesting that both social psychologists and leisure scientists trace the roots of their respective fields back to the same period and civilization in the history of humankind. Modern social psychologists regard Aristotle as their intellectual father and believe that he was the first to enunciate some of the basic principles of social influence and persuasion. Similarly, leisure scientists maintain that the Greeks discovered leisure and that leisure as a concept played a basic part in the systems of thought of such great philosophers as Aristotle and Plato. The identical ancient background of these two fields, therefore, suggests that the convergence of social psychology and leisure studies is a historical inevitability (Iso-Ahola, 1980). When reviewing the scientific literature, it becomes clear that the time has indeed arrived to combine social psychology and leisure. This convergence is needed for providing a more complete understanding and explanation of social influence processes in general and the social psychological nature of leisure cognitions and behaviors in particular.

LEISURE AS INDIVIDUAL AND SOCIAL CONCERN

Like most other areas of social psychological inquiry, the study of leisure can be justified on theoretical and practical grounds. Knowledge for the sake of knowledge has always been a powerful force behind human investigation, but the value of the obtained knowledge cannot be measured only by its capacity to extinguish researchers' need for curiosity. Knowledge has to have its utilitarian function as well.

Even a cursory review of the history of leisure shows that prominent philosophers have viewed leisure as a unique and irreplaceable opportunity for improving both intrapersonal and interpersonal behaviors. Generally, it appears that the main concern has been centered on the wise use of leisure, from the standpoint of developing one's mind and body. Some philosophers, most notably Aristotle and Marx, have seen leisure as providing the only opportunity to search for understanding of the individual's true nature and existence. This knowledge is supposed to free a person from external constraints, enabling him/her to achieve a true state of mind.

Other important functions frequently attached to leisure include (Iso-

Ahola, 1980) (1) socialization of the young into the mainstream of society through play and leisure participation, (2) enhancement of one's performance by improving work-related skills during leisure, (3) development and maintenance of skills for interpersonal behavior and social interaction, (4) social entertainment and relaxation, (5) enhancement of character and personality through wholesome leisure activities, (6) prevention of idleness and antisocial activities, and (7) development of a sense of community. It is immediately clear that these functions are sociopsychological in nature. Philosophers argue that if most people succeed in using their leisure wisely in accordance with the above functions, the entire society will benefit from such leisure orientation and the social climate will become conducive to psychologically healthful leisure participation. Consequently, individual leisure choices contribute positively to the sociopsychological leisure environment, which in turn advances "wholesome" leisure choices. This interrelationship between the individual and the social environment constitutes the core of the sociopsychological analysis of leisure.

The uniqueness of a sociopsychological study of leisure and recreation is evident when looking at the definition and basic approach of the field and practical implications thereof. Those who study leisure related phenomena from the sociopsychological perspectives indeed have something special: rather than calculating how many minutes people spend in various activities in various cultures, rather than trying to understand leisure behavior solely in terms of such social institutions as education, church, and family, or variables like income and occupation, sociopsychologically oriented leisure scientists start from an *individual* and emphasize that human beings do make decisions about their leisure needs, choices, and behaviors. Occupation and income do not make any decisions; it is the individual who does. For too long, leisure scientists have tried to unlock the secrets of leisure behavior by such variables as income, occupation, and socioeconomic status.

If we are to understand leisure behavior, we must consider how individual cognitions and behaviors influence and are influenced by those of others during a period of time subjectively designated as unobligated, free, or leisure. Leisure behavior does not exist in a social vacuum, because it takes place in a social environment in which the individual is at once the cause and consequence of his/her social leisure environment and society. Social leisure behavior does not exist in the time vacuum either, because the individual influences and is influenced by his/her social leisure environment, which thereby implies continual change — whether rapidly or slowly — in individual leisure behavior. These considerations give rise to viewing leisure behavior as a dialectical process according to which leisure behavior represents the interplay of two forces: a tendency to seek both stability *and* change, structure *and* variety, and familiarity *and* novelty in one's leisure. It then follows that the individual is in the process of a never-ending change, development, and evolution, suggesting that the social psychological inquiry cannot ignore the "historical context" (Gergen, 1973) of social leisure behavior.

TOWARD A SOCIAL PSYCHOLOGICAL THEORY
OF LEISURE BEHAVIOR

In attempting to understand and explain the "whys" of leisure behavior, a guiding question is, Why do people choose and participate in some activities as opposed to others? Or, as it is frequently stated in the context of children's leisure behavior, Why do children play? There is no paucity of attempts to answer these questions in the literature. Ellis (1973) found five "classical," six "recent," and two "modern" theories of play. These theories range from one extreme to another. At one end of the continuum is the instinct theory, according to which play is caused by inherited factors. Learning theory represents the other end, and to the exclusion of inherited forces, it emphasizes the role of environmental factors in the development of play behavior. Other theories fall somewhere between these two extremes.

Despite their great number, these theories suffer from two defects. First, they all focus on such narrow aspects of play and leisure that their explanatory

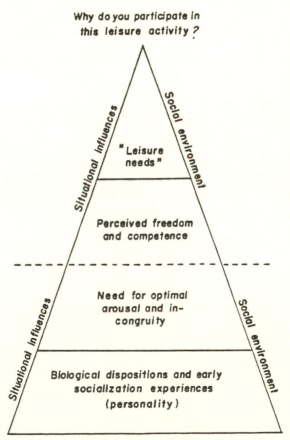

Figure 4-1. Levels of causality of leisure behavior. (From S.E. Iso-Ahola: *The Social Psychology of Leisure and Recreation*, 1980. Courtesy of William C. Brown, Dubuque, Iowa.)

power is inadequate. For example, in his famous theory, Patrick (1916) postulated that people play and engage in various activities because of their need for relaxation. While no one can deny the value of relaxation for leisure activities, it would be too simpleminded to assume that relaxation is the only or even the major motive for all leisure involvement. Second, these theories do not take into account the various levels of causality in leisure behavior. As a consequence, students often ask which of the frequent theories is "right." This confusion results from the authors' failure to point out the limits of their theories. Any given theory has been described as if it were *the* theory of leisure behavior. While small-scale theory construction and resultant mini theories dominate the initial stages of growth of any scientific field (Crane & Brewer, 1973), it is no excuse for ignoring that the "whys" of leisure behavior can and should be explained at different levels of causality, as illustrated in Figure 4-1.

Perhaps the most straightforward and popular way of explaining the reasons people participate in various leisure activities is to directly pose this question to them. As the above diagram demonstrates, it is also the simplest and most inadequate explanation, because research based upon this approach only "explores the tip of the iceberg." To ask subjects to rate the importance of a number of reasons ("leisure needs") for their leisure participation provides interesting information, but such knowledge is quite limited because it does not take into acount — at least in a measurable way — the fundamental forces of leisure behavior. For example, when a person is asked "Why do you participate in this leisure activity?" he does not, of course, answer "optimal arousal." Yet, the concept optimal arousal is essential for understanding the causes of leisure behavior. On the other hand, any isolated concept (e.g., biological dispositions, personality, childhood-adulthood socialization, optimal arousal, and intrinsic motivation) is insufficient and inadequate to fully explain the "whys" of leisure behavior.

Biosocial Basis

According to Figure 4-1, the fundamental cause of an individual's leisure behavior is his biological make-up, his inherited background. Recent empirical evidence has indicated that "there is a small but reliably heritable influence on the *patterning* of interests in individuals" (Grotevant et al., 1977, p. 637). In this study, members of biologically related families and members of adoptive families were administered an instrument to measure their interests. The results showed that biological parent-child and child-child relationships were all positive and significant, ranging from .19 (father-daughter) to .34 (sister-sister). None of the parent-parent, parent-child, or child-child correlations for adoptive family pairs were consistent and significant. Thus, these data indicate that the biological family members are moderately but significantly similar in their interest styles, whereas "adoptively related family members bear no more resemblance to each other than do parent-child pairs randomly selected from the population."

The results of Grotevant et al. (1977) also showed that the same-sex siblings (.36) were more similar to each other in the interest dimensions than the opposite-sex (.08) and parent-child (.17) pairs. This is an important finding because it demonstrates the effects of a social environment: the like-sex pairs have more similar rearing environments than do the parent-child pairs and consequently they are more similar in their interests. It should be remembered that biological parent-child and child-child pairs have, on the average, half of their genes in common, so that theoretically the correlation between the interests of a biological father and son should be about the same as the one between the brothers' interests. As the above correlations indicate, this is not the case because environment has begun altering these interest patterns. The Grotevant et al. (1977) study suggests that the *patterns* of leisure interests are biologically set, because "genetic differences among individuals contribute to interest differences among them." On the other hand, while genetic factors establish the overall orientation toward individual activity patterns, early socialization experiences tend to change them.

Further evidence of the importance of the early social environment to the development of play behavior was reported by Mueller and Brenner (1977). In this longitudinal study, two groups of boys, differing in the amount of peer acquaintance, participated for seven months in a laboratory testing of free play. Results showed that those toddlers who had 4½ months' acquaintance with their playmates more frequently engaged in sustained social interactions, being able to turn the fun into a sustained game, than those age-mates who had no peer acquaintance. Thus, social skills and social play are not the result of maturation or of immediate generalization from child-parent interactions. Rather, peer interaction in play enhances the child's social skills and ability to play socially, which in turn is the source of coordinated peer-orientated behavior.

Need for Optimal Arousal

Within one's biological dispositions, early social learning experiences influence in what specific activities a person becomes interested. For example, consider that many, if not most, people have biological tendencies toward many different types of leisure activities. Since a person cannot participate in all activities he is capable of doing, he must select in which activities to engage. Such selection, of course, is determined by his socialization experiences and the social environment in which he lives. The importance of the joint influence of biological dispositions and early socialization experiences is that they form the foundations for the individual need to seek optimal arousal and incongruity in leisure encounters.

The reason the individual seeks optimally arousing stimuli and environments is because too much or too little stimulation is damaging to him, both physiologically and psychologically. When the social environment provides too many stimuli, the individual withdraws; when these inputs are overly similar to the coded information and experience, he becomes bored and seeks novelty, complexity, and uncertainty (Hunt, 1969, 1972). In short, he strives for optimally arousing play. What is the empirical evidence for this theory?

Physiological and Physical Evidence

The first type of evidence comes from the stimulus deprivation studies revealing physical and physiological effects of the under- or over-stimulating environment. It is known that rearing animals under the conditions of complete stimulus deprivation leads to changes in biochemical and anatomical structures of their central nervous systems, resulting in deficiencies in the production of RNA (Hunt, 1969). Related studies on orphanage children suggest that human beings are also subject to detrimental effects of prolonged stimulus deprivation. In now-classic studies, Dennis and his associates (1957, 1960) showed that stimulus deprivation in the form of continuous homogeneity of auditory and visual experience reduced children's capacity to interact with their environment. The orphanage environment was deprived, in the sense that children were provided with practically no stimuli during the first four years of their lives. The resultant retardation in locomotor performance was indicated by these children's failure to sit up alone by two years of age and to walk alone by four years of age.

Fortunately, however, such detrimental effects in humans can be reversed by subsequent stimulating environments. Hunt reported that enrichment of experiences through progressively complex environments increases the growth of the central structures of the brain and augments one's problem-solving ability. Hunt (1972) found that the thickness of the cerebral cortex and the level of acetylcholinesterase activity of the cortex (which are indicators of high intelligence) increase with the complexity of the environment during early life. Similarly, other research reports (Dennis and associates, 1957, 1960; Kagan 1976) suggest that almost perfect recovery is possible, provided that later a stimulating environment is offered. On the other hand, Hunt (1969) suggested that "massive enrichment" is unnecessary and may even be counterproductive, presumably because "massive enrichments" provide too many stimuli for the child to handle, thereby resulting in withdrawal.

The above evidence suggests that social play environments have to be suitable to an individual child, not offering too little or too much arousal and incongruity. It is then clear that parents' roles are crucial in meeting children's needs for optimally stimulating milieu in which to grow. The optimally arousing play environments are also desirable because they give rise to the healthy development of personal control and mastery (Seligman, 1975) and because they enhance children's potential creativity (Bishop & Chace, 1971).

Evidence from Continuity/Discontinuity of Leisure Behavior

A different line of evidence of the support for the need for optimal arousal has been reported by leisure scientists. These researchers have found a statistically significant link between early childhood recreation and adult leisure behavior on the one hand and a significant difference in leisure participation between the two periods on the other.

Sofranko and Nolan (1972) reported that participation in youth was positively and significantly related to current levels of participation in the same activities. Similarly, Yoesting and Burkhead's (1973) data revealed that about 34-40% of outdoor activities were participated in similarly during childhood and adulthood, the link being statistically significant. The other half of their data indicated that about 60% of all outdoor recreation activities were participated in dissimilarly between the two periods. Based upon two large samples, Kelly (1974, 1977) found that of all the activities reported by respondents, 49% of them were begun in childhood and 51% in adult years. What is striking about this 50-50 differential for familiarity and change is that it is already present in infants. McCall (1974) found that 8½- to 11½-month-old babies spent about the same amount of time playing with their "old favorite toys" as with the new play objects in laboratory play setting.

Stability and Change

This continual change in leisure behavior throughout the life-span is due to the individual need to seek novel and arousing leisure experiences. The individual has a need for both stability (security) *and* change (novelty) in leisure experiences and behavior. Leisure behavior is then the result of two opposite forces simultaneously influencing the individual: the need for stability and the need for change. Over the life-span, these forces may take on the form and relative strength (Iso-Ahola, 1980, p. 176) depicted in Figure 4-2. It is noteworthy that even though the desire for permanence, structure, and psychological stability is relatively weak during childhood, adolescence, and adulthood, it nevertheless is important. For example, while expending most of his energy on exploring and investigating, a child can do so only if the social environment is also conducive to stability and security. In a way, the psychological stability and structure of the social environment is in the back of the child's mind, but in a stable and secure environment it does not dominate behavior. This is the principal reason a stable and secure family life is critical for the child. It permits attention to exploration, investigation, and manipulation in play, which is essential to cognitive maturation (Bruner, 1974). While the need for novelty seems to wane with increasing years, it nevertheless does not disappear in late adulthood but merely assumes different forms and appears within a much more limited leisure repertoire. Rather than seeking totally new leisure encounters, older people vary their leisure experiences within those activities they feel most capable of carrying out and which are expected to result in the most enjoyment.

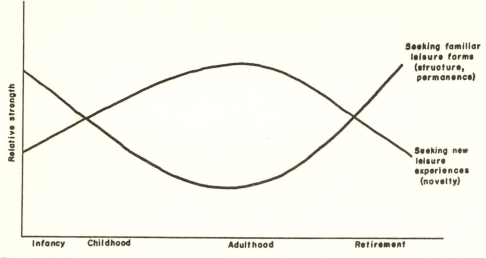

Figure 4-2. Relative strength of the tendencies to seek familiar and novel forms of leisure throughout the life cycle. (From S.E. Iso-Ahola: *The Social Psychology of Leisure and Recreation*, 1980. Courtesy of William C. Brown, Dubuque, Iowa.)

The need for stability *and* novelty (and thus optimal arousal) in leisure behavior can be pursued and fulfilled *within* and *between* play or leisure activities. A person may change from one activity to another in an effort to achieve optimally stimulating leisure. The desired level of change can also be achieved by numerous ways *within* the scope of a previously learned activity by changing (Iso-Ahola, 1980) (1) intensity of participation, (2) locus of participation (e.g., inside vs. outside of home), (3) social company, both quantitatively (few vs. many) and qualitatively (males vs. females), (4) time of participation (morning vs. afternoon), and (5) psychological reasons for participation (physical exercise, social interaction, etc.). These various dimensions of change are used differently by different people in order to achieve optimal novelty, complexity, arousal, and incongruity in all stages of the life cycle, and at any given time in a developmental stage. Such dimensions regulate persons' involvement in various leisure activities.

Thus, a person does not participate in one and the same activity, in the same manner, in the same place, with the same friends, etc. Even if he spends most of his free-time in one leisure activity, he seeks variety "within" the activity in order to meet the need for optimal arousal or incongruitry. While this need has its biological roots, it is influenced by one's social environment. What becomes optimally arousing may appear as "active" leisure participation to one person and "passive" leisure engagement to another, depending on social influences.

Implications

On the other hand, the fact that the need for change in leisure behavior can be satisfied within one and the same activity with little variety indicates human capacity to adapt to almost any condition (cf. Proshansky, 1973). This, in part, explains why people have become avid television-consumers and spectators, although they feel guilty of such passive behavior (Godby & Parker, 1976). That is, all one has to do is to change his reasons for watching television and he apparently gets enough variety and change. One day it is for education, the next day for social company, etc. By doing so, however, people diminish their level of optimal arousal. Instead of being active participants, people become passive consumers, which in turn is compatible with others' leisure habits and the social environment.

These ideas have important implications for leisure socialization. What becomes optimally arousing for an individual as a child is likely to affect his/her optimum level of arousal when an adult. Two different lines of research support this contention. First, Erickson (in Bruner, 1975) found that individuals who were able to keep a "sense of playfulness at the center of things" in childhood had the most interesting and fulfilling lives 30 years later. Second, Brooks and Elliott (1971) found that those who were fortunate enough to have satisfactory leisure activities between the ages of eight to eleven were psychologically better adjusted 20 years later than those who did not have such leisure activities in their early years, but rather learned to derive satisfaction from passive pursuits in childhood. These findings strongly suggest that if an individual's play is poorly stimulating throughout childhood, he may become accustomed to a low level of arousal and may learn to regard it as optimal. As a consequence, the tendency to seek novel, stimulating, and complex forms of leisure experiences in adulthood may be impaired.

Although it is theoretically possible for any free-time activity to become optimally arousing and thus psychologically rewarding, there are strong reasons to suggest that passive forms of recreation are not likely to do so. While the optimal level varies from individual to individual, some activities provide so little arousal and incongruity that they can meet few people's needs for optimal arousal. Activities categorized as "passive recreation" are such activities. Flanagan (1978) found in his nationwide survey that "active recreation" was one of the six areas showing the largest correlation coefficients with the overall quality of life. Similarly, Kornhauser (1965) reported that workers with high mental health scores were active in their nonwork behaviors, whereas workers with the lowest mental health scores tended to be escapist or passive in their free-time engagements, spending a lot of time watching television and little or no time in community affairs.

It follows from the above that there should be an inverted-U relationship between the perceived quality of life and leisure satisfaction and the level of arousal in leisure participation. This conjecture is strongly supported by data based upon a national probability sample of households in 48 states (Campbell et al., 1976, p. 357). The results indicated that people were most satisfied with their life and leisure when they felt they had an optimal amount of discretionary time available for their activities. Clearly, such data suggest that life and leisure satisfaction are at their highest when leisure behavior is optimally arousing and incongruous, and at their lowest when leisure behavior provides too little or too much arousal. Optimally arousing leisure is conducive to psychological well-being.

Given the importance of stimulating play environments in childhood, it is clear that children need parental guidance and encouragement for particiation in a variety of activities, but herein lies the problem. Since play (or leisure) consists of intrinsically motivated behaviors or activities performed for their own sake, play means the absence of external constraints. It can therefore be said that children are playing when their behavior is largely under their control, that is, when it is not extrinsically rewarded or externally sanctioned.

The "overjustification" research conducted during the last ten years (for reviews, see Lepper & Greene, 1978; Condry, 1977; Deci, 1975) has shown that adult intervention — whether in the form of extrinsic rewards or surveillance — undermines intrinsic motivation and free play, turning recreation and play into work. There is one important exception to this general pattern of results. Those rewards that signal competence enhance, not undermine, intrinsic motivation (Deci, 1975; Ross, 1976; Williams, 1980). In addition, verbal praise as compared to material or tangible rewards increases children's interest in play (Anderson et al., 1976; Dollinger & Thelen, 1978; Swann & Pittmann, 1977). Importantly, it has been found that when an adult rather than the child chooses a play activity, there is a signifiant decline in the child's intrinsic motivation for that activity (Swann & Pittmann, 1977).

Thus, an excellent social environment for seeking and achieving optimal arousal is provided by parents who do not use extrinsic rewards or otherwise force their children to engage in certain play activities, but who rather spend a considerable amount of time in talking with them about their self-directed play experiences of the day. Interspersed with pieces of advice, encouragement, praise, such comments will create an atmosphere and interaction that can sustain high intrinsic interest in a variety of play activities, or may even increase it.

Percieved Freedom and Competence

Perceived Freedom

According to Figure 4-1, at the next level of causation, leisure behavior can be explained in terms of intrinsic motivation. It is clear from the "overjustification" research that intrinsic motivation is at the heart of play and leisure behav-

ior. While there may be different types of intrinsic rewards for leisure participation and different labels for the same reward, two of them are more important than others: perceived freedom and perceived competence. It is important
to emphasize, however, that the influence of these factors occurs within the
framework of the need for optimal arousal. For example, a person who plays
tennis during free time because he feels he is good at it does not always play
tennis during his free time. At times, he participates in other activities he feels
good at, substituting from one activity to another. Even if he plays tennis most
of the time, he does not always play with the same opponent, nor does he select
the opponent who is much better or worse than he is — because such an opponent soon becomes repetitive, boring and unchallenging. Thus, a relative lack
of arousal drives a person to change or substitute either between or within
leisure activities, but the direction and speed of subsequent substitution is principally determined by perceived competence to participate with satisfaction in
various leisure activities.

For leisure involvement to become intrinsically motivated, it must meet one
critical condition: perceived freedom; that is, a person must have freedom initially to choose his activity. This is evident in the results reported by Iso-Ahola
(1979a, b). The significant interaction effects suggested that perceived freedom
forms a "threshold," after which the effects of other variables can be seen. When
free-time activities were unrelated to work, this low work-relation increased the
male respondents' perceptions of leisure only when they had initially had
freedom to participate in a given activity. When subjects had little or no
freedom to participate, even the fact that the participation produced such intrinsic rewards as feelings of competence did not notably increase the perception of leisure. When the participation was their own choice (high perceived
freedom), then the perception of leisure associated with participation not only
became high but was further augmented by intrinsic rewards of the activity.
Thus, perceived freedom appears to be the critical regulator of what becomes
leisure and what does not. It seems that perceived freedom involves the principle of all-or-nothing.

The results of other studies are consistent with these findings and suggestions. Mannell (1978) demonstrated in a laboratory setting that those subjects
who were given an opportunity to select (freedom of choice) a "leisure" activity
became considerably more involved in it than subjects who did not have
freedom of choice. For example, the former reported that time had passed and
flown much quicker than they had thought, thereby reflecting their deep involvement in the selected leisure activity. Wankel and Thompson (1978) reported a field experiment in which subjects (members of a commerical fitness
club) were divided into two groups, and their perceived choice was manipulated. Those who were told that the designed program was totally based upon
their own choices and perferences had a significantly higher average attendance rate than those who were told that their programs were based on "standardized exercise format." The difference in the average attendance between the

choice and nonchoice groups became greater as more time (5-6 weeks) elapsed from the beginning of the program. Taken together, these studies demonstrated that actual activity choice and perceived choice increased the degree and freqency of involvement in free-time activities.

Perceived freedom is critical not only for actual leisure involvement but also for subsequent physical and psychological well-being. Langer and Rodin (1976) showed that those nursing home patients who had freedom to control their everyday lives and recreational involvement exhibited greater increases in happiness, alertness, and activeness than those subjects who did not have such freedom of choice. Furthermore, enhanced perceived freedom and control increased patients' activity levels in general and their interpersonal activity in particular. More dramatically, the follow-up data (Rodin and Langer, 1977) indicated that enhanced perceived freedom and control significantly reduced subjects' morality rates. In a similar study, Schulz (1976) reported that among those nursing home patients who were able to predict or control social interaction (i.e. social visits by college students) the psychological and physical health was significantly better than among those who were not able to exercise such prediction or control.

The above studies demonstrate the importance of perceived freedom to the perceptions of leisure, leisure choices, actual involvement in leisure activities, and subsequent physical and psychological health. Given this importance of perceived freedom, it is unfortunate that much of leisure behavior seems to be externally motivated. Kelly (1976) found that 55% of all free-time activities are perceived as having "some or considerable obligation."

Perceived Competence

While perceived freedom is necessary, it nevertheless is not entirely sufficient for making leisure involvement intrinsically motivated. Once a person has been able to exercise freedom of choice in his leisure participation, he then expects to achieve certain intrinsic rewards, especially feelings of competence or mastery. As indicated earlier, people prefer and choose those activities in which they feel they are good.

At least two studies have reported data fully consistent with this supposition. In a large survey, Spreitzer and Snyder (1976) sought to determine the childhood antecedents of adult sports involvement. The results showed that perceived athletic competence was the strongest predictor of adult sport involvement for both men (.35 = path coefficient) and women (.32), indicating that if a person's perceived competence was high, his sports involvement was also high, and if perceived ability was low, so was sports involvement. In a related study, Csikszentmihalyi et al. (1977) asked subjects to carry a pocket-sized electronic paging device for a week and self-report, upon receiving audible beeps from the experimenter, at random times what they were doing and why they were doing it. The results revealed that the activities that were most frequently engaged in and that provided the most positive experiences were playing sports and games and talking with peers. It was further found that these activities were considered desirable because they were perceived to offer the greatest amount of challenge, required a high level of skills, and provided a strong feeling of control over their actions. At the same time, passive forms of leisure, like television watching, were perceived as the activities providing the least positive overall mood, offering virtually no challenge, requiring a low level of skills, and providing the least amount of personal control. Thus, the most enjoyable forms of leisure were strongly associated with perceived competence. This is not to suggest that people will always participate in activities as prompted by perceived competence, because it is not possible for practical reasons alone. Whenever they are participated in, the activities that provide feelings of competence or mastery and control are likely to be most enjoyable.

Toward a Unified Theory

The above evidence and discussion suggest that two motivational forces *simultaneously* influence the individual's leisure cognitions and behaviors. On one hand, leisure activities are sought because they provide change or novelty to daily routine. Thus, engagement in leisure activities allows one to leave the everyday environment behind. This is possible because leisure activities offer contrast to daily routine, mainly work. Research has shown that what is work for one can be leisure for the other. Csikszentmihalyi and Graef (1979) reported that men felt much freer than women in domestic and household chore activities, presumably because these activities had become routinized for women while they provided diversion for men. Therefore, it appears that routine activity undermines one's sense of freedom and hinders one from seeking diversion. Routine activities are seen as more worklike while nonroutine activities become to be seen as more leisurelike. Thus, it should not be surprising that people tend to place work in contrast to leisure and find the sense of freedom mostly in leisure. Of course, it is possible that leisure activity can become routinized and therefore lose its defining and central element — freedom. Unlike his work activity, a person can by himself modify his/her leisure involvement, so as to minimize routine and retain optimal variety and novelty.

It follows that the individual can do very little to avoid the dichotomy between work and leisure, so long as work is clearly structured, defined, and sanctioned as a 5-40 workweek (or whatever an arrangement). Obviously, one's job can be made psychologically richer by such arrangements as "flexitime" and increased individual responsibility in decision making. Nevertheless, these improvements do little, if anything at all, to knock down the fence between work and leisure. Leisure remains in contrast to work and has built into it a motivational force that allows the individual to leave the daily routine activity behind. Whether this force becomes a primary motivational force depends on social and personality factors and raises interesting empirical questions. It is possible that some leisure activities (e.g., tourism) are more conducive to the predominance of this force than other leisure activities. Similarly, individual differences (e.g., certain types of personality and individual experiences) and situational demands (e.g., marital problems) may influence the importance of this motivational force in leisure behavior. As shown in Figure 4-3, by escaping the everyday environment, a person can leave behind the personal and/or interpersonal world. In principal, he/she can escape personal problems, troubles, difficulties, failures, or the daily interpersonal world (e.g., roommates, friends, family members); or, he/she can escape both worlds.

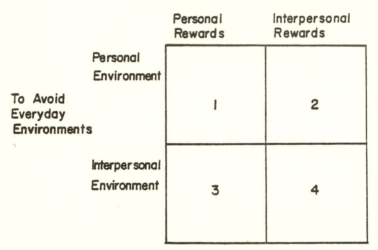

Figure 4-3. A social psychological model of leisure motivation.

The other motivational force is the individual tendency to seek psychological (intrinsic) rewards from participation in leisure activities. Self-determination in itself (i.e., one's ability to exercise freedom in choosing a leisure activity) is a major reward of leisure involvement. Psychologically, such freedom is important because it gives a sense of personal control over one's actions and behaviors. Thus, we can see that freedom in leisure is important for both motivational forces: it serves as a means for the tendency to escape the everyday environment and as an end itself for the tendency to seek intrinsic rewards through leisure participation.

The intrinsic rewards that the individual pursues through leisure participation can be divided into personal and interpersonal. The personal rewards include, in addition to self-determination, feelings of competence or mastery, challenge, learning, exploration, efforts, and relaxation. In other words, the individual participates in those leisure activities at which he/she is good, that are challenging and allow him/her to use and develop personal talent and skills.

The learning of new activities and things, acquisition of new skills, expenditure of effort, and exploration are all intrinsic rewards that a person can achieve when participating in leisure activities for their own sake. On the other hand, the seeking of interpersonal rewards means that in one form or the other, social interaction is the main intrinsic reward to be achieved. This can happen in many ways and different contexts: attending a party, dating, doing familiar leisure activities with new friends or a new activity with old friends, etc.

It is important to stress that the model presented above does not mean that

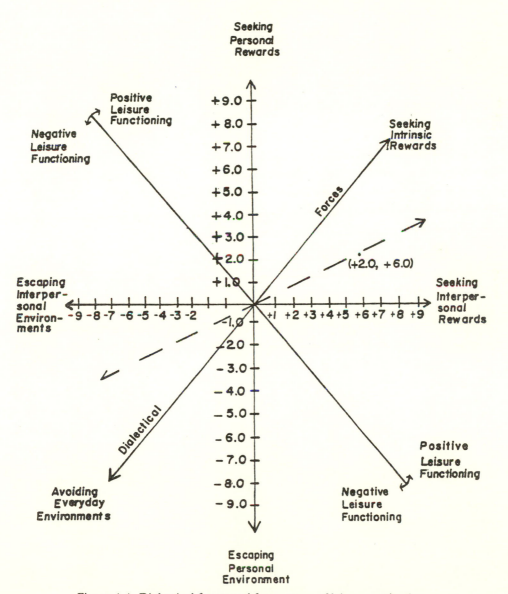

Figure 4-4. Dialectical forces and factor space of leisure motivation.

each person can be permanently placed in one of the four group (cells) in Figure 4-3. It is possible and likely that a person is influenced differently by the two motivational forces at different times. Although an individual, because of his personality, may show a tendency to use leisure in accordance with Cell No. 1 of Figure 4-3 most of the time, he/she may nevertheless at times participate in leisure activities for the reasons that are characteristic of other cells of Figure 4-3. He/she may go through all the four cells in the course of participation in one activity at one time only. Regardless of the cell a person is in through a given participation, his/her leisure behavior is simultaneously influenced by, and therefore represents an interplay of, the two motivational forces. Thus, it is not the question of "either-or" of these forces but, rather, one of approach *and* avoidance. The relative importance of these two forces remains to be determined by empirical investigation.

Based upon the model presented in Figure 4-3, a dialectical factor space of leisure motivation can be constructed. As can be seen from Figure 4-4, a person is influenced by two opposite (dialectical) forces, both of which have two end-poles pulling the person in opposite directions. First, the vertical axis presents the gamut that indicates the degree to which a person tends to seek personal rewards and to escape personal environment. The zero-point indicates the balance between the two tendencies. On the other hand, the horizontal axis shows the extent to which a person tends to seek interpersonal rewards and escape his/her interpersonal environment. Again, the center point reflects the equilibrium between the two forces.

Based upon self-reported data, it is possible to compute an axis for an individual or a group of individuals and thereby indicate the following things about leisure motivation:

(1) The steepness of the angle of the line (vector) shows the degree to which a person's leisure motivation is loaded by personal *versus* interpersonal orientation. The solid line of Figure 4-4 has an angle of 45 degrees, meaning that this individual (or group of individuals) is equally motivated by personal and interpersonal factors. The dotted line, on the other hand, is indicative of a person whose leisure motivation indicates a heavy interpersonal orientation. If this line (vector) conforms to the horizontal line, it then reflects the total interpersonal orientation in leisure motivation. If the vector conforms to the vertical axis, it then indicates the total personal orientation in leisure motivation.

(2) The distance from the gravity point (center) tells how far a person is from the completely balanced situation. If the person is located in the gravity point, it then shows that this person's leisure behavior is equally motivated by the tendency to avoid both personal and interpersonal rewards.

(3) The positivity/negativity of one's location (or vector) tells the degree of approach *versus* avoidance. Figure 4-4 reports the case of a person (or group) whose leisure motivation is influenced more by approach than avoidance. He/she is seeking personal rewards more than escaping the personal environment (+ 2.0) and is seeking interpersonal rewards more than escaping the interper-

sonal environment (+ 6.0). These two points locate him/her as a person whose leisure motivation can be characterized by "interpersonal approach" orientation.

This factor space can be used for many purposes. From a research perspective, it is possible to determine the location of a group of individuals and examine the amount of variation in the factor space of their leisure motivation from time to time. In this way, one can investigate which groups of individuals are similar and dissimilar in their leisure motivation. Also, the model invites research to discover factors that determine individual locations in the factor space. For example, are men and women located in the same quadrants? Do depressive and nondepressive individuals differ by their locations? What are the locations of various types of personalities? How are various types of leisure activities situated in the above space? In addition to these types of basic research questions, the factor space can be used for clinical and practical purposes. For example, a leisure counselor could determine the structure of a client's leisure motivation and the overall motivational tendencies. In this way, it would be possible to see whether the client is using his/her leisure effectively from the motivational standpoint. Similarly, any bias or one-sidedness in one's leisure motivation can easily be detected from the above factor space constructed for the individual client. The degree of variation in leisure motivation between activities in which one participates may be indicative or symptomatic of psychological problems or lack of them.

For example, a client whose referent points in the factor space are -7 (escaping personal environment) and -1 (escaping interpersonal environment) has a negative vector, with the degree of its angle approximating 90. Such a situation, especially if it is typical of a person's entire leisure motivation, not only indicates poor leisure functioning but may also reflect psychological problems or illnesses. This follows because the person is using his/her leisure almost solely to escape personal problems and difficulties. Psychologically, such motivation and behavior represents negative coping and can provide temporary solutions at best. Instead of hiding from problems, a psychologically healthier way of responding to the problems would be to seek intrinsic rewards (personal or interpersonal) from participation in leisure activities, because such seeking behavior is conducive to human development; on the other hand, the avoidance behavior amounts to seeking temporary hiding places and reflects poor or negative leisure functioning.

Thus, a therapist or counselor may use the above model to determine the client's location and vector in the factor space of leisure motivation and, based upon this information, can see what should be done to change negative leisure functioning into a positive one or how to increase positive leisure functioning. As Figure 4-4 indicates, the change from negative to positive leisure functioning can be accomplished by concurrently maximizing "seeking motivation" and minimizing "avoidance motivation." Since the essence of the motive to seek intrinsic rewards is the attainment of feelings of personal competence, mastery, or efficacy, and since leisure skills enable a person better to seek optimally arousing leisure experiences and combat boredom, the last section of this chapter focuses on implications for leisure counseling in terms of enhancing perceived competence and self-efficacy.

Empirical Support of the Model

A recent field study provides strong support for the above conceptualization. In this study (Iso-Ahola and Allen, 1982), over 40 intramural basketball players of 60 teams were administered a leisure need instrument and were asked to indicate how important each of 40 items or reasons was for their participation in the basketball program. A factor analysis performed for these ratings of perceived leisure needs (reasons) produced seven factors, of which the first four were entirely consistent with the four cells of Figure 4-3. The first factor, labeled "interpersonal diversion and control," indicated subjects' desire to *escape* their daily interpersonal environments and get away from other people through participation in basketball. The second factor, "personal competence," reflected their tendency to *seek* personal intrinsic rewards, mainly feedback about and feelings of personal competence and mastery. The third factor, "escape from daily routine," showed subjects' tendency to *escape* personal environment by attempting to change daily routine and get away from responsibilities through participation in basketball. Finally, the fourth factor, "positive interpersonal development," indicated subjects' tendency to *seek* interpersonal rewards through basketball participation, because such variables are talking to new people, building friendships, and bringing friends together loaded highly on this factor.

Taken together, these findings confirm the idea that leisure behavior is motivated by two dialectic tendencies or desires: to escape *and* to seek. Further, the data strongly support the notion that through leisure behavior the individuals are escaping the personal and interpersonal environment and that they are seeking intrinsic rewards that are both personal and interpersonal. Interesting empirical questions remain as to how various groups of individuals (e.g., males vs. females) differ in these tendencies, whether various activities invite the predominance of one tendency over another, and how much variation there is in these motivational tendencies within the same activity and person from time to time.

IMPLICATIONS FOR LEISURE COUNSELING

It is assumed that persons who seek leisure counseling services do so for one of the following principal reasons: (1) they have psychological problems that are expected to be alleviated or eliminated by improved leisure functioning with the help of a leisure counselor, and/or (2) they have problems with leisure functioning, which in turn are the source of psychological problems. In the first case, the individual approaches a leisure counselor mainly because of his/her psychological problems (e.g., depression) and expects to get a leisure treatment from the counselor in order to improve his/her psychological well-being. In this sense, a leisure treatment serves as a tool or medicine to bring about positive psychological changes in a person. The same is true of the second case, although the leisure treatment now becomes the end itself, because the inadequate leisure functioning is the main cause for a person's psychological problems. The important point to note is that leisure counseling cannot effectively be delivered without simultaneous psychological counseling. It should not be forgotten that having a leisure problem is the same as having a psychological problem. Diagrammatically, these relationships may be illustrated as follows:

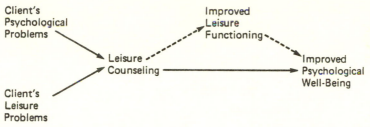

This approach requires that a leisure counselor be well equipped with psychological knowledge and skills. Counseling leisure activities without simultaneously addressing underlying psychological problems will not lead to desired outcomes. In short, leisure functioning does not exist in a psychological vacuum (Iso-Ahola, 1981; Dowd, 1981; Witt 1981).

At the core of one's psychological functioning is the belief that he/she is able to undertake various tasks and activities and is capable of performing them successfully. The strength of the belief in personal competency and effectiveness is the major component of intrinsic leisure motivation (Iso-Ahola, 1980); its reverse, perceived incompetence, constitutes the main constraint on leisure behavior (Iso-Ahola & Mannell, 1981). The more the individual believes in his/her abilities to do certain activities, the more he/she is motivated to participate in them and to expend effort in them, and the more he/she is capable of deriving satisfaction from them. In the face of obstacles and aversive experiences, a person with such a conviction in personal effectiveness has the strength to persist to overcome difficulties rather than attribute negative experiences to personal incompetence and helplessness. This all means that ineffectual leisure functioning results from a lack of perceived self-efficacy and causes psychological problems and even illnesses. It then follows that one important, if not the most important, task of the leisure counselor is to deal with the client's beliefs (or lack of them) about personal effectiveness or competence and raise such "efficacy expectations." What specifically can be done to impact upon these expectations?

Leisure Counseling: Improving Self-Efficacy

Performance Accomplishments and Personal Causation

Bandura (1982) has suggested and empirically shown that the mastery or efficacy expectations develop from four principal sources of information. First, *performance accomplishments or attainments* is the most influential source because it is based upon personal mastery experiences. While repeated successes increase and consecutive failures decrease perceived self-efficacy, in general, it is critical how an individual interprets his/her performance. An experiment showed that subjectively defined success is a more important determinant of subjects' causal attributions of outcome than is the objectively (externally) defined success (Iso-Ahola, 1978). Similarly, Bandura (1982) reported that *perceived* self-efficacy was a better predictor of subsequent behavior than was performance attainment per se. Whether an individual reads personal success as success depends on his/her cognitive appraisal of such relevant factors as task difficulty, the amount of effort expended, and situational/social support. Holding these other factors constant, personal accomplishments constitute the most powerful source of self-efficacy information. Seligman (1975), based upon empirical evidence supporting his learned helplessness theory, has offered an identical suggestion by reporting that the best way of immunizing people against learned helplessness is to expose them to a wide variety of mastery experiences on the one hand and to the difficulties that they are able to overcome by their own actions on the other. If the person is already in a state of uncontrollability or helplessness, the best way to get him/her out of it is to expose him/her repeatedly and progressively to authentic mastery experiences. Thus, to improve a client's leisure functioning, he/she should be counseled to those leisure experiences that authentically lead to mastery experiences and personal performance accomplishments (cf. Fig. 4-4). The resultant self-efficacy directly improves one's psychological well-being, as well as increasing his/her ability to cope with aversive experiences and encounters due to the increased sense of control over personal behaviors and life.

The important point is that a client should be counseled to self-directed mastery experiences. Otherwise, authenticity and generalizability of personal efficacy cannot be expected to materialize. This was clearly demonstrated by a recent experiment (Reich & Zautra, 1981). In this study, personal causation of participation in leisure activities was directly manipulated by inducing (or not inducing) subjects to initiate and perform self-chosen activities. One experimental group was asked to select 12 activities and the other group two activities that they had earlier rated as highly pleasurable and that they had not performed during the past two weeks. They were asked to volunteer to participate in these activities during the following two weeks, to sign a consent form in which they agreed to perform the self-selected activities, and to keep a record of those experiences with an activity log. The results showed that both experimental groups reported a higher quality of life and "a more pleasant outlook toward events in general" than the control group (who were not asked to engage in any activities). Importantly, the data indicated that prior negative life experiences interacted with the manipulation of personal causation in such a way that subjects with many prior negative life events benefited significantly more from the participation in self-chosen activities in terms of increased pleasantness and decreased psychiatric distress. Those subjects who were instructed to engage in 12 pleasant activities had less psychiatric distress than subjects who were induced to participate in two pleasant self-chosen activities.

This study and its results are important for several reasons. First, the methodology itself is noteworthy because it can be used as a simple but effective counseling tool. Clients are first asked to rate the pleasurableness of a long list of activities from different activity categories and are subsequently asked to select a few highly pleasant activities and participate in them for a period of time. This manipulation is effective because it emphasizes and focuses on personal causation of one's behavior. As the review reported research and discussion of the social psychological bases of leisure in the earlier part of this chapter revealed, perceived freedom or self-determination is critical to positive leisure experiences. The manipulation of personal causation was also effective because it was done in a way that was conducive to perceived self-efficacy. As Iso-Ahola (1980) has noted, those leisure activities that are rated pleasant are the ones that require the use of skills and offer challenge and feelings of control; in short, they are expected to lead to mastery experiences and thereby to increased self-efficacy.

Besides its methodology, the findings of the study themselves are important. By demonstrating the significant link between self-selected pleasant activities and psychological well-being or quality of life, the study provides compelling evidence for the need to counsel clients to those experiences or activities that are likely to lead to or heighten feelings of self-efficacy. Furthermore, the fact that subjects with many prior negative experiences displayed less psychiatric distress and greater pleasantness when counseled to participate in 12 rather than two activities (or none) suggests that a strong dosage of effective leisure functioning can and is needed to compensate psychological distress when individuals are under considerable life stress. In general, such a finding speaks strongly for the need for leisure counseling and recreational therapy.

Vicarious Experiences

The second source of information for efficacy expectations is vicarious experiences. Based upon the observation of similar or dissimilar others' leisure performances, a person makes inferences about his/her personal competence to perform the same leisure activity. If the person who is seen to perform a task successfully is believed to be of similar competence, such vicarious experience raises efficacy expectations in the observer. On the other hand, if a similar performer is seen to fail, such vicarious failures reduce observers' perceived competence and efficacy (Brown and Inouye, 1978). It is also worth noting that when a person is told that he/she is more competent than the ineffectual model performer, his/her efficacy expectations increase (Brown, 1979). In addition to social comparison processes, efficacy expectations can be altered by other means, for example, by being exposed to competent models who, by their performance, improve observers' skills or provide them with effective strategies for dealing with challenging and demanding activities (Bandura, 1982).

Two other relevant factors should be considered here. Langer (1979) reported that performing a task with an overtly confident individual produces an illusion of incompetence. Since many leisure activities structurally require the presence of others (e.g., tennis) or are chosen to be performed with others (e.g., golf), this finding has direct implications for the planning and conduct of such activities. Clearly, pairing of a person to perform a leisure activity with a highly confident (let alone cocky!) individual should be avoided. Another way of developing an illusion of incompetence is to allow someone else to perform an activity for oneself and thereby become a passive observer. This is especially likely to happen when performing with an overtly confident partner and when trying to learn new leisure skills. To relinquish too much control to another person (e.g., instructor) through the "you-do-it-I-watch" attitude in learning situations hamper a person's attempts to acquire leisure skills. Besides slowing down the learning process, passive participation is associated with the least positive overall mood (Csikszentmihalyi et al., 1977) and is deleterious to one's psychological and physical health (Langer & Rodin, 1976; Rodin & Langer, 1977; Schulz, 1976).

Two principal implications follow from the above ideas and findings. First, vicarious learning should not be a substitute for active learning and participation. Second, to increase efficacy expectations through vicarious (observational) experiences, a person should be exposed to those models whose behavior or performance allows him/her to infer, by implication, personal competence and efficacy. This includes the observation of a similar model who succeeds and an inferior model who fails in the leisure activity in question. It also includes, perhaps more realistically from the counselor's standpoint, giving clients information, for example through videotaped interviews, about similar others' problems and difficulties and their overcoming of the problems. This idea was strongly confirmed by a recent experiment (Wilson & Linville, 1982).

In this study, experimental subjects (college freshman) were shown statistical data and videotaped interviews with upperclassmen who reported that they had temporary problems as freshmen and that most freshmen improve their GPA with college years; the control group was given no such information. In addition, half of the subjects are asked to list all the reasons they could think of why students improve their grades from their freshman years to their upperclass years. The results were dramatic. Those who were shown videotaped interviews indicating that academic problems are temporary and typical of the early stage of the academic career significantly improved their GRE perform- ance, were less likely to leave college, and had better GPA scores one year after the completion of the study. On the other hand, the reasons manipulation had no such behavioral effects, through the listing of the reasons students in general improve their academic performance with years significantly increased sub- jects' moods. These findings can probably best be explained in attributional terms. That is, the attributional manipulation (the GPA information) allowed subjects to attribute their academic problems to unstable and temporary fac- tors, thereby enabling them to avoid attributions to lack of personal abilities. Such attributions, in turn, increased their academic expectations and im- proved moods, with the end result of positive changes in behavior (improved academic performance).

The findings have clear implications for leisure counseling. A relatively simple and inexpensive procedure of showing videotape interviews with former clients having had similar problems, and describing them as temporary prob- lems subsequently overcome, can be easily deployed in counseling service. The information conveyed by such videotaped interviews may become a powerful tool of changing clients' attributions of their problems, moods, efficacy expec- tations, and finally, their leisure behavior. Thus, these kinds of vicarious expe- riences, and those discussed earlier, can be very useful strategies in improving clients' perceived self-efficacy in efforts to help them overcome their leisure and psychological problems and should, therefore, be tried by practitioners.

Verbal Persuasion

The third source of information for efficacy expectations is verbal persua- sion. Accordingly, a person is led to believe that he/she has capabilities to do certain activities or tasks. This, of course, is the most obvious and perhaps the most widely used technique. On the other hand, the method is limited in its ef- fectiveness and has the best results when applied to those individuals who have some reason to believe that they can be successful in given tasks or activities (Bandura, 1982). If verbal persuasion or social reinforcement is unrealistic, it is not going to increase perceived self-efficacy and will not therefore help a per- son exert effort needed for the development of leisure skills. Bandura has shown that in comparison to performance accomplishments and vicarious ex- periences, verbal persuasion in a less effective technique in affecting efficacy expectations.

This all, however, does not mean that verbal persuasion is an insignificant source for self-efficacy judgments, as demonstrated by Bandura (1982) and his associates. A research program was designed to investigate the effects of per- suasive efficacy information on postcoronary patients' resumption of daily ac- tivities after having had a myocardial infarction. Based upon the idea that recovery from a heart attack is a social matter, wives' judgments of their husbands' (subjects) efficacy were investigated. The results indicated that wives who were actively involved in their husbands' treadmill exercises rated the husband's physical efficacy more highly than those wives who did not observe their husbands' treadmill exercises. The important point is that the patient's recovery from a heart attack is likely to be faster when both spouses' judgments of the husband's physical efficacy are high and congruent than when the judgments are low and congruent, as well as when the husbands and wives differ in their perceptions of the patient's physical efficacy to perform daily activities. Thus, wives' verbal persuasion in support of their husbands' physical capabilities may be critical for the patient's recovery and survival. Undoubtedly, these patients are strongly and positively influenced by such social support, especially when it deals with important leisure activities, such as sex.

This example has interesting implications for leisure counseling. Namely, it suggests that people other than leisure counselors, such as wives in the above case, may be in a better position to deliver realistic, and hence more effective, persuasion or judgment of others' capabilities to perform leisure activities. It is well known by the public in general as well as by those who seek counseling or therapeutic services that these professionals have been trained to make people feel good and to improve their self-concept and efficacy expectations. Thus, seekers of these services know that no matter what, they will get positive appraisal and feedback from counselors. Such cynical thinking of counseling services or therapy may in fact prevent many people from seeking the help of a leisure counselor. To make leisure counseling more effective for those who need and want it, counselors would do well to utilize a client's significant others' help in making verbal persuasion more realistic and authentic and hence more effective.

In part, the verbal persuasion process deals with changing clients' leisure values and attitudes. In a sport-oriented society, nonsport-related leisure activities become consensually demeaning (Iso-Aholo & Mannell, 1981). This suggests that persons who do not like sports or have not developed sport skills can easily develop an illusion of incompetence about their leisure behavior. Even though they may be capable of doing certain things with their hands well, they feel deviant and disenchanted with such leisure skills, because most people seem to think that it is more important to be able to play sports. The implication of all this is obvious. Leisure counselors may impact upon their clients' efficacy expectations by simply being able to change their leisure values and attitudes. Since people are narrow-minded about leisure in a sport-oriented society, the leisure counselor may provide the greatest service by simply opening clients' eyes about their leisure values and attitudes.

Physiological States

Finally, judgments of self-efficacy can be based on perceived physiological indicators. For example, a person may always get nervous and anxious before participating in, or performing, a certain leisure activity. If a person usually performs badly following the preparticipation arousal, the heightened anxiety subsequently becomes a signal warning about a likely failure or poor performance and, therefore, lowers the person's perceived capacity to perform the leisure activity in question. In an extreme case, the decreased efficacy expectations can develop into generalized fear or phobia. For example, it is not uncommon to find shy individuals to whom social interaction is anxiety-producing and efficacy-reducing and who, therefore, try to avoid leisure activities or experiences in which social interaction is a major component. For such individuals, leisure in general may become drudgery because many activities are based on social interaction. Similar problems arise for individuals who see physical risk or danger in most leisure activities. Such fears constrict leisure repertoire and reduce the quality of life.

To demonstrate that this kind of anxiety arousal or even phobia can be eliminated, Bandura (1982) and his associates performed experiments in which phobics are given treatments involving mastery, vicarious, emotive, and cognitive modes of influence. In one form of treatment, joint performance with a therapist (experimenter) was used to facilitate subjects' performances. In another, those performances or activities that intimidated subjects were broken down into easily mastered steps of increasing difficulty and were executed for increasingly longer periods. The objective of these treatments was to introduce performance aids that enabled subjects to perform the dreaded activities successfully. As noted earlier, progressive self-directed mastery experiences are critical for the development or improvement of efficacy expectations and hence to the overcoming of inhibitions. Other effective treatments included "imaginal conquest of fear" through visualization of threatening scenes or activities while deeply self-relaxing until anxiety arousal disappeared. Thus, clients can be taught to identify situational elicitors of anxiety and to manage anxiety arousal through thought processes and self-relaxation. As Bandura reported, by far the most effective technique is to arrange authentic and natural situations whereby subjects can achieve "field mastery experiences."

Leisure Counseling: Cultivating Intrinsic Motivation
Through Development of Perceived Competence/Self-Efficacy

As shown in the first part of this chapter, perceived freedom and competence are the two major components or mediating factors in the theory of intrinsic leisure motivation. Since intrinsic leisure motivation is positively correlated with self-concept, leisure satisfaction, and psychological well-being (Iso-Ahola, 1980), it follows that the cultivation of a client's perceived freedom and competence must be the central goal and task of leisure counseling. Gaining leisure knowledge and skills (from a leisure counselor) that makes it possible for a person better to fulfill internal standards increases perceived freedom and competence and, therefore, cultivates intrinsic leisure motivation. In this process, extrinsic rewards are useful to the extent that the level of reward reflects competence; that is, when higher rewards are given for greater competence, such rewards are attractive and become effective in the development of intrinsic leisure motivation (Williams, 1980), because competent performances are perceived as the reason for the rewards.

To enhance perceived competence or self-efficacy through performance accomplishments or mastery experiences, proximal goal-setting should be encouraged. As Bandura (1982) suggested, "self-motivation is best summoned and sustained by adopting attainable sub-goals that lead to future ones." Thus, leisure counselors could help clients set proximal subgoals for themselves so as to advance their leisure skills and thereby use this goal-setting as a vehicle of improving their feelings of personal competence and self-efficacy. The importance of proximal subgoals was demonstrated by an experiment (Bandura & Schunk, 1981) in which subjects (children showing gross deficits and lack of interest in mathematical tasks) were asked to work on mathematical tasks under one of the following goal-setting conditions: proximal subgoals, distal goals, or no goals. The results showed that those who worked for the proximal subgoals surpassed the other groups in terms of perceived self-efficacy, math skills, perseverance, and intrinsic interest in mathematics afterwards. These beneficial effects occurred apparently because the attainments of proximal subgoals provided these self-directed learners with relatively frequent boosts in perceived competence and self-efficacy, which in turn facilitated sustained involvement in the challenging activity. The use of proximal subgoals in the development and advancement of leisure skills and feelings of competence would therefore seem to be an excellent vehicle for cultivating intrinsic leisure motivation through leisure counseling.

While the above discussion suggests that a competence-enhancing intervention is always beneficial, a word of caution is in order. Recent experimental evidence points out that the positive effects of the competence-enhancing intervention occurs and lasts in the environment where people have a multitude of opportunities to accommodate different levels of personal competence (Schulz & Hanusa, 1979). Is there any value in having leisure skills, competencies, and feelings of personal efficacy if one cannot do anything with such skills? It is possible that the externally elevated feelings of competence in a constraining environment backfire and do the opposite of what was intended — they constrain rather than liberate (Iso-Ahola & Mannell, 1981). This may be an important point for leisure counselors to consider before initiating competence-enhancing interventions.

REFERENCES

Anderson, R., Manoogian, S.T., & Reznick, J.D. The undermining and enhancing of intrinsic motivation in preschool children. *Journal of Personality and Social Psychology*, 1976, *84*, 915-922.

Bandura, A. Self-efficacy mechanisms in human agency. *American Psychologist*, 1982, *37*, 127-147.

Bandura, A., & Schunk, D.H. Cultivating competence, self-efficacy and intrinsic interest through proximal self-motivation. *Journal of Personality and Social Psychology*, 1981, *41*, 586-598.

Bishop, D.W., & Chace, C.A. Parental conceptual systems, home play environment, and potential creativity in children. *Journal of Experimental Child Psychology*, 1971, *12*, 318-338.

Brooks, J.B., & Elliott, D.M. Prediction of psychological adjustment at age thirty from leisure time activities and satisfactions in childhood. *Human Development*, 1971, *14*, 51-61.

Brown, I., Jr. Learned helplessness through modeling: Self-efficacy and social comparison processes. In L.C. Perlmuter & R.A. Monty (Eds.), *Choice and perceived control*. Hillsdale: LEA, 1979.

Brown, I., Jr., & Inouye, D.K. Learned helplessness through modeling: The role of perceived similarity in competence. *Journal of Personality and Social Psychology*, 1978, *36*, 900-908.

Bruner, J. Play is serious business. *Psychology Today*, 1975, *8*, 81-83.

Campbell, A., Converse, P.E., & Rodgers, W.L. *The quality of American life: Perceptions, evaluations and satisfactions*. New York: Russell Sage Foundation, 1976.

Crane, W.D., & Brewer, M.B. *Principles of research in social psychology*. New York: McGraw-Hill, 1973.

Csikszentmihalyi, M., & Graef, R. Feeling free. *Psychology Today*, 1979, *13*, 84-90, 98-99.

Csikszentmihalyi, M., Larson, R., & Prescott, S. The ecology of adolescent activity and experience. *Journal of Youth and Adolescence*, 1977, *6*, 281-294.

Condry, J. Enemies of exploration: Self-initiated versus other-initiated learning. *Journal of Personality and Social Psychology*, 1977, *35*, 459-477.

Deci, E.L. *Intrinsic motivation*. New York: Plenum Press, 1975.

Dennis, W. Causes of retardation among institutionalized children: Iran. *Journal of General Psychology*, 1960, *96*, 47-59.

Dennis, W., & Najarian, P. Infant development under environmental handicap. *Psychological Monograph*, 1957, *71*, No. 7.

Dollinger, S.J., & Thelen, N.H. Overjustification and children's intrinsic motivation: Comparative effects of four rewards. *Journal of Personality and Social Psychology*, 1978, *36*, 1259-1269.

Dowd, E.T. (Ed.) Leisure counseling. *The Counseling Psychologist*, 1981, *9*, No. 3.

Ellis, M.J. *Why people play*. Englewood Cliffs: Prentice-Hall, Inc., 1973.

Flanagan, J.C. A research approach to improving our quality of life. *American Psychologist*, 1978, *33*, 138-147.

Gergan, K.J. Social psychology as history. *Journal of Personality and Social Psychology*, 1973, *26*, 309-320.

Godby, G. & Parker, S. *Leisure studies and services: An overview*. Philadelphia: Saunders, 1976.

Grotevant, H.D., Scarr, S., & Weinberg, R.A. Patterns of interest similarity in adoptive and biological families. *Journal of Personality and Social Psychology*, 1977, *35*, 667-676.

Hunt, J. McV. *The challenge of competence and poverty*. Urbana: University of Illinois Press, 1969.

Hunt, J. McV. *Heredity, environment and class or ethnic differences*. Paper prepared for the 1972 Invitational Conference on Testing Programs, 1972.

Iso-Ahola, S.E. Perceiving the causes of objective and subjective outcomes following motor performance. *Research Quarterly*, 1978, *49*, 63-70.

Iso-Ahola, S.E. Basic dimensions of definitions of leisure. *Journal of Leisure Research*, 1979, *11*, 28-39. (a)

Iso-Ahola, S.E. Some social psychological determinants of perceptions of leisure: Preliminary evidence. *Leisure Science*, 1979, *2*, 305-314. (b)

Iso-Ahola, S.E. *The social psychology of leisure and recreation*. Dubuque: Brown, 1980.

Iso-Ahola, S.E. Leisure counseling at the crossroads. *Counseling Psychologist*, 1981, *9*, 71-74.

Iso-Ahola, S.E. & Allen, J.R. The dynamics of leisure motivation: The effects of outcome on leisure needs. *Research Quarterly of Exercise and Sports*, 1982, *53*, in press.

Iso-Ahola, S.E. and Mannell, R.C. Social and psychological constraints on leisure. In M.G. Wade (Ed.), *Constraints to leisure*. Springfield, Il.: Charles C Thomas, 1983.

Kagan, J. New views on cognitive development. *Journal of Youth and Adolescence*, 1976, *5*, 113-129.

Kelly, J.R. Socialization toward leisure: A developmental approach. *Journal of Leisure Research*, 1974, *6*, 181-193.

Kelly, J.R. *Two orientations of leisure choices*. Paper presented at Annual American Sociological Association Convention, New York, 1976.

Kelly, J.R. Leisure socialization: Replication and extention. *Journal of Leisure Research*, 1977, *9*, 121-132.

Kornhauser, A. *Mental health of the industrical worker: A Detroit study*. New York: Wiley, 1965.

Langer, E.J. The illusion of incompetence. In L.C. Perlmuter & R.A. Monty (Eds.), *Choice and perceived control*. Hillside: LEA, 1979.

Langer, E.J., & Rodin, J. The effects of choice and enhanced personal responsibility for the aged: A field experiment in an institutional setting. *Journal of Personality and Social Psychology*, 1976, *34*, 191-198.

Lepper, M.L., & Greene, D. (Eds.) *The hidden costs of reward: New perspectives on the psychology of human motivation*. Hillsdale: LEA, 1978.

Mannell, R.C. Leisure research in the psychological lab: Leisure a permanent and/or transient cognitive disposition. In E. Avedon, M. LeLievre, & T. Stewart, (Eds.), *Contemporary leisure research*. Waterloo: Ontario Research Council on Leisure, 1979.

McCall, R.B. Exploratory manipulation and play in the human infant. *Monographs of the Society for Research and Child Development*, 1974, *39*, No. 155.

Mueller, E., & Brenner, J. The origins of social skills and interaction among play group toddlers. *Child Development*, 1977, *48*, 854-861.

Patrick, G.T.W. *The psychology of relaxation*. Boston: Houghton, 1916.

Proshansky, H.M. The environmental crisis in human dignity. *Journal of Social Issues*, 1973, *29*, 1-20.

Reich, J.W., & Zautra, A. Life events and personal causation: Some relationships with satisfaction and distress. *Journal of Personality and Social Psychology*, 1981, *41*, 1002-1012.

Rodin, J., & Langer, E.J. Long-term effects of a control-relevant intervention with the institutionalized aged. *Journal of Personality and Social Psychology*, 1977, *35*, 897-902.

Ross, M. The self-perception of intrinsic motivation. In J. Harvey, W.J. Ickes, & R.F. Kidd (Eds.), *New directions in attribution research*, Vol. 1. Hillsdale: LEA, 1976.

Schulz, R. Effects of control and predictability on the physical and psychological well-being of the institutionalized aged. *Journal of Personality and Social Psychology*, 1976, *33*, 576-573.

Schulz, R. & Hanusa, B.H. Environmental influences on the effectiveness of control- and competence-enhancing interventions. In L.C. Perlmuter & R.A. Monty (Eds.), *Choice and perceived control*. Hillsdale: LEA, 1979

Seligman, M.E.P. *Helplessness: On depression, development and death*. San Francisco: Freeman, 1975.

Sofranko, A.J., & Nolan, M.F. Early life experiences and adult sports participation. *Journal of Leisure Research*, 1972, *4*, 6-18.

Spreitzer, E., & Snyder, E.E. Socialization into sport: An exploratory path analysis. *Research Quarterly*, 1976, *47*, 238-245.

Swann, W.B., & Pittman, T.S. Imitating play activity of children: The moderating influence of verbal cues on intrinsic motivation. *Child Development*, 1977, 48, 1128-1132.

Wankel, L.M. & Thompson, C.E. *The effects of perceived activity choice upon exercise attendance*. Paper presented at the NRPA Research Symposium. Miami Beach NRPA Annual Convention, 1978.

Williams, B.W. Reinforcement, behavior constraint, and overjustification effect. *Journal of Personality and Social Psychology*, 1980, *39*, 599-614.

Wilson, T.D., & Linville, P.W. Improving the academic performance of college freshmen: The attribution therapy revisited. *Journal of Personality and Social Psychology*, 1982, *42*, 367-376.

Witt, P.A., et al. *The leisure diagnostic battery: Background, conceptualization and structure.* Grant report to the U.S. Department of Education/Office of Special Education. Denton: North Texas State University, 1981.

Yoesting, D.R., & Burkhead, D.O. Significance of childhood recreation experience on adult leisure behavior: An exploratory analysis. *Journal of Leisure Research*, 1973, *5*, 25-36.

Part II
APPLICATIONS

Chapter 5

LEISURE COUNSELING WITH YOUTH

L ARRY C. L OESCH

P EOPLE don't think much about leisure except that it's what people do to
"relax." People especially don't think about leisure among youth because
youth don't often complain about it. More typically, youth talk of all the fun
things they're going to do when they get older — which they equate with lots of
time, money, and freedom; their own cars; no commitments; no
responsibilities; and so on. There is thus a complacency about leisure among
youth; they *seem* happy enough, why bother? Yet the situation is nowhere near
as simple as it seems. Leisure is an extremely important aspect of the lives of
youth. In order to understand this importance, however, it is first necessary to
consider briefly the nature of the youth period in life.

The professional literature is replete with attempts to characterize the
"youth" period in people's lives. These attempts have ranged from relatively
simplistic ones, such as chronologically equating youth with the teenage years,
to much more complex and abstract ones, such as Erikson's (1969b) exposition
on youth as the period of "identity formation." Given the number and diversity
of the attempts made, it must be concluded that "youth" defies succinct
characterization and, accordingly, another attempt will not be offered here.
The previous attempts have not, however, been in vain because at least a few
generalizations about youth apparently have become widely accepted by
professionals. In the leisure context, the generalization of particular relevance
is that youth is a period characterized at least in part by intense needs for
stimulation (e.g., Cohen, 1979; Grinder, 1978; Manmaster, 1977). The often
seemingly insatiable needs for stimulation among youth pervade almost every
realm of their human functioning. Paramount among these is their need for
psychological stimulation (Smith, 1980). Given the opportunities, most youth
have and will invest almost boundless energy in psychologically stimulating
activities *they deem* appropriate to completion of their preadult developmental
life tasks and to crystallization of their self-identities. The problem, however, is
that many youth never find sufficient and/or appropriate opportunities, and as
a result, they become "bored" — with their life situations, with others, and with
themselves.

The boredom in the lives of youth manifests itself in many ways. At best it
serves as a motivator for activity to provide psychological stimulation. For

This chapter is based on an article of the same title that originally appeared in *The Counseling Psychologist*,
1981, *9*(3), 55-67.
The author wishes to express his sincere appreciation to Dr. Paul T. Wheeler and Ms. Barbara Loesch
for their assitance in the development of this article.

some youth, the resultant activities are positive and facilitate effective life development. Unfortunately, for many youth the resultant activities are considerably less than conducive to effective personal growth. Activities in this latter category would include behaviors such as delinquency, drug or alcohol abuse, inappropriate sexuality, and ineffective interpersonal interactions with peers or family members (Ausubel, Montemayer, & Srajian, 1977; McCandless, 1979). At worst, the boredom is self-perpetuating and leads to psychological (and perhaps physical) lethargy. The common result is that many of their significant and meaningful life experiences are delayed.

Leisure activity offers at least one sufficient and appropriate opportunity for youth to alleviate boredom and its associated negative ramifications. This may seem obvious, trite, or perhaps even mundane. However, as Neulinger (1974), Travers et al. (1978), and others have noted, a "leisure problem" exists within our society. The essence of the leisure problem is that many people do not know how "to leisure" effectively. Neulinger (1974) has identified three major dynamics experienced by people with a "leisure problem": (1) feelings of inner threat or discomfort due to lack of skills for effective leisure decision-making, (2) value conflicts that arise when work is viewed as "productive" and leisure is viewed as "nonproductive," and (3) feelings of "meaninglessness" or "time-wasting" during leisure activity. Clearly then, the leisure problem is primarily psychological in nature.

Two major aspects of the leisure problem are particularly important here. First, even though there is a multitude of leisure activities available, many youth are unable to identify and select those that are personally most appropriate and effective. Second, many youth fail to comprehend fully the importances of the functions of leisure in their lives, and therefore are unable to maximize the potential benefits of leisure activity participation. Thus, while the opportunity exists, many youth fail to capitalize upon it.

The response of the helping professions to the leisure problem has been the emergence of leisure counseling as a functional specialty (Overs, 1977). The goals of leisure counseling may be viewed (in general) from a relatively simplistic perspective. On a theoretical level, leisure counseling is an attempt to make the psychology of leisure an applied science (Avedon, 1974). On a practical level, leisure counseling is a process intended to enable people to achieve personally appropriate and effective leisure activities (Loesch, 1980b).

Leisure counseling is a new functional specialty and it has not yet reached full professional stature (Neulinger, 1978). In fact, most of the professional literature on leisure counseling, including both theoretical and research offerings, has been presented only within the last decade. Yet even in light of its recency, some startling and disappointing situations are apparent. For example, much (if not most) of the available leisure *counseling* literature has been authored by individuals with little or no formal preparation in counseling (Loesch, 1980a). Relatedly, with the notable exception of McDowell, useful and significant contributions to the leisure counseling literature by counseling psychologists (or persons with even roughly equivalent training and experience) are conspicuously absent. Finally, substantive theoretical and practical writings relative to leisure counseling with youth are almost nonexistent. These situations are disconcerting in light of the many potential benefits of leisure counseling in general and for leisure counseling for youth in particular (Hitzhusen, 1977).

Leisure in the Lives of Youth

The need for leisure counseling for youth is derived from the distinction between two basic types of leisure activities. The first is what may be called, for lack of a better term, "default" leisure activities. This type includes those behaviors engaged in either to "pass the time" until another activity begins or because of a perceived lack of alternatives ("what do you want to do?", "I don't know, what do you want to do?"). The second is what has been called "effective" leisure activities, a term stated or implied by numerous authors (e.g., Edwards, 1980; Loesch, 1980b; McDowell, 1976a; Neulinger, 1974). In general, this type includes those behaviors engaged in intentionally because of the potential for psychological benefit and satisfaction. One of the goals of leisure counseling is to minimize the frequencies of default leisure activity and to maximize the frequencies of effective leisure activity. The need for leisure counseling for youth therefore exists, in part, to the extent that youth engage in default leisure activities.

The precursor of leisure activity during the youth period of life is "play" during the childhood period. The distinction between play and leisure activity is primarily semantic; where play ends and leisure activity begins in life is unimportant. What is important is that play serves meaningful and necessary developmental functions during childhood (e.g., Bruner, Jolly, & Sylva, 1976). Play serves as the primary medium through which four major types of childhood developmental tasks are achieved: cognitive, social, personality, and physiological. Figure 5-1 outlines some of the major developmental tasks within each type that are to be achieved through play during the childhood years. Collectively, these tasks encompass almost all human functioning during childhood, with the notable exception of internal biological developments. Most of these developmental tasks remain to be reachieved at higher levels during the youth period of life (Ball & Meck, 1979), and indeed many remain across the life span (Vandenberg, 1978). It follows that if play is an appropriate medium for achievement of developmental tasks during childhood, then leisure activity should also be an appropriate medium for achievement of developmental tasks during the youth period of life. Unfortunately, childhood play is not always as effective as it should be in facilitating achievement of developmental tasks. In such cases, childhood play has to be "enhanced" by techniques such as developmental play (Brody, 1978) or play therapy (Jernberg, 1979). In a similar way, leisure activities do not always effectively facilitate achievement of developmental tasks. They, too, have to be enhanced, and this enhancement falls under the rubric of leisure counseling. Thus, a need for leisure counseling exists when leisure activities are not aiding effectively in the achievement of developmental tasks during the youth period of life.

I. Cognitive Development

    A. Acquistion of cognition (Elard, Bradley, & Caldwell, 1975; Montagu, 1978; Piaget, 1972).

    B. Establishment of reality orientation (Bruner & Sherwood, 1976; Stamm, 1976).

    C. Learning of cause and effect relationships (Fink, 1976; Garvey, 1977; Piaget, 1972; Piell, 1975).

    D. Assimilation of experiences (Klinger, 1969).

    E. Acquisition of problem-solving skills (Bruner, 1976; Piaget, 1962; Sylva, Bruner, & Genova, 1976).

II. Social Development

    A. Learning of social rules and conventions (Bruner, 1976; Butler, Gotts, & Quisenberry, 1978; Ohlsen, 1974).

    B. Attainment of self-control (Butler, Gotts, & Quisenberry, 1978; Weisler & McCall, 1976).

    C. Establishment of social relationships (Erikson, 1968a; Harlow & Suomi, 1970).

    D. Development of communication skills (Butler, Gott & Quisenberry, 1978; Erikson, 1972; Stern, 1974).

    E. Adaptation to new situations (Hutt & Bhavnani, 1976; Klinger, 1969).

III. Personality Development

    A. Individuation (Erikson, 1968; Weisler & McCall, 1976).

    B. Development of initiative and assertion (Bruner & Sherwood, 1976; Jones, 1976).

    C. Manifestation of self-esteem (Garvey, 1977; Piers, 1972).

    D. Improvement in emotional stability (Fink, 1976; Golomb & Cornelius, 1977; Piers, 1978).

IV. Physiological Development

    A. Improvement of functioning of bodily organs and systems (Butler, Gotts, & Quisenberry, 1978; Heron & Sutton-Smith, 1971; Hurlock, 1975).

    B. Development of sleep patterns (Montagu, 1978).

    C. Improvement of muscular and skeletal coordination (Hurlock, 1975; Jones, 1976).

Figure 5-1. Functions of play in child development. (Adapted from S. Sullivan, unpublished doctoral dissertation, University of Florida, 1980).

The onset of the youth period in life (used here as roughly synonomous with adolescence) brings with it three major changes pertinent here:

1. Developmental tasks appropriate for adolescence are encountered (added) while childhood developmental tasks are de-emphasized, but not totally eliminated.
2. The educational process (schooling?) and youths' involvements in it are elevated to a position of prominence.
3. The amount of time available for leisure activity is diminished from what it was during childhood.

Each of these changes alters the nature, functions, and potentials of leisure activity by youth and in turn contributes to the need for leisure counseling.

Havighurst (1951) was among the first to identify developmental tasks for adolescents; while many authors (e.g., Hurlock, 1975) have expounded on his ideas, his basic list is still appropriate today. He listed nine basic adolescent developmental tasks:

1. Accepting one's physique and developing a sex-appropriate self-image.
2. Developing new relationships with peers of both sexes.
3. Improving emotional independence from parents and other adults.
4. Initiating economic independence.
5. Selecting and preparing for an occupation.
6. Developing intellectual skills for civic competence.
7. Developing socially responsible behaviors.
8. Preparing for marriage and family life.
9. Crystallizing basic values.

Leisure activities are particularly well-suited for the achievement of these developmental tasks because they allow for "safe" experimentation. That is, youths often may explore and experiment with new behaviors during leisure activities without the (real or perceived) fears of reprisal or repercussion prevalent in other activities. For example, a youth striving for emotional independence may "test" an assertive behavior with an adult during a leisure activity before using the same behavior with a parent. Similarly, a youth may "test" a behavior with a parent during a leisure activity before using the behavior in other familial situations. Leisure activities, therefore, offer youth opportunities for "role-playing" in situations where the interpersonal dynamics are safer than in other situations.

Leisure activities also are often the only opportunities for behaviors for achieving developmental tasks. For example, opportunities for experimentation with socially responsible behaviors are limited in educational (school) and familial contexts. Schools and parents impart strong expectations about what constitutes socially responsible behavior. Consequently, if youths are to establish the most *personally* appropriate socially responsible behaviors, then behavioral experimentation leading to that establishment must occur in other contexts. Obviously leisure activities are an available other context.

During adolescence, education (schooling) receives a disproportionate emphasis as the most improtant activity in the lives of youth; an emphasis is imparted by parents, educational personnel, and society as a whole (Postman & Weingartner, 1973). The educational process obviously facilitates some aspects of cognitive development, yet the types of cognitive development enhanced by schooling are rather restricted (i.e., usually limited to accumulation of specified bodies of knowledge and to development of specified cognitive skills). The deficiencies of schooling in facilitating other types of cognitive development (e.g., creativity) as well as other types of development have long been recognized, sometimes rather humorously (e.g., Postman & Weingartner, 1969, 1973). Leisure activities may be the only other opportunities for these other types of developments.

The time available for leisure activity decreases rather dramatically during adolescence as the individual assumes more "nonchoice" responsibilities, usually educational and familial, and sometimes vocational. The result is that specific leisure activities engaged in by youth take on even greater importance than play in childhood because there is less time available for the completion of more developmental tasks. This situation does not preclude leisure activities from facilitating the achievement of the many adolescent tasks, but it does necessitate that the leisure activities engaged in be time-efficient if they are to be maximally effective.

Left to their own devices, it is unlikely that most youth will find sufficient opportunities for all the behavioral experimentation necessary for successful completion of all the adolescent developmental tasks. As a result, their behavioral experimentations may be unnecessarily prolonged, or their experimental behaviors may have unnecessarily severe consequences, or both. Since these situations are undesirable, there is a need for leisure counseling to help alleviate them.

As today's youth grow into adulthood, perhaps the only certainty in their lives that they will be facing a rapidly changing world. Accordingly adaptability and flexibility are key characteristics that must be established during adolescence. This is certainly true with respect to leisure activity since the rapidly changing world will influence their leisure activities in many different ways.

Among the changes today's youth will encounter in their lifetimes are those in the world of work. These changes will be both behavioral and attitudinal. The behavioral changes relate primarily to work patterns and schedules. The *Employment and Training Report of the President* (1978) concludes that (a) there is a continuing decline in the average number of hours worked per week and that this trend is expected to continue, and (b) there is a rapid and continuing trend toward earlier retirement among workers. In addition, "flexittime" scheduling of work hours for workers is an increasing trend in American businesses (Renwick et al., 1978). These trends imply that today's youth will have increasing amounts and longer blocks of leisure activity time available to them across their life spans.

The attitudinal changes about work relate to both its form and importance.

Renwick et al. reported that "78 percent (of the 23,008 respondents to their survey) would like to be able to set the hours they start and leave work — suggesting strong support for plans such as 'flexittime' " (p. 54). Even though their sample was highly biased with people in "professionals" occupations, the strength of their finding remains impressive. An even more important attitudinal change about work is the apparent decline of the Protestant (work) ethnic. Allen (1980), Hoyt (1977), Severinsen (1979), and Super (1976), among others, have all noted that the psychological importance attached to work that was so prevalent in earlier generations seems to be in a continuing decline. Conversely, as the psychological importance of work is decreasing, the psychological importance of leisure is increasing. These situations imply that attitudes about work and leisure will change significantly during the lifetimes of today's youth.

The changes in leisure that in part result from changes in the world of work necessitate that youth have effective leisure activity selections and decision-making skills. It is unlikely that youth will develop proficiencies in these skills through "trial-and-error" methods. They will need help in the form of leisure counseling to determine the most appropriate skills for their respective personal situations.

Today's youth will also encounter many changes in the natures of leisure activities. Many new ones will be created and some current ones may cease to exist. Witness the dramatic evolution of television video games: people who used to play Ping Pong® on a table now play Pong® on a television screen. Today's youth will need to be able to cope with these changes and have effective skills for evaluating the personal appropriateness of new leisure activities. Leisure counseling is needed now to help them avoid leisure related problems later.

Perhaps the greatest testimony for the need for leisure counseling comes from youth themselves. Their desire for leisure activity is undeniable. Further, they appear to have some understanding of the potential benefits of leisure activity participation. A study by Gholson (1979) illustrates these points well. Gholson surveyed approximately 2,500 students about the relative significances of extracurricular activities in their lives. Over 30% of his sample viewed extracurricular activities as more important than course-work in their school experiences. Approximately 56% of the students selected "participation in extracurricular activities" (as opposed to earning high grades, driving, etc.) as their primary means of establishing status and acceptance among their peers. Finally, each of the following reasons for participating in extracurricular activities were identified as "important" by more than 90% of the students polled: personal achievement and enjoyment, to have an outlet for individual (i.e., personal) needs and interests, for experiences not regularly available in school, to develop leadership skills, and broaden personal and social contacts.

Gholson also noted that a 1978 Gallup poll revealed that over 90% of parents with children in schools felt that extracurricular activities were "very important" or "fairly important" to their children's educations. In comparing student and parent attitudes Gholson concluded, "Thus students, like parents, believe that both immediate and long range benefits are to be gained from participation in extracurricular activity programs" (p. 67). Students know and want the benefits of effective leisure activities; leisure counseling can help them realize those benefits.

The final need for leisure counseling with youth arises from within the counseling profession. *The Counseling Psychologist* recently devoted an issue (Vol. 8, no. 4) to "Counseling Psychology in the year 2000 A.D." Among the many "themes" inherent in that issue was that counseling psychology will, or at least should, expand its service realm to encompass the totality of human functioning. While support for leisure counseling was implicit in many of the articles, Wrenn (1980) made the clearest case:

> The counseling psychologist of today is only beginning to be aware of the need of many clients for help in utilizing nonemployed hours in a life-satisfying manner. These satisfactions may be *complementary* to the client's self-involved or self-engrossing occupational activities or *compensatory* to an occupation that provides little sense of self-fulfillment. The satisfactions sought may be either personally creative or socially useful. They may be satisfactions that provide a sense of personal growth, a sense of contributing to the welfare of others or to a more healthy society, or a sense of personal or social enjoyment of the activity involved.
>
> It seems quite apparent that there will be available to the individual an increasing amount of nonemployed time that is now spent in self-indulgent or self-destructive ways. There will be also an increase in the number of jobs available that are life frustrating because they are repetitive, uninteresting, give little sense of dignity to the person, and give little hope for advancement. There is need now for the counseling psychologist to counsel others on developing a total pattern of life satisfactions. . . . (p. 33)

In the same issue, Super (1980) offered a rationale for counseling psychologists working specifically with youth: "Counseling psychology is, like the rest of applied psychology (and, looking sheepishly over our shoulders, experimental and developmental psychology), looking for new fields of endeavor, new areas of application, and new jobs. . . . Counseling psychologists are, more visibly and more audibly than ever, claiming a share of the work with school children."

Similar perspectives have been offered from other parts of the counseling profession (e.g., Edwards & Bloland, 1980; Fain, 1973; O'Morrow, 1970; Overs, 1975; Shank & Kennedy, 1976). It appears, therefore, that there is growing recognition and support of the need for leisure counseling as a functional specialty within the counseling profession. It is logical to extend this need for leisure counseling for youth.

These, then, are the major aspects of the need for leisure counseling with youth. Clearly, leisure activities are important parts of the lives of youth and just as clearly leisure counseling can help youths achieve effective leisure activities. However, in order to clarify *how* leisure counseling can be conducted so as to be helpful to youths, it is first necesary to establish a perspective from which to operate.

Perspectives on Leisure

Leisure is one of those words commonly used but not commonly interpreted; leisure means different things to different people. Unfortunately (because of the inhibiting impact on the evolution of leisure counseling), this situation exists among professionals as well as laypersons. In fact, quite a few definitions of leisure have been offered in the professional literature. For discussion purposes these definitions may be divided into four categories: time, work-related, psychological, and dynamic models. It should be emphasized that these categories are arbitrary and simply for clarity: some definitions may be rightfully placed in more than one category.

Most time-based definitions emphasize *residuality*. That is, leisure is time left over after time spent on something else, usually existence or subsistence activity. The strongest advocacy for this type of definition is that offered by Brightbill and Mobley (1977), "Leisure is best identified with time — time beyond that required, organically, for existence or subsistence" (p. 5). Similar definitions have been offered by Brightbill (1960), Clawson (1964), and Weiss (1964). Other authors have attempted to avoid the concept of residuality and have instead described different *types* of time. For example, Parker (1971) writes of work time and nonwork (leisure) time. More recently, some authors have moved beyond dichotomies and suggested multiple categories of time in a person's life. For example, Bolles (1978) writes of work time, nonwork time (e.g., going to and from work), personal care time, sleep time, house and family care time, and leisure time. However, even when time categories are used, the concept of residuality is implied (e.g., Bolles, 1978, p. 374). The unfortunate connotation of residuality is that it implies that some other type of time is more important in people's lives than is leisure time (which is true biologically but not necessarily psychologically).

Work-related definitions of leisure have been popular among counselors (apparently) because they fit well with current emphases on vocational development and counseling. These definitions are akin to time-based definitions in that residuality is stated or implied; the focus is on work and leisure is something secondary or supplemental. For example, Wilensky (1960) discusses two types of leisure. He describes *compensatory* leisure as that which helps an individual "compensate" for a lack of meaningfulness in work through "meaningful" leisure activity. Conversely, he describes *spillover* leisure as that which allows individuals who find meaningfulness in their work to find similar meaningfulness in (similar) leisure activities. Related perspectives on work and leisure have been offered by Allen (1980) and Parker (1971). Burch (1969) has raised insightful criticisms of Wilensky's types of leisure. He noted that the *compensatory* definition implies that leisure activities should be the "opposite" of work activities, a situation which may be neither desirable nor feasible. He also noted that the *spillover* definition may simply reflect "force of habit" and also may not be a desirable situation.

Psychological definitions of leisure focus on the subjective nature of human experience. These definitions typically reflect leisure as an attitude adopted by an individual. While numerous authors (e.g., Besag, 1975; de Grazia, 1962; Winters & Hansen, 1977) have alluded to the psychological nature of leisure, the foremost proponent of a psychological definition of leisure is Neulinger (1974) who wrote that, "Leisure is a state of mind; it is a way of being, of being at peace with oneself and what one is doing" (p. xv). He goes on to clarify this definition by emphasizing the aspect of personal freedom: "Leisure has one and only one essential criterion, and that is the condition of perceived freedom. Any activity carried out freely, without constraint or compulsion, may be considered to be leisure. To *leisure* implies being engaged in an activity as a free agent and of one's own choice" (p. 15-16). While this definition may find favor with (particularly humanistically oriented) counselors, it apparently has not been widely accepted by laypersons (Neulinger, 1976).

Dynamic models of leisure is a term used here to denote those conceptualizations of leisure that attempt to incorporate simultaneously two or more factors relating to or affecting leisure. Typical of this type is one presented by Kelly (1972). He suggested that there are two basic aspects of leisure: (1) discretion, which is divided into *chosen* and *determined*, and (2) work-relation, which is divided into *independent* and *dependent*. Kelly's model thus contains four quadrants: nonleisure (determined-dependent), complementary leisure (chosen-dependent), coordinated leisure (determined-independent), and pure leisure (chosen-independent). The model is "dynamic" in that quadrant sizes vary across persons and across times. Other models (as defined here) have been offered by Shepard (1974), Murphy (1975), and Kaplan (1960). Unfortunately, while these models may provide conceptual guidelines for counselors, their use with laypersons is typically limited by their complexities.

Individually, each of these types of definitions has at least one major limitation in regard to leisure counseling with youth. That is, any definition used in the context of leisure counseling with youth should be applicable, understandable, and acceptable to them. Time-based definitions would give the impression that other things (e.g., school, chores, work, etc.) are more important and would therefore be probably unacceptable and perhaps inappropriate for them. Work-related definitions may have the same receptivity problems as well as the difficulty in defining what constitutes "work" in the lives of youth. Finally, psychological and dynamic model definitions raise issues of understanding among youth because the former may be too abstract and the latter may be too complex to be easily interpreted.

The limitations in existing definitions lead to the development of yet another leisure definition. This definition was created with the intent of maximizing the positive aspects of previous definitions and minimizing their limitations. Thus the definition of choice here is that: Leisure is whatever activity an individual knowingly (i.e., consciously) defines to be leisure (Loesch & Wheeler, 1982).

This definition was created specifically for leisure counseling purposes (as opposed to the study or psychology of leisure in general). In this regard several aspects of this definition are worthy of note. First, this definition avoids the concept of residuality; leisure activity is significant in and of its own right. Second, it emphasizes personal freedom in choice, a component of many definitions of leisure. Next, it incorporates the concept of conscious awareness; how can anything be leisure if the person doesn't know it is? Finally, and most importantly, it is an *activity* based definition, one which emphasizes behaviors. This is a perspective that fits well with the views of counseling as a "behavioral" science and counselors as human "behavior" specialists. This is *not* to suggest that the attitudinal components of leisure and human functioning are unimportant. On the contrary, as will be emphasized later, these attitudinal factors are extremely important in the leisure counseling context. However, while an individual's attitudes or other affective dimensions may change during the leisure counseling process, a major goal of the process remains to have the individual recognize and/or select the most personally appropriate and effective leisure *activities* (i.e., behaviors).

The emphasis on leisure activity also does not imply that leisure counseling should be conducted only from one (e.g., behavioral) theoretical orientation. Indeed, leisure counseling has been, is, and should be conducted from a variety of counseling orientations depending on a counselor's personal preferences (Gunn, 1977b; McDowell, 1976a, 1977a, b). However, regardless of the orientation used, the effectiveness of leisure counseling should be interpreted in how the person behaves as a result of participating in the process.

The foundations of leisure counseling are by no means complete with the provision of a leisure definition. It is also necessary to consider the interrelationships among leisure activity and various aspects of human functioning.

Leisure and Mental Health

The primary goal of the counseling professions is the provision of services that enable people to achieve and maintain mental health. This is indeed a laudable goal. Unfortunately, the term "mental health" defies consensus about its definition. For example, an issue of *The Counseling Psychologist* (Vol. 4, no. 2) entitled "The Healthy Personality" offered the positions and counterpositions of many noted counseling psychologists on what it means to function effectively mentally. Each of the positions presented seems logical and defensible, but there certainly was not consensus about the nature of effective mental functioning. However, even though mental health defies consensual definition, there does seem to be agreement that various aspects of human functioning contribute to it. One of these is effective leisure. The ways that effective leisure contributes to mental health may be considered in terms of functions and potential benefits of leisure activity participation.

Witt and Bishop (1970) have suggested that the literature on leisure reveals four major functions of leisure in people's lives: catharsis, relaxation, compensation, and task generalization.

Leisure activities are *cathartic* when individuals engage in such activities for the purpose of purging themselves of certain emotions. Often the emotions to be purged are "negative" and the activities used are physical: people want to "do something" to get rid of fears, anxieties, frustrations, and so on. However, leisure activities may also be used for purging "positive emotional overloads" and be *relatively* passive; such as the "celebration" accompanying a promotion, the end of a school term, a salary increase, and so on. S.J. Perelman offers a poignant quote on the situation:

> I used to watch people leaving a Marx brothers film, their cheeks stained from tears of laughter. Then they would say, "Wasn't that silly?" If they had been equally churned up by a Garbo movie, they wouldn't say that. They'd think they had been purged — you know, catharsis. But with comedy, people do not trust their reactions. The trouble is people do not have the courage of their laughter.

The *relaxation* function is closely related to, but not synonomous with, catharsis. There are two parts of the relaxation function of leisure activities. The first is "restoration," where the individual uses leisure activities to regain, restore, or regenerate energy, particularly mental energy. The second is "diversion," where the individual uses leisure activity to "escape" physically and/or psychologically from other situations. The diversion function thus allows for periods of psychological calm. These relaxation functions are of course those most commonly asociated with leisure activity.

Leisure activity fulfills a *compensation* function when it allows individuals to "make up for" things lacking or deficient in other aspects of their lives. In this sense, leisure activity provides the mechanisms for attaining (personal) goals whose achievements are either not possible or only partially successful through other activities.

Behaviorally, *task generalization* may be defined as the tendency for a stimulus to which a particular response has been learned to evoke similar responses in other situations. Leisure activity task generalization is the tendency to choose leisure activities that are similar to other life activities (e.g., work, interpersonal or familial interactions, subsistence activities) because similar outcomes are expected. These outcomes would include such things as need gratification, feelings of personal satisfaction and/or accomplishment, and so on (Tinsley, Barrett, & Kass, 1977; Tinsley & Kass, 1978). Leisure activity task generalization and compensation functions are antithetical; the former serves to permit alternative behaviors.

Each of these functions of leisure activities is important in the lives of youth. Given the intense emotional states characteristic of youth, the need for at least occasional catharsis is apparent. Relatedly, the characteristically high physical and mental activity levels of youth support the need for both types of relaxation. The many developmental tasks confronting youth alluded to earlier attest to the need for the compensation and task generalization functions. Leisure activity functions therefore serve potentially meaningful and highly significant roles in the lives of youth.

The functions of leisure are important to leisure counselors because consideration of them may provide an enabling perspective for the leisure counseling process. Recipients of leisure counseling services are, however, often more concerned with the practicial benefits of effective leisure: they are concerned about the benefits for them. A considerable number of authors (e.g., Bolles, 1978; Compton & Goldstein, 1977; Edwards & Boland, 1980; Epperson, Witt, & Hitzhusen, 1977; Iso-Ahola, 1980; Overs, Taylor & Adkins, 1977) have suggested benefits of leisure activity participation. A synthesis of these offerings includes at least the following: creative expression, self-definition, autonomy, self-fulfillment, need gratification, and happiness. Clearly, these are personal benefits that people in general and youth in particular are seeking. Effective leisure activity is one way these benefits may be realized.

These functions and benefits are obviously important components of mental health. However, it is just as obvious that effective leisure activity in and of itself will not bring about total mental health. Effective leisure is a necessary but not sufficient condition for mental health; it must be supplemented by effective vocational adjustment, interpersonal development, and all the other components of human functioning. It is appropriate, therefore, to limit the relationships between leisure and mental health by considering "leisure mental health" as a special type. Leisure mental health may be defined as simultaneous effective emotional and behavioral leisure activity adjustment in both personal and social contexts (Loesch & Wheeler, 1982). While this is an esoteric definition, it at least provides a conceptual goal for the leisure counseling process.

A Framework for Leisure Counseling

As is probably true for any new counseling specialty, leisure counseling does not suffer from a lack of suggestions about how it should be conducted. Indeed, it seems as though everyone who has written about leisure counseling has their own "model" to offer. For example, the following are a few of the authors who have presented "models" or "guidelines" for leisure counseling: Connolly (1977), Dickason (1972), Edwards (1980), Fain (1973), Hayes (1977), McDowell (1976b), Mirenda and Wilson (1975), Overs (1970), Overs, Taylor, and Adkins (1977), and Witt, Campbell, and Witt (1975).

Unfortunately, most of the existing "models" (with the notable exception of McDowell's) focus (a) on *information-giving,* leisure *education,* or rather simplistic *guidance* services or (b) on the use of specific techniques (e.g., values clarification) within the "counseling" context. To the extent that these "models" lack substantive comprehension of the *counseling* process, they pose a threat to the development of leisure counseling. Neulinger (1977) aptly summarizes the situation: "At the threshold of a new discipline of leisure counseling it's tempting to develop quick programs, easy solutions, and 'workable' techniques. A simple solution would be ideal, but the nature of the problem is not likely to make such a solution possible, nor even desirable. Leisure counseling calls for a multiplicity of approaches." (p. 28)

I. Affective Dimensions

a. Feelings — emotional reactions to the concept of leisure and participation in various leisure activities.
b. Attitudes — opinions about the roles and functions of leisure and various leisure activities.
c. Values — beliefs about the relative importances of various leisure activities and participation in them.
d. Expectations — perceptions of benefits and liabilities from participation in various leisure activities
e. Interests — identified leisure activities that have potential for personal satisfaction
f. Personal characteristics — individual attributes that make some leisure activities more personally appropriate than others.

II. Behavioral Dimensions

a. Physical — current and desired behaviors relative to (physical) activity levels
b. Personal — current and desired behaviors characteristic of the individual when alone
c. Social — current and desired behaviors characteristic of the individual when with other people
d. Environmental — current and desired behaviors relative to various (physical) environments

III. Cognitive Dimensions

a. Intelligence — general levels of mental functioning available for various leisure activities
b. Aptitudes — specific mental abilities available for various leisure activities
c. Accomplishments — achievements relative to various past, current, or potential leisure activities
d. Thinking processes — characteristic styles of information processing and decision-making relative to leisure activities
e. Knowledge — amount of information possessed by the individual about various leisure activities

Figure 5-2. Dimensions of the triangulation leisure counseling model.

In response to Neulinger's charge, yet another model has been offered. The Triangulation Leisure Counseling (TLC) model (Loesch and Wheeler, 1982) is based on two generally accepted perspectives: (a) human functioning may be divided into affective, behavioral, and cognitive dimensions (as was popularized by the *Taxonomies of Educational Objectives*; e.g., Krathwohl, Bloom, & Masia, 1956) and (b) significant understanding results when three different types of information on a common topic are considered (an idea popularized in the program evaluation literature; e.g., Neigher, Hammer & Landsberg, 1977). The TLC model holds that affective, behavioral, and cognitive dimensions are unique to each individual as they relate to the individual's leisure activities. Accordingly, each dimension should be considered at least to some extent in every leisure counseling process. The dimensions to be considered are depicted in Figure 5-2.

Considered collectively, the affective dimensions allow for interpretations and understandings of an individual's *motivations* for participation in various leisure activities. In this regard, some other suggested models have placed a disproportionate emphasis on the evaluation of leisure interests as the means of inferring motivations. Such an inference is overly simplistic; human motivation reflects a composite of a variety of affective dimensions (Weiner, 1980). Since effective clarification and understanding of an individual's motivations are essential to the individual's identification and evaluation of potentially appropriate leisure activities, the affective dimensions must be explored thoroughly in the leisure counseling process. This is especially true for leisure counseling with youth since many youth will not have sufficient experience or skills to understand their own affective dimensions in general, and as they apply to leisure activities in particular.

Exploration of the behavioral dimensions allows for understanding for how the individual has behaved in the past and how the individual would like to behave in the future. This latter consideration is especially important because it permits determination of identifiable goals for the leisure counseling process. That is, the desired future behaviors related by the individual become the behavioral goals of the leisure counseling process. This (behavioral) goal setting part of the process may be particularly advantageous to youth because they are in the midst of setting many goals in their lives and this process may generalize beyond leisure activities.

Consideration of an individual's cognitive dimensions are important in that the natures of those dimensions will have bearing on which leisure activities are most appropriate for the individual. Perhaps even more importantly for youth, however, the exploration of cognitive dimensions (in terms of mental abilities and capabilities) may provide generalizable insights, that is, the ways that youth process information and make decisions about leisure activities is more than likely generalizable to other aspects of their lives.

In order to facilitate exploration of these dimensions, leisure counseling using the TLC model progresses through four stages:

I. *Joining* — the establishment of rapport between the leisure counselor and the individual(s) for whom the process is intended. This stage is similar in nature to the initiation of many other types of counseling and includes such things as empathic listening and facilitative responding.

II. *Exploration* — the consideration of the TLC model dimensions as they apply uniquely to the individual. This stage includes a variety of activities including assessments, experiential and didactic activities, self-evaluations, and so on.

III. *Action* — the experimentation by the individual with various potentially appropriate leisure activities and/or information processing and decision-making skills. This stage includes "practice" on the insight derived from the exploration stage, with particular emphasis on the individual's self-awareness and evaluations and reactions to the activities.

IV. *Termination* — the synthesis of the information and insights from the preceding two stages. This stage culminates with selection of potentially effective leisure behaviors (activities).

It should be noted that any of the first three stages may have to be "repeated" in any given leisure counseling process, depending on their respective outcomes.

This overview of the TLC model dimensions and stages has had to be brief by necessity. However, hopefully it has provided a perspective for leisure counseling with youth and further support that such counseling is anything but simplistic. What remains to be discussed is ways the leisure counseling process can be implemented with youth. The two basic ways are remedial and developmental leisure counseling.

Remedial Leisure Counseling

The term remedial leisure counseling denotes that some undesirable situation (i.e., set of behaviors) is to be "corrected." This situation may be one of two types. The obvious one is where youth are dissatisfied with their leisure activities and seek greater leisure satisfaction through alternative activities. The less obvious one is where effective leisure activity is the alternative to some other undesirable situation (e.g., delinquency). In either case, however, the nature of the remedial leisure counseling process is essentially similar.

The major component of any leisure counseling process is verbal interaction. In remedial leisure counseling, this interaction is bilateral; both the leisure counselor and the client listen and respond as is appropriate and desirable. The intent of this communication varies across the process. Initially, it seeks to clarify the exact nature of the problem. During a majority of the process it seeks to facilitate clarification of affective, behavioral, and cognitive dimensions as they relate specifically to the client. Toward the end of the process it seeks to facilitate finalizing decisions and plans as well as closure on the process. The form and style of verbal interactions will, of course, vary greatly depending on the personalities of the client and the leisure counselor and on the counselor's preferred counseling orientation.

During the *joining* stage of remedial leisure counseling with youth, the leisure counselor attempts to obtain several important pieces of information about (and from) the client in addition to establishing rapport with the client. The first piece of information needed is the specific nature of the problem for which (leisure) counseling was sought. For example, in some cases youth may seek leisure counseling because it is more "socially acceptable" than counseling for other types of problems such as relationships with parents or peers, shyness, vocational indecision, and so forth. In counseling terms, there may be a discrepancy between the "presenting" problem and the "real" problem. If such a discrepancy exists, the leisure counselor should either initiate a referral or shift to an appropriate type of counseling.

The second type of information desired is knowledge of the client's emotional, cognitive, and physical maturity. Such information is usually garnered by inference from communication with, and observation of, the client. However, supplemental information in this regard may sometimes be obtained from anecdotal records, if the client is a student. This inferring process necessitates that leisure counselors be well versed in developmental psychology. The information gained is useful in that it allows leisure counselors to know what the capabilities and potentialities of their clients are. For example, if a client has completed only a few of the developmental tasks appropriate for adolescence, the client may have difficulty clarifying values, making decisions, etc. In such cases the leisure counselor would have to "adjust" the leisure counseling process to the level of the client (e.g., go slower, use less complex sentences, do simpler activities, or explain concepts in greater detail).

General information relative to each of the various dimensions in the TLC model is the third type of information to be obtained during the *joining* stage. The leisure counselor should obtain global impressions of the client's affective, behavioral, and cognitive dimensions so as to form a comprehensive perspective on the client. This information is usually gained through open-ended questions about each of the dimensions. Further, these questions may relate to how the client perceives the dimenisons at present, or how the client would like the dimensions to be in the future, or, preferrably, both. Such information enables the leisure counselor, in conjunction with the client, to establish goals for the leisure counseling process.

The final type of information desired in this stage is assessment information (Howe, chapter 10). That is, if assessment instruments are to be used to supplement the leisure counseling process (e.g., for evaluating leisure interests, attitudes, values, satisfactions, etc.), the leisure counselor should initiate the administrations during this stage. While the assessments are typically not a part of actual counseling sessions, they should be administered early in the leisure counseling process so that the information will be available early to the leisure counselor and when appropriate later in the process.

The *exploration* stage of remedial leisure counseling is exactly what the name implies: exploration of each of the client's affective, behavioral, and cognitive dimensions as they relate to the client's (desired) leisure activities. The leisure counselor's purposes during this stage are to gain a holistic understanding of the client and to enable the client to have a holistic understanding of self.

The affective dimensions are usually explored through a combination of communication, experiential, and assessment activities. For example, feelings about leisure are usually explored through discussion with the client. Attitudes may be similarly explored, or one of the available leisure surveys (e.g., Crandall and Slivken, 1978) might be employed. Values are typically explored through the use of a values clarification activity. Such experiential activities also help to add variation to the counseling process. Client expectations (from leisure activity) are probably best explored through conversation. This discussion is extremely important for the leisure counseling process in that the client expectations derived are literally the "goals" for the process. Because of the potentially large number of leisure interests that need to be evaluated, such interests should probably be explored through the use of a leisure interest inventory (e.g., McKechnie, 1975). If a leisure interest was administered as an adjunct to the *joining* stage, this exploration would include discussion of the inventory results. Finally, the exploration of a client's personal characteristics should be done through client (verbal) self-report and subsequent discussion. While a personality inventory might be used for this purpose, the potentials for misuse, misinterpreation, and misunderstanding are generally too great to merit their use in the leisure counseling context (except by professionals specifically trained in the intricacies of personality assessment).

The exploration of the behavioral dimensions includes only discussion, and perhaps an experiential activity; there are no assessment instruments available for this purpose. Each of these four dimensions can be covered through client self-reports and subsequent discussions. In addition, the client might be asked to construct a "log" of typical leisure behaviors during a typical day, week, or month. The important task for these explorations is differentiation between current and desired behaviors. The desired behaviors should be closely aligned with the affective expectations discussed above; if not, the goals of the leisure counseling process may have to be realigned.

The cognitive dimensions are best explored through discussions. However, for leisure counseling with youth, supplementary information about mental capabilities may be obtained from anecdotal comments or standardized test scores in school records. It should be emphasized that "exact information in these regards is not necessary; global estimates of general mental ability, aptitudes, and accomplishments will suffice for leisure counseling purposes. Thinking processes used by the client and the client's leisure knowledge should be explored thoroughly because they have implications for how the leisure counseling process will proceed. For example, if the client generally lacks leisure knowledge, it may be desirable to have the client engage in some leisure educational activities.

The conclusion of the *exploration* stage involves summarization of important points by the leisure counselor and client. Remedial leisure counseling specifically implies helping the client *change* leisure behaviors. Thus a fundamental part of the summarization is elaboration of the possibilities for, and obstacles to, client leisure behavior changes.

The *action* stage of the remedial leisure counseling process involves having the client "try out" new and potentially appropriate leisure behaviors. This "trying out" process must be approached cautiously for several reasons. For example, an individual first participating in an activity is not likely to have proficiency in the activity and thus may be frustrated by a lack of immediate success and/or complete satisfaction. In addition, the client may not have fully appropriate equipment for the leisure activity and this may also limit proficiency. Finally, the trial participation may have some costs involved and the client may be reluctant to make the expenditures. For these reasons the leisure counselor should carefully structure the practice activities for the client. For example, if possible the leisure counselor should arrange to have the client participate in the activity with someone already proficient in the activity. Further, the leisure counselor might arrange for the use of equipment or facilities on a loan or low cost basis. In other words, the leisure counselor should do everything possible to make the practice experience a successful and satisfying one for the client.

The *termination* stage is intended to help the client solidify decisions. Accordingly, it integrates information from the *exploration* and *action* stages. For example, relationships among expectations, various leisure activities, and personal characteristics should be discussed toward the goal of helping the client fully understand the bases for the activities selected. Moreover, since people change, leisure activity preferences change, and therefore the client should also be helped to understand how leisure activity selections are effectively made. That is, the client should have understanding of the major components of the leisure counseling process so that the client may use a similar process in the future as appropriate.

Since remedial leisure counseling is intended to change previous leisure behaviors, the ultimate test of its effectiveness is whether the client actually changed behaviors. As with any counseling process, leisure counselors should carefully evaluate the results of their efforts. In remedial leisure counseling with youth, the evaluation process is often difficult because the changes are often subtle and therefore difficult to discern. However, outcome evaluation is essential if leisure counselors are to improve their counseling processes.

Developmental Leisure Counseling

The one certainty in the lives of today's youth is that the world around them, and their interactions with it, will continue to change as they grow older.

Consequently, it is important for them to develop basic skills that may be used effectively as they encounter the many changes during their lifetimes. Leisure skills and activities developed during this period will aid development during the entire life span (Dowd, Chapter 9) and will facilitate adjustment as an older adult (Myers, Chapter 6). This is particularly true for leisure activity identification, selection, and evaluation skills. In addition to their "natural" (physical and psychological) changes, youth will also encounter vocational, social, economic, and other changes that will affect their leisure activities. They need leisure-related skills that will enable them to cope with these changes and that enable them to maintain leisure mental health. Developmental leisure counseling is a process that facilitates their having such skills.

The purpose of developmental leisure counseling is to help youth develop leisure-related skills such as information processing, decision making, and evaluation of leisure activity personal appropriateness and effectiveness. Developmental leisure counseling is (theoretically) appropriate for any youth not in need of remedial leisure counseling; even youth with good beginnings of leisure-related skills can have their skills improved through developmental leisure counseling.

The major difference between remedial and developmental leisure counseling is that the former is "problem solving" oriented, whereas the latter is "skill building" oriented. It is in a sense, therefore, an educative process. The educative aspects of developmental leisure counseling necessitate that particular attention be paid to the ways information and ideas are presented, and the ways they are learned. Presentations may be divided into two major categories: (a) didactic, including lectures, readings, films, tapes, charts, and (b) experiential, including field trips, group activities, practice, and other situations where people learn by doing. Learning modes similarly may be divided into two categories: (a) visual, for people who learn primarily by seeing, and (b) aural, for people who learn primarily by hearing. Together, four combinations of presentation-learning styles are possible. In the developmental leisure counseling process it is best to use or allow for all four combinations to help insure that the communication processes used are personally effective for each participant.

The developmental leisure counseling process, under the TLC model, follows through the same four stages. However, since developmental counseling is usually done in small or large (e.g., classroom) groups, the nature of the leisure counselor's activities are different. For the sake of example here, the developmental leisure counseling process will assume the leisure counselor is working with a large group.

The *joining* stage again is intended to establish rapport between the leisure counselor and clients. However, it is also intended to establish rapport among the clients. Thus the *joining* stage of developmental leisure counseling often begins with an "icebreaker" exercise designed to help the participants get to know one another better. These exercises usually involve formation of small groups, an activity (e.g., completing a "shield"), and subsequent discussion.

Following this activity, the leisure counselor usually "sets the stage" for what is to follow. The leisure counselor should emphasize that the process is designed to help the participants gain coping skills for future situations and not to "correct" current or past leisure behaviors. This presentation should in large part be derived from the developmental constructs discussed earlier in this chapter.

As in the remedial leisure counseling process, if assessment instruments are to be used, they should be administered in conjunction with the *joining* stage activities. Also, if resource materials (e.g., books, films, etc.) are to be used, they should be identified and obtained at this time.

As distinct from remedial leisure counseling, experiential activities are used extensively during the exploration stage of developmental leisure counseling. This is because of the skill building orientation in the latter. That is, the experiential activities are intended to help participants learn skills they can actually use at later points in their lives.

Explorations of the affective dimensions are particularly amenable to the use of experiential activities. For example, feelings about leisure can be explored by having the youth list their feelings (about their leisure activities) and then having small and large group discussions about the similarities and differences among the lists. Expectations can be explored in a similar manner. Attitudes toward leisure activities might be explored through the use of leisure attitude surveys or by having the participants identify reflections of leisure attitudes in the various mass media and then having discussion about what was found. Leisure values can easily be explored through the use of values clarification activities adapted for the purpose at hand. Leisure interest can be explored through leisure interest inventories or through having the participants develop methods of locating information on various types of leisure activities and then discussing how to evaluate their interests in them. The exploration of personal characteristics, however, necessitates a diversion from the pattern. Such exploration in the large group context is best achieved by a presentation by the leisure counselor on how to do a "self-evaluation" and then individual applications by each participant. The use of experiential activities for this last exploration cannot be recommended because there is too much potential for psychological harm to the participants.

The exploration of the behavioral dimensions through experiential activities in a large group context necessitates considerable creativity on the part of the leisure counselor. This is because the concepts may be difficult to communicate in an abstract sense. However, the leisure counselor should strive to help the participants be able to evaluate their own various behaviors. For example, the participants could be asked to write a brief essay on their reactions to the environment (i.e., room) in which the developmental leisure counseling activities are being conducted. Similarly, structured fantasy exercises might be used for the exploration of desired social behaviors. Individual charting or logging activities could also be used to help participants evaluate the differences between their current and desired physical and personal leisure behaviors.

Exploration of the cognitive dimensions necessitates a cautious approach by the leisure counselor lest individuals feel threatened in the situation. That is, the participants should not have to divulge, or have divulged, any more of their personal mental abilities then they care to have known. In fact, the best tack is not to have any of this information presented to the large group. Rather, the participants should be helped to be able to make self (and therefore private) cognitive dimension evaluations. For example, the particiants should be informed as to where such information already exists (e.g., school records) and how they may obtain access to the information (e.g., through a parent conference). There are also a number of decision-making activities that could be used to help the participants learn about how they make decisions. Finally, small or large group discussions could be used to help participants generate resources for information about leisure activities, thereby supplementing their existing leisure activity knowledge.

The *action* stage of developmental leisure counseling has the same purposes as in remedial leisure counseling and therefore the same guidelines apply. There is, however, one distinct advantage in the small or large group content. It is often the case that two or more participants will have selected similar activities for trial participation. Thus participants can be "paired" for their trial participations. This usually has the effect of making each participant more comfortable in the activities. It also allows the "partners" to compare their subsequent reactions to the activities.

The *termination* stage of developmental leisure counseling again is primarily a synthesis function. However, whereas in remedial leisure counseling the emphasis is on making "final" leisure behavior decisions, in developmental leisure counseling it is on clarifying and enumerating the skills that have been covered. Thus, at the conclusion of the process, each participant should be able to make the statement, "I now have skills (___) which I did not have before the process began." Further, if the process has been fully effective, each participant should have the same, full set of skills. Therefore the primary activities of the *termination* stage are to have each participant complete that statement and to rectify any omissions that may appear. This is usually accomplished through large group activity and discussion. The resultant lists also serve as an evaluation of the developmental leisure counseling process.

Space limitations have necessitated that the preceding discussions of remedial and developmental leisure counseling be superficial at best. More complete discussions of these processes may be found in Loesch and Wheeler (1982). In addition, supplementary information regarding remedial leisure counseling may be found in Edwards (1980) and supplementary information regarding developmental leisure counseling may be found in McDowell (1976b).

Other Leisure Counseling Services

Leisure counseling consultation is the primary indirect service provided by leisure counselors (Edwards & Bloland, 1980). The need for leisure counseling consultation most frequently occurs when a leisure concern becomes evident as part of another type of counseling process. A common example is when youth are involved in vocational counseling. Since it is unlikely that any job will ever fulfill all of a person's needs, other life activities, particularly leisure activities, must be explored and evaluated in regard to potential need fulfillment (Severinsen, 1979). A vocational counselor working with youth might therefore need consultation as to how to help youth explore and evaluate leisure activities in conjunction with vocational counseling activities. A less common (although increasing in frequency) example lies in family counseling. The need for and potential of leisure counseling as a part of family counseling have been recognized, but to date have not often been realized (Gunter & Moore, 1975; Orthner, 1975, 1980). In order to realize this potential, it may be appropriate for leisure counselors to provide consultation services for family counselors. In sum, leisure counseling consultation may help youth by enhancing other types of counseling they are receiving.

Closely related to the leisure counseling consultation function is the provision of professional development services in leisure counseling for persons working with youth. Grossman (1980) has emphatically stressed that there are simply too many people with inadequate preparations providing leisure "counseling" services. The provision of inservice training, workshops, and other learning experiences in leisure counseling is one way to at least in part alleviate this situation. Such training is especially important for persons who want to do leisure counseling with youth because of the relatively unique characteristics of youth. A more complete description of what this training should entail may be found in Grossman and Kindy (Chapter 11). Suffice it to say here that such training and professional development is essential.

As a relatively new functional specialty, leisure counseling services in general, and for youth in particular, are not widely available. Consequently, there is a great need for the development of leisure counseling service delivery programs. Leisure counseling services now are apparently most frequently provided by counselors in private practice. It is therefore unlikely that the vast majority of youth will be able to avail themselves of such services. Program development activities should extend leisure counseling services for youth into schools, community agencies, youth programs, and other organizations and institutions that have frequent contact with youth.

Finally, research on leisure counseling with youth is yet another important indirect service function. The need for such research is glaringly apparent; there isn't any. If existing practices which have shown promise are to be improved and if ineffective practices are to be eliminated, then an empirical basis for leisure counseling with youth must be established. It should be acknowledged that some tangential studies with *implications* for leisure counseling with youth have been conducted (e.g., London, Crandall, & Fitzgibbons, 1977; Rimmer, 1979). However, it is necessary to move beyond implications into examinations of the effectiveness, and factors relating to it, of leisure counseling with youth. Studies of this genre should result in the provision of more and better leisure counseling for youth.

Innumerable professionals and innumerable lay-persons have lamented the difficulties of being a youth in our society. The lives of youth seem at once to be overly simplistic and overly complex. Yet the tasks youth face are not insurmountable obstacles and the difficulties they encounter are not unsolvable dilemmas. Some youth find resolutions through their own devices while others need considerable help, but all have some degree of difficulty in achieving those resolutions. Fortunately, the history of the counseling professions suggests that counseling interventions *may* alleviate some of the difficulties. Unfortunately, there is an insufficient number of counseling interventions to alleviate all the types of difficulties youth experience. However, as the counseling professions expand and extend their service realms, these areas of difficulty become fewer in number and lesser in degree. Leisure counseling with youth is part of the expansion and extension; it is needed and it has strong potential.

REFERENCES

Allen, L.R. Leisure and its relationship to work and career guidance. *Vocational Guidance Quarterly* 1980, *28*(3), 257-262.

American Psychological Association. *Standards for educational and psychological tests.* (rev. ed.) Washington, D.C. APA, 1974.

Ausubel, D.P., Montemayer, R., & Srajian, P. *Theory and problems of adolescent development.* New York: Grune & Stratton, 1977.

Avedon, E.M. *Therapeutic recreation service: An applied behavioral science approach.* Englewood Cliffs, N.J.: Prentice-Hall, 1974.

Ball, J.D., & Meck, D.S. Implications of developmental theories for counseling adolescents in groups. *Adolescence*, 1979, *14*(55), 528-534.

Besag, F.P. Work, leisure and school. *Counseling and Values*, 1975, *20*(1), 25-28.

Bolles, R.N. *The three boxes of life.* Berkely, Ca.: Ten Speed Press, 1978.

Brightbill, C.K. *The challenge of leisure.* Englewood Cliffs, N.J.: Prentice-Hall, 1960.

Brightbill, C.K., and Mobley, T.A. *Educating for leisure-centered living.* (2nd ed.) New York: Wiley, 1977.

Brody, V. Developmental play: A relationship-focused program for children. *Journal of Child Welfare*, 1978, *57*(9), 591-599.

Bruner, J. Nature and uses of immaturity. In J.S. Bruner, A. Jolly, and K. Sylva (Eds.), *Play: Its role in development and evolution.* New York: Basic Books, 1976.

Bruner, J.S. & Sherwood, V. Peekaboo and the learning of rule structures. In J.S. Bruner, A. Jolly, & K. Sylva (Eds.), *Play: Its role in development and evolution.* New York: Basic Books, 1976.

Bruner, J.S., Jolly, A., & Sylva, K. *Play: Its role in development and evolution.* New York: Basic Books, 1976.

Burch, R.J. Levels of occupational prestige and leisure activity. *Journal of Leisure Research*, 1969, *1*(3), 262-274.

Butler, A.L., Gotts, E.E., & Quisenberry, N.L. *Play as development*. Columbus, Ohio: Charles E. Merrill, 1978.

Clawson, M. How much leisure, now and in the future? In J.C. Charlesworth (Ed.), *Leisure in America: Blessing or curse?* Philadelphia, Pa.: American Academy of Political and Social Science, 1964.

Cohen, J. High school subcultures and the adult world. *Adolescence,* 1979, *14*(55), 491-502.

Compton, D.M., & Goldstein, J.E. (Eds.). *Perspectives of leisure counseling*. Arlington, Va.: National Recreation and Park Association, 1977.

Connolly, M.L. Leisure counseling: A values clarification and assertive training approach. In A. Epperson, P.A. Witt, & G. Hitzhusen (Eds.) *Leisure counseling: An aspect of leisure education*. Springfield, Il.: Charles C Thomas, 1977.

Corder, B., Whiteside, R., & Vogel, M. A therapeutic game for structuring and facilitating group psychotherapy with adolescents. *Adolescence*, 1977, *12*(46), 261-267.

Crandall, R., & Slivken, K. *The importance of measuring leisure attitudes*. Paper presented at the National Recreation and Park Association Convention, Miami, Florida, October, 1978.

de Grazia, S. *Of time, work, and leisure*. New York: The Twentieth Century Fund, 1962.

Dickason, J.G. Approaches and techniques of recreation counseling. *Therapeutic Recreation Journal*, 1972, *6*, 74-78.

Edwards, P.B. *Leisure counseling techniques: Individual and group counseling step-by-step*. (3rd ed.) Los Angeles: Constructive Leisure, 1980.

Edwards, P.B. *The Constructive Leisure Assessment Survey — II*. Los Angeles: Constructive Leisure, 1978.

Edwards, P.B., & Bloland, P.A. Leisure counseling and consultation. *Personnel and Guidance Journal*, 1980, *58*(6), 435-440.

Elrardo, R., Bradley, R., & Caldwell, B.M. The relation of infants home environment to mental test performance from six to thirty-six months: A longitudinal analysis. *Child Development*, 1975, *46*(1), 71-76.

Employment and training report of the President. Washington, D.C.: Superintendent of Documents, 1978.

Epperson, A., Witt, P.A., & Hitzhusen, G. (Eds.). *Leisure counseling: An aspect of leisure education*. Springfield, Il.: Charles C Thomas, 1977.

Erikson, E.H. A healthy personality for every child. In M. Almy (Ed.), *Early childhood play: Selected readings related to cognition and motivation*. New York: Simon & Schuster, 1968a.

Erikson, E.H. *Identity youth and crisis*. New York: W.W. Norton & Co., 1968b.

Erikson, E.H. Play and actuality. In M.W. Piers (Ed.), *Play and development*. New York: W.W. Norton & Co., 1972.

Fain, G.S. Leisure counseling: Translating needs into action. *Therapeutic Recreation Journal*, 1973, *7*(2), 4-9.

Fink, R.S. Role of imaginative play in cognitive development. *Psychological Reports*, 1976, *39*(3, pt 1), 895-906.

Garvey, C. *Play*. Cambridge: Harvard University Press, 1977.

Gholson, R.E. Extracurricular activities: Different perceptions but strong support. *Phi Delta Kappan*, 1979, *61*(1), 67-68.

Grinder, R.E. *Adolescence*. (2nd ed). New York: Wiley & Sons, 1978.

Grossman, A. Meeting the need: A professional preparation program for leisure counseling (editorial). *Leisure Information Newsletter*, 1980, *7*(1), 1ff.

Gunn, S.L. Leisure counseling: An analysis of play behavior and attitude using Transactional Analysis and Gestalt awareness: In A. Epperson, P.A. Witt, & G. Hitzhusen (Eds.), *Leisure counseling: An aspect of leisure education*. Springfield, Il., Charles C Thomas, 1977a.

Gunn, S.L. The relationship of leisure counseling to selected counseling theories. In D.M.

Compton and J.E. Goldstein (Eds.), *Perspectives of leisure counseling*. Arlington, Va.: National Recreation and Park Association, 1977b.

Gunter, B.G., & Moore, H.A. Youth, leisure, and post-industrial society: Implications for the family. *The Family Coordinator*, 1975, *24*(2), 199-207.

Harlow, H.F., & Suomi, S.J. Nature of love-simplified. *American Psychologist*, 1970, *25*(2), 161-168.

Havighurst, R.J. *Developmental tasks and education*. New York: Longmans & Green, 1951.

Hayes, G.A. Leisure education and recreation counseling. In D.M. Compton & J.E. Goldstein (Eds.), *Perspectives of leisure counseling*. Arlington, Va.: National Recreation and Park Association, 1977.

Hitzhusen, G. Youth recreation counseling — A necessity in therapeutic recreation. In A. Epperson, P.A. Witt, and G. Hitzhusen (Eds.), *Leisure counseling: An aspect of leisure education*. Springfield, Il.: Charles C Thomas, 1977.

Hoyt, K.B. *Refining the career education concept, part II*. (HEW Monograph on Career Education). Washington, D.C.: Government Printing Office, 1977.

Hurlock, E.B. *Developmental psychology*. (4th ed.). New York: McGraw-Hill, 1975.

Hutt, C., & Bhavini, R. Predictions from play. In J.S. Bruner, A. Jolly, & K. Sylva (Eds.) *Play: Its role in development and evolutuion*. New York: Basic Books, 1976.

Iso-Ahola, S.E. (Ed.) *Social psychological perspectives on leisure and recreation*. Springfield, Il.: Charles C Thomas, 1980.

Jernberg, A.M. *Theraplay*. San Francisco: Jossey-Bass, 1979.

Kaplan, M. *Leisure in America: A social inquiry*. New York: Wiley, 1960.

Kelly, J. Work and leisure: A simplified paradigm. *Journal of Leisure Research*, 1972, *4*, 50-62.

Klinger, E. The development of imaginative behavior: Implications of play for a theory of fantasy. *Psychological Bulletin*, 1969, *72*(4) 277-298.

Krathwohl, D.R., Bloom, B.S., & Masia, B.B. *Taxonomy of educational objectives The classification of educational goals Handbook II: The Affective domain*. New York: David McKay, 1956.

Loesch, L.C. *Leisure counseling (Searchlight Plus)*. Ann Arbor, Mich.: ERIC Counseling and Personnel Services Clearinghouse, 1980a.

Loesch, L.C. Life flow leisure counseling for older persons. *Journal of Employment Counseling*, 1980b, *17*(1), 49-56.

Loesch, L.C., & Wheeler, P.T. *Principles of leisure counseling*. Minneapolis, Mn.: Educational Media Corp., 1982.

London, M., Crandall, R., & Fitzgibbons, D. The psychological structure of leisure: Activities, needs, people. *Journal of Leisure Research*, 1977, *9*, 252-263.

Manmaster, G.J. *Adolescent development and the life tasks*. Boston: Allyn and Bacon, 1977.

Matheny, A.P., Jr., Donal, A.B., & Drantz, J.Z. Cognitive aspects of interests, responsibilities and vocational goals in adolescence. *Adolescence*, 1980, *15*(58), 301-311.

McCandless, B.R. *Adolescents: Behavior and development* (2nd ed). New York: Holt, Rinehart & Winston, 1979.

McDowell, C.F. Emerging leisure counseling concepts and orientations. *Therapeutic Recreation Journal*, 1976, *10*(2), 19-25. (a)

McDowell, C.F. *Leisure counseling: Selected lifestyle processes*. Eugene, Or.: University of Oregon of Leisure Studies, 1976. (b)

McDowell, C.F. An analysis of leisure counseling orientations and models and their integrative possibilities. In D.M. Compton and J.E. Goldstein (Eds.), *Perspectives of leisure counseling*. Arlington, Va.: National Recreation and Park Association, 1977. (a)

McDowell, C.F. Integrating theory and practice in leisure counseling. *Journal of Health, Physical Education, and Recreation*, 1977, *48*(4), 51-54. (b)

McDowell, C.F. *The Leisure Well-Being Inventory*. Eugene, Or.: Leisure Lifestyle Consultants, 1979.

McKechnie, G.E. *Manual for the Leisure Activities Blank*. Palo Alto, Ca.: Consulting Psychologists Press, 1975.

Mirenda, J.J., & Wilson, G.T. The Milwaukee leisure counseling mode. *Counseling and Values*, 1975, *20*(1), 42-46.

Montagu, A. *Touching: The human significance of the skin*. New York: Harper & Row, 1978.

Murphy, J.F. *Recreation and leisure service: A humanistic perspective*. Dubuque, Ia.: William C. Brown, 1975.

Neigher, W., Hammer, R.J., & Landsberg, G. (Eds.) *Emerging developments in mental health program evalation*. New York: Arnold Press, 1977.

Neulinger, J. Leisure counseling: A plea for complexity. *Journal of Health, Physical Education, and Recreation*, 1977, *48*, 27-28.

Neulinger, J. *Leisure counseling: Process or content?* Paper presented at the Dane County Recreation Coordinating Council Conference on Leisure Counseling, Madison, Wisconsin, September, 1978.

Neulinger, J. The need for and implications of a psychological conceptualization of leisure. *The Ontario Psychologist*, 1976, *8*(2), 18-20.

Neulinger, J. *The psychology of leisure*. Springfield, Il.: Charles C Thomas, 1974.

Ohlson, E.L. The meaningfulness of play for children and parents: An affective counseling strategy. *Journal of Family Counseling*, 1974, *2*(1), 53-54.

O'Morrow, G.S. Recreation counseling: A challenge to rehabilitation. *Rehabilitation Literature*, 1970, *31*(8), 226-233.

Orthner, D.K. Familia Ludens: Reinforcing the leisure component in family life. *The Family Coordinator*, 1975, *24*, 175-183.

Orthner, D.K. Leisure and conflict in families. *The Leisure Information Newsletter*, 1980, *6*(4), 10-12.

Overs, R.P. A model for avocational counseling. *Journal of Health, Physical Education, and Recreation*, 1970, *41*(2), 36-38.

Overs, R.P. Avocational counseling. *The Counseling Psychologist*, 1977, *7*(2), 85-88.

Overs, R.P. Avocational counseling: Gateway to meaningful activity. *Counseling and Values*, 1975, *20*(1), 36-41.

Overs, R.P., Taylor, S., and Adkins, C. *Avocational counseling manual A complete guide to leisure guidance*. Washington, D.C.: Hawkins and Associates, 1977.

Parker, S. *The future of work and leisure*. New York: Praeger, 1971.

Piaget, J. *Play, dreams and imitation in childhood*. New York: Norton, 1962.

Piaget, J. Some aspects of operations. In M.W. Piers (Ed.), *Play and development*. New York: W.W. Norton & Co., 1972.

Piell, E.J. *Invention and discovery of reality*. New York: Wiley & Sons, 1975.

Postman, N., & Weingartner, C. *Teaching as a subversive activity*. New York: Dell Publishing Co., 1969.

Postman, N. & Weingartner, C. *The school book*. New York: Dell Publishing Co., 1973.

Ragheb, M.G., & Beard, J.G. Leisure satisfaction: Concept, theory, and measurement. In S.E. Iso-Ahola (Ed.), *Social psychological perspectives on leisure and recreation*. Springfield, Il.: Charles C Thomas, 1980.

Renwick, P.A., Lasler, E.E., & staff. What you really want from your job. *Psychology Today*, 1978, *11*(12), 53 ff.

Rimmer, S.M. *The development of an instrument to assess leisure satisfaction among secondary school students*. Unpublished Doctoral Dissertation, University of Florida, 1979.

Severinsen, K.N. Should career education be founded in the Protestant Ethic? *Personnel and Guidance Journal*, 1979, *58*(2), 111-116.

Shank, J.W., and Kennedy, D.W. Recreation and leisure counseling: A review. *Rehabilitation Literature*, 1976, *37*(9), 258-262.

Shepard, J.H. A status recognition model of work-leisure relationships. *Journal of Leisure Research*, 1974, *6*(1), 58-63.

Smith, J.A. A survey of adolescents' interests: Concerns and information. *Adolescence*, 1980, *15* (58), 475-482.

Stamm, I. The multiple functions of play: A review and examination of the Piagetian and psychoanalytic points of view. In J. Travers (Ed.), *The new children*. Stamford, Cn.: Greylock Publishers, 1976.

Stern, D. Mother and infant at play: The dyadic interaction involving facial, vocal, and gaze behaviors. In M.L. Lewis & L. Rosenblum (Eds.), *The effect of the infant on its caregiver* (Vol. 1) New York: John Wiley & Sons, 1974.

Sullivan, S. *Development of an instrument to assess parental knowledge of parent-child play*. Unpublished Doctoral Dissertation, University of Florida, 1980.

Super, D.E. *Career education and the meaning of work* (HEW Monograph on Career Education). Washington, D.C.: Superintendent of Documents, 1976.

Super, D.E. The year 2000 and all that. *The Counseling Psychologist*, 1980, *8*(4), 22-23.

Sylva, D., Bruner, J.S., & Genova, P. The role of play in problem-solving of children three to five years old. In J.S. Bruner, A. Jolly, & K. Sylva (Eds.), *Play: Its role in development and evolution*. New York: Basic Books, 1976.

Tinsley, H.E.A. & Kass, R.A. Leisure activities and need satisfaction: A replication and extension. *Journal of Leisure Research*, 1978, *10*, 191-202.

Tinsley, H.E.A., Barrett, T.C., & Kass, R.A. Leisure activities and need satisfaction. *Journal of Leisure Research*, 1977, *9*, 110-120.

Travers, R.M.W., in collaboration with R. Harring, E. Start, L. Rynbrandt, & D. Fessler. *Children's interests*. Kalamazoo, Mi.: College of Education, Western Michigan University, 1978.

Vanderberg, B. Play and development from an ethological perspective. *American Psychologist*, 1978, *33*(8), 724-738.

Walshe, W.A. Leisure counseling instrumentation. In D.M. Compton and J.E. Goldstein (Eds.), *Perspectives of leisure counseling*. Arlington, Va.: National Recreation and Park Association, 1977.

Weiner, B. The role of affect in rational (attributional) approaches to human behavior. *Educational Researcher*, 1980, *9*(7), 4-11.

Weisler, A., & McCall, R.B. Exploration and play: Resume and redirection. *American Psychologist*, 1976, *31*(7), 492-508.

Weiss, P. A philosophical definition of leisure. In J.C. Charlesworth (Ed.), *Leisure in America: Blessing or curse?* Philadelphia, Pa.: American Academy of Political and Social Science, 1964.

Wilensky, H.L. Work, careers, and social integration. *International Social Science Journal*, 1960, *12*, 543-560.

Winters, R.A., and Hansen, J.C. Toward an understanding of work-leisure relationships. *Vocational Guidance Quarterly*, 1977, *24*(3), 238-242.

Witt, P.A., and Bishop, D.W. Situational antecedents to leisure behavior. *Journal of Leisure Research*, 1970, *2*, 64-77.

Witt, J., Campbell, M., & Witt, P.A. *A manual of therapeutic group activities for leisure education* (rev. ed.). Ottawa, Ontario, Canada: Leisureability Publications, 1975.

Wrenn, C.G. Observations on what counseling psychologists will be doing the next 20 years. *The Counseling Psychologist*, *8*(4), 1980, 32-35.

Chapter 6

LEISURE COUNSELING FOR OLDER PEOPLE

Jane E. Myers

INCREASED life expectancies combined with mandatory retirement policies have effected dramatic shifts in the demography of our elderly population, making today's older people "pioneers in the use of leisure" (Hess & Markson, 1980, p. 306). Whereas an individual born in 1900 could expect to live, on the average, 47 years, a person born today can expect to live 71 years. Further, due in part to advances in medical science and improved nutrition, life expectancy increases as a function of how long one has lived, so that a person who was 60 in 1980 could expect to live another 16 years.

The elderly American population includes 24,000,000 persons aged 60 and above, representing more than 12% of our total population or every ninth American (Brotman, 1980). An estimated 14% of these persons are in the labor market. This includes those who are working full- or part-time and those who are unemployed and seeking work (USDHEW, 1978). The remaining 86% are classified as retired, or perhaps as homemakers whose duties have lessened in relation to tasks such as childrearing. When young, these persons were strongly indoctrinated with the work ethic and taught to feel discomfort with nonproductive uses of time. As a result, many of them failed to develop leisure activities, hobbies, and other avocational interests.

Although now afforded increased time for nonwork activities, many elderly persons have substantial psychological barriers to the enjoyment of leisure. In addition to feelings of guilt over being nonproductive, they also are affected by a lack of role definition for their new found leisure. In short, they have learned neither to enjoy nor to value leisure, and they have large amounts of time to fill with functions other than the now obsolete work role. The potential for leisure counseling with older people appears both obvious and enormous, yet is complicated by another component of this age cohort's value system — a focus on independence, especially in regard to solving personal problems. Counseling, a commonly misunderstood profession among elderly people, is often equated with psychiatry. Thus, to seek counseling assistance is tantamount to an admission of mental illness. Also, counselors until very recently have avoided studying and working with older people.

In essence, then, today's elderly represent a group with potential for leisure counseling intervention, who may not actively seek such services and who may, if they do, encounter counselors untrained to deal with their specific needs. The intent of this chapter is to help alleviate this situation. Counselors who work with older people need a variety of information, including an overview of the aging process and needs of older people, and the integration of this knowledge into major theories of aging. This information is presented, followed by a discussion of the current state of the art in counseling with older people. Leisure counseling for older people is discussed in terms of preventive and remedial uses, with the overall goal of life satisfaction in mind. The application to older people of leisure counseling models described elsewhere in this book is then considered.

THEORIES OF AGING

All theories of aging are based on observations and represent attempts to integrate the known facts about older people. Biological theories originating in the medical sciences present explanations of the physical changes associated with advancing age. They stress the aspects of chronic debilitation and the inevitability of decline in body systems. Sociological theories evaluate age-related changes in terms of interpersonal or social dimensions, and stress role changes as a major outcome of the aging process. Psychological theories propose explanations to describe and account for personal coping behaviors and reactions to loss and change.

Research in these areas has resulted in a variety of theories to account for the coping behaviors of older persons and to define successful aging, or life satisfaction, in the later years of life. The discussion that follows is organized into biological, sociological, and psychological theories of aging. Of course, the impact of aging processes in all three areas of life is interrelated. The lack of a single, comprehensive theory to explain development in all areas of life necessitates a review of major theoretical efforts in each area. Each section includes some of the known facts about older people that are salient to the theories presented and facts that contributed to the development of these theories.

Biological Aging

Biological aging begins at conception and continues until death. It is an inevitable process that proceeds at a different rate for each individual, and eventually results in declining physical reserves and activity limitation. Normal biological changes predispose the older adult to both acute and chronic illness. Chronic diseases and disability affect older persons more than any other age group; in fact, an estimated 86% of all older people suffer from one or more chronic physical impairments that limit their ability to accomplish activities of daily living (Butler & Lewis, 1977). Yet, only 4 to 5% of older persons are institutionalized and only 10 to 15% are homebound as a result of illness or debilitation.

Most older people are physically capable of engaging in a variety of pursuits, from sedentary activities to sports activities, although many are handicapped psychologically by their conception of a "rocking chair" life-style as the norm for older adults. Slower paced activity is typical of older people (Gordon, Gaitz, & Scott, 1976), and represents normal adaptations to gradual physiological decline, including phenomena such as decreased reaction time. It is important to recognize that, during the course of progressive physical declines, most older people gradually modify their life-styles to maintain congruence between their physical capacities and other life needs or concerns. How they do this, and the extent to which they are successful, is the topic of social and psychological theories of aging.

Social Aging

Social aging presents a variety of challenges for older people because we have no norms for growing old (Kastenbaum, 1969). The work role is the preferred source of identity for most people, and the leisure role cannot replace work as a source of self-esteem because it is not a legitimate, normative role (Atchley, 1972). Retirement thus becomes a crisis in the meaningful use of time (Havighurst, 1972) and readily can be seen as a social embarrassment (Sinick, 1980), reflective of an abrupt transition out of the valued role of worker into the role-free life of retiree. Sheldon (in Ullmann, 1976) cites four common patterns of adjustment: maintenance, in which the individual tries to continue to work to satisfy the same needs after retirement as before; withdrawal, in which old activities are given up and new ones pursued; changes in activities to satisfy the same kinds of needs as before; and changes in both needs and activities as a result of freedom from previous external pressures. Attempts to explain the aging process from social perspectives have been based on observations of these role changes and adjustment patterns. Four primary theories that have emerged are known as disengagement, activity, identity continuity, and social reconstruction.

Disengagement Theory

Disengagement theory, the first major theory of aging, was proposed by Cumming and Henry (1961) to explain the observed facts regarding older people: that their behavior changes as they age, that the activities of middle age continue but are somehow decreased, and that the extent of social interaction decreases. This decreased social interaction is interpreted as a mutual process in which both society and the aging individual withdraw from one another. The aging person accepts this withdrawal and may even be desirous of it. The mutually satisfying process helps the elderly person and society to separate psychologically and socially so that the death of the older person is not disruptive to the equilibrium of society.

Activity Theory

The activity theory of aging was proposed by Neugarten, Havighurst, and Tobin (1961) to explain the same observed facts about aging as were "explained" by the disengagement theory. This theory was based on extensive research in the area of life satisfaction, and suggests that high morale is maintained principally among older persons who continue to be active, both socially and otherwise. Well-adjusted people live a personally satisfactory life that meets the expectations of society. They are healthy, active, independent, self-sufficient, and able to maintain satisfying interpersonal relations.

Identity Continuity Theory

Atchley (1972, p. 182) proposed the identity continuity theory based on evidence that "the adjustment problems sometimes associated with retirement are *not* the result of the loss of work and the identity it provides. . . . There is no indication that highly work oriented people are unable to take up the leisure role; in fact, just the opposite is true." Most people base their identity on several roles. Vocationally, their identity may be linked to an occupational skill, such as social interaction, rather than some abstract goal. A positive affirmation of leisure could result in continuance of the occupational skill after retirement or the "continuation of social relatedness" (Iso-Ahola, 1980, p. 122) through leisure. When a work activity, such as social interaction, continues after retirement, leisure may function as a work-substitute. This process results in the maintenance of identity or identity continuity.

In other words, the loss of the work function at retirement does not necessarily mean that leisure will increase. Rather, continued relationships and activities simply may expand to fill the available time. Radical change is much less characteristic of retired persons than is continuity (Atchley, 1971). Continuity of identity, or self-concept, occurs when activities remain stable during the retirement transition.

Social Reconstruction

Social reconstruction theory (Kuypers & Bengtson, in Bengtson, 1977) uses the social breakdown syndrome to explain the problems of aging as a "vicious cycle of increasing incompetence." The older person's social environment predisposes the individual to psychological breakdown (Step 1). Society labels the aged person as incompetent or deficient (Step 2), and induces him/her into a dependent or sick role (Step 3). Previous skills atrophy, the older person begins to identify him/herself as sick or inadequate (Step 4), and the spiral loop is established. Social reconstruction is characterized by input in three areas: First, efforts are made to change the functional ethic, which relates status to the productive work role, to a more humanitarian viewpoint, resulting in increased self-confidence and decreased susceptibility. Second, improved maintenance conditions (housing, income, etc.) result in increased self-reliance and reduced dependence. Third, the person begins to label him/herself as capable. Fourth, the encouragement of an internal locus of control results in the building and maintenance of coping skills, and hence, fifth, the internalization of a self-view as effective. It is logical to conclude that this theory goes further than most in linking social and psychological aspects of aging.

Psychological Aging

Psychological aging includes aspects of both cognition and emotion. Intelligence usually does not decline in old age, contrary to earlier assumptions based on cross-sectional data. Two types of intelligence have been isolated. The first, crystallized intelligence, includes knowledge gained as a result of experience, or the interactions between an individual and his/her environment. This capacity does not decline with age; a person's fund of stored knowledge may be expected to continue to grow until death. Fluid intelligence, or abstract reasoning ability, however, does decline with age beginning in early adulthood. The interactive effects of changes in these two types of intelligence in older persons tend to cancel out, as shown by Omnibus intelligence tests results. These tests give a composite score, which essentially averages scores for the crystallized and fluid dimensions, and these composite scores remain constant over the life span. What does change with age is speed of reaction time (Sterns & Sterns, 1981), not intelligence or ability to learn.

Old age has been variously defined as a time of loss — of physical health, social roles, status, relationships — resulting in a complex of identity crises for elderly people (Burkley, 1972). Retirement and the death of a mate, the two most shattering events of later life (Holmes & Rahe, 1967; Puner, 1977), result in the common, although usually transient, emotional reaction of grief, depression, and despair. The changes and losses that occur in late life present a new series of developmental challenges and offer unique opportunities for growth and development. Retirement from life is not a necesary concomitant of retirement from work or a necessary reaction to loss. Older people can and do develop avocational skills and activities to replace the functions that work supplied in their needs structure. Dealing with the loss of a spouse may be more difficult, based on research showing the presence of a confidant to be the primary factor that mitigates against a reduction in life satisfaction in old age (Lowenthal & Haven, 1969). Yet, most older people report that they are satisfied with their lives (Harris, 1975). Leisure can form the basis for continued social relationships to replace those lost due to retirement, thus contributing to the maintenance of life satisfaction.

Some authors believe old age to be the most stressful time of life (Butler & Lewis, 1977). One indication that this might be true is provided by statistics on the mental health of older people. Depression, the most common and potentially most treatable problem, affects an estimated 65% of all older people at some time (Select Committee on Aging, 1979). Suicide rates for older white males are the highest in the nation, and fully 25% of all reported suicides are among elderly people (Special Committee on Aging, 1980). Physical and mental health problems interact and create compounding difficulties for many elderly persons.

Nevertheless, the overwhelming majority of older people manage to cope with stress and change without outside intervention. Two primary characteristics of older people are worth mentioning here. One is that, due to the nature and extent of their individual life experiences, older people, as a group, are an extremely heterogeneous population. A second point is that they are survivors. Not only have they lived a long time, they also have lived through a greater variety of technological change than has occurred in the previous history of civilization. How they manage to cope and survive forms the basis for psychological theories of aging. The extreme diversity among older people makes the specifications of these theories somewhat difficult. The two primary theoretical orientations found in the literature include those that focus on life span development and those that focus on personality patterns.

Life Span Development

It is important to view aging within a context of life span development, a perspective that fosters the natural linkage between development and preventive intervention (Smyer & Gatz, 1979).

In general, developmental theories describe aging as an integral part of life span. Growth potential exists at all ages and is facilitated by developmental task accomplishment. Several developmental theories have proposed models to assist in this conceptualization.

The first of these theorists was Erikson (1950), whose theory of the eight stages in the life cycle of humans is well known to psychologists and counselors. The central psychological issue confronted by older adults is defined as ego integrity versus despair and disgust. The successful resolution of this issue prepares the older individual for death. Despair results when an older adult looks back over his/her life, is unhappy with one or more aspects of it, or perhaps has some unfinished business, and realizes that it is too late to make any changes. Ego integrity results when one looks back with a feeling of satisfaction over the course of one's life and activities. Changes in activities and attitudes, which may be brought about by the leisure counseling interventions discussed later, can have a marked effect on the resolution of this key psychological issue through increasing life satisfaction among older individuals.

Havighurst (1972) defined a number of developmental tasks that arise for persons at each stage of life. Older people must learn to cope with death of spouse and friends, retirement and reduced income, reduced physical strength and health, altered living arrangements, affiliation with age peers, development of new social roles, and development of constructive and satisfying leisure pursuits.

Yet another developmental theorist, Peck (1968), determined that older persons experience changes in the way they view and react to their environments. The primary changes are in four areas: valuing wisdom over physical prowess, socializing more and sexualizing less in human relationships, increasing emotional flexibility while reducing emotional impoverishment, and developing increased mental flexibility and decreased mental rigidity.

Personality Theory

Studies of personality indicate that some age-related changes do occur. These changes may include a tendency toward increased introspection, increased self-preoccupation, and decreased involvement with the outside world (Sterns & Sterns, 1981). In addition, a variety of personality types have been identified that are not related to chronological age.

Neugarten, Havighurst, and Tobin (1968) studied the relationship between social interaction and life satisfaction in old age. Their Kansas City Study of Adult Life led to the conclusion that personality type is the key factor affecting successful aging. They identified eight patterns of aging, defined by the extent of social role activity, and organized these into four basic personality types. Integrated individuals are those with competent egos who accept life, maintain control, and are flexible and mature. Armored individuals maintain tight control over their impulses and have high defenses against anxiety. Passive dependent persons have strong dependency needs and seek succorance from others. Unintegrated persons tend to have defective cognitive and affective processes. The first type is able to relinquish role responsibilities with some comfort and maintain life satisfaction; the other three types experience the lessening of role commitments somewhat more negatively. Those who maintain life satisfaction, the majority of older people, do not need counseling interventions. For those who could benefit from such interventions, counselors must be prepared with the full gamut of generic skills, plus special knowledge in the area of gerontological counseling.

COUNSELING OLDER PEOPLE

Based on their need to cope with changing life circumstances and life crises, we assume that older people need and can benefit from counseling. This assumption is backed up by at least one counseling needs assessment study (Myers & Loesch, 1981). In addition, most social service needs assessment surveys and national data surveys list counseling as an identified need of many older persons (Harris, 1975).

The major empirical support for the assumption that older people need counseling comes from research by Butler (1974) on the role of the life review.

Butler observed that people engage in a life review when they feel they are approaching death, and ask themselves questions such as who am I, who have I been, and how did I live my life (Waters & Weaver, 1981). Reminiscing can lead to a sense of pride over past accomplishments and a fuller appreciation of one's self-worth. While life reviews generally are positive, persons who see themselves as failures may find the process to be a painful one. Counseling interventions have proven effective in facilitating a positive outcome to the life review process.

Life review therapy may be both preventive and therapeutic. It includes taking an autobiography from the older person and his/her family and friends, with the purpose of evoking memories, knowledge, and self-understanding. The process may be used with retired persons to help them "take stock" of their lives — their interests, skills, values — and set goals for future life activities. This kind of planning was rare when people lived only a few years beyond retirement. Today, when people can expect to live 15 or more years beyond retirement, the preventive aspects of life review therapy are readily apparent.

A major therapeutic benefit of the life review process lies in its potential for building self-esteem. Counselors can always remind older people that they are survivors, as evidenced by the fact that they have lived a long time, and can focus their attention on the skills they utilizied to cope, change, and survive throughout their lives. Enhanced feelings of self-acceptance and self-worth result from this process, along with the achievement of what Erikson (1950) terms ego-integrity, described earlier.

The occurrence of the life review process when approaching death is not restricted to older people; however, it is much more common among the elderly cohort because the reality of death is, as it were, inescapable for them. Life review therapy is a primary technique used by gerontological counselors because it has important preventive and therapeutic aspects, and because of its relevance to the special needs of older people.

Another important area for counselor intervention, based on the special needs of older people, deals with support networks. Older people experience a shrinking social world, which often is naturally congruent with a slowing pace of life. Occasionally the increasing needs of older people, created by physiological decrements, social role changes, and psychological reactions, accompanied by decreasing resources resulting from retirement and other losses, lead to unmet needs. Decreased ability to meet one's needs without assistance can lead to a lowered self-concept. Finding new supports to replace old ones lost through death, geographic location, and other factors may be more difficult for older than younger people because they are out of the mainstream of work and social activities. Counselors can assist by establishing linkages with peer support groups and social agencies such as senior centers, through advocacy activities, and through individual and group counseling. Self-concept building can be an integral part of this process.

In addition to these specialized techniques, counselors use the full gamut of generic counseling skills when working with older people. Gerontological counseling, as a specialized area of study and practice, has been in existence only a short time, actually since the mid to late 1970s. Rapid progress is being made in the areas of counselor preparation and the development of programs to deliver counseling services to older people (see Myers, in press; Myers & Salmon, in press). We can anticipate the development of additional specialized techniques for working with older people as counselors continue to interact with them and to integrate knowledge of older people and their needs with knowledge of counseling theory and techniques.

We also can anticipate a lessening of the existing barriers to the delivery of counseling services to older people, which are due in part to both therapists and clients. Therapists often ascribe to common age stereotypes and biases, which lead them to believe, erroneously, that older people lack the potential for change and growth. Older people, on the other hand, tend not to seek counseling based on values of independence in problem solving. The stigma of mental illness is an added concern, as are misperceptions of counseling and counselors. Continued successful involvement in meeting some of the unique needs of older people, through techniques described in this section, will help to overcome those barriers that exist. Moreover, a variety of the goals of counseling with older people mentioned here — reminiscence, self-concept building, building support networks — can be accomplished through focusing on leisure. Some ways this may be done are explored in the remainder of this chapter.

LEISURE COUNSELING WITH OLDER PEOPLE

Increased leisure is not a universal concommitant of a reduction in unobligated time after retirement, as individual perceptions of freedom from stress and problems may not change (Iso-Ahola, 1980). Further, we cannot assume that all older people need leisure counseling, or that all who could benefit from it will accept it. What we can do is to become aware of the leisure needs of older people and their relationship to leisure counseling and services, and some possible uses of leisure counseling with older people. The latter includes both preventive and remedial aspects, and it leads to a final section on the application of leisure counseling models to older people.

Leisure Needs of Older People

Aging is accompanied by a changing time perspective. There is a shift in perception of time as time since birth to time left until death. Time left to live is indefinite, but it may be extended by involvement (Kimmel, 1976). Leisure offers substantial opportunities for involvement and reinvolvement, and an alternate means to status for older persons who no longer have a work role.

Attempts to define a "leisure role" for older people have described their leisure activities as largely sedentary, solitary, and home based (Binstock &

Shanas, 1976; Hess & Markson, 1980). Most older people prefer and participate in indoor activites, while their preferred outdoor activities tend to be non-
resource specific such as walking (McAvoy, 1979).

There is probably a shift to more sedentary leisure activities with advancing
age. In particular, the preferred activities for the young-old (ages 60-74) and
the old-old (ages 75 +) may be divergent. Studies such as the Harris Study
described below provide a conglomerate view of the older population, and they
fail to allow for the unique aspects of leisure activities of many older individuals. Many are community leaders, travelers, athletes, or engage in significant volunteer activities. Most but not all such individuals are young-old
persons.

The most popular activities for older people, determined in the Harris Survey (1975), were as follows: socializing with friends (47%), gardening or raising plants (39%), reading (36%), watching television (36%), sitting and
thinking (31%), caring for younger or older family members (27%), participating in recreational activities and hobbies (26%), and going for walks
(25%). Unfortunately, the Harris Study did not attempt to relate these activities to those engaged in at younger ages, nor did it examine the psychological
meaning the activities held for the older people. This omission has been a common methodological approach in descriptive research studies with older people.

Concomitantly, leisure services for older people have focused on activities,
primarily organized group activities such as singing, dancing, travelling, game
playing, camping, crafts, and hobbies (e.g., Fish, 1971; Merrill, 1967; Williams, 1962). Special attention has been devoted to the activity needs of handicapped, homebound, and institutionalized older persons; recreation often has
been viewed as therapy through encouraging social interaction and aesthetic
stimulation. Therapeutic crafts have been used to improve functioning to the
greatest degree possible, to prevent deterioration, and to enable the use of residual abilities (Hamill & Oliver, 1980). A basic philosophy underlying much
of this has been the belief that active participation is the key of alertness and
that recreation can be used as an aid to "growing old gracefully" (Moran,
1979).

A typical viewpoint expressed by Kraus (1971) is that "It is apparent that,
for the mass of retired persons, problems related to loneliness, boredom and
lack of meaningful personal and creative involvement pose serious difficulties.
It is to meet this need that organized recreation services for aging persons in
American society must play an increasing role" (p. iv). This viewpoint is evident in virtually all places where older people congregate and recreate, in senior centers, nutrition sites, retirement communities, city parks, recreation
centers, and so forth. The program planners in these settings share a common
failure to recognize that free time activities should have meaning. This is especially true for today's older people who have spent the majority of their lives in
a work-oriented society that looked on recreation as an indulgence.

Riley and Foner (1968) reported that more than 80% of persons over the age of 65 had some leisure time available each day. The average was five hours per day on weekdays and five to six and one-half hours on weekends. Access to life enrichment to fill these hours is a significant and universal problem. Educational, service, and voluntary activities are increasingly seen as important for older people (Lucas, 1962). The Report of the North American Regional Technical Meeting, prepared for the 1982 World Assembly on Aging, concluded that "Educational, recreational, cultural and leisure opportunities and activities contribute as much to the vitality and well being of a nation and its citizens, including old citizens, as other activities deemed more essential to physical survival" (National Council on the Aging, 1981, p. 59). The increasing recognition of the importance of leisure is accompanied by an awareness that many people, especially today's elderly, do not know how to leisure. Helping them learn how to leisure requires helping them examine the meaning and values they attach to their activities.

Loesch and Burt (1980) point out the need for new perspectives on leisure counseling for older people and note that "the idea that 'finding something for older persons to do' constitutes leisure counseling is simply too narrow in scope to be of much practical value for counselors" (p. 220). They also cite Neulinger's suggestion that leisure should not be viewed as a luxury but rather as an essential of life.

This latter suggestion has resulted in an emerging focus on leisure as a major part of one's life-style. While the implementation of this concept requires a reorientation in thinking over all phases of the life span, the implications for the older population are of particular interest here. In the past, various authors have viewed leisure as an alternate means to status for older persons deprived of the work role (e.g., Atchley, 1971; Overs, Taylor, & Adkins, 1976, 1977). The emerging concept of a leisure life-style implies intrinsic value for leisure apart from its replacement of the work function, the attribution of meaning to life through leisure without the guilt older people often feel as they engage in "non-productive" activities.

Until such time as we achieve a societal perspective on the value of a leisure life-style, individuals and groups of older people can be assisted in developing a similar personal orientation through counseling intervention. This intervention falls in two basic areas: prevention and remediation. Each area presupposes a goal of life satisfaction, and an understanding of the meaning of this concept is important to all leisure counseling efforts.

Life Satisfaction Among Older People

Life satisfaction among older people often is equated with successful aging. It has been variously defined and conceptualized and there seems to be some agreement that it comprises a feeling of well-being. This also is referred to as morale and/or a subjective feeling of contentment.

Studies of life satisfaction in older people are abundant in the literature, and they share a common goal of determining what factors result in a maintenance of morale, often in the face of very real difficulties. A national study conducted in 1975 (Harris & Associates) substantiated the major concerns of older people as poor health, finances, lack of independence, being rejected and neglected, and boredom (Lombana, 1976). These factors repeatedly surface as important in studies of life satisfaction (e.g., Atchley, 1971; Barfield & Morgan, 1978; Neugarten, Havighurst, & Tobin, 1961).

Not surprisingly, many studies of life satisfaction among older people focus on retirement, work, and/or leisure (e.g., Barfield & Morgan, 1978; McTavish, 1971; Peppers, 1976). The effects of the retirement transition on life satisfaction have been the most widely researched area, with prior planning emerging as the key variable in maintenance of morale. Where retirement is not a desired goal, planning for it often is neglected or resisted, and the loss of the work role can lead to a decrease in life satisfaction. Effective planning for leisure activities can mitigate against this occurrence.

It is actually the extent of activity, whether arising from work or leisure, that relates directly to life satisfaction in late life (Lubnau & Siggelkow, 1979). The key point seems to be one of attitude, as much as activity. The subjective state of well-being defined as life satisfaction has important parallels to leisure, defined by Neulinger (1981a) as a state of mind where one is at peace with oneself and what one is doing. Interestingly, those who have a wider range of interests at the time of retirement tend to have greater life satisfaction (Peppers, 1976). Such individuals can maintain the freedom to choose in at least some aspects of their lives. The loss of choice, one of the greatest losses of old age and one that promotes helplessness and loss of self-respect (Butler, 1975), can be avoided or compensated for by helping older people develop those areas in which choices are possible. Leisure is obviously such an area, and its potential may be operationalized through leisure counseling.

Preventive Uses of Leisure Counseling

The ability to develop and implement a leisure style of life must begin very early. In fact, the best way to assure an active and creative use of leisure in old age is to have this pattern in one's youth, because older people tend to continue the patterns they developed throughout their lives (Atchley, 1972). For those who fail to do this in their youth, increasing opportunities to learn how to leisure are provided for middle aged persons through preretirement planning programs. Virtually all such programs include attention to the use of time and activities designed to make life meaningful (e.g, Hunter, 1973; Morrow, 1980). Their common goal is to aid adjustment and to weaken resistance to retirement (Greene, 1969).

Preretirement planning is a major factor affecting postretirement adjustment. Some people never retire, some retire to a planned life circumstance, and some retire without previous planning. Persons in the latter group are likely to have strong needs for meaningful activity (Wexley, McLaughlin, & Sterns, 1975). Additional support for the need for preretirement preparation is provided in a study by Bosse and Ekerdt (1981) revealing a relative continuity in perception of leisure activity levels over the transition from work to retirement. Persons who retired did not see themselves as being more involved in leisure activities than their peers who continued to work. As was noted earlier in the discussion of theories of aging, radical changes do not occur after retirement. In fact, continuity is more characteristic of retired people. Continued relationships, activities, and tasks may expand to fill the time left available as a result of terminating employment (Iso-Ahola, 1980).

For many older individuals who maintain identity and activity continuity, leisure counseling may be inappropriate or not needed. For many others, however, the preventive aspects of the counseling process can have important implications. Life review therapy, used preventively, can assist older individuals to evaluate their skills, interests, attitudes, activities, and values, and also to set goals for the future. The lifelong tendency of most people to avoid confronting their own mortality must be dealt with in the later years if effective planning is to occur. With indeterminate time available to live, the enhancement of the individual's quality of life is a paramount concern.

Realistic planning will incorporate dimensions such as time ambiguity, potential physical declines, and resource availability. It is important in working with older individuals for counselors to help them confront the eventual "what if" situations, and plan for them. What if one loses a major source of support, such as a spouse? Is the older person's support system extensive enough to help them cope with an event of this magnitude? What if children move away? Are there other people to fill the need for social interaction and support? What if the individual becomes physically restricted due to disability? Are their interests and activities of such diversity that the only change need be one of expanding already existing interests? Or, is their investment in one activity, or more, so extensive that they will feel overwhelmed or depressed if unable to continue? These are the kinds of questions that must be raised and addressed as part of the leisure counseling planning process with older people.

One technique that may be used is to examine support systems. Having determined the major sources of support, an attempt might be made to examine and link these with the person's leisure support system. Helping people plan effective leisure support networks to deal with "what if" situations potentially could be useful to many older individuals. Discussions of support systems also are an excellent basis for emphasizing strengths and building self-esteem.

Another preventive use of life review therapy may involve focusing on leisure activities and activity changes over the life span. This process can be used to help older people understand the fluid nature of their activities and values, how the events and people in their lives gave meaning to the activities, and how their needs and values have changed over their life span. Such information will then form the basis for future projections of needs and goal setting to meet those needs.

Unfortunately, it is not always possible to plan for all eventualities, nor do all plans ever work out exactly as anticipated. Moreover, although the benefits of preretirement and retirement counseling appear obvious in facilitating optimal life adjustment, we cannot assume that all people will recognize and take advantage of these opportunities. Therefore, while preventive uses of leisure counseling are extremely important, the effective counselor must be prepared to work also with persons whose life satisfaction is low as a result of unforeseen or unplanned events, or simply ones for which they were not prepared.

Remedial Uses of Leisure Counseling

Those older persons who do not plan for their retirement may be confronted with an abundance of free time and question how best to use it. This free time may become a burden for those who fail to achieve a positive concept of leisure. Persons who simply do not know how to use their free time may benefit greatly from leisure education programs. Those who lack a positive perspective on leisure would benefit from leisure counseling. In both cases, relevant goals will include self-awareness, awareness of attitudes toward play and leisure, values clarification, and feelings, decision-making, and problem-solving skills related to leisure and goal setting activities (Peterson & Scott, 1977). These goals can be integrated effectively with the major gerontological counseling techniques discussed earlier.

The attitudes and values of elderly clients are of prime importance in the counseling interaction and may be the focus of goal setting in the leisure counseling process. In particular, the older clients' conception of the work ethic and attitudes toward play must be clarified. Negative attitudes towards leisure can effectively block all attempts at developing a positive leisure life-style, while positive attitudes will greatly enhance the ease with which the process is accomplished.

Both counselors and elderly clients need to develop a positive time perspective if counseling is to be effective. Basically this means that both view the older person's life not as time left until death but as time left to live. Free time is not time *left* to be filled due to loss of the work role, but rather time *available* to create and implement satisfying activities. By achieving and exemplifying a positive attitude toward time, leisure counselors can create the conditions for older people to thrive, not just survive. Fairly immediate improvements in life satisfaction can result from the development of positive attitudes toward time and leisure.

One way to help older persons achieve positive attitudes and satisfying uses of their leisure time is through life review therapy. Constantly focusing on the older person's strengths and survival skills can help build self-confidence, and exploration of the values attached to past life activities can provide clues to potentially meaningful leisure activities in later life. Where disability or some other objective difficulty has led to a loss or reduction in some favored activity, with concomitant lower level of life satisfaction, a focus on the transferability of skills to new activities may be warranted. Planning with these individuals should include both current and future activities.

Older persons with low levels of life satisfaction may fail to recognize the value of their support systems, especially in relation to leisure activities. Counselors can help them identify supports and focus on the interactive nature of the interpersonal ones. Not only is a spouse or friend a source of support for the older person, the older person also functions as a source of support for the spouse or friend. Fostering a sense that the person is needed can contribute to feelings of competence. These feelings, in turn, can lead to improved decision-making abilities.

Leisure support networks may be explored, expanded, and developed where they do not exist. A particularly effective way to accomplish this with older people is in a group setting, where the desirable goals of increased peer interaction can be met. Somewhat rapid improvements in self-concept are possible, given the dual opportunities provided through leisure counseling and leisure for peer interaction and identification and for engagement in meaningful activity. Helping older people make choices about their leisure activities can greatly enhance their feelings of competence and mastery.

Perhaps the major benefit of remedial leisure counseling for older people lies in the restoration of the freedom to choose, a loss seen earlier as the most common and devastating concomitant of aging. The potential for achieving affective life adjustment, the primary goal of leisure counseling (O'Morrow, in Loesch, Chapter 5), is significantly enhanced for older individuals who can feel a sense of control over at least part of their lives. Clearly, then, counselors may help older persons achieve this sense of control through the application of leisure counseling techniques within the framework of gerontological counseling techniques. Additional approaches to effective leisure counseling with older people may be considered from the standpoint of existing models of leisure counseling.

Applying Leisure Counseling Models to Older People

In any attempt at leisure counseling, theory should play an important role (McDowell, 1977). When dealing with older people, an additional consideration is that of theories of aging. An effective leisure counselor of older people, therefore, must be able to combine the theoretical formulations of both leisure and aging. This task may be far from easy, given the current developmental status and tentative nature of theories in both fields. In this section, three examples for combining leisure/aging theoretical bases are given, along with suggestions for counseling practice using each combination. These examples form the basis for a more general discussion of leisure counseling for older people.

Example 1: Applying Theories of Aging to Leisure Counseling

One way to examine the interactive effects of theories of aging and leisure is to determine the differences in applying various theories of aging based on a given leisure counseling model. Loesch (Chapter 5) proposed a seven-step model of leisure counseling for use with older persons. Briefly, these steps are as follows: (1) determination of the need for counseling, using formal and/or informal assessments, (2) evaluation of current leisure satisfaction to determine if the counseling need is in the area of leisure, (3) determination of an appropriate counseling orientation or approach (client-centered, behavioral, etc.), (4) comprehensive evaluation of the person, including affective, behavioral, and cognitive dimensions, (5) determination of which of two (or both) goals common to leisure counseling are to be achieved — the identification of those leisure activities that will contribute most to life satisfaction and the selection of leisure activities that will help the person change in some way, such as developing an improved self-concept, (6) determination of the most appropriate leisure activities for the older client, and (7) evaluation of the process. The question to be answered is whether this model would be applied differently if the counselor subscribed to one particular theory of aging. As an example, activity and disengagement theory will be used, since these represent quite opposite viewpoints concerning the aging process.

The activity theorist would follow steps 1 and 2 to determine if a counseling need existed and if that need was in fact for leisure counseling. This theorist might assume that, if a counseling need existed, assessment of leisure satisfaction should follow automatically. The process would ensue as described in the model, with emphasis on step 5, the determination of appropriate leisure counseling goals. The identification of which leisure activities would contribute most to life satisfaction would be a primary objective of counseling. Where life satisfaction was low, increased emphasis would be placed on the therapeutic value of various leisure activities in helping the person to change in a positive direction.

The disengagement theorist also would follow step 1 and determine if a need for counseling existed. In contrast to the activity theorist, the disengagement theorist would not treat a lack of life satisfaction as indicative of a need for assessment of leisure needs. Rather, this theorist would assume that the lack of satisfaction with life stemmed from a failure to disengage, which is the normal, desirable, and preferred reaction to aging. The focus of counseling would not be on activity selection so much as on self-acceptance in view of unchangeable social and personal realities. Leisure might become an important means to assist in changing the individual's values, but the goal would be only secondarily one of leisure satisfaction and primarily one of life satisfaction. The activity theorist, on the other hand, would emphasize leisure satisfaction as a necessary ingredient of overall life satisfaction.

Both theories would deal with the psychological meaning of leisure activities as part of the leisure counseling process; however, within the context of sociological theories of aging, subjective meaning plays a minor role. More psychologically oriented theorists would approach the process somewhat differently, perhaps placing the most emphasis on evaluation of personal feelings about leisure and activities.

Example 2: Applying Leisure Counseling Models to a Theory of Aging

Another way to examine the interactive effects of theories of leisure and aging is to determine the differences in leisure counseling approaches as a function of a given theory of aging. How, for example, would the process of leisure counseling according to Loesch (1981; Chapter 5) or Tinsley and Lindrud (in Tinsley & Tinsley, Chapter 3) differ based on a life span developmental theory of aging?

A counselor who ascribed to the Havighurst model of developmental stages would view an older person's life satisfaction as reflective of the individual's success in accomplishing a prescribed set of developmental tasks, such as adjusting to reduced physical strength and health and establishing an affiliation with an older peer group. The existence of counseling needs, according to Loesch, would be reflective of failure or inability to successfully accomplish these tasks. The role of leisure in facilitating developmental task accomplishment would be explored. The selection of leisure activities that would help with these tasks would be emphasized. For example, the selection of less strenuous activities would be a means of adjusting to reduced physical strength, while group activities with other older persons would assist in the process of peer identification.

Tinsley and Linrud (in Tinsley & Tinsley, Chapter 3) stress the need for self-actualization and modification of attitudes regarding work and leisure. (Developmental tasks and activities designed to effect successful task accomplishment would be seen as contributing to total life-style planning and personal development.) The resolution of these tasks would not become a focus for selection of leisure activities, as would be true using the Loesch model. Rather, development tasks would be seen as additional factors that affected a more holistic decision-making process in relation to modification of attitudes and self-actualization. In other words, the achievement of life satisfaction would involve more than developmental task accomplishment and the selection of activities to further this process.

Example 3: Leisure Life-Style and Social Reconstruction

Among theories of aging, the social reconstruction model described earlier (Bengtson, 1977) has received widespread acceptance among counselors, primarily because it offers a priori opportunities for counseling interventions. As was described earlier, environmental inputs can have a dramatic effect on the course of an older person's life and can help break the negative spiral of "inability to cope in a specific instance — labeling as incapable — increased/broadened inability to cope with various situations." Counselors can have an impact through both individual counseling and external advocacy activities.

This approach to viewing the problems of aging is entirely consistent with McDowell's (Chapter 1) description of leisure well-being, leisure style, and life-style as leisure counseling concerns. The four components of leisure well-being — coping, awareness/understanding, knowledge, and assertation — may be readily seen as essential to an older person's self-perception as capable. The four C's of choice, change, competency building, and confusion reduction may be viewed as client concerns for which the social reconstruction theorist should remain alert in terms of both need and possible intervention. Perhaps the key to the similarity in these two approaches, and their natural linkage, is that both are based in social learning theory, and thus stress the interaction of the individual with his/her environment. Coping behaviors are stressed, and the role of society in assisting individuals in meeting their unique needs is common to both theories.

Leisure Counseling and Older People

The preceding examples serve to illuminate the necessity for counselors to be aware of their theoretical beliefs in order to be effective. Theory helps both to set the goals for counseling interventions and to guide the counseling process to assure that desired outcomes are achieved. The task of the leisure counselor working with older persons is complicated by the variety of different theoretical orientations that must be integrated to form a solid base for counseling activities. At first glance, an attempt to combine the various theories of aging, counseling, and leisure can resemble an eclectic nightmare; however, the task is not really difficult if one first focuses on leisure, then gradually selects from aging and counseling theories those that best meet leisure counseling goals.

In working with older people, the central concern for the leisure counselor revolves around the question of how leisure can make the lives of older people more meaningful. The answer to this question becomes more clear if a life span developmental approach is used. Aging is one part of a continuous life cycle, a cycle in which growth and change is the norm from conception through all ages until death. The meaning of work and leisure changes throughout the life span and is not limited to changes at the time of the retirement transition.

Blocher and Siegal's (Chapter 2) concept of career as the organizing principle of life is relevant here, if one accepts the concept of career as incorporating both work and leisure. Career can remain constant even into old age if leisure assumes the functions supplied in the individual's life by work. This is not an either-or phenomenon; rather, it is a process and a challenge to the adult or aging individual for continued growth. This broad view of leisure as a way to impute meaning to life leads away from traditional activity-oriented approaches to work with older persons, and allows for treatment of them as unique individuals with unique psychological needs and potential. Viewing aging as part of the life span helps negate the tendency to see old people as having no future, and leads to a focus on human potential for life satisfaction based on needs, values, and functional meaning.

The central issue for the leisure counselor becomes one of helping older people obtain leisure and life satisfaction, or perhaps life satisfaction through leisure satisfaction. This counseling process provides unique opportunities for restoring to older people a sense of competency and mastery, and a realization of their freedom to make choices that will have an overarching impact on their lives. The important point for counselors is to treat each older person as a unique individual, and remember that the major characteristic of this population is its extreme heterogeneity. Each life experience we have makes us a more unique person. Each older person has a singular combination of life experiences. All are survivors. The task of the leisure counselor is to assure that all may thrive, as well as survive. Leisure offers an opportunity to put quality into the final years of those persons for whom the events of this century have yielded an increase in the overall quantity of life.

REFERENCES

Atchley, R.C. Retirement and leisure participation: Continuity or crisis? *The Gerotologist*, 1971, *11*(1), 13-17.

Atchley, R.C. *The social forces in later life*. Belmont, Ca.: Wadsworth, 1972.

Barfield, R., & Morgan, J. Trends in satisfaction with retirement. *The Gerontologist*, 1978, *8*(1), 19-23.

Bengston, V.L. *The social psychology of aging*. Indianapolis, In.: Bobbs-Merrill, 1977.

Binstock, R.H., & Shanas, E. *Handbook of aging and the social sciences*. New York: Van Nostrand Reinhold, 1976.

Bosse, R., & Ekerdt, D.J. Change in self-perception of leisure activities with retirement. *The Gerontologist*, 1981, *21*(6), 650-654.

Brotman, H.B. *Every ninth American*. Special Document prepared for the Special Committee on Aging, United States Senate, 1980.

Burkley, M. Counseling the aging. *Personnel and Guidance Journal*, 1972, *50*(9), 755-758.

Butler, R.N. Successful aging and the role of the life review. The *Journal of the American Geriatrics Society*, 1974, *22*(12), 529-535.

Butler, R.N. *Why survive? Being old in America*. New York: Harper and Row, 1975.

Butler, R.N., & Lewis, M.I. *Aging and mental health: Positive psychological approaches*. St. Louis: C.V. Mosby, 1977.

Cumming, E., & Henry, W.H. *Growing old: The process of disengagement*. New York: Basic Books, 1961.

Erikson, E. *Childhood and society*. New York: Norton, 1950.

Fish, H.U. *Activities program for senior citizens*. West Nyack, N.Y.: Parker Publishing Co., 1971.

Gordon, C., Gaitz, C.M., & Scott, J. Leisure and lives: Personal expressivity across the life span. In R.H. Binstock & E. Shanas (Eds.), *Handbook of aging and the social sciences*. New York: Van Nostrand Rheinhold, 1976, 310-341.

Greene, M.R. *Preretirement counseling, retirement adjustment, and the older employee*. Eugene, Oregon:

Oregon College of Business Administration, 1969.

Hamill, C.M., & Oliver, R.C. *Therapeutic activities for the handicapped elderly*. Rockville, Md.: Aspen Systems Corporation, 1980.

Harris, L., & Associates. *The myth and reality of aging in America*. Washington, D.C.: The National Council on the Aging, 1975.

Havighurst, R. *Developmental tasks and education*. New York: D. McKay, 1972.

Hess, B.B., & Markson, E.W. *Aging and old age*. New York: Macmillan Publishing Company, 1980.

Holmes, T.H., & Rahe, R.H. The social adjustment rating scale. *Journal of Psychosomatic Research*, 1967, 2, 213-218.

Hunter, H. *Preparation for retirement*. Ann Arbor: University of Michigan-Wayne State University, 1973.

Iso-Ahola, S.E. *Social psychological perspectives on leisure and recreation*. Springfield, Il.: Charles C Thomas, 1980.

Kastenbaum, R. The foreshortened life perspective. *Geriatrics*, 1969, 24, 126-133.

Kimmel, D.C. Adult development: Challenges for counseling. *Personnel and Guidance Journal*, 1976, 55, 103-105.

Kraus, R. *Recreation and leisure in modern society*. New York: Appleton-Century-Crofts, 1971.

Loesch, L.C. Leisure counseling for disabled older persons. *Journal of Rehabilitation*, 1981, 47(4), 58-63.

Loesch, L.C. & Burt, M.A. Leisure counseling for the elderly. It's time for a change. *Counseling and Values*, 1980, 24(4), 218-226.

Lombana, J.H. Counseling the elderly: Remediation plus prevention. *Personnel and Guidance Journal*, 1976, 55, 143-144.

Lowenthal, M.F., & Haven, C. Interaction and adaptation: Intimacy are a critical variable. *American Sociological Review*, 1968, 33.

Lubnau, E., & Siggelkow, H. The problem of leisure for the aged. *Zietschrift fur Alternsforschung*, 1979, 34(3), 231-235.

Lucas, C. *Recreational activity development for the aging in homes, hospitals and nursing homes*. Springfield, Il.: Charles C Thomas, 1962.

McAvoy, L.H. The leisure preferences, problems and needs of the elderly. *Journal of Leisure Research*, 1979, 11(1), 40-47.

McDowell, C.F. Integrating theory and practice in leisure counseling. *Leisure Today*, 1977, April, 27-30.

McTavish, D.G. Perceptions of old people: A review of research methodologies and findings. *The Gerontologist*, 1981, 21, 90-101.

Merrill, T. *Activities for the aged and infirm*. Springfield, Il.: Charles C Thomas, 1967.

Moran, J.M. *Leisure activities for the mature adult*. Minneapolis, Mn.: Burgess Publishing Company, 1979.

Morrow, P.C. Retirement preparation: A preventive approach to counseling the elderly. *Counseling and Values*, 1980, 24(4), 236-246.

Myers, J.E. Gerontological counseling training. The state of the art. *Personnel & Guidance Journal*, in press.

Myers, J.E., & Salmon, H. Counseling programs for older persons, Status, Shortenings and potentialities. *The Counseling Psychologist*, in press.

Myers, J.E., & Loesch, L.C. The counseling needs of older people. *The Humanist Educator*, 1981, 20(1), 21-35.

National Council on the Aging. The Report of the North American Regional Technical Meeting on Aging. Washington, D.C., June 15-19, 1981.

Neugarten, B.L., Havighurst, R.J., & Tobin, S.S. The measurement of life satisfaction. *Journal of Gerontology*, 1961, 16, 134-143.

Neulinger, J. *The psychology of leisure (2nd edition)*. Springfield, Il.: Charles C Thomas,

1981. (a)

Neulinger, J. *To leisure: An introduction*. Boston: Allyn and Bacon, Inc., 1981. (b)

Overs, R.P., Taylor, S., & Adkins, C. Avocational counseling for the elderly. *Journal of Physical Education and Recreation*, 1976, *48*(4), 445.

Overs, R.P., Taylor, S., & Adkins, C. *Avocational counseling manual: A complete guide to leisure guidance*. Washington, D.C.: Hawkins & Associates, Inc., 1977.

Peck, R. Psychological development in the second half of life. In B.L. Neugarten (Ed.), *Middle age and aging*. Chicago: University of Chicago Press, 1968.

Peppers, L.G. Patterns of leisure and adjustment to retirement. *The Gerontologist*, 1976, *16*(5), 441-446.

Peterson, C.A., & Scott, S.L. Leisure counseling: An aspect of leisure education. *Leisure Today*, April, 1977, 5-14.

Puner, M. Retirement and leisure. In S.H. Zarit (Ed.), *Readings in aging and death: Contemporary perspectives*. New York: Harper & Row, 1977.

Riley, M.W., & Foner, A. *Aging and society, Volume 1: An inventory of research findings*. New York: Russell Sage Foundations, 1968.

Select Committee on Aging, U.S. House of Representatives. *National Conference on Mental Health and the Elderly*. Washington, D.C.: U.S. Government Printing Office, 1979.

Sinick, D. Attitudes and values in aging. *Counseling and Values*, 1980, *24*(3), 148-154.

Smyer, M., & Gatz, M. Aging and mental health. *American Psychologist*, 1979, *34*, 240-246.

Special Committee on Aging, U.S. Senate. *Aging and mental health: overcoming barriers to service*. Washington, D.C.: U.S. Government Printing Office, 1980.

Sterns, H. and Sterns, R. Growing older: A few important points to consider. In J.E. Myers (Ed), *Counseling older persons, Volume III, A trainers manual for basic helping skills*. Falls Church, Va.: American Personnel and Guidance Association, 1981.

Ullman, C.A. Preretirement planning: Does it prevent post-retirement shock. *Personnel and Guidance Journal*, 1976, *55*, 115-118.

U.S. Department of Health, Education and Welfare. *Some future prospects for the elderly population*. Washington, D.C.: National Clearinghouse on Aging, 1978.

Waters, E.P., & Weaver, A.C. Specialized techniques to help older people. In J.E. Myers (Ed.) *Counseling older persons, Volume III, A trainers manual for basic helping skills*. Falls Church, Va.: American Personnel and Guidance Association, 1981.

Wexley, K.J., McLaughlin, J.R., & Sterns, H.L. A study of perceived need fulfillment and life satisfaction before and after retirement. *Journal of Vocational Behavior*, 1975, 7, 81-87.

Williams, A. *Recreation in the senior years*. New York: Association Press, 1962.

Chapter 7

LEISURE COUNSELING FOR FAMILIES

Dennis K. Orthner and Robert W. Herron

GIVEN the fact that much of our leisure behavior occurs in family groupings, it is not surprising that leisure problems are often inextricably linked to family problems — and, vice versa. Consider for a moment an actual case that a family therapist brought to the authors' attention while this chapter was being written:

> On a Thursday, mid-afternoon, a family of four appeared at the office of a local family counseling practice. They had no appointment but pleaded to see someone at once. They had just come from a golf course and were appropriately dressed in golf shoes, golf shirts, and so on. The two children, aged 9 and 11, looked just as frustrated as their parents. The father had broken one of his favorite clubs in anger and sadly exclaimed to the counselor, "We never have fun together anymore! I have provided all the material possessions I can for my family. We set aside all this time to be together but nobody ever has any fun. What can we do?"
>
> As the story unfolded, it became apparent that this day had begun with promise and ended in disaster, much as other days had done. The therapist explained, "In terms of healthy family systems, the family is obviously trying to be *too* close. They are trying to spend all their time together and they need to diversify, find some balance in their lives." In addition, the family needed to work on parent control issues, negotiation skills, and other relational matters. Still, what is interesting is the way in which leisure problems became the focal-point of this family's conflicts and how little information this therapist had available to suggest alternative leisure strategies.

Leisure counseling for families is not a new idea but its formal development as a process for improving family wellness is still in its infancy. Professionals in a variety of family and leisure/recreation professions have been offering counsel and advice on leisure options for families for many years. This has taken a variety of forms, ranging from suggestions for joint-family experiences from travel advisors and recreation leaders to prescriptions for families to spend time together by family counselors. All of this is under the assumption that "families that play together, stay together."

From a professional counseling perspective, these advice-giving efforts have done little to generate a systematic counseling theory of leisure behavior for families. At best, family counseling efforts in the leisure domain have focused on what Tinsley and Tinsley (Chapter 3) have labeled "leisure education" and "lesiure guidance" (i.e., an information-giving orientation to new leisure activity options). At worst, families have been simply provided with a range of recreational alternatives with little appreciation for the underlying quandry they may feel or the uncomfortableness they may have being either together or apart. Leisure counseling, with its important dimensions of value clarification, client-centered realization of leisure needs, and personal and interpersonal wellness orientation (McDowell, Chapter 1) has had little impact to date on the search of many contemporary families for leisure and family satisfaction.

In order to bridge some of the gaps between leisure and family professionals, this chapter will attempt to apply selected theoretical and empirical insights from leisure science and family social science to the more unified field of interpersonal counseling. This analysis will not focus on the assumption of leisure counseling per se, since these are outlined elsewhere in this volume, but on the particular assumptions that underlie the application of leisure counseling *to families*. Common symptoms of leisure dysfunctions in families are to be outlined, as well as strategies for leisure counseling interventions.

Assumptions of Leisure Counseling for Families

Any discussion of leisure intervention should be guided by a common understanding of leisure needs and normative activity preferences among the people in question. Studies over the past decade have begun to illuminate the role of leisure in family life and provide a basis for proposing means by which effective family leisure counseling can be introduced.

Leisure Needs and Family Interaction

First, it is important to understand that shared leisure time and experiences are valuable to families, not just to the individuals in those families. The family is a system based on a unique history and unique interaction patterns. A group without any common history would not be defined as a family, nor would a family last long if it had no interaction upon which to base its common identity and commitments.

Leisure experiences, we are now learning, serve as a critical foundation for these family bonds and interpersonal commitments. One of the most predictive elements in family commitment is open communication between family members, husbands and wives or parents and children (Powers & Hutchinson, 1979). However, discretionary time is necessary for open communication patterns to develop and this time must be sufficient for routine, patterned communication to evolve into open discussions that reveal the participants' values and needs. Shared leisure experiences provide this time and research confirms that family communication patterns are improved with increased joint leisure activities (Orthner, 1976).

In addition to improved communication, the sharing of leisure time can benefit families in other ways as well. Joint leisure activities have been related to increased marital satisfaction (Orthner, 1975), increased relational commitments (Goffman, 1961), greater value similarity (Adams & Cromwell, 1978), and lower levels of relational conflict (Orthner & Mancini, 1980). Certainly, as the case study mentioned earlier points out, leisure activities are not a panacea for all relationships but shared leisure time and experiences are often related to healthy family functioning. Leisure counselors must be aware of these linkages and prepared to assist families in selecting those activities that can enhance their relational development and strengthen their relational weaknesses.

Emerging Companionship Values

Companionship among family members has become a highly valued component of family life today. One study found that men and women ranked companionship highest on a list of nine goals of marriage (Levinger, 1964). In another study, a national sample ranked such things as liking the same kind of activities as more important to marital success than having children or financial security (Roper, 1974). Companionship — the sharing of time and experiences — has become a gauge of relational success not just to the "experts" but to most families as well. This means that the absence of companionship can lead to guilt and feelings of relational deprivation, problems commonly observed by family therapists (Beck & Jones, 1973).

Companionship has not always been held in such high esteem. Traditionally, men, women, and children were integrated into a family through the roles they contributed to one another rather than the times they shared together. Being a good cook or a good farmer was considered more valuable than being good company for one another (Orthner, 1981). Today, however, family success is determined more by the ability of family members to make flexible role adaptations than fixed role adoptions (Aldous, 1978). In a society in which sex roles and family roles are changing, role-making skills are now as important as role-taking skills were earlier.

Companionship facilitates role flexibility and role-making since leisure time permits the expectations behind the role behaviors to be explored and negotiated in contexts that are free from the constraint of normal family duties and responsibilities. For example, disagreements over household responsibilities are difficult to resolve when the pressure of those duties is immediate, when sex role patterns have been established, and when power issues are of concern to the parties. However, during shared leisure experiences, opportunities arise to more carefully discuss values and needs and to negotiate and practice alternate patterns of relating to one another. These patterns can, in turn, serve as the basis for new family roles. Leisure counselors should be aware that many families feel trapped between the comfortable, traditional family roles they grew up with and the new flexible, shared roles they see touted in the media. Not all families are able to easily adapt their leisure patterns to find that appropriate leisure mix that fits their personal and relational goals.

Leisure and Family Conflicts

When the potential sources of family conflicts are catalogued, it is easy to include such things as finances, children, sex, and in-laws. What may be surprising is that conflicts over leisure and recreation rank just as high as a source of tension and higher than some of those just mentioned. In a recent national survey, it was found that one-third of American families are experiencing stress from leisure conflicts (Straus et al., 1980). Only household roles and sex were more likely sources of family conflict. Similar findings occurred in a world-wide study of military families (Orthner & Bowen, 1982). Conflicts over the use of leisure time and opportunities for companionship were found to be more stressful in these families than child-rearing or finances.

These findings support the contention of Max Kaplan (1975) that "The concept of togetherness in leisure participation by all family members of a family is often a gestural cliche that is challenged by the disparity of meanings that they bring to the same activity" (p. 63). In contrast to the potential integrative role of leisure for encouraging family solidarity, many families find it difficult to reconcile their leisure preferences with their actual leisure behavior patterns. According to Carlson's (1976) research, three-fourths of all families experience this problem at some time.

In an attempt to outline some of the factors that stimulate leisure conflict in families, Orthner (1980) suggested the following:

1) leisure time and activity is discretionary and this leads to a peculiar vulnerability to sacrifice leisure needs when other needs arise.
2) family members often develop differential needs for leisure activities and these leisure divergences tend to increase over time.
3) family leisure activity patterns do not always reflect underlying family styles which can vary in their needs for joint leisure participation.
4) interruptions in normal leisure patterns often occur and make it difficult for some individuals to find adequate replacement activities, making them more unstable than before.
5) differences in circadian, daily rhythms of family members, can be related to conflicting leisure choices and leisure needs.

These and a host of other related factors impact upon leisure disagreements in families. Many of these families cannot sort out the bases for their particular conflict. Therefore, leisure counselors must be able to trace the sources of these conflicts and carefully assist families in negotiating mutually acceptable leisure patterns.

Life Cycle Variations in Families

A growing body of literature and research indicates that family leisure patterns vary according to family life cycle stage (Orthner, 1975; Rapoport & Rapoport, 1976). For example, the leisure concerns of young couples and young families are not typically the concerns of the middle aged. There appear to be common needs for a balance between togetherness and separateness throughout the life cycle, but the particular way in which these needs are met depends upon the primary developmental concerns of the time.

Young couples without children seem to benefit greatly from leisure activities balanced more heavily in the direction of joint participation. Marital satisfaction is strongly related to joint leisure activities at this time, while higher amounts of individual leisure activities are linked to marital dissatisfaction (Orthner, 1975). It is not that separation is unhealthy for these young couples; rather, this is a time in their relationship when roles and communication patterns are being established and companionship provides the time for these to develop in mutually satisfactory ways.

Families with young children have to find a balance between individual, marital, and parental needs. The stress of new career and family obligations brings about new pressures for the recuperation of private leisure moments, but there are also growing demands to participate with family members who are anxious for parental assistance. These personal pressures are coupled with longer work weeks, more household responsibilities, demands of "voluntary" organizations, and so on. Taken together, these young families often experience role overloads, and it is leisure needs that suffer the most. These families tend to experience significant drops in family companionship and satisfaction with their leisure time (Orthner & Bowen, 1982).

As children mature, time for companionship may increase (Orthner & Axelson, 1980) but leisure patterns often become more disparate (Pratt, 1976). In many families, husbands, wives, and children go their own separate ways for recreation. This pattern is functional in the sense that it follows on the heels of a period of increasing sex-role distinctiveness between husbands and wives. It can be dysfunctional in that neither partner can serve as a resource to the other during the personal, parental, and career transitions each faces in the middle years of their life. Couples who do share more joint activities at this time appear to benefit themselves and their marriage (Orthner, 1975). The rest tend to internalize their adult struggle for a sense of what Erikson (1964) calls "generativity" or they turn to others outside the family for support. Women, it appears, are more successful in developing new friends and support systems (Mancini & Orthner, 1978), while men find it more difficult to fulfill their social, leisure needs in mid-life (Levinson, 1978).

This brief overview suggests that relational leisure patterns and needs can vary over the life cycle and that leisure counseling must take into account the changing developmental needs of adults and children. The notion of individualizing leisure prescriptions is certainly recognized since the expectations families have for their leisure will depend upon the assumptions each individual brings into the family as well as the priorities they currently have established for themselves and their family. Integrating these potentially divergent life-style expectations can be a major challenge.

Needs for Leisure Intervention

Finding satisfaction with leisure is not always easy for individuals or families. Just as a skilled financial counselor may be needed to assist a family in recognizing and reconciling their economic priorities and expenditure patterns, some families need assistance in developing their time priorities and using leisure activities to strengthen their relationships. Without intervention, families often find that their activity patterns do not reflect their activities preferences.

Television watching is a good example of how leisure patterns do not always reflect preferences. National surveys point out that television watching is America's most common pastime (Robinson, 1977) but other surveys find that viewing television is rarely a preferred leisure activity (Mancini & Orthner, 1978). In many households, it is simply a tool for reducing personal tension and anesthetizing relational conflicts without having to use more creative means of resolving problems or encouraging togetherness (Rosenblatt & Cunningham, 1976). However, when interventions in this pattern occur, whether unplannned ("blackouts") or planned ("experiments"), the relationships involved are affected. First, conflicts increase because there is also an increase in communication between family members. This somewhat increases tension but it also tends to resolve the conflicts. Second, intimacy increases and results in more sexual activity and more family companionship (Orthner, 1981). Without this intervention, these new behaviors might not have time to be established.

The therapeutic literature also suggests that families can develop unhealthy leisure patterns that are very difficult to break (Nelson et al., 1970; Vale & Manning, 1980). Complaints like "we never seem to go out together any more" or "I wish I had more time to spend with the children but. . . . " are frequently heard in counseling sessions. Often, these patterns are longstanding and a source of deep resentment on the part of family members. Cuber and Harroff (1966) describe some of these families as "devitalized" — mutually and reluctantly resolved to a rather independent, sometimes sterile family relationship. Seidenburg (1973) describes other families as more openly angry and hostile over what is implied to be a rejection of their relational well-being. Still, no matter how deep the hurt, families today are less likely to survive a serious pattern of differences in their leisure expectations. Separation and divorce are all too easy to select. Leisure well-being has become very important to personal and relational well-being. The wise counselor is sensitive to the feelings of rejection that accompany reports of loneliness and leisure independence from a relationship that requires mutual support. The number of families seeking therapy is increasing, so opportunities for leisure intervention should increase as well.

Symptoms of Leisure Problems for Families

The presenting leisure problems that families report can vary a great deal. However, the underlying dilemmas families more often face largely fall into one of the following areas: relational enmeshment, relational differentiation, activity addiction, and incongruent activity preferences. Underlying each of these is an inability to find a balance between togetherness and separateness and an inability to reconcile different leisure expectations.

Relational Enmeshment

A good example of relational enmeshment is the family presented at the beginning of this chapter. Enmeshed families like these turn inward, developing extreme interdependency, and place a high premium on togetherness. Family members usually do not respect personal boundaries of individuality as much as they could. Obviously, it had become important for the golfing family to share the day together at any cost, even though it may not have been developmentally appropriate for all concerned.

Enmeshed families often feel guilt and almost a sense of betrayal when any one family member enjoys leisure alone with someone else. Vacations must be taken as a whole family and weekends are preplanned. Personal friendships are retarded in their development. As in the golfing family, there is a joint drive for happiness but little permission to find that happiness outside the close-uniting of the family.

Frequently, enmeshed families have difficulty dealing with unhappiness or conflict. There can be almost a pathological avoidance of problems out of fear that these will lead to loss of love, loss of commitment, and loss of the relationship (Miller, 1977). Therefore, it is threatening to have the children stay home from the game because of the fear that they will dislike being left, get angry, and potentially reject their already insecure parents.

The leisure counselor must be sensitive to the enmeshed family's fear of any cracks of separateness. At the same time, the counselor needs to convince the family that variety will enrich the individuals and the family in turn. Just as parents can be drawn together by vicariously enjoying the playful antics of their children, family members can profit by the individual growth and development that occurs when other members develop new leisure skills and interests. Enmeshed families fear these developments but can be helped to see their importance.

Relational Disengagement

Disengaged families lie at the other end of the continuum. They seldom if ever do anything together. The boundaries between family members are so rigid that they almost never are in contact with each other. Take, for example, a family with two adolescent children who are now seeing a family therapist. Until recently, they had few family problems because they saw very little of each other. The father fished and hunted in his free time but did not include his family in these sports. The mother was active in riding and showing horses. The two sons each had different activities, friends, and interests. This family had so little in common that other family members were rarely aware of special events in each other's lives, and they were unlikely to attend even if they were aware. Each person went their own way, supported in their individualism, and unencumbered by desires for family togetherness.

In disengaged families like these, each person is "doing his or her own thing." The family merely serves as an economic unit to provide food, clothing, and shelter. Emotional and recreational support comes from others, or perhaps from no one. Usually, the disengaged family functions relatively well until a crisis erupts. When this happens, the family is handicapped in its ability to respond effectively to the problem. So little time has been spent together that lines of communication are severely disrupted or nonexistent. In the above family, the crisis was stimulated by one of the sons being arrested for selling drugs. Not only was no one aware of the problem, they had no idea how to respond. They had to learn how to talk with each other, be together without feeling uncomfortable, and solve problems together — all skills that joint leisure activities can enhance.

Unfortunately, by the time a disengaged family comes in, crisis intervention may be more in order. However, the educational role of the leisure family counselor cannot be underestimated in convincing families before crises occur that investments in joint leisure activities will pay valuable returns.

Activity Addictions

Families characterized by an activity addiction are controlled by the demanding leisure pursuits of a minority of the family. For example, the husband-father in a Florida family liked to play golf. Unfortunately, his retail sales job permitted little free time and he used most of it on Wednesdays and Sundays for golf. He spent some time with his family, too, but family time had to be scheduled around his golf games. His family resented this relegation to second place, and they also resented the game of golf. This situation was further complicated by the rest of the family feeling guilty that they were angry over the father's absence; after all, he worked hard and deserved to enjoy himself. Therefore, no one said anything until this powder keg finally blew up.

This family situation could be replicated many times over. The problem can emerge out of extreme interest in almost anything, including hunting, fishing, baseball, bridge, or stamp collecting. None of these activities are basically problematic; it is just that the individual involved becomes so caught up in his/her own search for gratification that the needs of others, even family members, are ignored. Family vacations become golfing vacations; weekend trips are made to search for antiques; or evenings are spent at the races. Rarely are others asked what they want to do. It is assumed that this activity addiction is the driving force in all their lives.

If the addict is successful in winning the allegiance of the family and bringing them into a mutual search for gratification, then the problems are likely to be restricted to that of minimal socialization for leisure alternatives. This could be a major problem for children, who need to be able to explore other activity options and who may be ostracized by their peers if their family activity provides little status. For the adults, however, this can be a satifying joint venture. On the other hand, if the family grows resentful of the activity and is unable to participate willingly, this is very likely to lead to resentments, misunderstandings, and conflict. By that time, the activity addiction will have been complicated by many overlaying relational disagreements that will have to be sorted out and negotiated as well.

Incongruent Activity Preferences

The classic example of incongruent activity preferences is the debate between seashore or mountain vacation destinations. However, the potential problem is deeper in that some families are characterized by differing leisure interests to such an extent that it is a real challenge for them to find common ground. For example, a younger married couple in Virginia who said they still loved each other complained that they "did not seem to enjoy each other's company any more." She liked to go dancing and visiting with friends but he really preferred to see movies or to discuss the relative merits of a new piece of music. They both wanted to share their respective interests but it always seemed to lead to frustration for their partner. She was more active; he was more passive. She liked the crowd feeling at a lively party; he was more comfortable at a quiet dinner.

This couple reflects an underlying pattern of differences in their leisure preferences that makes reconciliation difficult. Previous attempts to conform to the activity needs of the other led to discomfort and conflicts. Their college courtship had earlier hid their differences with a demanding work and study schedule and the typical artificiality that comes from trying to make a good impression. Personal leisure interests and preferences had been submerged by limited time and money, and by romance.

Some preliminary studies suggest that problems like these can be related to biological rhythms in people (Adams & Cronwell, 1978). For instance, adults can often label themselves either "morning" or "night" people and leisure preference patterns frequently vary between these two orientations. Also, when married couples differ in their orientation, they are more likely to experience conflicts than if they are similar in their temporal-leisure orientations. Similar problems may be related to differences in psychological needs for physical exertion, outdoor activities, or social participation. Counseling these kinds of families will undoubtedly require finding new, common activities that will lead to mutual enjoyment as well as encouraging some separate activities for each person's personal fulfillment.

Integrating Leisure and Family Counseling

One of the major dilemmas facing the integration of family and leisure counseling is the reference point of the counseling: leisure counseling has traditionally been oriented towards individual development while family counseling has been oriented towards family system development. This is a practical as well as a theoretical dilemma.

To illustrate the leisure counseling focus on individual growth and needs, it is noteworthy that there have been no serious writings to date on how to include leisure counseling in family therapy or families in leisure counseling. Edwards' *Leisure Counseling Techniques* (1980), while a traditional approach, focuses almost entirely on counseling with individuals or with individuals in groups. Little attention is given to family leisure needs. A recent special issue on leisure counseling in *The Counseling Psychologist* (Dowd, 1981) did not include any significant references to family leisure counseling, with the exception of Loesch's comment that "The need for and potential of leisure counseling as a part of family counseling have been recognized, but to date have not often been realized" (64).

Assumptions

To be successful, family leisure counseling must seriously take into account the inherent tension within any family system between the needs of the family group and those of the individual. In any family, autonomy needs pull against the needs of the system for togetherness and intimacy. Most family system researchers and practitioners (Beavers, 1977; Minuchin, 1974) contend that healthy family members need both independence and closeness. Family leisure counseling will not be effective until this dialectic is taken into consideration and counseling skills are developed for dealing with this dialectic. Rather than viewing them as opposites, it is important to understand that these two drives can reinforce and enrich each other.

The differing, sometimes conflicting, needs of individuals and family systems are outlined in Table 7-I. Probably the most basic individual need is a sense of responsibility for his/her identity and behavior. Often this entails time for privacy and solitude. Autonomy gives a priority to freedom to do as one wants whether alone or with others. Across from autonomy stands a fundamental relational need — intimacy. One of the characteristics of healthy family systems is a sense of emotional bonding, family identity. Intimacy involves much more than physical togetherness. It means giving temporal and energy priority to the relationship. Intimacy grows out of the free choice of the autonomous individual to be with other members of the group. Usually this results in some curtailment of individual freedom. Family leisure cannot occur without this kind of choice. While time together limits personal freedom, it can also serve to enrich the individual.

Table 7-I

Individual Needs	Family Systems Needs
Autonomy	Intimacy
Freedom	Responsibility
Solitude	Togetherness
Awareness of Self	Communication With Others
Needs	Problem Solving
Attitudes	Mutual Reinforcement

A second polarity stems from the need for awareness of self and needs for communication with others. In order for anyone to function satisfactorily in today's society, they must be in touch with their unique physical, emotional, mental, and spiritual needs. Once the individual enters the family group, this awareness is not available unless it is communicated effectively to other family members. Frequently, individual needs and preferences clash. Thus, skills in negotiation and problem solving are essential. Successful family leisure must include heightened sensitivity on the part of the individual, a willingness to communicate his/her needs, and a willingness to listen empathetically to the feelings and wants of others.

Characteristics of Healthy Family Systems

To work effectively with the leisure needs of families, the family leisure counselor must consider the nature of healthy family systems. Fortunately, family research has been turning its focus from a study of family pathology to understanding family health and well-being. The theoretical model of Lewis and his colleagues (1976) is built on this research and is a helpful guide to understanding fundamental family needs. According to their classification, healthy family systems usually possess five characteristics.

The first characteristic is a mutually understood, explicit power structure. The research of Lewis and others supports the value of a strong parental coalition in families. The leisure counselor needs to be aware that someone is nearly always in charge in a family. Goals can usually be accomplished more efficiently if parents assert their authority and then delegate responsibilities as much as is developmentally appropriate.

Second, just as individuals have a self-concept, so a family needs a mythology or a picture of how it functions. It is helpful for both individuals and families if these concepts are fairly accurate and congruent with their joint reality.

Any time leisure counselors have the opportunity, they should encourage families to recall experiences of the past that have molded them into the family they are today.

Third, because of the tension between individuals and systems, healthy families are able to negotiate and solve problems as they arise. This will be discussed more fully below.

Fourth, there is a sense of autonomy in a healthy family system. Each person feels responsible for his/her thoughts, feelings, and actions, as well as not being threatened by other family members. For leisure, this means respect for the preferences and activities of others, even though each person may not enjoy the activities as much as someone else.

The fifth variable relates to family affect. In a healthy family, individuals can express their emotions clearly and freely as well as empathize with the feelings of others. A healthy family can jointly experience the whole gamut of feelings from joy to sorrow. Leisure should be one of the primary ways that growing families can celebrate with each other.

Principles of Leisure Counseling With Families

Because of the features of healthy family systems discussed above, a set of principles and skills are needed for the leisure counselor to intervene in families.

Communication

When the leisure professional begins to work with more than one person, the ability to facilitate communication is crucial. Communication theory and skills have been explicated in many sources (Satir, 1967; Miller, Nunnaly, & Wackman, 1975), but the most basic assumption of communication theory rests on the belief that each person is unique and experiences life in a different way. Therefore, each member of a family — regardless of age — has ideas about leisure that can be contributed. Frequently, families get in "ruts" because they do not draw upon the rich resources within themselves.

The implication of systems and communication theory is that the family leisure counselor in most cases must work with as much of the family unit as possible. Leisure needs will always impact on other family members and it is vital that these be discussed and negotiated together, not apart.

The most important communication skill for the leisure counselor to teach families is for each person to speak for him/herself. In exploring issues, it is essential that the counselor make sure that each family member has the opportunity to share his/her ideas. Frequently, this will mean intentionally "going around the circle" to hear from individuals. In almost all cases, families have a "spokes-person," and the counselor must sensitively guard against their domination of sessions. Likewise, the counselor must intervene when one member speaks for the group or for another family member.

Behavioral Exchanges

The family leisure counselor must convince the family that everyone will gain if all are willing to take a collaborative stance. All parties gain or regress to the extent they are willing to work cooperatively.

Exchange theory is explicated in many sources (cf. Scanzoni, 1972; Jacobson & Margolin, 1979). Essentially it involves the simple concept of trade-offs — "if you'll play badminton with me, I'll watch a movie with you." In spite of its simplicity, however, many families become polarized and need guidance from a leisure counselor on how to strike bargains with each other so that everyone benefits.

The assumption behind behavioral exchange is that each person has needs. They will experience greater happiness and satisfaction if those needs are met to a large degree. The family leisure counselor must affirm that a majority of needs can be met if family members can assist each other in achieving these needs.

Many times exchange can be accomplished by alternating activities. "We will go to the beach if next summer we can go to the mountains." Another option is to meet separate needs concurrently, "I will go see the Shakespearean play while you watch the baseball game."

Exchange stands as a healthy antidote to both relational enmeshment and disengagement. The exchange perspective takes the needs of the individual seriously but it also nurtures the health of the family system.

Problem-Solving

Many leisure opportunities and problems do not lend themselves to only behavioral exchange. More serious conflicts require problem-solving skills. There are many guides for problem-solving and one of the most helpful is *Marital Therapy* by Jacobson and Margolin (1979). While it focuses on the marriage relationship, it is equally relevant for families.

The first principle of problem-solving is obvious but frequently ignored: only one problem or issue should be worked on at a time. The family leisure counselor must insist that the family develop an agenda to focus its attention. Often, each family member feels their issue is the most pressing. Assurance should be given that everyone will have their time.

Second, the leisure counselor must help family members learn how to make positive requests instead of statements about what one does not want to do. "I don't want to play that dumb game" will exacerbate the problem. "I would like to have a family picnic and walk around the lake afterwards" will have a much better chance of success.

A third principle the counselor must move the family towards is being specific about their leisure needs. Obviously, wanting "to be a happier family" is not adequate. The family leisure counselor must be adept at asking process questions that help family members clarify in more concrete terms what would make their interaction more enjoyable. "I would like for us to have a family game night once a week" offers a proposal that can be negotiated.

Fourth, within a family context a number of solutions or alternatives should be examined. In some cases it is useful to brainstorm in order to generate possibilities.

Finally, in family problem-solving, one person should serve as a facilitator who summarizes what he/she understands to be the consensus. Without this summary, plans are often not finalized. Various people frequently have different notions about what was planned. The family leisure counselor must press the family to set dates and assign specific responsibilities. It usually is helpful to record on paper plans and decisions. If there are differing interpretations, the document can serve as a reference. The fewer ambiguities subject to memory and misinterpretation, the more likely the family will succeed at its leisure goals.

Cognitive Assumptions

The final principle of family leisure counseling centers on the cognitive element. This is important because the assumptions persons make about themselves and others have a determining effect on the enjoyment they receive from life. Rational emotive therapy (Ellis, 1973) and cognitive behavioral therapy (Meichenbaum, 1977) have based their psychotherapies on this premise.

Assumptions about work most often influence both the quantity and quality of leisure. Recently, one of the authors counseled a middle age couple who have the resources to travel anywhere they please. The wife, however, often balks at her husband's enthusiastic ideas. After exploring this issue, it was found that the wife did not feel worthy of such extravagance. In her family of origin, any leisure could only be enjoyed at the price of hard work. Until now, she has not felt comfortable going on trips until she has earned it — which has never been achieved.

Because of the pervasiveness of the work ethnic in our culture, many people feel guilty when they have time for leisure. It is important for family leisure counselors to view themselves in part as educators who help people realize that leisure is not only a right but that it can significantly improve the quality of their lives.

At times it may be necessary for the leisure counselor to discuss what McDowell (Chapter 1) has termed "Seven Leisure Assertive Rights in Guilt-free Leisure Style." The rights are as follows:

1. The Right to do Nothing.
2. The Right to Procrastinate.
3. The Right to be Uncertain.

4. The Right to be Alone.
5. The Right to be Playful.
6. The Right for Self-Expression.
7. The Right to be Childlike.

All of the principles discussed here are relevant to the leisure needs of families. The leisure counselor must be certain that he/she has competent skills in these areas, as well as the sensitivity to utilize them when they are appropriate.

Selected Techniques For Family Leisure Counseling

Flexibility and creativity are essential ingredients for any type of counseling. Still, here are a variety of strategies, techniques, and resources that may be particularly useful in family leisure counseling.

Guided Fantasy

Guided fantasy (McDowell, Chapter 1) believes that Americans tend to approach leisure more from the left or rational side of their brains. This often results in activities that are more stressful than recreational, more worklike than playlike. Whether treating individuals, groups, or families, the leisure counselor should begin to stimulate the exploration of ideas and possibilities that are not always deduced logically. One of the easiest means of accomplishing this is to use guided fantasy. In this approach, the counselor asks family members to relax and to close their eyes. One option would be to allow themselves to go anywhere and do anything that they would like to do. There would be no time or financial restrictions on what they could experience. After each person has had time to follow their inner journey, time should be allowed for the entire family to share where their fantasy took them. The counselor should stress that our fantasies often contain a germ of what is important and attainable for us.

Another way of opening up this mode of consciousness is to give an assignment to the family that they only have a limited amount of time left to live. How would they ideally like to spend that time? This exercise will help them clarify what is important and what will probably be some of their family leisure priorities.

A final variation is to do brainstorming. The method requires the family to throw out ideas about their leisure interests but no idea is critiqued. They are all recorded on paper or tape and later examined for patterns and differences. Nevertheless, regardless of the technique used by the counselor, the goal is to enable family members to begin dreaming instead of being locked into linear thinking.

Inventories and Tests

We now move to the left side of the brain. In this area, psychological tests and family interaction inventories can be invaluable tools in helping the counselor understand the family and individuals who compose it.

First, the Myers-Briggs Type Indicator (Briggs & Myers, 1976) is widely administered and can be a useful tool in family leisure counseling. It provides a psychological profile of the family members and their orientation towards others. For example, it is useful to know whether family members are introverts or extroverts in their orientation. This information can help balance the needs of the individual to be alone with the togetherness of family. "Sensing" individuals are more concerned with details while "intuitive" types focus more on relationships and possibilities. One other significant factor the measure provides is how people order their lives. "Judging" persons like their lives organized; "perceiving" individuals like spontaneity.

As an example of how this inventory might be used, recently one of the authors encountered a couple who said they have never had satisfactory leisure activities because the husband (perceiving) likes to travel with no plans. The wife (judging) feels uncomfortable unless she knows where they are going, how they will get there, and so on. Both have thought something was wrong with the other. Such testing can help people realize there is nothing wrong with either orientation. They are just different. Each can contribute to the richness of the relationship if their personality is seen as a complementary strength.

Another instrument well suited to the assessment of the family is FACES (Family Adaptability and Cohesion Evaluation Scales), developed by David Olson and his colleagues (Olson et al., 1978). The cohesion dimension of the instrument is especially relevant to family leisure counseling. It measures the independence of family members, whether the family is open or closed to outside influences, time and space together and apart, friendship patterns, and decision making. It also has a subscale on interests and recreation. By administering FACES, the family leisure counselor will have a picture of whether a given family needs more time apart or whether there needs to be a concerted effort to spend more quality leisure time together.

One other type of inventory is specifically designed for leisure counseling and can be adapted for families as well. Leisure and avocational activity instruments, such as the Constructive Leisure Activity Survey (Edwards, 1980) or the Milwaukee Avocational Satisfaction Questionnaire (Overs et al., 1977) can serve as a stimulus for family members to consider those activities in which they have some interest and satisfaction. These inventories give the counselor an overview of the family's interests. They can also be used profitably in situations where there is a need for the family to discover what their leisure attitudes are and as a source for new leisure alternatives.

For some families, leisure inventories can be adapted in a way that may be more lively for the whole family. Q-Sort is a research-diagnostic technique in which cards are sorted in order of preference. This activity can be done individually or can be used as a family assignment. In order to use the Q-Sort the counselor would need to compile a list of 75-100 family leisure activities. Each of these is then typed on a card. Five boxes with slots are then provided, each ranging from strongly like to strongly dislike. It is useful to require that an equal number of cards be allocated to each slot. In this way, preferences can be clarified as well as the stimulation of new leisure possibilities.

Family Meetings or Councils

For families that exhibit adequate communication skills and the ability to negotiate regular meetings, planned family activities can be very useful. The Mormon Church has institutionalized a weekly family night for its members and the program has been very successful. With the pace of life in many homes, families must be intentional about having time together for sharing and planning. In this way, family members learn to be able to enjoy leisure as a family unit.

Family meetings are an ideal setting to practice the skills of negotiation and problem-solving that were discussed earlier. One person should be designated as the moderator (possibly on a rotating basis) and another as the recorder for plans and decisions. One of the authors' families evolved a system whereby each family member was able to choose on a rotating basis what the family activity would be for that particular week.

Some families must be stringent about meeting regularly. Others find it more helpful to meet as needed. The crucial element is to set aside time in which leisure and other concerns can be considered.

For families who are socially isolated and in need of a wider social and recreational support network, there are family enrichment models that broaden the family base to include other families as well. The "family clusters" model developed by Sawin (1979) brings together families and individuals at different points in their development for a common purpose, frequently, for intergenerational understanding and support. Clusters usually contract to meet together for a specified number of weeks and during this time, the members often learn to expand their concepts of recreation and fun beyond themselves and their family, to others as well.

Resources

There are a variety of other tools also available to the leisure counselor working with families. For example, the Million Dollar Round Table of the Life Underwriters Association commissioned a book and program, *Family Time* (Nutt, 1976), which can be used by families to stimulate family interest in and create new family experiences. Helpful suggestions are also offered by Zinkiewicz (1979) on ways to improve family communication, creatively manage television, and develop family rituals.

A family enrichment program that can also be useful has been developed by Carnes (1981) based on the research and theory behind the FACES program.

In the four sessions of the "Understanding Us" program, families examine themselves in terms of adaptability and caring (cohesion). Through creative exercises, each family develops its own family map and explores ways in which they can move toward greater health.

Family leisure counselors can also take advantage of the current popularity of noncompetitive games. The opportunity to play without competing can be very liberating and stimulating for many families. A number of board games, including the *Ungame*, have been created just for this purpose. They can be used as "outside assignments" for families and will serve to reorient leisure attitudes as well as interpersonal relationships.

Conclusions

The linkages between leisure problems and family problems and between leisure gratifications and family gratifications are increasingly being made. While it is often difficult to sort out cause and effect factors in families experiencing stress or confusion, it is not difficult to see that improvements in the quality of time families spend together can pay off in better understanding, communication, problem solving, and commitment. This can be a reasonable objective of the family leisure counselor.

At the present time, the major stumbling block to improvements in family leisure counseling appears to be lack of information. Family counselors are often unaware of leisure treatment methodologies, and leisure counselors are just as unaware of family treatment methodologies. There are exceptions, no doubt, but this appears to be the norm today. It is our hope that this chapter can stimulate others to explore this valuable relational environment through which most of us have learned our early leisure orientations and to which we now devote much of our time and energy. Nurturing family leisure processes not only lessens the problems of today, it also sets the tone for healthy leisure patterns in future generations.

As a final caution, it is our feeling that leisure counseling with families will require some specialization on the part of the counselor. Family counseling requires a solid understanding of family dynamics, some examination of family intervention techniques, and a definite concern for family growth and dynamics. Not all leisure counselors can be assumed to have the training to intervene effectively in family systems but these intervention skills can be acquired and developed. Even though some techniques for intervention have been suggested here, we must remember that no technique can be used without proper understanding of how to use it, when to use it, or if it should be used at all with a particular family. To paraphrase a common proverb, leisure counseling is like sex — "an emphasis on technique usually leads to impotence." Likewise, the wise leisure counselor who wishes to work with families should learn to really understand the needs of families, how they vary, and then practice the intervention techniques by which these systems can attain maximum stimulation and enjoyment.

REFERENCES

Adams, B., & Cromwell, R. Morning and night people in the family: A preliminary statement. *The Family Coordinator*, 1978, *27*, 5-13.

Aldous, J. *Family careers: Developmental change in families*. New York: Wiley, 1978.

Beavers, W.R. *Psychotherapy & growth: A family systems perspective*. New York: Brunner/Mazel, 1977.

Beck, D., & Jones, M.A. *Progress on family problems*. New York: Family Service Association, 1973.

Briggs, K.C., & Myers, I.B. *Myers-Briggs Type Indicator*. Palo Alto, Ca.: Consulting Psychologist Press, 1976.

Carlson, J. The recreational role. In F. Ivan Nye (Ed.), *Role structure and analysis of the family*. New York: Sage, 1976.

Carnes, P. *Understanding us*. Minneapolis, Mn.: Interpersonal Communication Programs, 1981.

Cuber, J., & Harroff, P. *Sex and the significant Americans*. New York: Appleton-Century, 1966.

Dowd, E.T. (Ed.) Leisure counseling. *The Counseling Psychologist*, 1981, *9*(3).

Edwards, P.B. *Leisure counseling techniques: Individual and group counseling step-by-step* (3rd ed.). Los Angeles: Constructive Leisure, 1980.

Ellis, A. *Humanistic Psychotherapy*. New York: McGraw-Hill, 1973.

Erikson, E. *Insight and responsibility*. New York: Norton, 1964.

Goffman, I. *Encounters: Two studies in the sociology of interaction*. Indianapolis: Bobbs-Merrill, 1961.

Jacobson, N., & Margolin, G. *Marital therapy*. New York: Brunner/Mazel, 1979.

Kaplan, M. *Leisure: Theory and theory*. New York: Wiley, 1975.

Levinger, G. Task and social behavior in marriage. *Sociometry*, 1964, *27*, 433-448.

Levinson, D. *The seasons of a man's life*. New York: Alford Knopf, 1978.

Lewis, J., Beavers, W., Gossett, Jr., & Phillips, V. *No single thread*. New York: Brunner/Mazel, 1976.

Mancini, J.A., & Orthner, D.K. Recreational sexuality preferences among middle-class husbands and wives. *Journal Of Sex Research*, 1978, *14, 96-106.*

Meichenbaum, D. *Cognitive-behavior modification*. New York: Plenum, 1977.

Miller, M.V. Intimate terrorism. *Psychology Today*, 1977, *11*, 79-82.

Miller, S., Nunnally, E., & Wackman, D. *Alive and aware*. Minneapolis, Mn: Interpersonal Communication Programs, 1975.

Minuchin, S. *Families and family therapy*. Cambridge, Ma.: Harvard, 1974.

Nelson, B., Collins, J., Kreitman, N., & Troop, J. Neurosis and marital interaction: II. Time sharing and social activity. *British Journal Of Psychiatry*, 1970, *117*, 47-58.

Nutt, G. *Family time*. Chicago: Million Dollar Round Table, 1976.

Olson, D.H., Bell, R., & Portner, J. *Family adaptability and cohesion evaluation scales*. St. Paul, Mn., 1978.

Orthner, D.K. Familia Ludens: Reinforcing the leisure component in family life. *The Family Coordinator*, 1975, *24*, 175-183.

Orthner, D.K. Patterns of leisure and marital interaction. *Journal of Leisure Research*, 1976, *8*, 98-11.

Orthner, D.K. *Families in blue*. Washington, D.C.: Dept. Of The Air Force 1980.

Orthner, D.K. *Intimate relationships: An introduction to marriage and the family*. Reading, Ma.: Addison-Wesley, 1981.

Orthner, D.K., & Axelson, L. Effects of wife employment on marital sociability. *Journal Of*

Comparative Family Studies, 1980, *11*, 547-561.

Orthner, D.K., & Bowen, G. *Families in blue: Phase II*. Greensboro, N.C.: Family Development Press, 1982.

Orthner, D.K., & Mancini, J.A. Leisure behavior and group dynamics: The case of the family. In S. Iso-Aloha (Ed.), *Social psychological perspectives of leisure and recreation*. Springfield, Il.: Charles C Thomas, 1980.

Overs, R.P., Taylor, S., & Adkins, C. *Avocational counseling manual: A complete guide to leisure guidance*. Washington, D.C.: Hawkins & Associates, 1977.

Powers, W.G., & Hutchinson, K. The measurement of communication apprehension in the marriage relationship. *Journal Of Marriage And The Family*, 1979, *41*, 89-95.

Pratt, L. *Family structure and effective health behavior: The energized family*. Boston: Houghton Mifflin, 1976.

Rapoport, R., & Rapoport, R. *Dual-career families re-examined*. New York: Harper & Row, 1976.

Robinson, J. *How Americans use time*. New York: Praeger, 1977.

Roper Organization. *The Virginia Slims American Women's Opinion Poll*. New York: The Roper Organization, 1974.

Rosenblatt, P., & Cunningham, M. Television watching and family tension. *Journal of Marriage and the Family*, 1976, *38*, 103-111.

Satir, V. *Conjoint family therapy*. Palo Alto, Ca.: Science and Behavior Books, 1967.

Sawin, M. *Family enrichment with family clusters*. Valley Forge, Pa.: Judson, 1979.

Scanzoni, J. *Sexual bargaining*. Englewood Cliffs, N.J.: Prentice-Hall, 1972.

Seidenburg, R. *Corporate wives — corporate casualties*. New York: Doubleday, 1973.

Straus, M., Gelles, R., & Steinmetz. *Behind closed doors*. New York: Doubleday, 1980.

Vale, W.H. & Manning, D.E. *Leisure and the marital relationship*. 1980.

Zinkiewicz, C. *The anytime book for busy families*. Nashville, Tn.: The Upper Room, 1979.

Chapter 8

LEISURE COUNSELING WITH SPECIAL POPULATIONS

PETER A. WITT, GARY ELLIS, AND SHARON H. NILES

Leisure counseling with handicapped individuals has been a concern without any agreed upon method of solution. Fundamental to this concern has been the observation that many handicapped individuals do not work and, thus, "free" time activities are the major sources of fulfillment in their lives. Coupled with the observation that there are both environmental (e.g., architecture) and personal (e.g., lack of skills) barriers that prevent optimum functioning, some form of effort to upgrade ability to maximize fulfillment via leisure involvement seems justified. In addition, even when handicapped people work, free time experiences are often less than optimally fulfilling or meaningful, again due to some combination of external and internal constraints.

Over the past 25 years there have been numerous proposals suggesting how to remediate, upgrade, educate, or counsel the handicapped individual so that leisure functionally improved. Epperson, Witt, and Hitzhusen (1977) documented numerous approaches to counseling and Tinsley and Tinsley (Chapter 3) have compiled an extensive review of leisure counseling models. It is clear from these reviews that there has been little agreement as to the nature of the problems. For example, the leisure problem has been variously seen as not having enough information, having problems in decision-making, and having problems due to lack of personal awareness. McDowell (Chapter 1) has probably done the best job of identifying the myriad of concerns that leisure counseling may choose to tackle.

Given the above situation, it would seem counterproductive to add yet another view of the "problem" and offer another direction for solution to an already abundant leisure counseling literature. However, growing understanding of the full implications of the leisure-as-a-state-of-mind view (see McDowell, Chapter 1) and of the conceptual strengths of attributional and helplessness theory (see Iso-Ahola, Chapter 4) offers promise for finding a conceptually sophisticated and practically applicable approach to leisure counseling for the handicapped.

To help understand a proposed approach to leisure counseling for the handicapped, it will be necessary to discuss the nature of leisure itself with particular emphasis on leisure as a state of mind (as opposed to an activity). This will be followed by a discussion of problems that handicapped individuals may have in achieving leisure, followed by an approach to remediating or overcoming these problems. Much of what follows has been developed as part of the Leisure Diagnostic Battery project, which has been a three year effort to develop instrumentation to assess leisure functioning of handicapped individuals and to suggest appropriate remediation strategies (Ellis & Witt, 1982).

While the focus of the chapter will be on the handicapped, much of the conceptualization of the problems faced by individuals during leisure and suggested counseling approaches to overcome these problems is applicable to the population at large. The major differences in conceptualization or approach have to do with nuance. Even if the chapter only focuses on the handicapped it would be difficult, if not impossible, to include principles that have exact applicability to individuals with a wide diversity of handicaps and who may live under a wide variety of conditions. Thus, it is left to the reader to make adjustments or place emphasis where necessary to account for specifics of individual differences and situations.

What is Leisure

There have been three traditional views of leisure: time, activity, or a state of mind. The adoption of each view has different potential implications for counseling. The time view sees leisure as nonwork time. The purpose of leisure in this sense is to prepare oneself to go back to work refreshed and ready to be a productive citizen. For the handicapped who do not work, this view of leisure is obviously problematic. Our society views much of what to do in free time as earned as a result of work. If one does not work, how is leisure to be justified? This belief has led to a view by society and, often, the handicapped themselves that much of what they do is somehow useless, unearned, and of no purpose or value.

The activity view of leisure is also problematic. For one thing, it is hard to get exact agreement as to what activities are to be counted as leisure. More problematic, however, is that there is increasing evidence (Iso-Ahola, 1980) that it is not what you do but how you feel about what you do that really matters and ultimately determines satisfaction. In addition, the activity view of leisure is also problematic for the handicapped. Often because of architectural and other barriers or because of personal limitations, they are not able to participate in "normal" activities or measure up to standards of success based on "normal" criteria. Thus, the activity view of leisure tends to reinforce a perception of the handicapped as unable and out of the mainstream.

Each of these views of leisure have had their proponents and have spawned particular counseling methodologies to deal with perceived problems in functioning. Thus, resource guidance and skill learning were aimed at getting handicapped people into "normally" acceptable activities. Decision-making strategies were seen as valuable for dealing with time use problems. Unfortunately, there has been the growing feeling that these perspectives do not get to some of the root problems that handicapped people experience with leisure. Emerging interest in a state of mind view of leisure, however, has opened the door to a better conceptual framework for understanding leisure problems and deriving approaches to optimizing leisure functioning.

Although largely ignored until recently as an actual basis for program provision or actual service delivery, the state of mind view has been discussed by utopians and scholars over the past 2000 years. The basic view is that leisure is not something you do, but rather something you experience, something you feel, and a way of perceiving your experience — thus, a state of mind. In the state of mind view, it is not what activity you do that is important; rather, it is the subjective perception of the individual about his/her experience that is ultimately related to satisfaction or well-being. Thus, maximizing leisure functioning involves maximizing conditions that provide a positive state of mind.

Conceptual Foundation: Perceived Freedom and Leisure

Perhaps the most universally agreed upon condition that is characteristic of the state of mind view of leisure is the concept of freedom. The profound and intimate relationship between freedom and leisure is widely recognized by leading researchers and conceptual thinkers in the leisure services field. For example, Bregha (1980) has stated that, "leisure is undoubtedly the most precious and also most fragile expression of our freedom." Achieving this perception of freedom may have many positive consequences such as the ability to maximize playfulness (Lieberman, 1977) or depth of involvement or flow (Csikszentmahalyi, 1975).

Given that freedom is a critical regulator of leisure functioning, remediation of deficiencies in functioning requires careful analysis of an individual's perception of his personal freedom. Through such an analysis, several elements of freedom become evident. Each of these elements may be considered to be part of one of two major aspects of freedom: "freedom from" or "freedom to."

An individual's leisure functioning may be optimal when he/she is free *from* constraints in the environment. An individual may, for example, lack knowledge of leisure opportunities in his/her community. Without this knowledge, the individual is restricted to a more limited range of alternatives, many of which may not be compatible with interests and competencies. Thus, knowledge of such aspects of opportunities as what services are offered, who may participate, where the services are offered, and how much they cost provides the individual with "freedom from" a particular personal barrier to optimal leisure functioning.

In addition to knowledge of leisure opportunities, numerous other personal and environmental barriers to optimal leisure functioning may exist. These barriers might include lack of accessible facilities, overbearing time constraints, lack of needed financial resources, lack of available opportunities, and poor social skills. Such barriers might also include prohibitive values, attitudes, and social norms the individual believes are held by friends and acquaintances or by the society as a whole. The existence of one or more of these barriers may create a general overall perception of many prohibitive barriers in an individual's environment. If such barriers are present, the enhancement of the individual's leisure functioning must involve not only the elimination of the barrier itself but also the elimination of the perception of that barrier. In the process, the individual must be "freed from" both personal and environmental barriers.

Besides being "free from" personal and environmental barriers, an individual must feel "free to" pursue leisure in the manner of his/her choice. Although these "freedom to" elements may be considered personal barriers, they are also considered to be associated with a particular emotion, feeling, or state of arousal. Three elements of this feeling of "perceived" freedom are discussed by Iso-Ahola (1980; Chapter 4). These elements include a perception of control, personal competence, and intrinsic motivation.

One aspect of "freedom to" is *perceived control*. The individual who believes that he/she has the ability to control the process and outcome of an experience or situation through his/her own efforts and abilities is considered to be internally controlled. On the other hand, the individual who believes that the process and outcomes of experiences are mostly determined by fate, luck, and/ or powerful others is considered to be externally controlled. A perception of internal control is facilitative of freedom because the individual believes that he/she is able to determine outcomes or consequences of his/her involvement in activities or situations. The more one feels capable of determining these consequences, the more freedom he/she feels to become involved or to pursue leisure. Leisure functioning, therefore, is enhanced.

For many handicapped individuals, a sense of internal control is lacking due to the debilitating effects of an injury or accident or the degree to which professionals or family members make decisions for them. In either case, handicapped individuals may begin to perceive themselves as lacking in the ability to make decisions or undertake actions that will affect processes or outcomes in their life. While this tendency to perceive lack of control may pervade all aspects of the individual's life, it may be particularly evident in leisure situations, where handicapped individuals may not be allowed to choose their own involvements or, within a given situation, to decide how they wish to be involved. This is particularly true in institutional or agency settings and may also be the case in home settings due to the overprotective attitudes of caregivers. In addition, if a handicap is due to injury or illness, the perception of external control may be due to the initial unfamiliarity with the new condition and the extent to which prior skills are missing or unusable in a current situation.

Perceived Leisure Competence

In order to feel comfortable or feel free to participate in an activity, one must feel some degree of personal *competence* in that activity. This perception of competence provides the individual with a degree of assurance that his/her involvement will be rewarding and satisfying and that the probability of failure resulting in an embarrassing or frustrating experience is unlikely. Perceived competence, therefore, becomes a probabilistic belief about the likelihood of a positive experience resulting from a given endeavor based on the individual's perception of his/her abilities in that activity or situation. The individual who feels competent in a variety of activities is more amenable to a high degree of leisure functioning because he/she can expect a positive experience to result from participation in many different activities and situations. The individual who perceives self as competent, therefore, is in a position to feel a sense of "freedom to" pursue leisure.

It should be noted that competence is multi-faceted. Competence can be subdivided into four domains: cognitive, social, physical, or general perceptions of competence (Harter, 1980). Cognitive competence deals with one's perception of one's ability to make decisions and complete tasks such as thinking of new things to do and new ways to participate in familiar activities. Social competence deals with one's perception of one's ability to make new friends, meet people, and feel comfortable with others involved in leisure activities. Physical competence deals with one's perception of oneself to perform gross and fine motor skills. Finally, general competence deals with the individual's personal perception regarding, "I'm good at _____" or "I'm a good person at _____."

Competence can also be judged from three different reference points: (a) with reference to personally delineated standards, (b) in comparison to "normally" accepted standards, and (c) in a comparison to others with similar abilities or disabilities. Each frame of reference comes into play at some point in an individual's life. Adequate leisure functioning probably depends on knowing when certain standards are applicable and attainable. Wortman and Dintzer (1978) suggest that adaptive responding is dependent on making *accurate* attributions and knowing which and when standards are appropriate. Thus, there is a need to teach people to make these judgments.

Together, attributions of competence and internal control are powerful forces enabling the individual to feel a sense of "freedom to." It should be noted that these feelings are highly associated with positive affect, which is often labeled fun or enjoyment. At the opposite extreme, individuals may perceive themselves as helpless and experience a feeling of avoidance or dislike for a given situatuion. Worse, however, is the possibility that individuals will generalize feelings of helplessness across a variety of situations. They may see themselves as generally low in ability, lacking in control, and in addition, perceive environmental problems as insurmountable.

It is also possible, however, that feelings of helplessness are more *discriminated* (i.e., they are limited to specific activities, types of activities, or situations). Thus, while individuals may feel highly competent in art and feel a high degree of control over outcomes and circumstances in this activity, they may feel quite incompetent in sports. Finally, an individual may exhibit *avoided helplessness* in certain situations. An individual may, for example, utilize avoided helplessness as a tactic to preserve a high perception of competence by attributing specific failure to chance or to specific situational conditions. In this case, avoided helplessness is a healthy response that serves to facilitate the individual's leisure functioning.

The distinction between types of helplessness (generalized, discriminated, or avoided) is useful both in understanding individual responses and in planning strategies for helping individuals change to more adaptive responses. In this regard, discriminated or avoided helplessness responses may be preferable to behavioral manifestations of generalized helplessness. It should also be noted that generalized helplessness may be more difficult to affect as a result of the nonspecific and stable nature of attributions producing such perceptions.

A third aspect of "freedom to" is *intrinsic motivation*. Intrinsic motivation refers to the extent to which individuals engage in certain behaviors for intrinsic reasons, such as pleasure, enjoyment, curiosity, or the satisfaction of internal needs (Deci, 1975). An extrinsically motivated behavior, on the other hand, is one in which the individual becomes involved due to the presence of external influences such as rewards and prizes or threats and sanctions. Intrinsic motivation, therefore, is characteristic of adequate leisure functioning. The leisure behavior of the intrinsically motivated person is determined by his/her preference and interests rather than being determined by outside influences. Intrinsic motivation describes the individual who feels "free to" pursue personally preferred leisure involvements. Increasing the degree of intrinsic motivation, thus, becomes a critical goal of helping handicapped individuals improve their leisure functioning.

Several aspects of the relationship between perceived competence, perceived control, and intrinsic motivation are important to delineate because of their usefulness in understanding the dynamics of leisure functioning. First, having a perception of personal control may be a necessary condition for achieving a sense of personal competence or intrinsic motivation. Thus as Iso-Ahola (1980; Chapter 4) suggests, perceived control acts as a threshold after which the other components are attainable. For example, individuals may feel competent at tossing horseshoes, but if they feel forced to participate, they perceive that the situation is not under their control. They may consequently not be able to achieve satisfaction even though they are able to adequately do the activity. Thus, external causes for potentially positive outcomes minimize feelings of satisfaction because the focus is on regaining control and freedom. Competence in this case is of little consequence in satisfying the individual's needs and thus voluntary participation may be curtailed.

It should also be noted that intrinsically motivated behavior or involvement may play a role in making involvement in a given situation seem less critical. In this sense, the individual may have a better opportunity to experience competence and control. Thus, there is a potentially circular relationship between the sense of competence and control necessary for initial involvement and higher degrees of these perceptions resulting from successful experiences.

So much of what besets handicapped individuals centers on self-perceptions in these areas being inevitably/continually/consistently reinforced by societal stereotypes and environmental obstacles that it is not surprising many handicapped individuals fail to function adequately. It is also not surprising that the handicapped often require a large degree of extrinsic as opposed to intrinsic motivation to become involved in a situation.

Deci (1975) suggests that personal control and competence are internal needs, that they are intrinsically motivated. The individual, therefore, has a desire to seek optimal challenges in order to satisfy these needs (Ellis, 1973). Researchers on intrinsic motivation (DeCharms, 1968) suggest that individuals who engage in intrinsically motivated activity are characterized by total involvement and absorption in the activity, commitment to the activity, and lack of anxiety or feelings of threat. This is related to the "flow" concept delineated by Csikszentmihalyi (1975). These attributes suggest that feelings of control and competence lead to satisfaction of basic needs and that perceived freedom is one result.

Depth of Involvement or Flow

As discussed earlier, the flow concept, as delineated by Csikszentmihalyi (1975), is important to understand as a potential indicator of adequate leisure functioning. As just described, absorption and commitment to an activity are a result of feelings of intrinsic motivation, which in turn seem to be more possible when there is a personal perception of control and competence in a given situation. In the common vernacular, "flow" is the ability to be "into" something. This being "into" something enables the individual to transcend concerns about his/her handicap or the "cannots" or "shoulds." In essence, the achievement of perceptions of competence and control and the resultant feelings of intrinsic motivation open the door to feelings of leisure involvement that are characterized by excitement, enthusiasm, commitment, and absorption. The transcendency of small concerns and limitations when this state is achieved is one of the chief advantages of leisure pursuits. For the handicapped, the type of involvement characterized here provides an arena for self-enhancement and personally derived meaning and satisfaction.

Playfulness

In addition to helping to achieve a sense of absorption and involvement, the perceived control-competence-intrinsic motivation paradigm also points to the possibility of the individual developing a high degree of playfulness in their leisure involvements. Playfulness, according to Lieberman (1973) is composed of cognitive, physical, and social spontaneity as well as manifest joy and sense of humor. Although manifest joy and sense of humor may reflect freedom via social competence, the spontaneity elements are perhaps most associated with freedom. In order to be spontaneous, one must feel a degree of freedom. Spontaneity is the ability to make something of nothing, to take chances, to be creative.

Again, for the handicapped person spontaneity, joy, and humor may easily disappear or not be reachieved after a traumatic injury. Rehabilitation processes, institutional settings, and/or community circumstances may give no basis for playful behaviors. In addition, playful behaviors may be viewed as unacceptable and thus lead to negative consequences such as failure, peer or adult disapproval. This diminuation of the range of "acceptable" behaviors will, in turn, lead to a decrement in perceived freedom. In essence, there is the player in all of us. It can be nurtured or squelched.

Goals of Leisure Counseling

Given the above context and variables, particular goals of the leisure counseling process can be identified (see Table 8-I). While the list is not exhaustive, it provides a basis for operationalizing the preceding theoretical perspectives.

Table 8-I

GOALS FOR LEISURE COUNSELING

- *Increase Perceived Control in Leisure Experiences*
  Increase knowledge of opportunities
  Increase decision-making ability
  Increase ability to perceive and make choices before, between, and during experiences.
  Increase positive feelings toward one's own rights and needs
  Increase ability to assert one's own rights and feelings
- *Increase Perceived Competence in Leisure Experiences*
  Increase personal perception of "success" in leisure involvements or activities
  Decrease need for interpersonal comparisons
  Increase perception of incremental improvement
- *Increase Intrinsic Motivation*
  Increase "want tos" and decrease "have tos," "shoulds," and "musts"
  Increase personal sense of wants, needs priorities
  Increase sense of personal responsibility for making decisions
- *Increase Depth of Involvement*
  Increase personal ability to match ability to task demands
  Increase personal ability to narrow attention to experience at hand
  Decrease personal emphasis on winning and losing as opposed to enjoyment and participation
  Decrease influence of time dimensions
- *Increase Playfulness*
  Increase willingness to be spontaneous
  Increase ability to show joy and sense of humor
  Increase ability to "see" possibilities or generate alternatives

---

The list provides direction and potential structure of leisure counseling efforts. Many of the traditional counseling models deal specifically with elements of the above goals (e.g., assertive training with perceived control; transactional analysis with playfulness; and values clarification with intrinsic motivation). However, it should be clear that counseling alone will not help achieve all of the listed goals. Thus, leisure counseling needs to be put in an overall framework that involves (a) environmental planning or structuring, (b) leadership and programming efforts, and (c) counseling (or education) efforts. Only when these three efforts are combined into a total service package will efforts to facilitate the leisure development of handicapped individuals be fully successful. The counseling profession in general is recognizing the advantages of this multi-faceted approach that includes an ecological component (e.g., Rusalem, 1973; Lewis and Lewis, 1977). Counseling need not be limited to the dydactic interview or even the group interview. Thus, the following sections outline the interactive role of each of these components in an overall leisure facilitation process.

Components of a Comprehensive Leisure Facilitation Process

The leisure facilitation process needs to begin with some form of assessment of the individual's current level of leisure functioning. In essence this phase answers the question: What is the problem? This is followed by a determination of objectives for remediation or change. Next, specific strategies are determined and implemented for achieving identified goals. Finally, postassessment is undertaken to determine the effectiveness of implemented strategies in overcoming initially discovered problems. Postassessment is the beginning of a reiterative process that seeks to identify additional or unaccomplished goals and accompanying strategies that subsequently need to be implemented.

The actual assessment process may take several forms. It may include formal instrument-based assessment, interviews, observation, etc. Some available assessment instrumentation available for this purpose is reviewed by Howe (see Chapter 10). Unfortunately, few of these instruments are based on a conceptualization of leisure functioning based on attribution theory and the "freedom from — freedom to" paradigm described earlier in this chapter.

Over the past three years, however, the Leisure Diagnostic Battery project has attempted to fill this void (Ellis & Witt, 1982). Thus, specific instrumentation has been developed to measure the "freedom to" and "freedom from" domains. Although initially developed for 10-14-year-old handicapped individuals, the developed scales have been adapted for use with adults as well.

Utilizing the LDB, assessment is conducted in two phases. Five scales corresponding to aspects of the "freedom to" domain are initially administered. These consist of the following instruments: Perceived Leisure Competence Scale, Perceived Leisure Control Scale, Leisure Needs Scale, Playfulness Scale, and Depth of Involvement Scale. The 95 items in these scales can be summed to achieve a "Perceived Freedom" score. If the attained score indicates the value and need for remediation efforts (i.e., an initial diagnosis of limited perceived freedom), then three additional follow-up instruments are given. These include Knowledge of Leisure Opportunities Test, Barriers to Leisure

Involvement Scale, and a Preferences Inventory. The first two of these scores deal with aspects of the "freedom from domain described earlier.*

Scores from the "freedom from" scales along with the individual scale scores comprising the "freedom to" domain are used as a basis for setting remedial objectives and determining specific remediation strategies. The counselor/therapist/leader administering the instruments will also want to use other information they have about the client based on other relevant instruments, personal observation, case records, etc. In other words, the LDB should ultimately be used as only one source of information in a comprehensive assessment effort. For example, instruments to assess social, decision-making, and psychomotor skills may be useful as part of the "freedom to" assessment effort.

Based on the assessment data, goals for remediation such as those outlined in Table 8-I can be set. The next step is to determine appropriate remediation strategies. As noted previously, these strategies may be oriented toward environmental manipulation or design, leadership and programming methods, and/or counseling techniques. For example, identified problems in the area of perceived control can be dealt with from several perspectives.† From the point of view of environmental design, clients may not perceive themselves as able to interact successfully with impending/existing environmental factors. Steps may be taken to change environmental circumstances to allow more client choice, more control over outcomes, or self-determined criteria. All of these "manipulations" can be leader-free in that they involve provision or adjustment of environmental elements that in and of themselves emphasize choice.

On the other hand, specific leadership or programming strategies may be undertaken to facilitate personal perceptions of control. For example, the leader may plan experiences to maximize client choice among and within activities. Facilitation of choice can be part of the normal communication process between client and leader as opposed to counseling per se. The process may be as simple as, "What would you like to do now?" or "Let's plan what we're going to do next."

Finally, more structured counseling may be called for. Making appropriate personal choices may be facilitated via one-to-one or small group structured sessions that utilize any of the myriad counseling techniques. In the current example, values clarification processes may be appropriate followed by processes emphasizing support to the client who has difficulty implementing choices.

---

*Further information about the Leisure Diagnostic Battery can be obtained from the Leisure Diagnostic Battery Project, Division of Recreation and Leisure Studies, North Texas State University, Denton, Tx. 76203. Extensive field testing has indicated acceptable reliability (alphas in excess of .85 for most scales) and evidence of construct, concurrent, and discriminant validity.

†The Leisure Diagnostic Battery has an accompanying remediation guide describing specific strategies related to results from the Leisure Diagnostic Bettery assessment process (Ellis, Witt, & Niles, 1982).

The importance of this comprehensive approach to counseling cannot be overstated. In particular, it emphasizes several key points about leisure counseling and helps to provide a framework for overcoming past conceptual and methodological difficulties.

First, the approach makes it clear that leisure counseling for the handicapped is not separate from other attempts to facilitate leisure functioning of handicapped individuals. Counseling is appropriate as a specific methodology designed to accomplish a specific goal. Its usefulness as a strategy must be weighed against other available remediation options (e.g., environmental manipulation or leadership/programming) and will usually be effective only if done as part of a comprehensive plan involving all three elements.

Second, the approach helps overcome the blame-the-victim mentality inherent in so many treatment approaches (Ryan, 1976). Many counseling strategies are aimed at helping the client adjust to an inhospitable environment. Thus, in an environment that discriminates against handicapped individuals to the point of exclusion or only accepts normative definitions of success and failure, it is the handicapped individual who is blamed for the inability to cope and successfully participate. On the other hand, the comprehensive approach places equal emphasis on efforts to change environments as well as programming and leadership strategies to make them more hospitable and appropriate to the functioning level and needs of handicapped participants. It recognizes individual perceptions of success/failure and satisfaction/happiness as more important than external situational definitions of these outcomes. Indeed, it suggests that leisure counselors may need to act more as advocates or environmental change agents than personal "therapists" (Edginton & Compton, 1975). The need for a preventative or developmental approach (Lewis & Lewis, 1977) that builds on both individual and community strengths (Rappaport et al., 1975) is also apparent.

Third, the comprehensive approach to remediation together with the conceptual model outlining potential areas of leisure dysfunctioning discussed earlier argues strongly against the activity-matching or resource guidance mentality that is emphasized in many so-called leisure counseling strategies. Many leisure counseling strategies are dependent on a model that assumes that all will be solved if clients were matched with or directed toward preferred activities. Thus, "interest finders" are used to help clients choose appropriate activities. Unfortunately, however, interest finders are too often used as a crutch transferring counselor responsibility to activities, rather than as one element in a comprehensive remediation approach.

Too often clients are asked about interests or preferences without any effort to ascertain "why" they prefer what they do or whether choices are fulfilling or satisfying (Witt & Groom, 1979). For example, due to external pressure and feelings of incompetence, individuals may "prefer" activities that are minimally satisfying. Because interest finders place emphasis on activities and not on the feelings that participants have about their involvements, too often interest finders are ineffective and inappropriately used. They may only serve to perpetuate involvement within the confines of a low perception of control and competence.

In essence, there is a necessity to change emphasis from activities to experiences, and in particular, to the meaning of experiences to clients. The aim of all interaction with the client must be the facilitation of client's perceptions of freedom rather than participation per se. Thus, the comprehensive approach to leisure facilitation is useful because it emphasizes the meaning of the involvement to the client and the interrelated roles of environmental planning, leadership and programming, as well as leisure counseling in maximizing clients' perception of freedom as opposed to simply maximizing client participation.

Given the above rationale, the following section is devoted to specific strategies for increasing "freedom to." As discussed in the previous section, some of these ideas are based on work undertaken as part of the Leisure Diagnostic Battery Project (Ellis, Witt, & Niles, 1982). The strategies discussed include means to (1) increase client ability to perceive and make choices before, within, and during experiences and (2) increase depth of involvement. Discussion of these specific areas should provide further examples of how leisure might be facilitated.

Increasing Ability to Perceive and Make Choices

Perceiving that choices are available and being able to choose between available choices is basic to the concept of freedom. Part of the problem faced by many handicapped individuals is the perception that there are few things to do and few people to do things with, and that the ability is lacking to do what is available. While part of this perception may be accurate, in many instances a perception of lack of choice may be due to mis-reading environmental cues, failing to see opportunities that are available, and/or fearing change itself, albeit positive. Part of this problem can be dealt with via counseling. Attitudes, past experiences, and future opportunities can be explored. Through specific exercises that are available, alternatives can be generated, possibilities for participation analyzed, and means of becoming involved developed.

In discussing available choices, attention should be paid to particular activities and preferred styles of participation (risk/no risk, alone/with others, active/passive). Equally important, emphasis should be placed on the process of choice within activities and during experiences. Thus, the individual who chooses a given activity as desirable can also be helped to see the possibility for choice within the activity (e.g., what position to play, what art class to take, what movie to see). In addition, clients can be helped to see that the process of making choices goes on even during experiences (e.g., whether to sit through an entire boring movie).

Facilitating a perception of available choices also needs to go on within the actual participation process either as a follow-up to counseling or in lieu of counseling. If activity leaders and planners would communicate the right and the responsibility to make choices as well as reinforce efforts to choose in actual activity situations, counseling might be avoided. Thus, leadership is seen in this case to involve efforts to maximize a sense of control and freedom by planning and leading activities so that choice is optimized. Highlighting an awareness of choices as they arise, suggesting that the client seek alternative solutions in difficult situations, or informing that the client's decisions are valued and should be implemented are all ways of maximizing the perception of choice.

Of course, the ability to perceive choice will also be facilitated if there are in fact choices to make. Too often parent, leader, or public attitudes restrict activity offerings or the way particular offerings are to be undertaken. The handicapped individual may in this case realistically perceive restrictions on opportunity, discriminatory attitudes concerning abilities or needs, and perhaps over-protection concerning potential harm emanating from risk situations. In these cases, advocacy of the rights and needs of the handicapped may be just as important as efforts to overcome perceptions of the handicapped themselves. In this sense, much can be done to prevent perceptions of lack of control rather than simply remediate problems when they arise.

Increasing Depth of Involvement

Increasing depth of involvement can be accomplished via a combination of all three facilitative strategies noted above. Being able to maximize depth of involvement requires that the individual is able to totally focus on the activity at hand. In other words, the individual needs to feel a sense of "freedom from" and "freedom to." The depth of involvement experience involves both the ability and opportunity to lose track of clock time as opposed to inner time, to ward off distraction by other environmental elements, and to feel a sense of competence and control in the current involvement. Achieving this state requires both an environment conducive to facilitating involvement or flow and an individual prepared to take advantage of such circumstances.

Again, facilitation of feelings of personal control and competence may be useful. The individual also needs to be helped to match ability to the difficulty or demand requirements of a given situation. Helping handicapped individuals overcome fear of failure or more realistically assess demands may be appropriate here.

In addition, efforts need to be made to create an environment that facilitates involvement or flow. Ellis, Witt, and Aguilar (1982) have noted six requirements for structuring this type of setting:

1. Attention must be attracted.

2. Complexity of the situation must be arranged so that an optimal challenge to the individual is present.
3. Stimulus field must be narrowed.
4. Extrinsic rewards must not be the most prominent motivation for involvement.
5. Feedback must be immediate.
6. The individual's awareness of consequences of winning and losing must be minimized.

Each of these must be considered by the leader in designing an environment conducive to flow. Each element is discussed in detail.

Novelty is a primary means of *attracting attention*. In addition to traditional methods of advertising, such as posters, flyers, word of mouth, and other media, the leader might consider special gimmicks to attract the attention of clients who are exhibiting deficiencies in leisure functioning. If the activity is a fishing trip, the leader might bring along a fish when he invites the client to participate. if the activity is a craft, the tutor might present a finished project representative of the product to be produced. If the activity is music, the invitation might be sung to the client. If it is drama, a mime act or magic act might be arranged as a novel means to attract attention. The possibilities are endless; they are limited only by the creativity and imagination of the leader.

After attention has been attracted through novelty, it must be held through *complexity*. As mentioned previously, this is a task of creating an optimal level of challenge, commensurate with the individual's skills and perceived competence. This challenge, it should be noted, may be created within activities or between activities. Rule changes can simplify or make an activity more complex. If running is called for in the activity, the rule might be changed to require hopping. If paint brushes are generally used, the leader might substitute sponges and a toothbrush. If the activity is a nature hike, participants might be challenged to find a rainbow of colors or to locate specific flora or fauna. Like novelty, complexity in task is primarily a matter of the leader's imagination and creativity.

The third consideration in establishing an "involvement environment" is to keep the *stimulus field narrow*. It is difficult to maintain focus of attention when novel aspects of the environment irrelevant to the activity are competing for the individual's attention. In planning to enable focusing of attention, the leader may consider the elimination of background music unrelated to the activity, the segregation of activities requiring a great deal of noise and movement from activities requiring little noise and fine motor activity, and the minimization of excessive and continual encouragement from outside sources. If an experience is to be optimal, the environment must enable participants to focus their attention on the task or activity at hand.

The fourth consideration in establishing an involvement environment is to de-emphasize the importance of *extrinsic rewards*. In his studies of flow, Csikszentmihalyi (1975) found that extrinsic rewards prevent the flow experience. The individual working toward leader approval, a trophy, a ribbon, or a piece of candy seems to focus on these outcomes rather than on the self-rewards emanating from depth of involvement and the flow experience. This detrimental effect of external rewards on intrinsic motivation provides further evidence of the importance of attracting attention to activities and generating participation through novelty rather than through the more common and more traditional methods of coercion and offers of extrinsic rewards.

The *immediacy of feedback* is another area of concern in facilitating flow. Feedback, in this context, refers to the effect of the individual's action. It would be erroneous to assume that this guideline suggests that the tutor constantly provides verbal feedback to the client throughout the process of the activity, since such feedback would be an extrinsic reward and would add breadth to the stimulus field. Feedback, in this context, refers explicitly to the individual's perception of the consequences of specific actions. According to Furlong (1976), games and sports are good examples. The ball is in the air; we catch it or not. In this case, the feedback is direct, unambiguous, and inherent in the activity. The extent to which tasks within preferred activities provide this feedback is an important consideration in planning an involvement environment.

The final consideration in the creation of an involvement environment is related to *minimizing the individual's awareness of the consequences of winning and losing.* If the client focuses on the consequences of success or failure, winning or losing, rather than on involvement, flow is harder to attain. This guideline has important implications for well-meaning spectators, observers, leaders, and ancillary personnel who may design their encouragement and interaction with the client around success and failure rather than around the process of participation. In order to achieve flow, the individual's cognizance of the consequences of success or failure must be minimal.

Conclusion

Leisure counseling has been characterized in this chapter as one part of an overall leisure facilitation process. An effort has been made to avoid laying the blame for leisure problems totally with the handicapped client. Teaching coping skills or helping a person adjust to difficult life circumstances is acceptable if efforts are also taken to change environmental circumstances to be more hospitable and facilitative of the leisure experience. The mutuality of responsibility of the person (client) and of the environmental circumstances for optimizing leisure functioning has been emphasized.

While the presented material does not exhaust potential strategies for facilitating leisure for the handicapped, it does provide a conceptual framework and direction for practical application. Efforts have been made to avoid a cookbook approach. Rather, attempts have been made at identifying the concerns that leisure counseling for the handicapped must address and to suggest some avenues for directing such efforts.

REFERENCES

Bregha, F. Leisure and freedom reexamined. In T. Goodale and P. Witt (Ed.), *Issues in an era of change*. State College, Pn.: Venture Publishing, Inc., 1980.

Csikszentmahalyi, M. *Beyond boredom and anxiety*. San Francisco: Josey-Bass, 1975.

Deci, E. *Intrinsic motivation*. New York: Academic Press, 1968.

DeCharms, R. *Personal causation*. New York: Academic Press, 1968.

Edginton, C.R. & Compton, D.M. Consumerism and advocacy. *Therapeutic Recreation Journal*, 1975, *9*(1), 23-27.

Ellis, G., & Witt, P. *The Leisure Diagnostic Battery: conceptualization and development*. Project Report. Denton, Texas: North Texas State University, Division of Recreation and Leisure Studies, 1982.

Ellis, G., Witt, P.A., & Niles, S. *The Leisure Diagnostic Battery Remediation Guide*. Denton: North Texas State University, 1982, (Leisure Diagnostic Battery Project Report).

Ellis, G., Witt, P.A., & Aguilar, T. Facilitating "flow" in therapeutic recreation settings. *Therapeutic Recreation Journal*, in press.

Ellis, M.J. *Why people play*. Englewood Cliffs: Prentice-Hall, 1978.

Epperson, A., Witt, P.A., & Hitzhusen, G. *Leisure Counseling: An Aspect of Leisure Education*. Springfield, Charles C Thomas, 1977.

Furlong, W.B. The fun in fun. *Psychology Today*. June, 1976.

Harter, S. The perceived competence scale for children. *Child Development*, in press. 1980.

Iso-Ahola, S. *The social psychology of leisure and recreation*. Dubuque, Iowa: William C. Brown, Co., 1980.

Lewis, J.S., & Lewis, M.D. *Community counseling: A human services approach*. New York: John Wiley and Sons, 1977.

Liebermann, J.N. *Playfulness: Its relationship to imagination and creativity*. Brooklyn: Academic Press, 1977.

Mannell, R.C. Social psychological techniques and strategies for studying leisure experiences. In S.E. Iso-Ahola (Ed.), *Social psychological perspectives on leisure and recreation*. Springfield, Charles C Thomas, 1980.

Neulinger, J. *The psychology of leisure*. Springfield: Charles C Thomas, 1982.

Rappaport, J. et. al. Alternatives to blaming the victim of the environment. *American Psychologist*, 1975, *30*(2), 10-18.

Rusalem, H. An alternative to the therapeutic model in therapeutic recreation. *Therapeutic Recreation Journal*, 1973, *7*(2), 10-18.

Witt, P.A., & Groom, R. Dangers and problems associated with current approaches to developing leisure interest finders. *Therapeutic Recreation Journal*, 1978, *13*(1), 19-31.

Wortman, C.B., & Dintzer, L. Is an attributional analysis of the learned helplessness phenomenon viable? A critique of the Abramson-Seligman-Teasdale reformulation. *Journal of Abnormal Psychology*, 1978, *87*(1), 75-98.

Chapter 9

LEISURE COUNSELING WITH ADULTS ACROSS THE LIFE SPAN

E. THOMAS DOWD

Mental health has always been an elusive concept, especially insofar as theories of personality and psychopathology have focused on disturbance of functioning and remedial interventions. Only recently has there been much consideration of mental health as more than the absence of pathology and a concomitant emphasis on development of intervention strategies to promote healthy functioning. This chapter will describe several models of mental health and then turn to a discussion of the function of leisure in optimizing mentally healthy functioning. Various conceptualizations of the stages of adult life will be presented and the function of leisure in assisting in the resolution of the developmental tasks of each stage will be discussed. Finally, the process of leisure counseling with adults will be described, with particular attention being paid to stages in the adult life span during which leisure counseling interventions might be especially useful and powerful.

Concepts of the Mentally Healthy Adult

Psychoanalytic Theory

According to psychoanalytic formulations, the individual personality structure consists of three parts: the id, the ego, and the superego. The id operates according to the demands of the Pleasure Principle and demands immediate gratification, while the ego operates according to the Reality Principle, which takes into account the demands of the external world. The superego represents the "internalized conscience," the values and prescriptions of parental and other societal authority figures.

Another crucial feature of the psychoanalytic theory of personality is the concept of stages of development. The stages of childhood psychosexual development, from oral to genital, are well known and require no discussion here. It is important to note, however, that an individual who does not progress normally through these stages is considered maladjusted or "sick."

A third major concept is that of repression. Psychoanalytic theory postulates that basic instincts are socially unacceptable if expressed directly; they must be brought under control either by repression (which absorbs a large amount of psychic energy) or by sublimation of these desires into more socially acceptable activities. For example, oral gratifications can be achieved by such activities as smoking and chewing gum; genital gratifications by sex within marriage.

Several implications for the emerging construct of the healthy personality follow from the above concepts. First, the personality structure of the mentally healthy adult would consist of a dominant ego, which is able to restrain both the demands of the id and the superego, leaving the individual relatively free from the instinctual forces of the id as well as from the structures of an overactive conscience. Second, the mentally healthy adult should have progressed satisfactorily through all the stages of psychosexual development, without having become fixated at any one stage. Third, the person would have learned how to suppress or sublimate rather than repress basic instinctual drives into socially appropriate outlets. Such an individual should be free in the most profound sense of the term, free of repressed, energy-sapping conflicts and thus possessing the energy to engage in joyful, creative activity without having his/her behavior unduly constrained either by internal or external forces. Such a person would be able to do what Freud once said a healthy person should be able to do: "Lieben und Arbeiten" (to love and to work). Such a person would also be free enough to fuse effort with spontaneity in a commitment required of *both* work and leisure (Bordin, 1979).

Behavioral Theory

The behavioral approach provides the clearest example of the cultural relativity of the concept of normality, or mental health. Behaviorism (cf. Skinner, 1953) postulates that behavior is governed by its conseqences; if an action is reinforced, the probability of its occurring in the future will increase, but if it is not reinforced or is punished, the probability of its occurring in the future is diminished or extinguished. The implications of this simple principle are far-reaching and profound. Normal behavior is that which is reinforced most often in most people, thus equating the concept of normality to the statistical concept of the norm. Different behaviors are obviously reinforced in different cultures, or even in different subcultures, so the assumption that a specific set of behaviors constitutes normality becomes meaningless. Whatever most people do is by definition normal. Therefore, the mentally healthy adult is one whose behavior is governed by the reinforcing consequences of the society in which he/she lives, and who is able to adapt to the behavioral constraints of this society with a minimum of strain. There are obviously no universal standards of mental health across radically different societies; since different societies reinforce different behaviors, what is mentally healthy in one society may be indicative of mental illness in another. Mental health is measured by degree of adjustment to the culture and the ability to achieve one's goals within its framework. In fact, goal-achievement — of whatever goals are seen as appropriate for that culture — can be viewed as the result of behavior of mentally healthy adults. Obviously, however, similar societies are also similar in many of their reinforcing consequences and behaviors reinforced.

Social Learning Theory

Bandura (1977) has developed two concepts that have particular relevance for this discussion: efficacy expectation and outcome expectation. The latter refers to an individual's estimate that a given behavior will lead to a given outcome. The former refers to the conviction that one can successfully accomplish the behavior required to produce that outcome. It can be readily seen that it is possible to have high levels of both, low levels of both, or to be high on one and low on the other. Implicit in social learning theory is the notion that the mentally healthy person possesses a high level of efficacy expectation across a wide variety of situations; that is, the person sees him/herself as able successfully to accomplish behaviors required to produce desirable outcomes in many different settings. However, high outcome expectancies are not as related to good mental health as are efficacy expectations, since individuals may see themselves as personally efficacious but still be unable to effect desired change due to situational and environmental constraints. One may feel personally efficacious but still not be able to obtain a desired outcome simply because the situation is such that no one would be able to obtain that outcome in those circumstances. However, it would be expected that consistently low outcome expectations across many situations would eventually have an impact on one's mental health.

Dowd (1976) has presented a related definition of mental health. He sees mental health as resulting from one's perception of control over one's environment. Individuals who do not feel a sense of control in one area may attempt to compensate by striving for more control in the other, thus those who feel a lack of control over their immediate environment may compensate by seeking increasing control over themselves. Likewise, those who feel on the ragged edge of losing personal control may compensate by stressing their control over others in their environment, such as work subordinates or family. Especially intriguing is the idea that some individuals may purposefully choose to fail as the only perceived way of establishing control (i.e., choice) in their lives. One thinks of students who, after repeated academic failures, find failure to be a way of life and give up in relief.

These concepts of perceived efficacy or control have been linked to feelings of helplessness; those who see themselves as lacking a sense of self-efficacy or control are likely to feel helpless. Helplessness in turn has been experimentally linked to depression (cf. Seligman, 1975). Thus, there is evidence that those who lack a solid sense of self-efficacy may be especially prone to depression.

Competence Theory

More directly than others, White (1963, 1973) has addressed the issue of what constitutes the healthy personality. He considers that a sense of competence or mastery is crucial to an individual's self-esteem of mental health and appears to regard striving for competence as a universal motive. He further feels that competence and interests are related in such a way that healthy individuals possess strong interests in one or more activities. These interests are often sufficiently strong, White says, to organize an entire life pattern and to provide meaning and direction in life.

A number of important concepts regarding the healthy personality emerge from the above discussion as aspects of the mentally healthy adult. First, the healthy individual should have a sense of competence, mastery, and control over self and large sections of the environment, especially the former. Second, the healthy adult should have the ability to operate successfully in "the world as it is" and to achieve his/her goals and objectives within the context of that culture. Third, the healthy person should be able to distance sufficiently from basic needs and the demands of society to feel a sense of internal freedom. Fourth, the healthy individual should be capable of expending sustained effort in the pursuit of some strong interest or interests involving a substantial degree of commitment over time.

The Function of Leisure in Optimizing Mental Health

There appear to be a number of potential contributions that leisure can make to the formation of the healthy personality. Several are implicit in the literature on adult development, while others can be drawn from the literature on basic human needs and their modes of satisfaction. These contributions will now be discussed.

Promoting Identification Through Leisure

Identification can be defined "as an automatic, unconscious mental process whereby an individual becomes like another person in one or several aspects" (Moore & Fine, 1968, p. 50). Identification aids in the learning of a variety of interests, ideals, personal attributes, goals, and language. It has been widely discussed as a primary mechanism in childhood development, but it has recently been seen as important in adult development as well. An especially important form of adult identification is seen in the mentor relationship, where a younger worker forms a close working relationship with an older worker and thus is aided in learning the social aspects of a trade or profession (Colarusso & Nemiroff, 1981). Levinson, Darrow, Klein, Levinson, and McKee (1978) have also discussed the importance of the mentor relationship, both to the development of the mentor and to the one who is mentored.

Identifications most commonly revolve around occupational relationships and personal characteristics, but they can also involve interests, goals, and values. The latter are especially important in leisure identifications. The noted columnist Sidney Harris recently observed that when young people were asked to choose whom they most admired, they almost invariably chose prominent

figures in the entertainment field. Harris went on to lament the absence of figures in business, science, and education as identification objects. Whom we
identify with says a lot about how we see ourselves as individuals. As leisure
has become more important in our lives, we appear to have increasingly identified with leisure figures, often, however, of the most transitory type. It would
appear that a conscious effort to promote identification with leisure figures of
greater solidity might be helpful to assisting young people and adults to develop different interests, values, and goals. As Iso-Ahola (1980) has noted,
leisure can be destructive as well as constructive.

Providing for Increased Autonomy Through Leisure

White (1976) has described the process of adult development and coping as
one of increased autonomy, as the individual constantly assimilates material
from the environment in order to expand the range of functioning and to
enhance self-determination. Likewise, Neulinger (1981) considers that the task
of leisure education is to teach people to be autonomous and independent in
thinking. Both advocate a high degree of autonomy as conducive to good mental health. It is readily apparent that many individuals do not have much opportunity in their lives for expression of autonomy, especially those for whom
work is highly routinized. These people can be helped to express through their
leisure activities the autonomy that is missing from the rest of their lives and
that is widely considered to be important to mental health. Leisure counseling
that is devoted to the expansion of autonomous and creative activities can significantly add to human happiness.

Providing for Mastery Experiences Through Leisure

The importance of a sense of mastery and competence in the healthy personality was noted earlier. Colarusso and Nemiroff (1981) have also described
mastery of various tasks as an important aspect of adult development in all cultures. Gould (1978) has described not only the shift towards increasing mastery
of events and feelings that characterizes the transition from childhood to adulthood, but also the left-over "childhood demons" of lack of mastery that plague
all adults. He considers that the evolution of adult consciousness involves gradual elimination of these residual fears of not being able to cope. Likewise, Iso-
Ahola (1980; Chapter 4) has presented considerable data indicating that
individuals tend to choose those leisure activities that help satisfy their need for
competence, activities they can do well. However, there is also evidence indicating that the process of learning new leisure skills provides for an increased feeling of competence and control (Iso-Ahola, 1980). Many people have few
opportunities in their lives to engage in competence-enhancing or mastery experiences. Unfortunately, these are precisely the individuals who all too often
fill their leisure time with passive activities, such as watching television and

spectator sports, activities that contribute essentially nothing to a sense of mastery and competence.

It may seem strange that, given the data indicating that people tend to choose competence-enhancing activities, so many people rely on passive leisure activities. Individuals are often not aware of alternatives, however, and inertia and habit are powerful forces in determining our leisure (as well as other) pursuits. Leisure counseling devoted to increasing awareness of competence-enhancing experiences and actual participation in competence-enhancing activities can significantly aid to developing an individual's sense of mastery and control.

Providing for an Increased Sense of Freedom Through Leisure

If one attribute can be considered as the defining characteristic of the leisure experience, it would be the perception of freedom to participate or not, as one chooses (Iso-Ahola, 1980, Chapter 4; Neulinger, 1981a). Freedom appears to be the central defining characteristic of what constitutes leisure. One who feels constrained to perform even the most enjoyable task will likely not feel at leisure.

Furthermore, the perception of freedom appears to involve freedom from external constraints, rather than internal (Bordin, 1979). An individual may feel tremendous inner compulsion to perform an activity, or to achieve well in it, but only as long as the compulsion is perceived to emanate from within will he/she be likely to label the activity as leisure. For example, a violinist may spend long hours and much effort in practicing for an amateur concert and feel a great deal of internal compulsion to perform well, yet label the experience as leisure. Thus, although leisure activities may involve a high degree of intense, concentrated effort, to the extent that they are free of external constraints they contribute to the individual's sense of personal freedom and the leisure experience.

Providing for Spontaneous Commitment and Involvement Through Leisure

Bordin (1979) has recently discussed the historical differentiation between play, which epitomizes freedom and spontaneity, and work, which requires effort and compulsion. What is needed, he argues, is a fusion of spontaneity and disciplined effort and commitment such that the traditional distinction between work and leisure is reduced. Commonly held is the idea that leisure involves little effort and no commitment. However, if leisure is to play a significant role in the enhancement of mental health, it is necessary that this notion be overcome, lest the leisure experience be trivialized. Already in some circles leisure is equated with inconsequential and ephermeral diversion, resulting in a certain contempt and scorn for the "leisure life-style." The lives of many adults are relatively free from serious commitments and disciplined, long-term effort. Leisure activities, properly understood, can provide a source of spontaneous commitment so important for a healthy life-style. This is especially significant for those individuals who have few other sources for the expression of commitment and disciplined activity in their lives, such as the retired (see Myers, Chapter 6).

Promoting a Sense of Community and Relationship with Others Through Leisure

People, as the saying goes, need other people; the ability to relate easily and well with others is an important attribute of the mentally healthy adult. Yet, there are relatively few opportunities in modern life for adults to relate to others and satisfy their need for community. With the decline of churches as important institutions in many people's lives, and the disappearance of the extended family and the immediate neighborhood as primary sources of community, a large number of people find their primary relationships with others deriving from work and the nuclear family. In some subcultures, of course, neighorhood and extended family relationships, as well as churches, provide important sources of relationships. For the majority of adults, however, the neighborhood is simply a place to live and close relatives live at some distance.

For these individuals leisure activities may provide a major and perhaps the only source of significant interpersonal relationships. Work was never intended to be a major source of interpersonal gratification and those who attempt to meet their interpersonal needs through their occupation risk disillusionment and burnout if others do not respond in like fashion. In addition, one can seldom surround one's self with like-minded people at work, while one can choose leisure activities on this basis. Therefore, leisure activities engaged in with individuals similar to one's self and organized around common interests can contribute greatly to a sense of community and close interpersonal relationships. This function of leisure in developing and maintaining interpersonal skills and a sense of community has been discussed in some detail by Iso-Ahola (1980; Chapter 4).

Promoting Life Balance Through Leisure

Many individuals lead very unbalanced lives, where their daily activities are narrow in scope, channelized in direction, and routinized in nature. For example, many adult men engage primarily in occupational activities designed to ensure career advancement, while many adult women engage primarily in home- and child-centered activities. As a result of this lack of balance, many psychological needs may go unmet.

There is substantial evidence that people will seek to satisfy unmet needs (Bloland & Edwards, 1981); when they are unable to do so satisfactorily, the result is often frustration and discontent. As stated earlier, work was not intended to satisfy all of an individual's needs, relationship and otherwise. Therefore, many leisure activities are designed, deliberately or not, to be either compensatory or supplemental to work (Allen, 1980).

Compensatory and supplemental leisure activities are similar in that they both seek to provide experiences, associations, and settings that are missing in the individual's daily round of activities. Thus, the university professor who spends his/her day in abstract, intellectual pursuits may engage in leisure activities of a strenuous physical nature. Blocher and Siegal (Chapter 2) have discussed this point and its implications in some detail. The human duality expressed so well by Robert Louis Stevenson in *Dr. Jeykll and Mr. Hyde* is a part of all of us; needs that are consistently denied or unexpressed will seek expression with increasing force as we age (Levinson et al., 1978), a point to which we will return later. Leisure may be the only area of life in which people have the freedom and flexibility to engage in activities designed to restore balance and satisfy unmet needs.

Promoting Creativity and Self-expression Through Leisure

The correct use of leisure can foster creative and divergent thinking. Most of the intellectual and physical activities of people are problem-solving, goal-directed, and convergent in nature. Leisure experiences provide one of the few opportunities in the lives of most individuals to engage in exploratory and creative activity, where the end result is a satisfying process rather than an end product. Perhaps it is precisely those people whose occupations foster divergent thinking who appear to have little need for leisure or who seem to have effectively fused work and leisure (Allen, 1980). Blocher and Siegal (Chapter 2) refer tangentially to this point when they note that leisure can provide "an opportunity to explore, with less constraint, novel interests and conceptualizations." The increase in self-expression that lesiure experiences can provide is another method of restoring balance to life, which was discussed earlier.

Providing Personal Meaning to Life Through Leisure

The search for life meaning is a central developmental task of adulthood, especially for the elderly (see Myers, Chapter 6). As discussed later, there are several times in adult life where questions of life meaning become especially salient. Until recently (and still true in many cases), men found primary meaning in their lives through their occupations, while women found primary meaning through their homes and interpersonal relationships. That this is changing is too obvious to require further discussion; what is not so obvious is that nothing has replaced these activities as creators of meaning. Leisure is especially well-equipped to provide meaning to life, in part because leisure satisfaction and perceived quality of life are significantly related (Iso-Ahola, 1980; Neulinger, 1981a, b), and in part because the leisure experience involves intrinsic motivation (Iso-Ahola, 1980; Neulinger, 1981a). Intrinsic motivation, which arises from within the individual, is much more likely to result in personally meaningful activity that that extrinsically motivated. The meaningless tasks of life tend to be those that are done because one must.

Stages of Adult Development

Leisure needs and activities differ over the life span, as even the most casual consideration will suggest. The next section will address the stages of adult development and developmental tasks that must be mastered within each stage, according to several models of adult development. This will set the stage for a discussion of the role of leisure in adult life.

The period with which we are concerned in this chapter, from early adulthood in the early 20s to retirement at about 65-70, has been described by several writers. This section will describe the major stages of this period as proposed by these authors and provide a synthesis of the kinds of tasks and transitions that face adults during this critical time.

Perhaps the most widely known stage theory of adult development is that presented by Erikson (1963), in which the entire life cycle is divided into stages with tasks and dangers for each stage. The stages with which we are concerned here include Intimacy versus Isolation and Generativity versus Stagnation. Erikson's work is seminal and subsequent developmentalists have built heavily on his ideas.

In the Intimacy versus Isolation stage, the young adult, having just discovered his/her identity, must now in part risk losing it in achieving intimacy with another person. This is much more than genital intimacy, but includes the willingness and ability to share mutual trust and long-term commitment with another, with whom one regulates cycles of work, play, and procreation. The danger of this stage is isolation, the unwillingness to involve oneself with and commit oneself to another individual. At its most fundamental level, this isolation is an unwillingness or inability to become involved with others, whether individuals or groups, in the multitudinous tasks of daily life.

Generativity can take many forms, but the central task is that of establishing and guiding the next generation. Although the most common form is the raising of children, other forms of generativity include any activity designed to produce something that outlasts the individual, such as founding a company, mentoring younger workers, or teaching school. Indeed, generativity could almost be redefined as productivity and creativity, in which there is an increasing expansion of interests and involvement with other people, institutions, and the world with a heavy investment in the outcome.

Stagnation occurs when this expansion fails to take place and the individual becomes increasingly obsessed with self and increasingly unwilling to take risks. Withdrawal from involvement with others occurs as the person turns all energies and concern upon self, resulting in a sense of personal impoverishment.

As a result of closely studying the adaptive coping styles of the Grant Study men, and drawing heavily on Erikson, Vaillant (1977) has described the life cycle of adult men in our culture. His stages include Intimacy and Career Consolidation (20-30), Generativity - A Second Adolescence (the 40s), and Keeping the Meaning vs. Rigidity (the 50s). In the first stage, the tasks are to achieve intimacy (generally defined as a stable marriage) and to begin carving a career (i.e., "making it"). During this period, the men focused largely, sometimes almost exclusively, on their careers, with a corresponding impoverishment in their interpersonal and expressive behavior.

By age 40 or so, the stage of generativity had begun, and the men were much more concerned with assisting others and achieving results through the efforts of others. They had often embarked on a rebirth of activity and energy, sometimes in entirely new directions. They showed more signs of being vitally alive, had obtained a sense of perspective on themselves and their accomplishments, and were generally able to laugh at themselves. There was a lessening of the career push and a greater involvement in interpersonal relations, as they reached out more to others.

During the fifties, the men reported a greater contentment with what they had, were increasingly likely to know what they valued and to take a stand, and were devoted to seeing the culture carried on rather than replaced. As John Kennedy once said, "The torch is passed."

Gould (1978) has described adult development through the midlife decade in terms of the following stages: Breaking loose from parents, "I'm nobody's baby now" (22-28), Opening up to what's inside (28-34), and the mid-life decade (35-45). The first stage is characterized by the ambivalences of separating from parents, yet retaining them as a safe harbor in case of trouble. The second stage involves the questioning of the rules and patterns of the twenties, while remaking the implicit contracts that had been made with others. There is a more realistic sense of one's powers and limitations, and where one wants to go. During the mid-life decade, one comes to terms with death and the limitation of time and with one's vulnerability and splits. Levinson and his colleagues (Levinson et al., 1978) have provided the most detailed look at adult male development in their intensive study of 40 men. They divided adult life into three eras, with several periods within each era. Of particular concern here are the periods Entering the Adult World (22-28), the Age Thirty Transition (28-33), Settling Down (33-40), the Mid-Life Transition (40-45), and Entering Middle Adulthood (45-50).

Levinson et al. essentially describe an adult life-style characterized by fits and starts. Thus, during the Entering the Adult World period, a man is making some initial choices and building first commitments in a provisional life structure. Then, during the Age Thirty Transition, he becomes increasingly uneasy and convinced that something is missing in his life. Often, changes and new directions are initiated during this stage or previous commitments are reaffirmed.

The Settling Down period involves the establishment of a definite life structure in which certain aspects of one's life are accorded primacy, most notably career and instrumental actions, and others are put aside and suppressed. The two tasks of this period are to establish one's niche in society and to advance. The suppressed aspects of man include expressive and interpersonal behaviors and (often) home and family life.

During the Mid-Life Transition, everything is reappraised again as the individual reviews his life and its meaning up to this point, begins to change negative parts of his present life and to test new choices, and begins to deal with the polarities in his life. Often, whole new life structures are created at this time and radical changes made in life-style, although more commonly the changes made are relatively minor. What is apparent, however, and what has given rise to the term "mid-life crisis" is that this period is characterized by a profound reappraisal of the meaning of one's life to that time and a setting of directions for the remainder of one's life.

If the reevaluative tasks of the Mid-Life Transition are handled satisfactorily, the individual is prepared to enter Middle Adulthood. This period is characterized by the development of a new life structure that can endure for the remainder of the person's life and often by a period of renewed vigor and purpose. Of especial interest is the fact that those individuals who underwent the most upheaval during the Mid-Life Transition are generally the ones who create the most stable structure during Middle Adulthood.

Several significant themes emerge from Levinson's work. One is the importance of the Dream, which is a youthful view of the future self that never dies. The Dream is suppressed during the period of Settling Down, only to reemerge during the Mid-Life Transition. The Dream can often provide the organizing principle for middle adulthood and beyond. Another important theme is the reemergence of the suppressed aspects of the self during the Mid-Life Transition; for men this is generally the expressive and interpersonal parts of the personality. This period is thus a time of increased openness to new experiences, both internal and external, and a time of increased sensitivity to others and a more objective view of self and reality. The third important theme is the crucial significance of mentoring in the lives of people. It is important to the mentor since it gives significance to his life at the period of Mid-Life Transition and it is significant to the one who is mentored since it is a way of introducing him into the occupation or social situation. It is an important aspect of becoming one's own man.

Most of the research on adult developmental stages to date has been done on men, and the development of women in adulthood is less clear. Nevertheless, it appears that many of the stages discussed above apply to women as well, especially those who have independent careers (Levinson et al., 1978). However, there do appear to be some significant differences. Women may tend to be governed more by the "vicarious achievement ethic" in which they gain their identities from the activities of significant people in their lives, rather than from themselves (Lipman-Blumen, 1972). More significantly, it appears that as men are rediscovering the more intuitive, expressive side of themselves during the Mid-Life Transition, women are at the same time discovering the more instrumental, assertive side of themselves (Neugarten & Gutman, 1958; Gould, 1978). Finally, since women are usually involved with childbearing and rearing during their early years, the appearance of the stages appear to occur later than the corresponding stages in men (Gould, 1978).

In the light of the above discussions, how can developmental stages in adult life be summarized? The research done to date seems to point to the existence of a common pattern of adult development. The basic tasks of the 20s seem to be the initial creation of a tentative career and life direction and intimacy with another person. Around age 30, there is a reevaluation of this life direction and major or minor changes may be made, or the present direction may be confirmed. The subsequent period is characterized by intensive goal-directed behavior primarily (at least in men) of an occupational nature. During this time, significant aspects of the personality are generally suppressed. Around age 40 there is an even more far-reaching reappraisal of one's life, often resulting in major changes in activities and life direction. Assisting the next generation becomes of primary importance, and the previously suppressed parts of the personality begin to emerge. Those who go through a profound reexamination at this time are ultimately better able to chart a meaningful direction for the remainder of their lives than those for whom this transition is less profound. In middle adulthood there is an increasingly comfortable sense of who one is and what one has accomplished and an increased emphasis on guiding others and achieving through others. In women, this time may be one of increased self-exploration and self-direction as well as a newly found assertiveness. Psychologial and even physical differences between men and women become less pronounced (Dacey, 1982) and a new spirit of acommodation between spouses is often apparent. The life-cycle is beginning to wind down.

The Role of Leisure in Adult Life

In light of the above discussion of adult developmental stages, how can leisure activities assist individuals in successfully coping with the transitions of adult life and furthering growth and change? This section will outline the changing role that leisure can play throughout the life span and various rationales for different leisure pursuits at different stages of life.

Recall that the 20s are characterized by the creation of a tentative career and life-style, as well as beginning of intimacy with another. It is typical of this age, however, that leisure tends to be relatively unplanned, formless, inchoate, and directionless. In part this may be an outgrowth of the "default" leisure activities that are engaged in by so many youth (Loesch, Chapter 5) or the destructive leisure patterns referred to by Iso-Ahola (1980) that result from inadequate leisure socialization of youth. Just as leisure activities of youth must often be enhanced, so too should those of early adults. Unfortunately, young adults are generally too occupied with the other developmental tasks of that period to pay much attention to their leisure development; they are more concerned with "lieben und arbeiten."

It is not enough to love and to work, one must also learn to play in order to achieve a sense of balance in life. This stage of life is noted for its trial behaviors and its tentative commitments; as noted by Dowd (1981), leisure can provide a trial preparation for a multitude of tasks that can add richness and depth to life in a sort of "laboratory for learning." Blocher and Siegal (Chapter 2) make a similar point when they state that leisure provides an opportunity to explore novel interests and concepts with fewer constraints. Levinson et al. (1978) have stated that an important task of this period is to discover and generate alternative options. Leisure experiences, deliberately chosen to be dissimilar to other life activities, can help to maintain this exploratory stance by providing additional experiences and preventing premature closure. In leisure, roles and tasks can be experimented with under conditions of low threat and with minimum commitment and accountability. Carefully chosen leisure experiences can add the spontaneity and joy called for by Bordin (1979) and can provide an occasion and a setting for the development of further intimacy with a significant other (see Orthner & Herron, Chapter 7). Few areas of an individual's life provide the opportunity for the expression of intimacy; leisure has that potential. Many relationships, especially at the beginning, have foundered on the rocks of overinvolvement with individual activities such as work.

The danger of this stage, as noted by Erikson (1963), is that of isolation. Leisure experiences, insofar as they involve social activities, can do much to reduce incipient isolation and can provide an opportunity for the development of a variety of social skills. Likewise, the kind of leisure one engages in during this stage can have a significant impact on subsequent life-style and quality of life. Havighurst and Feigenbaum (1968), for example, found that a leisure-style described as community centered, in which the individual participated in a wide variety of community activities, was characteristic of people who scored uniformly high on performance in the eight social roles of work — parent, spouse, homemaker, leisure, friend, citizen, and clubs, and associations. As Myers (Chapter 6) has noted, the best way to assume a good use of leisure in old age is to inculcate it in youth. The past is the best predictor of the future.

The age 30 transition is a time for reevaluation of the life-style and an opportunity for renewal, change, and growth. Some life changes are usually made during this period, although they may be relatively minor in nature. If a vital program of leisure activities has not yet been initiated, now is a good time to begin. Since they are already asking questions regarding further life direction, people are more receptive to change than they have been up to this point or will be again until the mid-life transition. As has been noted frequently in the crisis intervention literature, individuals are more open to change and more receptive to influence from others during times of change, stress, and transition. Leisure counseling at this point can help provide for a broader range of experiences in the years to come and, by reducing the progressive narrowing of interests that characterize the 30s, can contribute to a smoother mid-life transition.

The theme of the 30s is work, work, and work! Levinson et al. (1978) refer to this period as that of "settling down" and state that the tasks are to establish one's niche and to work at advancement in one's career. Erikson (1963) refers to this period as that of Generativity (although that stage for Erikson incorporates the remainder of life up to old age) and considers that it is akin to productivity and creativity. Vaillant (1977) refers to this period as that of career consolidation. Thus, especially for men, the 30s are equated with a work-oriented lifestyle, more appropriately perhaps named a work-style.

The 30s are a particularly humorless time (Levinson et al., 1978; Vaillant, 1977). Men especially during this period take themselves very seriously and have great difficulty looking at themselves and their lives in an objective, detached fashion. They are extremely goal-oriented, often sacrificing most other aspects of life to career advancement and seldom stopping to "smell the flowers." It is generally during this period that the "workaholic" syndrome flowers, which is often difficult to shake in later life. Leisure often plays a small part in an individual's life during this period.

The work-leisure relationship has been one of the more frequently examined topics in the leisure literature. Winters and Hansen (1976) argue that the literature on work-leisure relationships boils down to polarity or fusion: polarity in that leisure is a means to escape work and fusion in that one participates in leisure as part of the work process. Polarity seems to be the process for the semiskilled or unskilled, while fusion is more characteristic of those in managerial positions. Allen (1980) discusses these concepts in more detail and considers that the common element among the fusion, spillover, and extension concepts is that work and leisure involvement are seen as similar, in that each has an effect on the other. The polarity, compensatory, and opposition concepts stress the differences between involvement in leisure (see Blocher & Siegal, Chapter 2, and Loesch, Chapter 5, for a description of these terms). Bordin (1978) advocates the fusion of effort and compulsion that characterizes work with the freedom and spontaneity that characterizes leisure in a creative whole.

Several writers have gone even further and have viewed work and leisure as different aspects of the same process. Thus, McDaniels (1977) considers that leisure can and should complement work and give meaning to an individual's life. He has developed the equation, *Vocation* = *Work* + *Leisure* (V = W + L). Blocher and Siegal (Chapter 2) present a detailed rationale for viewing work and leisure as subjects of the general concept of career.

Leisure can have a significant psychological impact on a person's life during the 30s. In particular, carefully chosen leisure experiences can provide for novelty and a level of optimal arousal (Blocher & Siegal, Chapter 2; Iso-Ahola, Chapter 4) in a period characterized by decreasing novelty and static arousal. A life devoted to career and "making it" is hardly conducive to increasing novelty in life. Yet according to Iso-Ahola (1980; Chapter 4), the tendency to seek novel forms of leisure arises from early adulthood in middle adulthood, subsequently declining throughout the remainder of life. Simultaneously, the need for familiar forms of leisure is at a low ebb during early adulthood, rising continuously after middle adulthood. Thus, a deliberate focus on novel leisure experiences providing for optimal arousal can assist the individual in adding diversity, interest, and balance to life.

In a similar vein, Blocher and Siegal (Chapter 2) have proposed that adult development is characterized by increasing attraction to stimuli involving higher levels of novelty, complexity, ambiguity, and abstraction. To deny these is to risk stultifying the growth and development of the individual; yet the lives of many people in their 30s (except those at higher executive levels) lack all or most of these elements. Leisure experiences can insure that these needs of the developing person are met and leisure counseling can assist in providing those experiences.

The period of the 30s is characterized primarily by extriniscally motivated activities, revolving around "must do" activities both at home and at work. As noted by Iso-Ahola (Chapter 4), intrinsic motivation is at the heart of leisure behavior. Lesiure experiences may likely be, in fact, the *only* area in an individual's life where intrinsic motivation or activities freely engaged in may be possible at all (Dowd, 1983) during this time of life. As noted earlier, a sense of freedom and autonomy is important for good mental health in adults, so the sense of freedom provided by leisure can be crucial.

The existence of a "mid-life crisis" has been widely discussed in both the popular and scholarly literature during the last few years. Although the term "crisis" may be a bit strong (Levinson et al., 1978; Neugarten, 1964), there seems to be little doubt that adults go through a period of doubt and questioning during the late 30s to middle 40s. The issues dealt with at this time include a reappraisal of the past and making choices about the future (Levinson et al., 1978), an increased exploration of the inner world (Vaillant, 1977), an increased sense of the pressure of time (Gould, 1978), and the discrepancy between career aspirations and career achievements (Colarusso & Nemiroff, 1981). During this period, the individual is more open to changes and new experiences than almost any other time of life. It appears that, paradoxically, those people who undergo the most profound agony and reappraisal during this period are precisely those who emerge with renewed energy, purpose, and productivity during their middle and later years. Likewise, those individuals who go through the mid-life transition without a ripple are often those who lose their sense of purpose and productivity in later years and stagnate (Gould, 1978).

A major theme during this period is that of meaning: meaning of life, of one's activities to that point, and of future endeavors. Heretofore, especially for men, meaning in life has tended to be derived from occupational accomplishment, while for many women, meaning has been derived from home activities and child-raising. With the slowing down or ceasing of occupational advancement and the "empty nest," both men and women are forced to find other activities in life from which to derive meaning and significance (Colarusso & Nemiroff, 1981).

Leisure is potentially well equipped to provide the life meaning increasingly not provided by work. Thus, McDaniels (1977) argues that at mid-life, leisure can provide a sense of self-fulfillment and mastery not found in work. Furthermore, leisure interests developed during this period can be continued into retirement and provide continuity from full-time work to full-time leisure. Similarly, Wilkinson (1975) states that as work has lost much of its ability to give meaning to life, a leisure orientation can be especially useful for (1) workaholics, to avoid stress from too much achievement; (2) alcoholics, who have made a satisfactory vocational and social adjustment, but who cannot cope with free time; (3) disadvantaged, in that jobs they usually get cannot satisfy their intrinsic needs; and (4) severely disabled, in that it is an alternative to free time emptiness.

Especially significant during the adult years are problems related to stress and burnout. Selye (1974) has defined stress as the nonspecific response of the body to any demand made upon it, although popular language seems to equate it with stimulus overload. Burnout is the lack of interest or response that results when individuals can no longer see any results or rewards for their exertions. Both reach their peak in the period just prior to middle adulthood.

Although the popular notion is that all stress is bad and must be reduced whenever possible, in actual fact one can suffer from too little stress as well as too much. Stress can be thought of a simply stimulation. Selye (1974) has identified two types of stress: distress, which is bad stress, and eustress, which is good stress. The following discussion will focus on ways in which leisure activities can reduce the former and enhance the latter.

Distress, or stimulus overload, can be reduced via leisure activities in a number of ways. It has been known for some time that physical exercise can significantly reduce stress responses (Cleaver & Eisenhart, 1982; Sachs, 1982; Sachs & Buffone, 1983). In particular, running or jogging appears to be beneficial in reducing anxiety and depression (cf. Morgan, 1980; Buffone & Dowd, 1981), although the effects of physical activity are relatively transitory in nature. In order for exercise to be maximally beneficial, one must *keep* exercising. For those individuals for whom strenuous activity is not appropriate, more passive activities have been found to be of help in reducing stress as well (Cleaver & Eisenhart, 1982), especially if participants are enabled to "lose themselves" in a feeling of timelessness (see McDowell, Chapter 1). Some level of physical activity, however, is helpful for almost everyone.

Despite the wide publicity given to the effects of distress, or stimulus overload, the effects of eustress are perhaps even more insidious, partly because they are less obvious. Recall from the previous discussion that leisure experiences have the function of enhancing feelings of competence and mastery and increasing one's level of optimal arousal (see also Chapter 4), and that these are important in optimizing mental health. Bunting (1982) has advocated participation in challenging activities as a way of providing for a higher level of stimulation and arousal as well as increasing focused attention on a task. Mitchell (1982) has discussed the novelty value inherent in leisure stress and has pointed out that there are today few opportunities in the lives of most individuals for complete expression of personal creativity, freedom, and commitment, all of which have been mentioned earlier as important to mental health. Restrictive social and occupational structures often stifle our best abilities. James (1982) has conceptualized bordeom as the stress of predictability and has suggested that leisure activities can provide novelty value and expand limits, as well as increasing feelings of mastery and consequent self-esteem.

Burnout results when individuals can no longer see results to themselves or others from their efforts, and is expressed in lack of energy, lack of interest, and irritability. It is especially prevalent in the human services professions, where it is responsible for a significant turnover of staff each year. Participation in leisure activities where one can see a result from one's efforts can help in alleviating this serious problem.

Appropriate leisure activities, developed through leisure counseling, can thus do much to reduce both the effects of overstress as well as the less obvious efforts of understress. The effects of the latter are especially insidious, as they are less noticeable and can rob large numbers of individuals of their energy, creativity, and zest for life. Ultimately, the cost in reduced effectiveness is borne by society.

By middle adulthood, the individual is ready to make a commitment to new choices and a new life structure (Levinson et al., 1978), is more concerned with helping people than achieving (Erikson, 1963), has become more inner-directed (Gould, 1978), is more concerned with questions of ultimate meaning, and has developed a secure and comfortable identity (Vaillant, 1977). Unfortunately, there is often a concommitant rigidity that can result in less willingness to change and less tolerance for unusual behavior in others. However, a new flowering of creativity and productivity can also develop if the individual has worked through the previous mid-life transition.

Leisure patterns have shifted somewhat by the late 40s and early 50s, from active pursuits to more sedentary activities (Myers, Chapter 6) and from physical leisure to more intellectual leisure (Colarusso & Nemiroff, 1981). Although there are large individual differences in the magnitude of this shift, in general, adults in the middle years are less physical active than they were earlier. However, it is important to maintain a certain modicum of physically activity in order to maintain health and vigor in later years.

It is in this period that preretirement planning can profitably begin and, indeed, is one of the most significant targets for leisure counseling services. Myers (Chapter 6) has discussed the need for preretirement counseling and the contribution it can make towards life adjustment in later years.

A crucial need during this period is for leisure experiences to be as diverse as possible and to allow for the incorporation of new activities as well. With increasing rigidity comes the danger that *all* activity patterns, including those of leisure, will ossify. Although, as Iso-Ahola (Chapter 4) points out, there is a greater tendency to seek familiar forms of leisure and a corresponding reduction in the tendency to seek novel leisure activities, everyone needs *some* novelty.

Although lesiure activities may have become less physical and more intellectual by this time, this can be viewed as positive. Leisure chosen wisely in previous years should have aided the individual in achieving higher cognitive levels, which in turn should make intellectual forms of leisure even more enjoyable in the middle and late years. Thus, as Blocher and Siegal (Chapter 2) suggest, aging persons may be increasingly attracted to leisure stimuli of higher cognitive complexity.

Summary

This chapter has developed a concept of mentally healthy adulthood drawn from a variety of theoretical writings on the healthy personality and has described in detail the role that lesiure experiences can play in optimizing mental health. After a review of the stages of adult development, the role of leisure in each of these stages was described. It can be seen that leisure counseling interventions are more likely to be successful during periods of searching and questioning, such as the Age 30 Transition and the Mid-Life Transition, as the individual is already receptive to change. While preventive efforts might be best focused at these times, remedial efforts can and should occur at any time. The overall framework for analysis consisted of a description of the psychological deficits that occur in each stage of adulthood and suggestions as to how leisure experiences could remedy these deficits and increase balance in life at all stages. The notion of balance is central to this chapter; leisure is seen as providing for a richness and diversity to life that is difficult to acquire in other ways. Lives that consist of a relatively narrow range of activities providing for limited stimulation are seen as detrimental to both the individual and society, whereas lives enriched by a wise and productive use of leisure are ultimately of great benefit both to the individual concerned and to the larger culture. Societies that foster and develop a wide range of stimulating leisure activities are truly civilized.

REFERENCES

Allen, L.R. Leisure and its relationship to work and career guidance. *Vocational Guidance Quarterly*, 1980, *28*, 257-262.

Bandura, A. *Social learning theory.* Englewood Cliffs, N.J.: Prentice-Hall, Inc., 1977.

Bloland, P.A., & Edwards, P.B. Work and leisure: A counseling synthesis. *Vocational Guidance Quarterly*, 1981, *27*, 101-108.

Bordin, E.S. Fusing work and play: A challenge to theory and research. *Academic Psychology Bulletin*, 1977, *1*(1), 5-9.

Buffone, G.W., & Dowd, E.T. *Psychological changes associated with cognitive behavioral therapy and an aerobic running program in the treatment of depression.* Paper presented at the Association for Advancement of Behavior Therapy Convention, Toronto, 1981.

Bunting, C.J. Managing stress through challenge activities. *Journal of Physical Education and Recreation*, October, 1982, *53*, 48-49.

Cleaver, V., & Eisenhart, H. Stress reduction through effective use of leisure. *Journal of Physical Education and Recreation*, October, 1982, *53*, 33-34.

Colarusso, C.A., & Nemiroff, R.A. *Adult development.* New York: Plenum Press, 1981.

Dacey, J.S. *Adult development.* Glenview, Ill.: Scott, Foresman & Co., 1982.

Dowd, E.T. The Goetterdaemmerung syndrome. *Counseling and Values*, 1976, *20*, 139-142.

Dowd, E.T. Leisure counseling: Summary of an emerging field. In E.T. Dowd (Ed.), Leisure counseling. *The Counseling Psychologist*, 1981, *9*(3), 81-82.

Dowd, E.T. Leisure counseling. *Wiley encyclopedia of psychology.* New York: Wiley, 1983.

Erikson, E.H. *Childhood and society.* New York: W.W. Norton & Co., Inc., 1963.

Gould, R.L. *Transformations: Growth and change in adult life.* New York: Simon and Schuster, 1978.

Havighurst, R.J., & Feighenbaum, K. Leisure and life-style. In B.L. Neugarten, *Middle age and aging.* Chicago: University of Chicago Press, 1968.

Iso-Ahola, S.E. *The social psychology of leisure and recreation.* Dubuque, Iowa: Wm. C. Brown Co., 1980.

James, A. Boredom — The stress of predictability. *Journal of Physical Education and Recreation*, October, 1982, *53*, 35-36.

Levinson, D.J. Darrow, C.N., Klein, E.B., Levinson, M.H., & McKee, B. *The seasons of a man's life.* New York: Knopf, 1978.

Lipman-Blumen, J. How ideology shapes women's lives. *Scientific American*, January, 1972, *226*(1), 34-54.

McDaniels, C. Leisure and career development at mid-life: A rationale. *Vocational Guidance Quarterly*, 1977, *25*, 344-349.

Mitchell, R.G. The benefits of leisure stress. *Journal of Physical Education and Recreation*, October, 1982, *53*, 50-51.

Moore, B., & Fine, B. *A glossary of psychoanalytic terms and concepts.* New York: American Psychoanalytic Association, 1968.

Morgan, W.P. Psychological benefits of physical activity. In F.J. Nagle & H.J. Montoye (Eds.) *Exercise, health and disease.* Springfield, Il.: Charles C Thomas, 1980.

Neugarten, B.L. & Gutman, D.L. Age-sex roles and personality in middle life: A thematic apperception study. *Psychological Monographs*, 1958, *72*, No. 17 (Whole No. 470).

Neugarten, B.L. *Personality in middle and late life.* New York: Atherton, 1964.

Neulinger, J. *The psychology of leisure* (2nd ed.). Springfield, Il.: Charles C Thomas, 1981a.

Neulinger, J. *To leisure: An introduction.* Boston: Allyn and Bacon, 1981b.

Sachs, M.L. Running therapy: Change agent in anxiety and stress management. *Journal of Physical Education and Recreation*, October, 1982, *53*, 44-45.

Sachs, M.L. and Buffone, G.W. (Eds.). *The psychology of exercise and running: Research and application.* Lincoln, Nebraska: University of Nebraska Press, 1983.

Seligman, M.E.P. *Helplessness: On depression, development and death.* San Francisco: W.H. Freeman & Co., 1975.

Seyle, H. *Stress without distress.* New York: Lippincott, 1974.

Skinner, B.F. *Science and human behavior.* New York: Macmillan, 1953.

Vaillant, G.E. *Adaptation to life.* Boston: Little, Brown and Co., 1977.

White, R.W. (Ed.). *The study of lives: Essays on personality in honor of Henry A. Murray.* New York: Atherton Press, 1963.

White, R.W. The concept of the healthy personality: What do we really mean? *The Counseling Psychologist*, 1973, *4*(2), 3-12.

White, R.W. Strategies of adaptation: An attempt at systematic description. In R.H. Moos (Ed.), *Human adaptation: Coping with life crises*. Lexington, Mass.: D.C. Heath & Co., 1976.

Wilkinson, M.W. Leisure: An alternative to the meaning of work. *Journal of Applied Rehabilitation Counseling*, 1975, *6*(2), 73-77.

Winters, R.A., & Hansen, J.C. Toward an understanding of work-leisure relationships. *Vocational Guidance Quarterly*, 1976, *24*, 238-243.

Chapter 10

LEISURE ASSESSMENT AND COUNSELING

CHRISTINE Z. HOWE

AS professionals interested in assessment and leisure counseling, it is certainly in order for us to conceptualize leisure as a psychological experience or a state of mind. A contemporary leisure philosopher, Murphy (1977, p. 7), discusses two common and contrasting concepts of leisure: the discretionary time view and the holistic view. The discretionary time view probably appears most frequently in the popular recreation literature. This view equates leisure with free time. Leisure is a portion of time that remains when the obligations of work and tasks of daily living are met. Free time is earned through work and gained only when subsistence responsibilities are met (see Blocher & Siegel, Chapter 2). Thus, we can infer that this "leisure" must be productive. Leisure is largely identified with amusement, activity, diversion, and/or recreation. Leisure is not an end in itself, but a means of refreshing ourselves before we return to work. Leisure finds meaning only through work because work is the central focus of our lives. This view prescribes an activities orientation to leisure in which unobligated time is "constructively" occupied.

The holistic view of leisure is grounded in the ancients' definition of leisure as an attitudinal state that bears no relationship to clock time. The ancients viewed leisure as an end in itself with the highest order of enjoyment being found in contemplation and celebration. Leisure is the enjoyment of experiences for their own sake, without regard to work. Work is a temporary absence from leisure because the purpose of work is to enter into leisure. Work thus finds its meaning only in relation to leisure for leisure is the basis of culture and the very center of life (Bundy, 1977).

In expanding upon this, the holistic view suggests that through our leisure experiences (which may occur while at work or at play) we are of a state of mind that encourages self awareness; the disclosure of our aspirations and feelings; and the expression of them. Assuming that this quest towards self actualization or fulfillment is desirable, then collectively our values may be shifting from the work ethic towards a leisure ethic (Murphy, 1977).

These concepts are important for us individually as professionals to be aware of as we examine the various assessment instruments that exist for use in leisure counseling today. If indeed we accept leisure as a psychological state, then leisure can be interpreted as the opportunity to fulfill a variety of intrinsically motivated needs (Iso-Ahola, 1980). Satisfaction is derived through meeting needs such as competence, mastery, socialization, relaxation, novelty, arousal, and relief from stress. When we feel free to pursue whatever experience we feel meets these needs, then we are intrinsically motivated. We are more likely to find ourselves more deeply into a leisure state (Iso-Ahola, 1982, pp. 32-33). This implies that as counselors, when we are conducting assessments, we are well advised to use instruments that probe beyond simple interest inventories into the identification of intrinsic needs, leisure attitudes, and leisure behaviors or patterns. Leisure is a complex and dialectical process, and assessment is one means of helping us along the path of somehow improving and enhancing the behaviors of our clients. Assessment can be the first step in leading to change in client behavior as a consequence of services delivered (Witt, Connolly, & Compton, 1980, p. 6).

Thus, it can be seen that our philosophical position affects what we deem is important to assess. If "state of mind" is the preferred leisure perspective, then motivation, attitudes, values, perceived freedom, choice, and opportunity will be influential in our choice of variables to "measure" (Witt et al., 1980, pp. 6-7) and, accordingly, what instruments to use.

Overview of Leisure Assessment

There are a variety of ways to define assessment that reflect whether we are narrowly or broadly conceiving the phenomenon. For our purposes, leisure assessment is broadly defined as a process of identification and discovery about client needs, attitudes, values, and behaviors where change, clarifications, improvement, or reinforcement of behavioral functioning is desired. These data are used as a guide in either the provision, development, or facilitation of leisure experiences for the client based upon the changes, clarification, improvement, or reinforcement needed. It is an integral part of the total leisure counseling process that helps us as professionals to make informed decisions with and about our clients (Witt et al., 1980; Loesch & Wheeler, 1982).

This description, at first glance, makes the assessment process sound rather simple. However, when we examine assessment within the context of leisure counseling, the complexity of the entire endeavor becomes apparent. Many professionals are coming to believe that leisure counseling is a developmental process as well as a remedial process, especially when viewed as a component of leisure education (Peterson & Gunn, 1977). Leisure counseling can be described as helping clients to become involved in leisure experiences that are intrinsically meaningful, satisfying, and personally effective (Loesch, 1980, p. 7). This descrption fits nicely with McDowell's framework for approaches to leisure counseling (McDowell, Chapter 1). The framework allows the use of the assessment process under four leisure counseling foci: leisure related problem solving; leisure awareness; leisure resource guidance; and leisure skills development. These foci cover the range from remedial to educational.

The complexity of leisure counseling reflects upon the task of assessment and leisure assessment instrumentation. The "state of the art" relevant to instrumentation will be discussed later, but suffice it to say that the reviews are mixed at best. Nevertheless, there are some good reasons for using the assessment process.

Rationale for Conducting Leisure Assessment

There is a growing body of knowledge that is available for use in leisure assessment and counseling. This information comes from several fields: psychology, sociology, rehabilitation, leisure, and counseling. There are journals and magazines, books and newsletters, and college courses that all address these topics.

A variety of clients have received leisure counseling and have served to "field test" various instruments and techniques. Such client groups include older persons (more specifically retirees), the criminally incarcerated, college students, individuals with disabilities, disadvantaged youth, and the adult public (Loesch, 1980, pp. 18-20). The primary recipients have been older people and the disabled.

Assessment processes, to some extent, reduce subjectivity in leisure counseling, and the degree to which the processes are standardized also facilitates comparison between and within clients. This can lead to amassing a fairly large amount of information in a relatively short period of time that is current, accurate, and engenders discussion that is basic to informed decision making on the part of the counselors (Loesch & Wheeler, 1982, pp. 111-112). What does this mean for counseling psychologists who become involved with assessment and leisure counseling?

Special Implications for Counseling Psychologists

Assessment and leisure counseling are yet emerging into the domain of counseling psychologists. As a result of this, there are still some questions or concerns that remain about this process. What education and training is needed to be qualified in leisure counseling? (See Grossman & Kindy, Chapter 11.) What code of ethics, standards, or guidelines for practice should exist? (See Fain, Chapter 12.) How can the theoretical basis for leisure counseling be more thoroughly established through scientific research? (See Blocher & Siegel, Chapter 2; Iso-Ahola, Chapter 4.) What role do we have in educating our clients and/or the public at large about the nature and value of leisure? To what extent should we attempt to increase the numbers of persons receiving leisure counseling? Should we expand leisure counseling services to groups such as military personnel (especially those placed overseas), families, persons in mid-life, single adults, homemakers, mid-career persons, children, long-term institutionalized people, and unemployed individuals? How can we cautiously but optimally use existing standardized assessment instrumentation and develop valid and reliable new ones?

As persons practicing within an already established profession, it would seem appropriate for counseling psychologists to lend our wisdom to this emerging speciality and to provide some leadership in answering these questions. This implies an attitude of meeting the challenge of nurturing and guiding a new interdisciplinary endeavor that is growing increasingly important as persons in our society seek more and more leisure opportunity and fulfillment.

It may also be inferred that counselors as individuals must be cognizant of the roles we assume as we interact with our clients. If we elect to be quite visionary, then we will likely work with our clients to promote self-determination and independent functioning in leisure. We (with our clients) may arrive at goals such as heightened leisure consciousness, a broadened leisure knowledge base, and growth through leisure (Kinney & Dowling, 1981, p. 71).

Review of Instrumentation

During the 1970s, authors in recreation and leisure paused to reflect upon the assessment instruments that were developing in the field of leisure counseling. In the 1980s, persons in psychology also become involved in this endeavor. Each attempt has contributed to the betterment of the body of knowledge relevant to instrumentations. Thus, only a few general comments are in order before we move to our present review of instruments.

General Comments on the "State of the Art"

Loesch (1980), Witt et al. (1980), and Loesch and Wheeler (1982) are among the authors who have most recently systematically examined the status of leisure assessment instrumentation. As stated earlier in this chapter, the reviews are mixed at best. Loesch had some rather discouraging findings from his 1980 computer-assisted literature search. At that time he found that "fewer than ten leisure interest assessment instruments are commonly mentioned in the professional literature, and two of those are no longer available . . . only one . . . is published by a major publishing company; the others typically are available only from their respective authors. In sum, even the few available assessment instruments directly relevant to leisure counseling are hard to obtain" (Loesch, 1980, p. 16).

In addition to the lack of availability of instruments, Loesch (1980) and Witt et al. (1980) are extremely concerned about the general lack of quality in terms of validity, reliability, and level of sophistication of assessment instrumentation. The instruments tend to be underdeveloped in terms of having a substantive research base of support and having been subjected to norming procedures using large and representative samples.

We can either be devasted or inspired by the statement that —

> The current state of the art reveals a dominant emphasis on interest inventories and profiles related to leisure activity involvement. Additionally, current assessment efforts seem to be largely agency-specific, focused on isolated developments in

assessment procedures to address unique agency needs or services. There appear to be very few developments in assessment procedures that are designed to address the general concept of leisure competence or clientele needs in relation to leisure functioning, (Witt et al., 1980 p. 7)

Loesch and Wheeler (1982, pp. 111-112) acknowledge the aforementioned criticisms of assessment instruments. They further caution us of the danger of relying upon the results in a way that depersonalizes the leisure counseling process. This also may lead clients to interpret the results as irrefutable "facts" thereby inhibiting their growth. The authors conclude that —

> Since the state of the art of assessment in leisure counseling is not good, many of the instruments available (seemingly) have as much potential for harm as for help in their current stages of development. Hopefully many of these instruments will be refined as additional data are gathered. If they are, they could become valuable resources for leisure counseling, (Loesch & Wheeler, 1982, p. 134)

Thus, it is ever incumbent upon us as professionals to strive to improve the quality of leisure assessment instruments so that we may confidently use them as resources in the leisure counseling process. Using assessment instrumentation is an important professional function that should aid us in providing effective services and opportunities through the acquisition, interpretation, and use of valid and reliable information of our clients' needs (Witt et al., 1980; Loesch & Wheeler, 1982).

Leisure Assessment Instrumentation

Loesch and Wheeler's (1982) six categories of instrumentation form the framework for the presentation of leisure assessment instruments in this section. A manual review of the literature occurred in February and March of 1982 and a computer-assisted literature search was conducted in February. Key words or descriptors that were used either individually or in combination included leisure, leisure time, assessment, values, behavior, leisure counseling, attitudes, testing, measurement, preferences, scales, interest inventories, surveys, questionnaires, opinions, measurement techniques, motivation, needs, participant satisfaction, recreational activities, personality traits, older adults, test validity, attitude measures, adult counseling, vocational interests, and self-concept. Major data bases such as ERIC, NCMH, Dissertation Abstracts Inernational, Psychology Abstracts, and Sociology Abstracts were perused. Various persons in park, recreation, and leisure education were also contacted for unpublished and "in house" documents. This last effort yielded a list of instruments that was prepared by Mundy (1981) while she was at the Department of Recreation and Leisure Studies at the California State University-Long Beach. Wehman and Schleien's (1980, pp. 14-15) table of leisure assessment tools was also uncovered. A modification of those two lists using the Loesch and Wheeler categorization system appears in Figure 10-1.

Category	Instrument/Developer	Referencing Norm	Referencing Criterion	Relia-bility	Validity	Comments
LEISURE ATTITUDES	Leisure Orientation Scale (Burdge, 1961)			Deterio-rated	Deterio-rated	Historical value
	Study of Leisure (Neulinger, 1974)	X		Good	Good	
	Leisure Ethnic Scale (Slivken & Crandall, 1978)	X		Good	Good	
	Leisure Attitude Scale (Ragheb, 1980)	X		Good	Good	Stepping stone to later work
LEISURE VALUES	Survey of Leisure Values (Loesch, 1980)	X		Good	Good	Initial phase of development
LEISURE STATES	Walshe Temperament Survey (Walshe, 1977)					
	Leisure Well-Being Inventory (McDowell, 1979)					
LEISURE BEHAVIOR	Mundy Recreation Inventory for the Mentally Retarded (Mundy, 1966)					Psychomotor/cognitive domain

Figure 10-1. Leisure assessment instruments.

Figure 10-1. (*continued*)

Category	Instrument/Developer	Referencing Norm	Referencing Criterion	Relia-bility	Validity	Comments
	Joswiak's Leisure Counseling Assessment Instruments (Joswiak, 1975)	X			Good	Affective domain
	Comprehensive Evaluation in Recreation Therapy Scale (Parker, 1975)	X		Good		Affective domain
	Recreation Behavioral Inventory (Berryman & Lefebvre, 1979)					Psychomotor/ cognitive
LEISURE SATISFAC-TION	Milwaukee Avocational Satisfaction Questionnaire (Overs, Taylor & Adkins, 1977)					
	Leisure Satisfaction Sacle (Beard & Ragheb, 1980)	X		Good	Good	Appeared earlier in unpublished docs.
	Leisure Satisfaction Inventory (Rimmer, 1979)	X			Good	

Figure 10-1. (*continued*)

Category	Instrument/Developer	Referencing Norm	Referencing Criterion	Relia-bility	Validity	Comments
LEISURE INTERESTS	Leisure Interest Inventory (Hubert, 1969)	X		Good	Good	
	Avocational Activities Interest Index (D'Agostini, 1972)					
	Mirenda Leisure Interest Finder (Mirenda, 1975)	X			Good	
	Self-Leisure Interest Profile (McDowell, 1973)		X			
	Leisure Activity Blank (McKechnie, 1975)	X		Good	Good	
	Avocational Activities Inventory (Overs) Taylor & Adkins, 1977)					
	Constructive Leisure Activities Survey (Rev. Ed.) (Edwards, 1980)		X			
	State Technical Institute Leisure Activities Project (Navar, 1979)					

This figure is limited to only those instruments that are readily available through a publisher or those that are cited in journals or textbooks. In-house or agency specific materials were not included, partially in order to keep the listing manageable, broadly applicable, and reasonably accessible.

Usability of Instruments for Counseling Psychologists

Each of us as professionals — based upon our philosophy, education, and experience — has developed criteria for use in selecting among the various instruments that are available to us. To some extent our criteria may also be colored by the purpose of our assessment, how it will actually be implemented, and by whom the assessment will be conducted and the results used (Witt et al., 1980, p. 6).

Beyond this, we probably further consider whether the instruments are norm-referenced or criterion-referenced, easily administered and readministered, and designed for the population with which we intend to use the instruments. We may also be concerned with the mode of response and the validity and reliability of the instrument (Wehman & Schlein, 1980, p. 12).

Finally, Carver (1974, pp. 512-518) provokes our thoughts by suggesting that we address both the psychometric and edumetric dimension of tests (or instruments) as we make judgments about their usefulness.

> The tests that have focused on measuring between-individual differences have been called psychometric tests. Therefore, this dimension of tests will be called the *psychometric dimension*. A test may be evaluated in terms of its psychometric properties, that is, the extent to which it reflects the stable between-individual differences that traditionally have been of primary interest to psychological testing. The other dimension of tests will be called the *edumetric dimension* . . . A test may be evaluated in terms of its edumetric properties, that is, the extent to which it reflects the within-individual growth that traditionally has been of primary interest of educational testing. Teacher-made tests, for example, usually focus more on the edumetric dimension rather than on the psychometric dimension. (Carver, 1974, p. 512.)

The implication is that even though all instrumentation to some extent reflects both between-individual differences and within-individual growth, some will do a better job in one dimension over the other due to design, development, and application.

Of further interest to us is Carver's contention that —

> A failure to keep the psychometric and edumetric dimensions conceptually separate has resulted in a certain amount of confusion when evaluating tests. For example, the American Psychological Association's (1966) *Standards for Educational and Psychological Tests and Manuals* states that "reports of reliability studies should ordinarily be expressed in the test manual in terms of variances for error components (or their square roots) or standard errors of measurement, or product-moment reliability coefficients" (p. 29). This focus on variances and correlation coefficients is of high relevance to the psychometric properties of a test but is completely irrelevant to the edumetric properties of a test. A test may be perfectly reliable from an edumetric standpoint while at the same

time it is perfectly unreliable from a psychometric standpoint. The *Standards* does not make this kind of discrimination, however, but reflects a tendency to evaluate all tests from a psychometric standpoint. There is little recognition of the fact that is quite possible for a test to be extremely good from the edumetric standpoint and extremely bad from the psychometric standpoint. (Carver, 1974, pp. 512-513.)

The following discussion of the assessment instruments listed in Figure 10-1 attempts to take into account much of the aforementioned criteria. The discussion is neither a comprehensive nor definitive evaluation of instrumentation. It is hoped that the counselor would be the "final" judge of the utility of a particular instrument for a particular situation or client. In addition, the evolutionary and/or sketchy status of many of the instruments prohibits a summative detailed evaluation. However, there are some data that should be helpful in at least making some formative judgments.

Discussion of the Instruments As Used In The Counseling Process

Burdge's (1961) Leisure Orientation Scale (LOS) commences this discussion because of its historical significance within the category of Leisure Attitudes. Burdge is credited with being the first person to recognize the need for a scale of specifically measure leisure attitudes (Slivken, 1978, p. 9). In his master's thesis, Burdge presented evidence of the unidimensionality, internal consistency, and validity of the instrument (1961). However, in 1976, Yoesting and Burdge reviewed the data on the use of the LOS and found that in use, the original scale had undergone numerous modifications in wording and in the number of items used. The "changed" scales did not have measures of validity and reliability reported with their trials, and Yoesting and Burdge thus felt that the scale had "deteriorated" over time. They concluded by encouraging the development of new scales (Yoesting & Burdge, 1976, pp. 345-366).

That suggestion brings us to Neulinger's Study of Leisure (SOL), published in 1974. Within his book *The Psychology of Leisure* Neulinger thoroughly outlines the development of the instrument and presents data with regard to the norming procedures and the content, construct, and empirical validity of the SOL. There is less information given on its reliability (Neulinger, 1974). However, Loesch and Wheeler (1982) find the SOL to be sufficiently reliable and among the most psychometrically credible of the leisure assessment instruments. This conclusion is in part due to the extensive analysis to which the various forms of the instrument were subjected. They cautiously recommended using the SOL in leisure counseling when a large amount of information is desired and it is anticipated that the client will be able to respond to an approximately 150 item forced-choiced questionnaire. Neulinger's book provides complete directions for the administration and scoring of his instrument.

In the course of her master's thesis Slivken (1978) and Crandall (her advisor) reduced their Leisure Ethic Scale (LES) to ten items to unidimensionally measure affinity towards leisure. They, as Neulinger does, report the development and refinement of the LES in terms of validity, reliability, and norming procedures. Slivken's vast presentation of data (1978, pp. 64-88) indicates that the LES demonstrates face, content, and construct validity (through both convergent and discriminant validity) and shows good reliability via split-half and test-retest correlations. The scale also demonstrates internal consistency. Psychometrically, they feel that LES appears to be a sound indicator of affinity towards leisure.

The LES is certainly more narrowly focused than the SOL, inasmuch as the selected aspect of leisure stems from one of the SOL's *five* factors. Slivken thought that Neulinger's affinity factor was the most important one and has reduced the number of items measuring that to ten. However, Loesch and Wheeler (1982, p. 117) are concerned about the brevity of the scale from a psychometric viewpoint and find the LES to be basically a gross indicator of leisure attitude. This implies that the SOL could give a finer indication of leisure attitude, but at the expense of greater effort and time consumed. Both must be judged within the context of their utility as leisure counseling aids. The determination of clients' attitudes towards leisure is only one of the many questions that must be answered.

Ragheb's (1980) Leisure Attitude Scale (LAS) is another instrument that underwent extensive development in the 1970s. It is the most recent published entry into the category of leisure attitudes. Ragheb's intent is to assess the cognitive, affective, and behavioral components of an attitude. Thus, his instrument uses six original forced-choice items assessing the cognitive component in the form of views and beliefs on leisure. He employs Neulinger's question number 15, Form 0769 in a slightly modified manner for the affective component and Triandis' (1964) Behavioral Differential Scale to measure the behavioral intentions of respondents toward leisure (p. 142). The LAS is not intended to specifically serve as a leisure assessment tool, but as a means of investigating the interrelationships among leisure participation, leisure satisfaction, and leisure attitudes. At this point then, the LAS might best be considered an investigatory instrument that may be used to uncover any dissatisfaction that has occurred in client leisure experiences. Counselors may use the results to work on increasing the leisure awareness of the clients thereby perhaps making their future involvement more attractive and rewarding (p. 148). It seems that the LAS is better used as a heuristic device for the purposes of inquiry. Its psychometric characteristics are largely defined by Neulinger's and Triandis' work and seems to have formed the basis of Beard and Ragheb's later work with their leisure satisfaction index.

The single entry in the leisure values category is the Survey of Leisure Values (SLV) developed by Loesch in 1980 as reported in Loesch and Wheeler (1982). This instrument still needs further field testing, but preliminarily has demonstrated content validity and test-retest reliability within five subscales. Because the SLV is still in the trial stages, it is not yet recommended for actual use in assessing clients' leisure values.

As opposed to examining specific behaviors or parts of personalities, instruments in the category of leisure states attempt to assess the totality of the personality as it relates to leisure, so this category might also be more broadly labelled "psychological states." Walshe (1977) sees personality as being a blend of four temperaments: melancholic, phlegmatic, sanguine, and choleric, with one or two tending to dominate (p. 94). Her Walshe Temperament Survey (WTS) assesses which temperament(s) is dominant, allowing the counselor to help the clients to select leisure experiences in light of their dominant temperament.

Walshe's discussion does not report any normative, validity, or reliability data. Efforts are, however, being made regarding these psychometric characteristics (Loesch & Wheeler, 1982, p. 121). The WTS consists of 48 items for each of the four temperaments requiring about one-half hour from clients in which to respond. Assuming that counselors accept Walshe's concept of personality and temperament, once traditional measures of reliability and validity become available, the WTS will fully join the ranks of leisure assessment instrumentation.

McDowell's (1979) Leisure Well-Being Inventory (LWBI) also falls into the category of leisure states. Unfortunately, traditional indices of validity and reliability and norming procedures are not available. The LWBI determines how prepared and able the client is to maintain leisure well-being based upon McDowell's four aspects of psychological health: coping, awareness/understanding, knowledge, and assertion. Four subscales measure these attributes by means of 125 forced-choice items. There are ranges of scores that McDowell interprets to show leisure well-being. However, without psychometric data to examine this instrument, it too must be considered a heuristic device as opposed to a fully developed assessment tool. Thus, the LWBI is a further attempt at gleaning additional information from clients to aid in discussions relevant to their leisure needs.

Underlying the category of leisure behavior is the professional's desire to know what the client reports he/she *actually* does within the context of leisure. Ideally, a truer indication of actual leisure behavior would be found through extensive and probably unobtrusive observations occurring within the client's natural environment, but that type of opportunity is rarely available. Thus, the instruments in this category seek to uncover what clients do through self-reported data.

The Mundy Recreation Inventory for the Mentally Retarded (MRIR) assesses leisure behavior in the psychomotor and cognitive domains. The instrument is specifically directed towards mentally retarded individuals. For further information it is suggested that the author be contacted (Mundy, 1981).

The Recreation Behavioral Inventory (RBI) emerged from Berryman and Lefebvre (1979). It too assesses leisure behavior in the psychomotor and cognitive domains. It is specifically designed for use by therapeutic recreators for individuals with disabilities. For further information about RBI, the authors should be contacted.

A set that is available from an established publishing house is Joswiak's (1975) Leisure Counseling Assessment Instruments (LCAI). These instruments focus on the affective domain, have demonstrated content validity, and gone through norming procedures throughout their development. They stem from Joswiak's master's thesis and have been used for leisure counseling purposes by persons in the field of therapeutic recreation. Reliability information is not available, but the instruments appear to be generally credible, again as a vehicle for collecting information for discussion purposes.

Parker, Ellison, Kirby, and Short (1975, pp. 143-152) developed the Comprehensive Evaluation in Recreation Therapy Scale (CERTS) to identify, define, and rate client behaviors relevant to the therapeutic process. Formal evaluation of the validity of the scale was in progress in 1975 and the results of the activity have not entered the published literature as of this time. The authors were especially interested in predictive and content validity. Tests of reliability were conducted and the instrument was found to be consistent between observers (Parker et al., 1975, p. 147). The scale was designed for use in short term, acute-care psychiatric settings to provide information on 25 different behaviors. This is accomplished by the professional completing a 155 item force-choiced checklist that looks at a variety of individual and group behaviors (pp. 149-152) and characteristics. This checklist allows the professional a broad view of the behaviors and characteristics of the client at the time at which it is completed. The checklist is not purely limited to behavior and thus may reflect the values of the developers and the times of which it is a product.

Leisure satisfaction is a category in which some of the better known assessment instrumentation is contained. Pioneering work in the field was done by Overs, Taylor, and Adkins (1977, pp. 106-136) with Milwaukee Avocational Satisfaction Questionnaire (MASQ). Reliability, validity, and normative information is limited to what was found during field testing with the Milwaukee Avocational Counseling Project. The instrument has 24 forced-choice items to which the client responds. It is of practical value in forming the basis of discussion in a counseling situation.

Rimmer's (1979) Leisure Satisfaction Inventory (LSI) demonstrates factorial and concurrent validity and was initially normed with persons of high school age. The reliability coefficients are moderate but significant. The instrument consists of 40 forced-choice items to examine leisure satisfaction through intrinsic dimensions. Loesch and Wheeler (1982, p. 127) suggest that the LSI has good potential, but is in need of further development.

Satisfaction is an important feeling that is expressed by persons when they report they have had a positive leisure experience (Iso-Ahola, 1980). As with attitude, satisfaction is a key element of the totality of assessing client leisure experiences for counseling purposes. Beard and Ragheb's (1980) Leisure Satisfaction Scale (LSS) is a vital new contribution to this category.

The original LSS has 51 forced-choice items with an alpha reliability coefficient of .95, while a reduced form with 24 items has an alpha reliability coefficient of .93. The original questionnaire has six factors or components (each of which demonstrates good subscale alpha reliability): psychological, educational, social, relaxational, physiological, and environmental/aesthetic. The instrument also demonstrates good content and "face" validity as judged by a group of experts and was normed using a wide variety of subjects (Beard & Ragheb, 1980, pp. 30-31). Most respondents complete the instrument in 20 mintues. The authors suggest that —

> The LSS could be used in a counseling situation as a vehicle for examining the use of an individual's free time, and for discussing ways in which leisure activities could be altered to better serve one's needs. At the least, minimal discussion of the LSS results should cause an individual to develop an awareness of, and interest in, the time available for leisure activities, and to develop priorities among competing leisure activity choices (p. 31).

They also state that the LSS should be used as a heuristic device to explore various constructs, relationships, and items on the scale in terms of leisure satisfaction theory. Thus, the psychometric data available about this instrument allows us to use it confidently in both counseling and research situations.

The final category of leisure assessment instrumentation, leisure interests, holds the greatest number of questionnaires, checklists, and inventories. The Leisure Interest Inventory (LII) was developed in 1969 by Hubert as part of her doctoral program. As described in her dissertation, the LII has a sound theoretical base, demonstrates both content and concurrent validity, and has good internal consistancy and stability coefficients for its subscales. Normative data are also available.

The LII has 80 forced-choice items, which represent five typologies that are taken from the work of Max Kaplan: sociability, games, art, mobility, and immobility. If counselors agree with the typologies as being an adequate indication of leisure interests, then the LII is a psychometrically acceptable inventory to use.

D'Agostini's (1972) Avocational Activities Interest Index (AAII) was designed to detail activities by her self-constructed classification system. For further information, the author must be contacted directly.

The Self-Leisure Interest Profile (SLIP) came about in 1973 as a result of McDowell's master's thesis, wherein it was designed for self-administration by the general public and is criterion-referenced. Thus, the instrument may be used to examine changes within a single individual's self-reported leisure interests. Once again we must use SLIP cautiously because of a lack of information about its psychometric characteristics.

The Mirenda Leisure Interest Finder (MLIF) developed by Mirenda and reported in 1975 by Mirenda and Wilson is another self-administered instrument using forced-choice items. According to Wehman and Schlein (1980), the MLIF is norm-referenced and designed for use by the general public. It is quickly administered and demonstrates good validity. Thus, it would seem to be a credible instrument for use in assessing interests and in making comparisons with others who have completed it. As with many of the other categories, leisure interests are but one element worthy of assessment within a program of leisure counseling. The information derived from such devices should be used in concert with other data that are gleaned from and about the client.

That brings us to one of the most widely distributed and applied leisure interest inventories, McKechnie's Leisure Activities Blank (LAB), whose manual was published in 1975. The LAB consists of 120 forced-choice items that elicit information about past and future involvement with selected activities. Normative, validity, and reliablity data are available, along with guidelines on interpreting various subscale score patterns. The LAB has high internal consistency and test-retest reliability. Loesch and Wheeler (1982, p. 129) state that counselors can use the LAB with confidence in its validity. It serves well as a basis for discussion about self-reported leisure activity and because of the rigor used in its continued development, the LAB is a good resource for both practical and theoretical purposes.

The Avocational Activities Inventory (AAI) is yet another product of the Milwaukee Project. The AAI (Overs et al., 1977) lists over 800 leisure activities and was intended to be used to classify avocational activities. This classification system formed the foundation for the MASQ described earlier in this chapter, and other instruments that are directed towards special populations. The AAI might best be used to stimulate conversation about the breadth of activities that may be available to the client in order to enhance his/her leisure awareness. It may serve as a starting point for that person who may have little knowledge of the range of leisure experiences that exist.

A revised edition of Edwards' Constructive Leisure Activities Survey (CLAS-2) as discussed by Edwards and Bloland (1980) is subject to psychometric limitations in terms of validity and reliability data. However, it is criterion-referenced and designed to determine clients' past, present, and future leisure activities and interests, along with their needs and preferences. The instrument is an interview schedule that typically takes 20 minutes to complete and includes five categories: physical and outdoor activities, arts and crafts, learning, general welfare, and personal satisfaction. CLAS-2 is not focused solely upon leisure interests, so it may provide a broader insight into clients. With additional testing and development, this instrument could prove to be a valuable asset to standardized assessment.

Navar and Clancy brought the State Technical Institute Leisure Activities Project (STILAP) into the published literature in 1979. Navar (1979) uses STILAP as an activities checklist to obtain data on participation patterns of adult clients through inquiring about 14 competency areas. STILAP also seeks to measure how often leisure skills are used and what skills the clients are interested in further developing. STILAP demonstrates construct and face validity. At this time there is no evidence available regarding reliability or norming procedures. The 14 competencies were drawn from the literature surrounding investigations of adult leisure behavior. The competencies range from physical to mental to social skills, with skills being perceived as the means to an end of responsible independent leisure functioning. STILAP can be used as a basis for direction regarding the involvement of clients in leisure experiences.

This brief recounting of selected assessment instruments by no means exhausted all of them. The few that touched upon individuals with disabilities were primarily limited to the developmentally disabled, and only highlighted. Upon deeper examination, it can be seen that the instruments can easily cross categories. Thus, the categories in Figure 10-1 should not be construed to be mutually exclusive. There is duplication and overlap among the instruments that fall within them.

It appears that the tension between the "applied" and the "theoretical" dimensions of research exist also within the confines of the assessment process and the instrumentation used therein. If this tension is used to spark continuing research and development in the area of leisure assessment instrumentation, then the practice of leisure counseling will benefit. However, if the tension is channeled into bickering and in-fighting, then there is some likelihood that the entire parks, recreation, and leisure profession may suffer.

It is good to systematically review the tools of our trade. We are bound to continually monitor our practices and the tools that we use to aid the decisions that we make. That particular responsibility is of the utmost importance at this particular stage of development in the practice of leisure counseling. We must endeavor to be fully accountable to the clients that we serve. Using our assessment instruments ethically and judiciously is one means of doing this.

Concluding Comments

A final resource for use in leisure counseling is Connolly's (1981, pp. 27-29) listing of selected textbooks and reference books. Full bibliographic entries and annotations are given for seven references. These books focus on established psychological tests that are not specifically directed towards leisure assessment and counseling. Surely the contents would be useful in concert with the instruments described in this chapter.

Reliability, validity, objectivity, and credibility are among the concerns that we have as we judge the relative merits of different instruments. In leisure assessment, we must also consider the availability of the instrument, the qualifications needed to accurately use it, the degree to which the affective domain is explored, the ultimate purpose of the insrument, the nature of the client with whom the instrument will be used, and the final practical criterion of cost in terms of resources used, such as time and money. None of these concerns is truly unique to the practice of leisure assessment and counseling.

However, if we do accept the psychological definition of leisure and we acknowledge the privacy of the affective domain, it seems we also should consider, if not separately then at least strongly, the social aspect of the leisure experience. The affective domain involves emotions and feelings, and typically, these are experienced towards other persons or in a social context. Therefore, work remains to be done in assessing how we conduct ourselves socially in terms of maturity, authority, cooperation, and fulfillment. The interaction that occurs through the social aspect of leisure as it relates to our behavior in group situations is worthy of continued study as we strive to further understand ourselves as human beings.

Recommendations for the Future

Throughout the course of this chapter, we have tried to examine leisure assessment instrumentation. In order to accomplish this task with the full care that it deserves, we have ended up taking a look at the broader area of leisure counseling as an emphasis within the profession of counseling psychology. Dowd (1981, pp. 81-82) nicely summarizes this relationship between leisure counseling and counseling psychology.

He begins by stating that counseling psychology has "broadened into a profession which assists relatively intact persons in maximizing their developmental potential in all areas of their lives . . . (by) making use of a wide variety of sophisticated psychological interventions" (1981, p. 81). In part because of this, there is some overlap with the other helping professions. Leisure counseling is indeed illustrative of this. Because leisure counseling has evolved from being merely activity selection, it may be perceived as complimentary to the other tasks of counseling psychologists, since leisure counseling is another means of aiding the development of the entire individual.

This point of view results because, within leisure counseling, the motives behind the selection of leisure options, leisure decision-making and problem-solving skills, and the meaning of leisure in the lives of people are psychological phenomena that are increasingly being emphasized. Patterns of human development that are leisure related are multidetermined and fall within the overall life adjustment patterns of people. Thus, leisure counseling can encourage an environment or an awareness that helps clients to choose leisure experiences that enhance and fulfill their lives (Dowd, 1981, p. 81). The use of assessment instrumentation *helps* to make leisure counseling a more efficient and effective process for both counselors and clients.

Art and Science of Leisure Assessment

We have seen the multiplicity and strengths and weaknesses of instruments used in the assessment process. It stands to reason that no one means of collecting information about a client should be used in isolation or as the sole criterion for decision making and planning. To merely rely upon a "paper and pencil test" is to miss the richness of information to be gained from extensive and candid dialog. The systematic observation of client behavior (or body language) communicates so much to the trained eye, that it is essential to triangulate our methods of inquiry. Listening and watching does not relieve us, however, of our responsibility to continue to develop valid and reliable tools to guide our inquiry. Rather, this condition of multiple inquiry allows for the fusion of the "artistic" and the "scientific" or the intuitive and the rational as a comprehensive approach to better aid in the development and enrichment of our clients' lives as they grow in their own independent functioning and self-determination. The emergent and subjective nature of the leisure experience itself probably provides the best rationale for clients' taking collegial roles in the assessment and leisure counseling process. It is, after all, ultimately they who will be at play.

Need for Improved Instrumentation

To be responsive to accurately identified needs of our clients is just one of the many roles of counseling professionals. The assessment process and its instrumentation are intended to help us be more accurate in fulfilling this responsibility. In 1981, Sessoms asked, "Do we have the instrumentation necessary to assess recreation interests, potential, and optimum leisure behavior?" (p. 65). Perhaps, in terms of edumetric dimensions of tests, the answer is yes. In terms of the psychometric dimensions, the answer is no. Qualifiers? Yes, there are, so what we should do in light of this dilemma is acknowledge it and proceed with courage towards its resolution. That may be our biggest contribution to the future of leisure assessment and counseling.

REFERENCES

Beard, J.G., & Ragheb, M.G. Measuring leisure satisfaction. *Journal of Leisure Research*, 1980, First Quarter, 20-32.

Berryman, D.L., & Lefebvre, C.B. *Recreation Behavioral Inventory*. Unpublished manuscript, 1979. (Available from C.B. Lefebvre, 2225 East McKinney, Denton, Texas 76201.)

Bundy, R. Leisure: The missing future perspectives in educational policy. *Journal of Education*, 1977, *159*(2), 93-104.

Burdge, R.J. *The development of a leisure orientation scale*. Unpublished master's thesis, The Ohio State University, 1961.

Carver, R.P. Two dimensions of tests: Psychometric and edumetric. *American Psychologist*, 1974, July, 512-518.

Connolly, P. Selected references on assessment. *Therapeutic Recreation Journal*, 1981, Third Quarter, 27-29.

D'Agostini, N. *Avocational Activities Interest Index*. Unpublished manuscript, 1972. (Available from N. D'Agostini, Sutter Memorial Hospital, Sacramento, California 95819.)

Dowd, E.T. Leisure counseling: Summary of an emerging field. *The Counseling Psychologist*, 1981, *9*(3), 81-82.

Edwards, P.B. *Leisure counseling techniques: Individual and group counseling step-by-step* (3rd ed.). Los Angeles: Constructive Leisure, 1980.

Edwards, P.B., & Bloland, P.A. Leisure counseling and consultation. *Personal and Guidance Journal*, 1980, *58*,(6), 435-440.

Hubert, E.E. *The development of an inventory of leisure interests.* Unpublished doctoral dissertation, University of North Carolina at Chapel Hill, 1969.

Iso-Ahola, S.E. *The social psychology of leisure and recreation.* Dubuque: Wm. C. Brown Co., 1980.

Iso-Ahola, S.E. Intrinsic motivation: An overlooked basis for evaluation. *Parks & Recreation,* 1982, *17*(2), 32-33.

Joswiak, K.F. *Leisure counseling programs materials for the developmentally disabled.* Washington, D.C.: Hawkins and Associates, 1979.

Kinney, W., & Dowling, D. Leisure counseling or leisure quackery? *Parks and Recreation,* 1981, *16*(1), 70-73, 106.

Loesch, L.C. *Leisure counseling.* Ann Arbor, Mi.: ERIC/CAPS, 1980.

Loesch, L.C., & Wheeler, P.T. *Principles of leisure counseling.* Minneapolis: Educational Media Corp., 1982.

McDowell, C.F. *Approaching leisure counseling with the self leisure interest profile.* Unpublished master's thesis, California State University, 1973.

McDowell, C.F. *The leisure well-being inventory.* Eugene, Or.: Leisure Lifestyle Consultants, 1979.

McKechnie, G.E. *The structure of leisure activities.* Berkeley, Ca.: Institute of Personality Assessment and Research, 1974.

McKechnie, G.E. *Manual for the Leisure Activities Blank.* Palo Alto, Ca.: Consulting Psychologists Press, 1975.

Mirenda, J.J., & Wilson, G.T. The Milwaukee leisure counseling model. *Counseling and Values,* 1975, *20*(1), 42-46.

Mundy, C.J. *Leisure Assessment Instruments.* Unpublished manuscript, 1981. (Available from Dr. C.J. Mundy, Department of Human Services and Studies, Florida State University, Tallahassee, Florida 32306.)

Murphy, J.F. Leisure, aging and retirement: Changing patterns and perspectives. *Leisure Today,* October 1977, pp. 6-7.

Navar, N. *State Technical Institute Leisure Activities Project.* Unpublished materials, 1979. (Available from Dr. N. Navar, Department of Leisure Studies, University of Illinois at Urbana-Champaign, Champaign, Illinois 61820.)

Neulinger, J. *Psychology of leisure.* Springfield, Il.: Charles C Thomas, 1974.

Overs, R.P., Taylor, S., & Adkins, C. *Avocational counseling manual: A complete guide to leisure guidance.* Washington, D.C.: Hawkins and Associates, 1977.

Parker, R.A., Ellison, C.H., Kirby, T.F., & Short, M.J. Comprehensive evaluation in recreation therapy scale: A tool for patient evaluation. *Therapeutic Recreation Journal,* 1975, Fourth Quarter, 143-153.

Peterson, C.A., & Gunn, S.L. Leisure counseling: An aspect of leisure education. *Leisure Today,* April 1977, pp. 5-6.

Ragheb, M.G. Interrelationships among leisure participation, leisure satisfaction and leisure attitudes. *Journal of Leisure Research,* 1980, Second Quarter, 138-149.

Ragheb, M.G., & Beard, J.G. Leisure satisfaction: Concept, theory, and measurement. In S. E. Iso-Ahola (Ed.), *Social psychological perspectives on leisure and recreation.* Springfield, Il.: Charles C Thomas, 1980.

Rimmer, S.M. *The development of an instrument to assess leisure satisfaction among secondary school students.* Unpublished dissertation, University of Florida, 1979.

Sessoms, H.D. Leisure counseling: A frank analysis of the issues. *Parks & Recreation,* 1981, *16*(1), 64-69, 107.

Slivken, K.E. *Development of a leisure ethic scale.* Unpublished master's thesis, University of Illinois at Urbana-Champaign, 1978.

Triandis, H. Explanatory factor analyses of behavioral component of social attitudes. *Journal of Abnormal and Social Psychology,* 1964, *68*, 420-430.

Walshe, W.A. Leisure counseling instrumentation. In D.M. Compton & J.E. Goldstein

(Eds.), *Perspectives of leisure counseling*. Arlington, Va.: National Recreation and Park Association, 1977.

Wehman, P., & Schleien, S.J. Relevant assessment in leisure skill training programs. *Therapeutic Recreation Journal*, 1980, 9-20.

Wilson, G., & Mirenda, J. The Milwaukee leisure counseling model. *Counseling and Values*, 1976, *24*(3), 238-242.

Wilson, G.T., Mirenda, J.J., & Rutkowski, B.A. Milwaukee leisure counseling model. *Leisurability*, 1975, *2*(3), 11-17.

Witt, P.A., Connolly, P., & Compton, D.M. Assessment: A plea for sophistication. *Therapeutic Recreation Journal*, 1980, Fourth Quarter, 5-8.

Yoesting, D.R., & Burdge, R.J. Utility of a leisure orientation scale. *Iowa State Journal of Research*, 1976, *50*, 345-356.

Part III
PROFESSIONAL ISSUES

Chapter 11

PROFESSIONAL PREPARATION FOR LEISURE COUNSELING

Arnold H. Grossman and Joan H. Kindy

INTRODUCTION

IN order to assess the "state of the art" of leisure counseling at the time of this writing, a survey instrument was included with the *Leisure Information Newsletter* (Volume 8, Number 4, Spring 1982) and in *Programming Trends in Therapeutic Recreation* (Volume 3, Number 1, February 1982). Approximately five hundred questionnaires were sent in these mailings to the subscribers of these professional publications. Because of the short response time required, the questionnaire was mailed only to the *Leisure Information Newsletter* subscribers in the United States and Canada; however, it was mailed to all of the subscribers of *Programming Trends in Therapeutic Recreation* (the large majority of whom are in the United States and Canada), as it was the first page of the journal.

Forty complete surveys were returned. Thirty-two persons indicated that they do or have provided leisure counseling services, and eight persons indicated that leisure counseling is not a part of what they do.

The academic degrees of persons providing leisure counseling services are as follows: nine individuals had a Ph.D. or Ed.D.; eleven, a M.A. or M.S.; one, a M.S.W.; and eleven, a B.A. or B.S.

The academic majors of these persons are as follows: thirteen individuals majored in therapeutic recreation; nine in recreation; two in counselor education; two in leisure studies; and one each in recreation administration, physical education, philosophy, psychology, sociology, and clinical social work.

Two questions were designed to determine where these individuals work and what they do. The setting responses are as follows (some individuals indicated more than one setting): fourteen individuals work in public or private hospitals; eight in public agencies; five in private business or private practice; five in universities; three in private agencies; one each in a residential school, voluntary agency, and developmental center.

The wide range of position titles listed or functions performed by the thirty individuals who responded to that question is indicative of the various professional roles in which leisure counseling is included. They are as follows: five individuals are recreation managers; three are program directors; two each are residence directors, directors of leisure services, senior recreation therapists, and therapeutic recreators; and one each is a teacher of leisure counseling, teacher of therapeutic recreation, social activities consultant, counselor assessment specialist, teacher of recreation, treatment team leader, assistant director of activities therapy, director of a counseling psychology program, agency director, adjunctive therapist, mentally handicapped coordinator, activity therapist, and manager of a leisure consulting firm.

The questionnaire requested that the individuals indicate the number of academic courses taken in the areas of counseling, leisure counseling, recreation/leisure studies, and assessment. For the twenty-four usable responses, the ranges and means are as follows:

Types of courses	Number of courses, range	Mean number of courses
Counseling	0 - 15	2.75
Leisure counseling	0 - 4	.78
Recreation/Leisure studies	0 - 60	14.70
Assessment	0 - 8	1.90

In addition, for the foregoing question, one person reported having earned a Ph.D. in counseling and one person a M.S. in counseling; two persons reported having taken "many" courses in recreation/leisure studies; one individual reported "many" assessment courses; and one person indicated a question mark in this area. Seventeen individuals reported having attended conferences and institutes focusing on leisure counseling.

Two other descriptive areas of interest were the nature of the leisure counseling services provided by these persons and the types of clients to whom the service are/were provided. Regarding the former, activity selection, resource guidance, leisure information and referral were provided by a large majority of the respondents. Some leisure counselors also engage in assessment of leisure interests, follow-up, placement, and life planning with their clients. A few teach leisure counseling, provide opportunities for assertiveness training, values clarification, and socialization training. One person indicated that he/she helps clients to learn coping skills in general. Twenty-one of these individuals provide leisure counseling services both on a one-to-one basis and in groups, and two of these persons are providing consultation services as well. Of the nine other respondents to this question, five are working only with groups, three only on a one-to-one basis, and one provides leisure counseling as part of a leisure counseling curriculum.

The clients of the respondents are from all age groups, from children to seniors; represent well persons and physically and emotionally disabled persons; represent all levels of socioeconomic status; are institutionalized and outpatients, as well as participants in community recreation programs; and represent all levels of intellectual functioning.

Thus, the "typical" leisure counselor, according to the results of our survey, seems to be the holder of a master's or a bachelor's degree; works in a hospital setting or for a public agency; and is an administrator. This person's academic major was recreation/therapeutic recreation, and he/she has taken approximately fourteen courses in recreation/leisure studies, three courses in counseling, two courses in assessment, and less than one course in leisure counseling.

He/she has probably attended a conference or institute focusing on leisure counseling. This leisure counselor provides direct service to a wide range of individuals and groups in the areas of activity selection, resource guidance, leisure information, and referral.

In any emerging field, there is a great deal of variability and lack of consensus concerning definitions of key concepts. Leisure counseling is no exception. The respondents were asked to answer the question: "How do you define leisure counseling?" Definitions ranged from a very specific response — "advice giving and activity alternative seeking" — to a response that could be characteristic of all counseling — "a process during which a counselor and client work together to clarify and diagnose the client's concerns to identify mutually agreed upon long and short term goals for counseling and to develop and implement a treatment plan to achieve these goals."

One respondent accurately reflected the sentiments of the authors of this chapter: "I am very much concerned about the number of people in the field practicing leisure counseling with a very limited knowledge and experiential level." Thus, this chapter on "Professional Preparation for Leisure Counseling" will address the needs for knowledge and supervised experience.

Prior to a discussion of the specific rationale for professional preparation of leisure counselors and presentation of a curriculum guide for such preparation, it is necessary to present the definition of leisure counseling and its contextual framework that has influenced the thinking and writing of the authors. The definition is the one presented by Loesch and Wheeler (1982):

> Leisure counseling is a process which uses verbal and nonverbal techniques to assist individuals to increase their affective, behavioral, and cognitive leisure awareness and to develop effective leisure activity selection and evaluation skills, thereby facilitating movement toward leisure mental health. (p. 71)

The value of such a definition lies in its clarity in presenting leisure counseling as an important process in itself, which can be addressed by counselors as a part of life span counseling and by individuals specializing in leisure counseling. Furthermore, this definition permits consideration of various client populations, various counseling techniques, and various purposes of interventions.

The contextual framework is best characterized by Morrill, Oetting, and Hurst (1974). They presented a model that enables understanding of the targets, purposes, and methods of intervention that most commonly concern counselors and that can serve to assist leisure counselors in conceptualizing the dimensions of their functioning. The model is presented as a cube with three dimensions (a figure in their article). According to this model every counseling intervention has three dimensions: (1) target of intervention, which answers the question of who or what constitutes the "client" (i.e., individual, primary group, associational group, institution, or community); (2) purpose of intervention, which answers the question of why the intervention is taking place (i.e., remediation, prevention, development); and (3) method of intervention, which serves as a framework for choosing a particular set of counseling techniques (i.e., direct service, consultation and training, media).

For the leisure counselor, the client may be an individual, a primary group (family, close friends), an associational group (organized club), or an institution (hospital, neighborhood). The purpose of the intervention may be remedial (because of "leisure lack"), preventive (hospitalized patients being discharged), or developmental (leisure decision-making). The method used may be one or a combination of direct service (individual and/or group counseling), consultation and training, and media (television, movies, printed materials). A "model" professional preparation program would provide for education encompassing all of the aforementioned knowledges and skills.

THE NEED FOR PROFESSIONAL PREPARATION

The need for professional preparation in the disciplines of counseling and recreation/leisure services is well recognized; in response there have emerged accepted standards for professional preparation programs in these areas. Traditionally, these disciplines responded to societal needs in relation to the "work ethic." Counseling focused on educational/vocational counseling in schools, colleges, and agencies, while recreation services operated from a residual time concept (i.e., the time remaining after existence and subsistence needs were met) and focused on re-creating people to return to work. With the emergence of the postindustrial society with its concomitant technological advances, shorter work weeks, increased holidays and vacation periods, longer life spans, and changing social norms and values (e.g., The Civil Rights Movement, Women's Liberation, Gay Liberation), these disciplines (as well as others) have been called upon for new and changing services. Consequently, the nature of preparation within each of these disciplines changed as well.

One of the changes was the emergence of "recreation counseling" in the field of recreation. As the "umbrella" of the field grew to "recreation and leisure studies," the study of "leisure counseling" entered curricula as a course or a unit of a course. As research related to this new specialty was virtually nonexistent, course content was based on the knowledge, skills, and experiences of the individuals in the recreation and leisure services profession. There is still limited research; however, the discipline of counseling has shown a recent interest in leisure counseling (see Edwards & Bloland, 1980; Loesch & Wheeler, 1982; *The Counseling Psychologist*, 1981) and some joint efforts with the recreation and leisure service profession are emerging.

To date, the authors know of only two professional preparation *programs* for leisure counselors in the United States: the post-master's "Certificate of Advanced Study in Leisure Counseling and Consultation" in the Department of Recreation and Leisure Studies at New York University, which was developed jointly with the Department of Counselor Education; a master's and a doctoral program at Oklahoma State University, with leisure counseling options in the

Department of Leisure Services.

The "Certificate of Advanced Study in Leisure Counseling and Consultation" at New York University requires a minimum of 33 credit-hours beyond the master's degree in recreation and leisure studies. The total program is developed for each student in relation to previous education, professional experience, and projected career goals. In addition, specific prerequisites have been established for the program, and these must be completed prior to commencing study in the Leisure Counseling and Consultation program. The prerequisites are a basic course in concepts of leisure, recreation, and play; a basic course in leisure counseling; and basic courses in theories of personality and developmental psychology. The required courses for the program are one course each in the following areas: counseling — theory and process; group counseling; counseling the adult; individual counseling practice; interdisciplinary approaches to play and leisure; leisure education and recreation program development; the consultant's role in leisure services; contemporary concepts in counseling for leisure; a graduate internship in leisure counseling and consultation; a broad liberal/cultural arts course; and an integrative experience in leisure counseling and consultation. While professional work experience is not required prior to matriculation, the Certificate is granted only after the student has had three years of satisfactory, related professional experience obtained either before or during the pursuit of the Certificate.*

Both master's and doctoral programs with options in leisure counseling are offered at Oklahoma State University. The master's degree requires a minimum of 32 graduate credit-hours. Students may have competency deficiencies and are required to make up these deficiencies by taking specified prerequisite courses or by completing appropriate individualized learning experiences to be negotiated with the student's major advisor. The master's program has two core courses in the areas of research and research design for health, physical education, and leisure services. There are four required courses, in the following areas: social aspects of play and sport or social foundations of recreation and leisure; administration of recreation or recreation service delivery systems; introduction to leisure counseling; and advanced methods in leisure counseling. The leisure counseling specialty requires six credit-hours in general counseling and six or more elective credit-hours in a specialized counseling area (e. g., special populations, industrial and community leisure counseling). The doctoral program has the same requirements with regard to deficiencies as the master's program; however, it includes competencies required of master's students. The program requires a minimum of 60 credit-hours beyond the master's or a total of 90 credit-hours of graduate work. These include four courses as follows: critical issues in higher education; effective teaching in college and university;

---

*For more information, write to the Department of Recreation and Leisure Studies, School of Education, Health, Nursing, and Arts Professions, New York University, 70 Press Annex, Washington Square, New York, N.Y. 10003.

curriculum development in higher education; and development and organization of higher education. The two required leisure science courses are an advanced seminar in leisure counseling theory and research, and special problems in leisure counseling — internship. In addition to the above listed requirements, a minimum of 42 credit-hours are required outside the department, which are distributed in the following areas: advanced research and/or statistics; human behavior; advanced counseling; dissertation research; and electives.*

With only two known professional preparation programs in the country, it is not surprising that many individuals providing leisure counseling services have limited, if any, professional preparation. This is supported by the findings of the survey reported at the beginning of this chapter (with due recognition of its small sample). The resulting situation, which has been previously stated by Grossman (1980) but bears repeating, is as follows:

1. Recreation professionals without training in leisure counseling have established programs or services in the area.
2. Individuals without training in either recreation or leisure counseling are attempting to establish themselves as "leisure counselors."
3. Most alarming, individuals (recreational professionals and others) are establishing leisure counseling programs and services after taking one or two courses or workshops.

The "call" for professional preparation is not new. Others (Hayes, 1977; Epperson, 1977; Neulinger, 1981) have indicated the need for professional preparation and some individuals have specified "suggested minimal education" for leisure counselors (Neulinger, 1981, p. 198), the major topics to be included in a professional preparation program (Loesch & Wheeler, 1982, pp. 252-255), and the requisites of the "The Leisure Counselor as a Professional" with implications for professional preparation (Hayes, 1977). What is new in this chapter is the presentation in the next section of a "Curriculum Guide for the Professional Preparation of Leisure Counselors" based on the current knowledge in the area of leisure counseling and presented in a format of units, each of which focuses on a basic core competency. This approach emanates from joint expertise in the professional preparation of leisure counselors at New York University over the past two years and communicates the essential components of a professional preparation program for leisure counselors more clearly than just college course titles and descriptions).

CURRICULUM GUIDE FOR THE
PROFESSIONAL PREPARATION OF LEISURE COUNSELORS

The "Curriculum Guide for the Professional Preparation of Leisure Counselors" consists of the following eleven units:

---

*For more information, write to the Department of Leisure Services, School of Health, Physical Education and Leisure Services, Oklahoma State University, 103 Colvin Center, Stillwater, Oklahoma 74078.

- Unit I   — Behavioral Science Foundatons
- Unit II   — Special Populations
- Unit III   — Counseling: A Helping Profession
- Unit IV   — The Roles of the Leisure Counselor
- Unit V   — Concepts of Leisure and Leisure Education
- Unit VI   — Leisure Counseling: Philosophy and Objectives
- Unit VII   — Leisure Counseling: Approaches and Models
- Unit VIII   — Leisure Counseling: Intervention Strategies
- Unit IX   — Leisure Counseling: Evaluation and Research
- Unit X   — Professional Development for Leisure Counselors
- Unit XI   — The Internship: Supervised Leisure Counseling Practice

Each of the units consists of three sections: (1) the *rationale*, which is a statement explaining why the competency of that unit is requisite for the effective leisure counselor; (2) the *basic core competency*, or the behavior which the individual should be able to demonstrate upon completion of the unit, indicating the achievement of specified knowledge and practices; and, (3) the *content* to be covered to achieve the competency.*

The "Curriculum Guide for the Professional Preparation of Leisure Counselors" is exactly what its name implies — it is a guide. It should *not* be interpreted as units of a single college course or an 11-session workshop. It is envisioned that the "Curriculum Guide" can be used in a variety of settings [e.g., colleges and universities (in degree and nondegree programs), training institutes and workshops sponsored by professional organizations, work settings (in developmental training programs)]. The nature and length of the education experience, no matter what the setting, will depend on a number of factors [i.e., the competencies of the instructor(s) in each of the units, the competencies the participants bring to the training, the resources of the sponsoring organization, the limitations of the sponsoring organization (as a college offering courses of semester length only)]. In any event, the "Curriculum Guide" should not be used to give a "quickie" course with the implication that the individuals who "complete" it are qualified leisure counselors. That would only contribute to the alarming state of affairs that now exists — many unqualified individuals providing leisure counseling.

In preparing the "Curriculum Guide for the Professional Preparation of Leisure Counselors," we made some basic assumptions, which should be communicated at this point:

1. The individual coordinating the professional preparation program will have achieved each of the competencies and will be able to involve other qualified individuals in teaching those units that are not his/her particular strength.

---

*Recognition is given to the American Camping Association for the format of this curriculum guide, which is part of the format presented in *Camp Director Education Curriculum Guide*, edited by Sue Stein (Martinsville, Indiana: American Camping Association), 1981.

2. The instructors will be able to assess the competencies of the participants at the beginning of the educational experience and if they have achieved the basic core competencies for each of the units.
3. The instructors will have knowledge of the educational resources (e.g., books, journals articles, films) for their own as well as the participants' use.
4. The instructors will possess current knowledge of the state of the art of leisure counseling and related research.
5. The instructors will have knowledge of and skills in adult education, and they will be able to design educational experiences to facilitate the learning of the content of each unit so that the participants will be able to achieve the core competencies.
6. The coordinator will be able to establish a system for the selection of individuals to be admitted to the professional preparation program.

Unit I — Behavioral Science Foundations

Rationale

Leisure counselors must have a broad understanding of the principles and psychosocial foundations of human growth, development, and behavior, since knowledge in these areas forms the theoretical underpinning of the professional delivery of counseling services. Knowledge should encompass both general and special populations.

Basic Core Competency

Leisure counselors should demonstrate knowledge of the primary theories of developmental psychology across the life span, should be aware of the ways in which people learn and unlearn attitudes, values and behaviors, and should be able to apply these knowledges to the understanding of various populations and institutions with which they work.

Content to Achieve Competency

a. Nature of intellectual, social, and emotional development in childhood, adolescence, and adulthood for nondisabled and disabled persons.
b. Processes of human learning.
c. Personality theories and their behavioral implications.
d. Social-psychological concepts and theories, and their relationship to individuals and groups.
e. Theories, conceptions, and descriptions of behavior disorders and physical/emotional disabilities.
f. The implications of cultural factors (e.g., mores, values, customs, religious teachings, and ethnic influences) on growth and development, life-

style selection, sexual behavior, family patterns, and parenting.

g. Nature of work, career patterns, occupational choice, job satisfaction, leisure satisfaction, work, and leisure as integral parts of educational and vocational development.

Unit II — Special Populations

Rationale

Leisure (then called recreation) counseling has its roots in services with special populations, and this is one area in which the need for leisure counseling has been firmly established. Whether the services are provided in a rehabilitation institution, a camp, or a senior center, it is incumbent on leisure counselors to have an understanding of special populations so that they can assist individuals with disabilities in enhancing the quality of their leisure experiences.

Basic Core Competency

Leisure counselors should demonstrate knowledge of the characteristics of special populations, disabling conditions, and their implications for recreation planning and participation.

Content to Achieve Competency

a. Characteristics of special populations, disabling conditions, and their implications for levels of functioning.
b. The effect of developmental and acquired disabilities on the self-concept of individuals.
c. Societal perceptions of individuals with disabilities and the resulting attitudinal and architectural barriers.
d. Methods of activity analysis, activity selection, and adaptation, and their use in recreation planning and participation.
e. Segregation, integration, and mainstreaming of disabled individuals in recreation services.
f. Community services and resources (including accessible facilities) to assist individuals with various disabilities.
g. Legislation pertaining to, advocacy for, and the rights of individuals with disabilities.

Unit III — Counseling: A Helping Profession

Rationale

Building upon the behavioral science foundations, professionals who deliver effective leisure counseling services must possess understanding in four areas: counseling theory; counseling process; counseling outcomes; and self-understanding.

Basic Core Competency

Leisure counselors must demonstrate not only theoretical knowledge of the major counseling theories and processes associated with them but also the personal skills and understandings necessary for effective counseling, regardless of theoretical persuasion. They must be able to evaluate critically major research efforts with regard to counseling with specific populations for specific purposes.

Content to Achieve Competency*

a. Study of counseling as a form of professional assistance in processes of development and adjustment.
b. Affective approaches to counseling (e.g., person-centered, gestalt, existential, psychoanalyatic) with associated process and research.
c. Cognitive approaches to counseling (e.g., rational-emotive, transactional analysis, trait-factor) with associated processes and research.
d. Behavioral approaches to counseling (e.g., behavioral counseling, reality therapy) with associated processes and research.
e. Application of a, b, and c to individual and group counseling.
f. Patterns of interaction and dynamics in large and small groups.
g. Ability to objectively compare and contrast differing sets of values as stated by other persons.
h. Abilities to be empathetic, understanding, and genuine; to communicate and relate effectively with others; and to respond to verbal and nonverbal behavior in meaningful ways.
i. Abilities to think, reason, and solve problems and to discover problem areas through intelligent inquiry.
j. Ability to respect the uniqueness and worth of individuals and to place confidence and trust in their potential for growth, including the capacity to cope with persons of varying physical, mental, cultural, ethnic, and religious backgrounds in effective ways.
k. Ability to understand but not overly identify with the problems of individuals.
l. Ability to be perceptive of one's own feelings and unique needs system.
m. Building (a) personal theory(ies) of counseling.

---

*Recognition for some of the content areas is given to "Proposal for Recertification of the School Counselor, K-12, Program," Department of Counselor Education, Health, Nursing, and Arts Professions, New York University, February, 1978 (unpublished).

Unit IV — The Roles of the Leisure Counselor

Rationale

In order to meet the commitments and challenges of an emerging field, leisure counselors should have a knowledge of the potential roles they can fulfill and the relationships of these roles to their profession and other professions, to a variety of human service delivery systems, and to themselves as individuals.

Basic Core Competency

Leisure counselors should demonstrate knowledge of the roles and expectations of leisure counselors in a variety of human service delivery systems in relation to their own philosophy of leisure counseling and the philosophy of the system; their assessment of their personal strengths and professional competencies; their perceptions of themselves and other leisure counselors; and their impact on their own profession, other professions, and the delivery system.

Content to Achieve Competency

a. Leisure counselors in counseling settings who specialize in leisure counseling or provide leisure counseling concurrently with other counseling services (e.g., career counseling).
b. Leisure counselors in recreation and leisure service settings who specialize in leisure counseling or provide leisure counseling concurrently with the delivery of other recreation and leisure services.
c. Leisure counselors in private practice who have their own clientele and/or provide leisure counseling for organizations on a contractual basis.
d. Leisure counselors as leisure service consultants who recommend and/or assist organizations in establishing leisure counseling services.
e. Leisure counselors as educators.
f. The relationship of leisure counselors to the various types of delivery systems.
g. The relationship of the philosophy of leisure counseling and the personal philosophy of the leisure counselor to the philosophy, goals, and objectives of the various types of delivery systems (see a to e).
h. Individual's perception of self as a leisure counselor.
i. The leisure counselor's perception of others in the same delivery system.
j. The perception of self in relationship to others in the same delivery system.
k. The impact of the leisure counselor on the delivery system, his/her own profession, and other professions.
l. Assessment of professional competencies and personal strengths in relation to the roles of the leisure counselor.

Unit V — Concepts of Leisure and Leisure Education

Rationale

Because the word *leisure* is used to describe a variety of phenomena in society, from time to activity to clothing, leisure counselors should have an understanding of the multifaceted uses of the term so that they can assist individuals and groups to identify and clarify their values, attitudes, and views of leisure and the implications of these for quality leisure experiences.

Basic Core Competency

Leisure counselors should demonstrate an understanding of the phenomenon of leisure from a variety of conceptual frameworks and their implications for analyzing and enhancing the quality of the leisure experiences of individuals and groups in contemporary American society.

Content to Achieve Competency

a. Historical and philosophical perspectives of leisure and their influence on leisure in American society.
b. The phenomenon of leisure from sociological, psychological, economic, and environmental perspectives.
c. Models and paradigms for categorizing leisure concepts (e.g., the works of Kraus, Murphy, Kaplan, Neulinger).
d. Concepts of leisure (e.g., free-time, activity, state of mind) and their implications for examining the leisure experiences of individuals and groups in contemporary American society (e.g., through the life cycle, in relationship to work, socioeconomic status, sex, disability).
e. The quantity versus quality aspects of leisure experiences.
f. Educational processes to enable individuals to identify and understand their values, attitudes, and goals in relation to leisure and to enhance their options for quality leisure experiences.

Unit VI — Leisure Counseling: Philosophy and Objectives

Rationale

In order to provide professional leisure counseling services, it is essential that leisure counselors formulate a philosophy of leisure counseling, based on historical and contemporary philosophies of leisure counseling, from which goals, objectives, and an organizational structure emanate.

Basic Core Competency

Leisure counselors should demonstrate the ability to state, interpret, justify, and perhaps modify their philosophy, goals, and objectives of leisure counseling and how they relate to the delivery of leisure counseling services and societal trends and needs.

Content to Achieve Competency

a. Historical foundations of leisure counseling and their implications for the development of a philosophy and objectives for leisure counseling.
b. Contemporary philosophies and objectives of leisure counseling and their relationships to current and future societal trends and needs.
c. Operational definitions for the terms *philosophy, goals,* and *objectives*.
d. Professional and personal experiences that influence the development of a philosophy of leisure counseling.
e. A personal philosophical statement of leisure counseling and the formulation of goals and objectives for leisure counseling practice.
f. The justification of leisure counseling and leisure counseling practice as a component of a counseling or recreation and leisure service delivery system.
g. The relationship between the philosophy, goals, and objectives of leisure counseling and the organizational structure for the delivery of leisure counseling services.
h. Current professional issues in leisure counseling.

Unit VII — Leisure Counseling: Approaches and Models

Rationale

Because no unified field of leisure counseling exists at present, it becomes the responsibility of those individuals providing leisure counseling services to identify the strengths and weaknesses of existing approaches to and models of leisure counseling and to draw implications for theoretical and practical applications.

Basic Core Competency

Leisure counselors should demonstrate the ability to contrast and compare approaches to and models of leisure counseling and to identify implications for the conceptual development of leisure counseling as well as their implications for leisure counseling practice.

Content to Achieve Competency

a. Operational definitions of the terms *theory, model, paradigm, concept.*
b. The relationship of philosophy, goals, and objectives to theories, models, and paradigms.
c. Analysis of approaches to or models of counseling and leisure counseling in terms of nature, purpose(s), goals, intervention techniques, appropriateness for which individuals under what conditions.
d. The relationship between approaches to or models of leisure counseling to theories, models, or concepts of leisure and play.
e. Implications of approaches to or models of leisure counseling to a conceptual development of leisure counseling.
f. The relationship between personal philosophical statements of leisure counseling, approaches to and/or models of leisure counseling, and leisure counseling practice with specific individuals in specified settings.

Unit VIII — Leisure Counseling: Intervention Strategies

Rationale

Because leisure counseling is a helping process that can be provided in a variety of settings with many different types of individuals and groups, it is incumbent on leisure counselors to learn how to use a multitude of intervention methods and techniques so that those appropriate to specific individuals or groups in specific settings will be employed.

Basic Core Competency

Leisure counselors should demonstrate the ability to use a variety of intervention techniques to assess the leisure needs and interests of specific individuals in specific settings so as to assist them in increasing their leisure awareness, developing their leisure activity selection and evaluation skills, and enhancing the quality of their leisure experiences.

Content to Achieve Competency

a. Role and function of assessment in leisure counseling.
b. Existing instruments used in leisure counseling to assess the needs and interests of individuals to be served.
c. Interviewing: purpose, types, basic components, techniques.
d. Listening: purpose, types, techniques.
e. Observation (including nonverbal communication): purpose, types, methods.
f. Problem-solving and decision-making (including brainstorming, goal set-

ting, and possible outcomes): approaches, processess, methods.

g. Role playing, simulation games, guided discovery: purposes, types, methods, and techniques.

h. Values clarification: approaches, types, techniques.

i. Activity analysis: purpose and methods.

j. Approaches to and processes of recreation program planning and development.

k. Strategies for implementing leisure education.

l. Stress management: approaches and techniques.

m. Establishing behaviorally oriented objectives in relation to assessed leisure needs and interests of individuals and/or groups.

n. Design and implement individual and/or group program to achieve objectives.

o. Resource information file: purpose, methods of establishing and using.

p. Making referrals: when, purposes, basic components, techniques.

q. Modification of intervention techniques to meet the needs of special populations.

r. Record keeping and reporting.

Unit IX — Leisure Counseling: Evaluation and Research

Rationale

In order to improve planning, effect better services and management, establish greater accountability, and contribute to the knowledge base of leisure counseling, it is necessary for leisure counselors to understand and apply the principles and components of evaluation and research.

Basic Core Competency

Leisure counselors should demonstrate the ability to design and implement a systematic approach to individual, group, and program evaluations in relation to their services and to formulate and conduct research studies in the area of leisure counseling.

Content to Achieve Competency

a. The need for and purpose(s) of individual, group, and program evaluations in leisure counseling.

b. Definition of *evaluation* and issues surrounding it (e.g., degree of formality, judgment vs. descriptions, time frame, preordination vs. responsive, values).

c. Who is the evaluation audience(s) (i.e., for whom are the evaluations being prepared).

  d. Selecting evaluation strategies consistent with purposes and audience(s) (e.g., measurement, professional judgment, goal free, discrepancy).

  e. Analysis of the results of evaluations.

  f. Using and communicating evaluation results.

  g. The need for and purpose(s) of research in leisure counseling.

  h. The relationship between theories, paradigms, models, and concepts to research.

  i. Basic research designs and methods and their potential applications to leisure counseling.

  j. Samples of questions or problems in leisure counseling for which research is needed.

Unit X — Professional Development for Leisure Counselors

Rationale

In order to provide leisure counseling in a professional manner, it is necessary that leisure counselors learn the attributes of a profession and a professional against which they can measure their own strengths and limitations, themselves as individuals engaged in a helping profession, and the field. Also, as leisure counseling is an emerging field with limited consensus in terms of an accepted knowledge base and established practices, it is incumbent on leisure counselors to engage in activities of continuing professional development so that they obtain a repertoire of up-to-date knowledge, intervention techniques, and resources.

Basic Core Competency

Leisure counselors should demonstrate the ability to assess their strengths and limitations in relation to the attributes of a helping professional providing assistance to individuals and groups in the area of leisure counseling; and they should demonstrate a knowledge of activities related to continuing professional development.

Content to Achieve Competency

  a. Attributes of a profession, including code of ethics.

  b. Motivating forces toward professionalization (e.g., increase and insure competency, accountability to public, protection of "turf," control over work, job security).

  c. Attributes and responsibilities of a professional, including ethical behavior and confidentiality.

  d. Values, beliefs, and understandings of individuals in the helping professions (e.g., high capacity for empathy, flexibility, sufficient personal strength to make sharing/helping possible, extraordinary self-discipline to transcend self and give attention to the needs of others, respect for individuals as human beings, conscious use of self in a helping relationship).

e. Assessment of personal strengths and limitations in terms of c and d.

f. Assessment of personal beliefs, meanings, and experiences in relation to asking for and receiving help, leisure counseling, the quality of various leisure experiences, and the implications of these for leisure counseling practice.

g. The leisure counselor's professional responsibility as an advocate in relation to a variety of issues (e.g., the relationship of leisure to the quality of life, the need for leisure education, financial support for recreation services).

h. Continuing professional development for leisure counselors (e.g., courses, conferences, institutes, professional literature, professional writing, research).

i. Legal aspects of counseling practice in general and leisure counseling specifically.

Unit XI — The Internship: Supervised Leisure Counseling Practice

Rationale

Leisure counselors must have the opportunity to apply the academic components of their professional preparation to actual professional practice, under the joint supervision of academic faculty and persons who are experienced in providing leisure counseling services "in the field." Supervised leisure counseling practice enables the student to "learn by doing" and to assess strengths and limitations as a leisure counselor.

Basic Core Competency

Leisure counselors should demonstrate the ability to complete successfully a supervised leisure counseling practice experience by meeting the accepted standards established by the professional preparation program.

Content to Achieve Competency *

a. Apply, under professional supervision, the knowledge, skills, and attitudes acquired in the academic or workshop setting.

b. Gain knowledge of particular leisure counseling delivery systems and their relationships to other leisure delivery systems.

*Recognition for some of the content areas is given to Arnold H. Grossman, *Fieldwork & Internship: A Practicum Manual for Students, Faculty and Agency Supervisors*, Department of Recreation and Leisure Studies, School of Education, Health, Nursing, and Arts Professions, New York University, 1980.

   c. Test, develop, and/or enhance leisure counseling skills.

   d. Apply assessment techniques for the purpose of determining the leisure needs and interests of individuals and groups, including special populations.

   e. Assess own skills in establishing helping relationships.

   f. Determine appropriateness for the student of leisure counseling as a professional activity.

   g. Learn to make effective use of supervision for continued professional development.

   h. Test, develop, and enhance skills and competencies in counseling, supervision, consultation, and education.

   i. Diagnose the socioleisure needs of an individual or group; develop an appropriate intervention plan; implement the plan; and evaluate the outcomes.

CONCLUDING REMARKS

Writing a chapter on professional preparation for an emerging discipline is never an easy task, and when it involves the "territory" of two professions it becomes more difficult. There will be those individuals who will applaud the effort ("It is long past due!") and there will be others who will say it is too soon to undertake such an endeavor ("We need more research!"). There will be others who will say that one aspect of leisure counseling was given insufficient emphasis and others who will state that the same aspect was overemphasized. These reactions were anticipated, but there are individuals desiring and/or in need of leisure counseling services today and they should not be "written off." Furthermore, they are entitled to receive the services of the most competent professionals that society can prepare with its present state of expertise.

The "Curriculum Guide" is not envisioned as the ultimate program for professional preparation. In fact, it is hoped that it will be modified as professionals continue to add to the body of knowledge of leisure counseling and to resolve some of the crucial issues facing the field.

There are many issues regarding leisure counseling today that have implications for professional preparation and that have not been discussed here. They have been addressed in other chapters of this book and elsewhere by many competent professionals. For the purposes of informing the reader of our awareness of these issues and the need to incorporate them in a professional preparation program, a short listing is in order: (1) Which profession, if any, has a public mandate to provide leisure counseling?; (2) What is the nature of the ideal leisure state?; (3) Are recreation and leisure services personnel on the "bandwagon" of leisure counseling because it will give the profession status (bring it closer to the medical model)?; (4) Are individuals in the recreation and leisure profession providing leisure counseling because it gives each of them the status of "counselors" and/or the power to manipulate clients in their search for power and influence?; (5) Does the necessary instrumentation exist to assess leisure interests, potential, and behavior?; (6) Is there too much reliance on instrumentation and not a sufficient amount on the humanistic processes in leisure counseling practice today?; (7) Is the emerging abundance of free time "the social ill" that the recreation and leisure service profession should address through leisure counseling practice?; (8) Does (or should) leisure counseling occur in isolation? and (9) Are counselors creating the subfield of leisure counseling in response to a real need, or simply for professional enhancement? These issues are important and their eventual resolution will affect the nature of leisure counseling as a discipline. They should be addressed in any professional preparation program; and it is urged that a discussion of them be included in the previous units as appropriate. Only informed professionals can contribute to the most desirable resolution of these issues.

In addition to the aforementioned issues regarding leisure counseling in general, specific issues regarding the professional preparation of leisure counselors have emerged. Some of these follow: (1) Who is providing leisure counseling and what is their training and/or ability?; (2) Should leisure counselors be trained as counselors with a speciality in leisure or as leisure service professionals with training in counseling?; (3) What is the number of courses in counseling that should be required of recreation professionals and what is the number of courses in recreation and leisure that should be required of counselors?; (4) Should an individual be trained only as a *leisure* counselor?; (5) Who should educate leisure counselors? and (6) What should the ideal curriculum be? Some of these issues are important (e.g., What should be the training and abilities of a leisure counselor? and Who should educate leisure counselors?). Some questions are of much less importance (e.g., Should they be trained as counselors with a speciality in leisure or recreation professionals with a speciality in counseling? and What is the *number* of courses in counseling and leisure?).

The important questions can be incorporated into two basic issues: (1) the academic background of the persons providing leisure counseling services, and (2) the qualifications of those who are responsible for their instruction. With regard to the first issue, it would seem, from the responses to the survey reported in the beginning of this chapter, that formal study in counseling is not the predominant model. The counseling competencies presented in the "Curriculum Guide" make explicit the need for expertise in the theory and practice of counseling. Whether this expertise is developed through traditional independent courses in counseling, such as at New York University, or through coordinated modules as part of a training program, the point is that the client has the right to expect that his/her leisure counselor has counseling expertise. Likewise, the identified competencies make clear the need for expertise in the area of recreation and leisure.

The second specific issue regarding professional preparation of leisure counselors concerns the expertise of those who "teach" the competencies. Only those professionals who have demonstrated their own expertise should be responsible for attesting to the attainment of others. In the absence of a definitive leisure counseling profession, with its attendant certification or licensing, code of ethics, accreditation of curricula, and a professional organization, a coordinated effort to provide professional preparation must take place. Counseling *and* leisure service professionals must undertake cooperatively the designing of curricula and instruction. It is not an issue of which comes first, counseling *or* leisure competencies. Both areas of competency are equally important, and those now separate professions are responsible for meeting the needs of those who desire to practice leisure counseling.

One final remark is necessary. Truax and Carkhuff (1967, p. 207) report a growing list of studies showing that by the time a counselor had been trained, he/she had less empathy than when the training started. There is something about professional preparation and becoming "professional" that alienates some people from humanity's wavelength. It appears that "professionals" begin to identify with their profession first and the human beings with whom they work only secondarily. It is our hope that the individuals who use the "Curriculum Guide" presented in this chapter will work to see that this does not happen to those being trained in leisure counseling and that the consumers of their services will continue to demand an accountability for the effective types of services they have a right to expect.

REFERENCES

Edwards, P.B., & Bloland, P.A. Leisure counseling and consultation. *The Personnel and Guidance Journal*, 1980, *58*(6), 435-440.

Epperson, A.: Educating recreators for leisure counseling. *Journal of Health, Physical Education and Recreation*. 1977, *48*, 39.

Grossman, A.: Meeting the need: A professional preparation program in leisure counseling. *Leisure Information Newsletter*, 1980, *7*, 1ff.

Hayes, G.A.: Leisure education and recreation counseling. In D.M. Compton & J.E. Goldstein (Eds.), *Perspectives of leisure counseling*. Arlington, Va.: National Recreation and Park Association, 1977.

Loesch, L.C., & Wheeler, P.T.: *Principles of leisure counseling*. Minneapolis: Educational Media Corporation, 1982.

Morrill, W.H., Oetting, E.R., & Hurst, J.C.: Dimensions of counselor functionig. *The Personnel and Guidance Journal*, 1974, *52*, 354.

Neulinger, J.: *To leisure: An introduction*. Boston: Allyn and Bacon, 1981.

The Counseling Psychologist, 1981, *9*(3).

Truax, C.B., & Carkhuff, R.R.: *Toward effective counseling and psychotherapy*. Chicago: Aldine, 1967.

Chapter 12

TOWARD A PHILOSOPHY OF MORAL JUDGMENT AND ETHICAL PRACTICES IN LEISURE COUNSELING

GERALD S. FAIN

Introduction

THE purpose of this chapter is to establish the foundations for questions pertinent to ethical practice in the field of leisure counseling and to draw implications for practice. Its intention is not to generate a rationale for the creation of a set of principles or beliefs. As the reader will find, codes exist in related disciplines, the principles of which have been tested as part of the legal process, professional experience, and scholarly debate. The literature offers abundant evidence that those who *seriously* engage in the helping professions — social work, medicine, psychology, or other human service fields — discuss, struggle, and learn to live with the disciplines of conduct established by their peers.

Moreover, fundamental principles that help the individual distinguish between essentially "good" and "bad" actions have long been studied. It is, however, quite another task to interpret these general principles into the context of professional practice in any particular field of service. To date, however, pointed discussions of ethical practices in leisure counseling have not occurred.

The need to attend to questions of ethical practice is accelerated because of the age in which we live. Today, sophisticated legal mechanisms, combined with strong consumer movements, do not allow the time or provide the support for nurturance of those professionals who cannot attend to questions of ethical practice responsively. Such questions reduce quick, precise, and rational responses by professionals in the 1980s more than at any other period in history. A great deal of attention has been focused on the questions of ethics in the past few years. Perhaps stimulated by a post-Watergate awareness or linked to fundamental concerns of human rights, it is clear the public is thinking about issues of right and wrong. This includes the issues of abortion, the right to life movement, the right to die movement, Equal Rights Amendment, nuclear power, clean air and water, world hunger, and Solidarity, all of which affect the ways we behave as individuals in a civilized order.

A study of dealing with ethical conduct was published in the November 1981 issue of *Psychology Today*. Author James Hassett based his study upon the responses of more than 23,000 respondents. For the most part, the survey documented what many people already know, but are reluctant to admit. In Hassett's words, "I was amazed how many people said, 'this is wrong, but I'd do it anyway.'" The study clearly points in the direction that morality, as we have traditionally understood and practiced it, is being challenged. Our understanding that "guilt is a powerful motivator" may apply here, as *Psychology Today* "received about 4,000 letters, the largest number of responses ever." He concludes, "Given the amount of rule breaking our survey documents, it would seem unwise to place too much faith in the honor system" (Hassett, 1981).

With specific regard to leisure counseling, we need to be fairly certain that its practice is of sufficient substance or power to justify our intervention. Without careful scrutiny of action, innocent people and society as a whole may be at risk. It is one thing to proclaim that leisure counseling may be of utility in helping people address life problems associated with their leisure and quite another to hold the professional accountable for providing adequate protection against harm.

In order to establish these understandings, it is first necessary to become familiar with the discipline of ethics, the process of ethical practice formulated in related fields of service and inquiry, and then to examine the existing phenomenon of leisure counseling as it has evolved.

The Discipline of Ethics

Ethics is that part of philosophy that deals with the study of what people *ought to do*. Unlike psychology, anthropology, and sociology, which seek to interpret and understand the behavior of people, ethics pertains to the questions of "rightness" or "wrongness" of actions.

Ethics derives from the Greek *ethos* meaning custom. In this sense, we seek to study human customs. *Mores* is the Latin word from which we draw the meaning of morality. Both concepts are inextricably linked, morality being the sole interest of ethics. Ethics then, also referred to as moral philosophy, deals *not* with the conventions of everyday living, addressing, styles, or fashions in the way of manners, but instead deals with fundamental customs such as telling the truth, respect for individual rights and the freedoms and responsibilities protected by the society. "The fact that men do make judgements of right and wrong, is the basic fact of experience from which ethics takes it start" (Fagothey, 1972, p. 4).

In our civilized world we recognize that when people do what they want to do, without regard for what they ought to do, they are considered outlaws. This principle is fundamental to the tenets of human rights articulated by John Stuart Mill.

> The sole end for which mankind are warranted, individually or collectively, in interfering with the liberty of action of any of their number, is self-protection. That the only purpose for which power can be rightfully exercised over any member of a civilized community, against his will, is to prevent harm to others. His own good, either physical or moral, is not sufficient warrant. He cannot rightfully be compelled to do or forbear because it be better for him to do so, because it will make him happier, because, in the opinions of others, to do so would be wise, or even right. (John Stuart

Mill, *On liberty*, in Reiser, Dyck, & Curran, 1977).

The study of ethics is based upon the natural order of things. Those who study ethics do not invent or interpret the world in ways that are contrived or arranged in a manner that is purely political or self-serving. In this respect, it is a classical discipline that transcends the space of everyday living. Should one wish to apply the principles of the discipline to a particular field of practice, it is necessary that the field in question have a discrete body of knowledge. Simultaneously, the process designed to resolve questions pertaining to "proper" conduct reveals the phenomena. By studying what we "ought" to do we better understand what it is that we do.

The Hippocratic Oath, presented by Hippocrates (c 460-c 377 B.C.), was far more than a statement pertaining to ethical behavior of physicians. The oath clearly separated, for the first time in history, medicine from the practice of religion, superstition, and magic. Without understanding the empirical nature or natural order of the field, it is not possible to establish the essential boundaries of inquiry. This becomes evident when we accept the proposition than an action, in and of itself, is neither good nor bad. Each action must be considered with respect to its consequence and context. For example, taking a group of children into the woods could be considered therapy: a deliberate action. If so it would likely require a licensed practitioner who might even receive third party reimbursement. In contrast, the same type of activity (taking children into the woods) could be a summer camp experience in which high school or college students assume a primary role in structuring the childrens' experience. The resulting difference between CAMP COUNSELOR and COUNSELING PSYCHOLOGIST should clearly illustrate this point.

"Self-Realization Through the Disciplined Ego"

A morally good or a morally bad act is a kind of self-assertion or self-expression. When we judge a person's acts from a moral point of view, we judge them as his/her acts, part of his/her whole system of actions. Our judgment might have been different if someone else had acted similarly or brought about the same consequences. Our actions tell us and those around us who we are and what we value.

To be truly moral our actions must in some sense be consistent. They must arise out of a consistent character and manifest that character if they are to be valid. This is a principle by which the individual or the group is judged.

This consistency of action, within the context of professional practice, is represented in codes of ethics. These codes require the practitioner to exhibit behavior that is stylistically and substantially in accord with that of the members of the guild. The content provides direction in technical or ontological actions as well as aesthetics. Therefore, the manner of one's dress, hygiene, or style, while not necessarily explicitly stated with a code, is included. These code behaviors are expected by those in the profession and the public at large, and in all but the most severe instances interpretation and enforcement would be attended to by members of the licensing body.

The degree to which a code becomes more concerned with style than with ontology is of concern. Strictly defined, in the view of the ontologist, emotional involvement may be considered of secondary importance. To illustrate the point, therapeutic intervention or medical treatment can then be seen to have a beginning and end. Given the grave nature of the life and death situations one must deal with in medicine on a daily basis, it is understandable that a view eschewing involvement outside of the acts performed would prevail. A code of ethics is then attractive to the physician because by discouraging compassion "it helps free the physician of the destructive consequences of that personal investment" (May, 1977, p. 69). However, in matters of aesthetics where style is the consequence, then it is the timelessness of the acts that would rightly prevail with respect to the code.

Hence, medical practice in a hospital setting attends to different issues than those of the performing artist whose actions transcend the technical. The former may be considered to have ontological interests while the latter is more concerned with aesthetics.

This is not to imply that the two live in separate worlds. Rather we can accept the reality that the *actions* upon which codes are based require a different rationale. Therefore, for physicians to pronounce their respect for human life in the delivery of surgical treatment without debating questions of abortion or brain death would be irresponsible and unacceptable. Equally unacceptable would be the actions of a performing artist that did not demonstrate mastery of the technical skills shared by disciplined colleagues.

Successful counseling, in the most generic sense, requires a mastery of both technical and aesthetic domains. Discipline of the individual's creative desire as a helper is necessary for coherence in the field of practice. Yet, addressing human problems as a counselor often is dependent upon one's ability to build interpersonal relationships, and interpret experiences in the manner of the artist.

Intuitionism and Utilitarianism

Over the past 200 years moral philosophy has advanced a variety of views. Some of these views have compelling relevance to the unique interests of those who study and practice in the area of leisure. By reviewing two in particular, intuitionism and utilitarianism, as ways of understanding the world, we may be more able to postulate pertinent questions that underscore ethical considerations in leisure counseling.

The views of moral philosophy associated with intuitionism and utilitarianism rest in two different worlds. The intuitionists believe that human beings are able to differentiate between what is morally right or wrong on the basis of their individual conscience. Morally right acts are those that are right in themselves. These acts are intrinsically representative and objectively real. In this sense, reason is the mechanism that drives people to create rules. William Whewell (1794-1866), a scientist and professor of moral philosophy at Cambridge, was a major influence in this movement. He firmly believed that reason is the "light of man's constitution which reveals him to himself" (Hudson, 1980, p. 4). Further, the intuitionists held that virtue must be freely chosen so as to be approved by one's conscience.

In contrast, the utilitarians expound the view that a person's actions are good or right only to the extent to which they create or increase human happiness. This school of thinking is most frequently associated with Jeremy Bentham (1748-1832) who, like his disciple John Stuart Mill (1806-1873), believed that the primary motive directing each of us to act is the desire for our own pleasure. Therefore the Greatest Happiness Principle, a theory long discussed by philosophers, serves as the basis for utilitarianism. Perhaps of greatest interest and application to the subject of leisure counseling is the *Ethica Nicomachea*. Here, Aristotle debates the rightness or wrongness of pleasure. He asks about the ineptness of the drive to avoid pain and the consequence of an existence founded only upon the pursuit of pleasure.

One fundamental difference seems to be present in the thinking of Mill and Bentham. Mill believed in the conscience and that we prove the morality of action by experience. Bentham held that conscience revealed little and opted for a more simplified, scientifically objective standard of morality (Hudson, 1980).

Our present interest in considering the views of intuitionism and utilitarianism is important for several reasons. When we consider the role that the conscience plays in deciding what is good and bad, we begin to understand how difficult these decisions usually are. Conscience is seen as having a reference to the individual and the society. Knowing what one "ought" to do comes from past experience that dynamically interacts with circumstances of the moment. Prevailing values of one's culture and mores of subgroups, in combination with what the individual believes to be right or in the self interest, leads to the actualization of "ought." A second issue to be raised comes from discussion of the "Greatest Happiness Principle." Certainly those involved in leisure counseling, perhaps more than any other human service professions, should address this question. The moral philosophical belief system of leisure is founded on this very point. Leisure represents to contemporary society a resource that holds the singular potential for nothing else but happiness, happiness in that it is expected to be "pleasureable" and highly "satisfying." Here lies the problem.

If in happiness a person is to achieve a state of pleasure, a state of being that is without pain, will this bring satisfaction? Should we answer yes, it would follow that we support a type of hedonism and encourage people to follow self-interest as a rule. Yet, social psychology reminds us that the reality of others (our group and society) has direct impact on personal happiness and life satisfaction. We do have an awareness of others whose beliefs and actions affect our abilities to experience happiness. Thus, our acceptance of intuitionism or utilitarianism as a basis for moral action has implications for our pursuit of leisure and ultimately for the practice of leisure counseling. The fundamental question to be asked is, What is the goal or end to which leisure counseling is devoted?

As we approach the end of the century, there appears to be an increasing interest in the study of ethics in professional practice. Interest in ethics is so strong that the *Boston Globe* newspaper ran a fifteen article series in 1979 on the subject. Included were numerous references to current university-based professional preparation programs that have recently created courses explicitly on ethics. This series was followed by a three-part series in 1981 that focused on ethics in business. In 1982 the *Globe* reported that a course on ethics at Harvard attracted 300 students from across campus.

More pointedly, the Carnagie Council on policy studies in higher education found "signs are proliferating that some colleges and universities — and some of their students — are engaging in ethically dubious, if not illegal, behavior" (Scully, 1979). This is followed by a Hastings Center Report that found, after a two-year survey, a sharp increase in courses on ethics at both the undergraduate and professional school levels. This included more than 2,000 courses from the areas of bioethics (abortion, genetic counseling, use of human subjects, etc.) to journalism (invasion of privacy, censorship, accepting gifts, etc.). The study went on to criticize some of the coursework for their lack of theoretical framework and rigorous moral thought (Winkler, 1979).

Before beginning this section on ethics in related fields of practice it should be asked, Why do professions need ethical codes of practice? What is it that distinguishes these people from the rest of the population? Everyone must accept the "laws of the land" as established by the citizens of that society, regardless of career, social and economic status, or political or religious beliefs. Members of professional groups are not different in this respect as they too are citizens. In general, the reasons can be clustered into three broad categories.

First, the actions taking place in professions are so specialized that the lay population is unable to judge rightness or wrongness. Responsible people question their own work out of an interest in improving their ability to deliver services. Second, members of the profession demand of themselves and their colleagues certain standards of practice. When those standards are violated, it affects each individual practitioner's ability to work. Without discipline, expectations for outcome would vary greatly, undermining clarity of inquiry and public acceptance of the profession. Discipline allows for the creation of a common set of principles and practices. Codes of conduct also create the mechanisms that allow for review and reprimand of violators. Third, the public at large has legitimate concern that in the absence of control exercised by the profession, the likelihood of harm is great. This "felt need" is expressed as outrage when a public trust is violated. From reviewing established professions, it could be concluded that public support is directly proportionate to the degree of perceived harm. Because we have great concern for avoiding pain and death we require physicians to be highly trained and licensed. By means of licensing, the public is saying that without control the possibility of harm to innocent members of society is great. Codes of ethics, therefore, provide assurance to the public that the profession is also concerned about misconduct.

Without specialized knowledge, disciplined practice, or perceived opportunity for harm, it is understandable that little discussion of ethics in leisure counseling has taken place. Yet, it is equally understandable that there be concern to guard against misconduct. Absence of rules should not be interpreted as license to behave without conscience.

The fields of medicine and law have historically provided and stimulated debate for the moral philosopher. From studying the time of Hammurabi or Hippocrates to the present, one could learn a great deal about the evolution of professional ethics. However, for the present purposes, a review of ethical codes in psychology and human service fields may be sufficient. In contrast to medicine and law, helping professions have rather short histories.

Human Services

Other professions, recognizing the importance of moral foundations for the intellectual development and public acceptance of their work, have studied ethics. Because the advancement of any particular field of practice is based upon its meaningful distinctiveness in responding to need, professional uniqueness is necessary. However, it is also recognized that in general *all* helping professions have much in common.

With an interest in applying ethical principles, Levey (1974) studied the codes of ethics of 89 human service occupational groups. As a social worker he was interested in commenting on the Code of Ethics of the National Association of Social Workers of 1971. Without an analysis of underlying moral assumption, he concluded that ethical conduct would be classified into four broadly conceived categories.

I. *The Practitioner*

"The practitioner, should be: '. . . in full command of his personal faculties when performing his occupational functions or when he might be called on to do so.' " (p. 210)

II. *The Client*

"The practitioner, as a faithful agent, owes it to his client to provide him with the best qualitative and quantitative care, protections, and service, and to treat him with empathy, consideration, and fidelity. He must apply himself to the maximum extent of his capacity, not only to safeguard the client's interests, but also to advance the client's cause as far as his knowledge, ethics, and competence permit." (p. 210)

III. *Professional Colleagues*

". . . pertains to the relationships between the practitioner, his fellow practitioners, and the occupational group. The principles involved related to etiquette, fairness, and professional orientation." (p. 213)

IV. *Society*

"The principles in this category demand great care and responsibility in the manner the practitioner presents himself to, deals with, and helps the community in which he is a part." (p. 213)

In conclusion, he urges that the social work profession become active in refinement, implementation, and enforcement of their Code of Ethics. Levey argues that the future of the profession depends upon this work.

This clustering of ethical principles is representatiave of Human Service fields. The four categories do serve to identify shared areas of concern.

Higher Education

Dill (1982), outlining the history of ethics within the academic profession, begins by noting that John Dewey was the creator and first chair of the Committee on Professional Ethics of the American Association of University Professors (AAUP). Dewey left office in the 1920s; the committee did not meet again until 1956. "Not until 1966, fifty-one years after founding of the association and twenty-six years after adopting a statement on academic freedom and tenure, did the AAUP finally adopt a statement on professional ethics" (Dill, p. 244). Dewey had argued that statements regarding "freedoms," addressing issues of academic freedom and tenure as articulated by the AAUP, required an understanding of responsibilities and disciplined conduct of behaviors.

Dewey not only was instrumental in directing educational practice but was also dynamically invested in the philosophy of the ethics. His contribution was one that brought the evolving theoretical, psychological, and human development theory into the thinking of that day. Through awareness of the principles of human growth and development, ethical thinking was enriched as well as the oral development of children and the dynamics of personality-informed theory.

The university community has recently become interested in questions of ethics. Courses in the area of ethics from the view of specific disciplines, such as law, medicine, theology, and the liberal arts, have proliferated. *The Journal of Higher Education* devoted one of its 1982 issues entirely to the issue of ethics. It is important to note that academicians have ignored the question of ethical practice as it relates to the profession of university teaching. We have courses on medical ethics, legal ethics, and other fields of practice, all taught by professionals, yet no evidence of concern for the question of ethical practices as they exist in the classroom.

Emily Robertson and Gerald Grant (1982) have discussed this apparent reluctance to develop a code of ethics within academia. They argue that a code of academic ethics would not necessarily improve the conduct of people in the profession and that due to the complexities of the university it would be impossible to create a code that was other than too general or too specific.

Their position addressed a most perplexing question. Is university teaching a profession in and of itself, or is the university just a place where scholars from specific areas of practice explore knowledge and share information with students? If we believe that a professor of law is a lawyer who is employed by the university to teach, that infers a different conclusion that if we considered him/her a teacher employed for his/her knowledge of law. More importantly we would want to explore the *responsibility* of the university, professor, and student within the broader context of education and democracy.

Psychology

The most recently revised *Ethical Principles of Psychologists* (formerly, Ethical Standards of Psychologists) was adopted by the American Psychological Association's Council of Representatives on January 24, 1981 (*American Psychologist*, June 1981). The document includes ten principles that are identified in the preamble.

> Psychologists respect the dignity and worth of the individual and strive for the preservation and protection of fundamental human rights. They are committed to increasing knowledge of human behavior and of people's understanding of themselves and others and to the utilization of such knowledge for the promotion of human welfare. While pursuing these objectives, they make every effort to protect the welfare of those who seek their services and of the research participants that may be the object of the study. They use their skills only for purposes consistent with these values and do not knowingly permit their misuse by others. While demanding for themselves freedom of inquiry and communication, psychologists accept the responsibility this freedom requires: competence, objectivity in the application of skills, and concern for the best interest of clients, colleagues, research participants, and society. In the pursuit of these ideals, psychologists subscribe to principles in the following areas:
>
> 1. Responsibility
> 2. Competence
> 3. Moral and Legal Standards
> 4. Public Statements
> 5. Confidentiality
> 6. Welfare of the Consumer
> 7. Professional Relationships
> 8. Assessment Techniques
> 9. Research with Human Participants
> 10. Care and Use of Animals
>
> Acceptance of membership in the American Psychological Association, in particular, the member to adherence to these principles.
>
> Psychologists cooperate with duly constituted committees of the American Psychological Association, in particular, The Committee on Scientific and Professional Ethics and Conduct by responding to inquiries promptly and completely. Members also respond promptly and completely to inquiries from duly constituted state association ethics committees and professional standards review committees.

The process followed by the American Psychological Association in the formation of their ethical practices is outlined by Golann (1969). This sequence of events spanned important development stages from 1948 to 1963.

- 1948: 7,500 APA members generated 1,000 reports citing case material that raised ethical concern. The ethics committee organized into these six categories:

Public Responsibility
Client Responsibility
Teaching
Research
Writing and Publication
Professional Relationships

- 1951: A draft document was prepared and sent to all members for comment. For the next several years formal study of the document was conducted at professional meetings and within departments. Some 200 reports were submitted.

- 1953: After the next set of revisions were completed, the membership adopted the Ethical Standards of Psychologists.

- 1959: Eighteen general principles were abstracted from the standards and field tested for three years.

- 1963: The revised Ethical Standards of Psychologists were adopted.

- 1981: Since 1963 a number of substantive changes in the code had occurred. The 1981 revision included minor language changes and the addition of principle number 10, dealing with care and use of animals.

The variation and acceptance of standards is an important achievement for a profession. The work of APA over the past 35 years demonstrates a commitment to addressing questions of moral substance energized by sensitivity to the human problems psychologists attend.

> Much of what counselors and other mental health professionals do, even though time-honored, is truly experimental. Counselors will be hard pressed to name those personality, vocational, and ability tests that are so valid that the margin of error is almost nil. The same is true for intervention techniques. Counselors may need increasingly to think of their clients as participants in research and surround them with the protections that such persons deserve. (Goldman, 1978)

With specific regard to issues of morality, Kendler (1980) cautions as to the dangers of the psychologist assuming the position of authority. The process of directing an individual through treatment to a prescribed set of beliefs or values based upon "scientific fact" raises concern. This concern is heightened when one considers the science from which this practice has evolved.

Perhaps the strongest critique of psychological knowledge as "science" has been Sigmund Koch. Koch (1981) is one who does not believe psychology is a single or coherent discipline. Among other criticisms, he believes that psychology has been misconceived, full of jargon, single-minded, rigid, and profession-centered. Despite a somewhat hopeful view of the future, he generally feels these professions are failing.

> It is that there are times and circumstances in which able individuals, committed to inquiry, tend almost obsessively to frustrate the objectives of inquiry. It is as if uncertainty, mootness, ambiguity, cognitive finitude, were the most unbearable of the existential anguishes. Under these conditions, able and sincere inquirers become as autistic as little children; they seem more impelled toward the pursuit and maintenance of security fantasies than the winning of whatever significant knowledge may be within reach. (p. 259)

Koch reminds us of the vulnerability facing the social and behavioral sciences, a criticism that reflects the basic skepticism people may have in accepting explanations for the complex phenomena of human behavior. The interaction between person and environment, each with its own unique history and disposition, provides a dynamic state difficult to describe and predict. Unlike basic chemical reactions that can be replicated with great accuracy, individual actions are the products of the interaction of a large number of constantly changing variables.

However, the science of psychology has advanced in the past 50 years to a point of social acceptability. Insurance companies pay for psychological services in the same way they pay for hospitalization or for an x-ray. Psychologists have become part of the marketplace, advertising services that include sex therapy, drug treatment, behavior management, hypnosis, career counseling, marriage counseling, and biofeedback. There is no reason to suspect that this trend of continuing advancement will be seriously impeded. On the contrary, it appears that the number of licensed psychologists will continue to grow.

Sport Psychology

The North American Society for Psychology of Sport and Physical Activity (NASPSPA) is a relatively new organization. One of their first tasks has been the establishment of Ethical Standards for Provision of Services by Sport Psychology Educators, Researchers, and Practitioners. After three years of committee work, drawing heavily from the existing work of the American Psychological Association, NASPSPA present two documents to its membership: Ethical Standards of Sport Psychology Consultants and the Guidelines for Psychological Testing Within Sport and Other Physical Activity Settings. The documents were approved. Of significant note was an editorial comment:

> The documents would serve as NASPSPA's agreed upon guidelines for ethics and testings and, therefore, would represent sound practices which the membership would voluntarily follow. The documents do not implicitly or explicitly indicate mandatory adherence and therefore, do not involve adjudication if not followed. If at some later date the membership desires mandatory adherence and subsequent adjudication, then these issues will be considered with the advice of legal counsel. . . . the only individuals who are qualified to call themselves sport psychologists are those

professionals who have been licensed as "psychologists" by various state governments. These individuals, by their training and licensure, are required to abide by the ethical standards that have been adopted by the American Psychological Association. These individuals (without a license to call themselves "psychologists") however, may not call themselves "sport psychologists". Because licensure restricts the use of the term psychologist, NASPSPA is considering the adoption of new titles in order to avoid confusion and legal problems. (p. 3)

It appears that similar concerns and possibly similar courses of action may lie ahead for those seeking the title of Leisure Counselor, should acceptance by psychology be desired.

Recreation and Leisure

In the late 1800s there was substantial evidence of the need to address questions of moral responsibility. Leaders of that day like John Dewey, Joseph Lee, and Jane Addams, who shaped social policy, believed in the value of recreation. They tended to view recreation and leisure as an important part of living in a free society. The playground, in particular, was thought to require the same high quality leadership as the school or clinic.

Over the past 100 years the recreation and leisure professions have not carried this responsibility very far. While such discussion is conspiciously absent from present day texts in the field, Miller and Robinson (1963) address the issue directly. They not only cite an interest in moral theory by the profession but also reference efforts at the state level to establish codes of professional conduct.

> The transition from the conception of the workers role as just a job to that of being a professional can perhaps be most clearly marked at that point when an individual establishes standards for himself and subscribes to a code of ethics to govern his behavior and conduct . . . . The American Recreation Society, The Group Work Section of the National Association of Social Workers, National Recreation Association, and the American Institute of Park Executives have adopted codes of ethics; numerous state recreation societies have followed suit. (pp. 383-384)

The code for the American Recreation Society to which they refer considers ethics as "a part of science and philosophy dealing with moral conduct, duty and judgement. It establishes a standard of professional right and wrong conduct and behavior" (p. 2).

At present there is little evidence of interest by recreation and leisure professionals toward the study or promotion of ethical practice. Little attention to advising the work of the ARS is evidenced in the literature, professional meetings, or university curriculum. Ethics has not been addressed as an issue of scholarly concern since that time.

It may be important to point out that in 1966 the American Recreation Society along with seven other organizations joined together in creating the National Recreation and Park Association (NRPA). As a result, the professional movement was somewhat redirected. NRPA is, by design, a lay-professional organization. The strictly "professional" issues assume a relatively lower priority than those representing the general public. This NRPA code of ethics committee began its work in 1973. It was not until 1977 that NRPA adopted its own set of principles. The Suggested *Principles of the Code of Ethics of the Recreation and Park Profession* is recommended as a model for individual states to follow.

The American Alliance for Health, Physical Education, Recreation and Dance (AAHPERD), like the NRPA, offers professional membership for recreation and leisure practitioners. With a close tie to public education, AAHPERD has not expended effort in creating a unique set of principles or guidelines.

Of significant importance is the jointly sponsored curriculum accreditation program of NRPA, AAHPERD, and the American Alliance of Leisure and Recreation. Indicative of prevailing views within the profession, this program, which grants accreditation of two year, Baccalaureate, and Masters degree programs in leisure or recreation, does not include explicit standards or guidelines for the study of moral theory or professional ethics.

The end result is that recreation and leisure service practitioners have no effective means in place to review matters of ethical import. Should one member of the profession seek to question the behavior of a colleague, there is no single authority to which one can appeal. Given that this responsibility with respect to legal sanction rests with state government, it is important to recognize the dependence for enforcement on licensing bills. The point is that without legal recourse, such as the revocation of one's right to practice, review of suspected ethical misconduct is without enforcability.

When Dr. Robert Hayes, a professor of recreation, was found guilty of the largest welfare fraud in the history of the Commonwealth of Massachusetts in 1981, he was sent to prison. Upon his release, he has the option to continue his career in recreation without sanction brought against him by colleagues in recreation. Dr. Hayes is certainly not the first recreator to be found guilty of criminal charges, and there is no reason to believe that all other members of the profession are necessarily of higher moral character. The disgrace of one person's actions damages the reputation of all persons with whom they associate. Unfortunately, that damage is compounded when colleagues neglect the opportunity to formally disassociate themselves from such action.*

Some state recreation and park societies have addressed issues of ethical practices. The State of Illinois' Therapeutic Recreation Section has prepared a code of ethics and accompanying case book. Not only does this provide guidance to the practitioner but it also is foundational to other acts of professionalization.

There is no reason to suspect that issues of moral or ethical substance will be

---

*We hasten to add that the profession of university teachers in the state is also without a mechanism for removal for conduct as a university professor.

vigorously pursued by the recreation and leisure professions in the near future. Fundamentally, this field has emerged as a "Free Market," without stringent and consistent standards of practice. In general, neither the public nor the practitioner has required such standards.

Influence of the Courts

There is no area of everyday life unaffected by the legal system. We live in a society that uses law as a means of controlling and protecting the individual. Rulings in our courts have set clear directions for health care practices, educational services, consumer protection, and civil rights. The impact has had a civilizing effect on our society. Through a comparatively orderly process of the courtroom, disputes can be settled with a high degree of fairness. Might is not necessarily going to prevail if all parties are seen as having equal opportunity for representation.

The outcome of court action and its effect on society is undoubtedly influenced by public expression. The busing of school children for the purpose of achieving desegregation may appear, in the eyes of the court, a clear vision. Yet when implemented there are many questions and issues raised to which the court must respond. In a similar way, simple statements of ethical beliefs should not be considered of practical value until they have sustained the review of our courts and field testing.

For our purpose we will review a selected few cases that illustrate the impact of the courts as it may apply to leisure counseling.

Confidentiality

One of the few studies dealing with ethics in the field of recreation was completed by Sylvester (1981). His interests, while confined to the practice of therapeutic recreation, offer a good beginning to necessary case building. Within the field of counseling, many pertinent cases can be found. One of the most well-reported resulted in review by the Supreme Court of California (Tarasoff v. Regents of University of California, December 23, 1974).

Tatiana Tarasoff was killed by Prosenjit Poddar on October 27, 1969. The parents of Tatiana brought suit against the University of California regents, doctors, and campus police. It was their contention that the psychotherapists who had been treating Prosenjit had prior knowledge of his intention to kill Tatiana, and that they did not take the necessary action to warn her. Furthermore, they charged that the campus police, who also had knowledge of his intention (having been advised by the psychotherapists), also failed to warn her of the potential violence. The police did take Poddar into custody. After release, he discontinued psychotherapy.

This case reached the Supreme Court of California. The lawyers representing the University argued that the psychotherapeutic relationship demands confidentiality and that free and open communication between therapist and patient is essential. If patients believed that the communications with the psychotherapist were not confidential and could be shared with police and others, they would not freely express their feelings, emotions, thoughts, and problems. Without complete confidence in the relationship, the psychotherapist would not be able to provide treatment. On the side of the parents, the lawyers argued that it was the duty of the therapist to warn Tatiana.

The court cited sections of the California Evidence Code, rulings in similar cases, and the Principles of Medical Ethics of the American Medical Association (1957) Section 9: "A physician may not reveal the confidences entrusted to him in the course of medical attendance . . . unless he is required to do so by law or unless it becomes necessary in order to protect the welfare of the individual or of the community."

In this case the treatment of the patient terminated two months prior to the time he committed the tragedy. The court felt this was significant in that the termination of treatment increased the risk of violence.

The Supreme Court, in a reversal of a lower court's findings, held that the psychotherapists could not avoid liability for failure to warn the intended victim or those who could reasonably have been expected to notify her. In addition, the Court held that the Campus police could be held liable for failure to warn the victim, although neither they nor the therapists were liable for failure to confine Poddar. Thus, psychotherapists are expected to exercise reasonable care in preventing injury or violence of which they are aware.

The case serves to show that while there are general principles that guide our intentions and behaviors, each act must be viewed within its context. While confidentiality in general is to be respected within the therapeutic relationship, in this instance the courts found the application to be wrong. We also note the reliance of the legal system on the established standards of care within the profession. Great consideration was given to the nature of psychotherapy with regard to accepted practices for treatment and ethical behavior.

Related issues of concern for confidentiality were raised by the Amerian Psychiatric Association in 1970: "threats to the confidentiality of the physician-patient relationship in modern society are not abating; they are increasing and must be thwarted."

This position is easily understood given the increasing pressure of the public to obtain information. The debate is ongoing, as is the involvement of the courts. Telling or not telling a patient about his/her condition often presents problems. Other problems are raised when we enlarge the question to include the public's right to know. This latter issue has been raised in the case of political figures who have received treatment for some form of emotional disorder.

Structuring a discussion based heavily on "common sense and good judgement" as outlined by John Dewey, the APA drew eight examples in which confidentiality MIGHT be broken:

**A patient will probably commit murder; the act can be stopped only the interven-
tion of the psychiatrist. Can confidentiality be broken?

**A patient will probably commit suicide; the act can be stopped only by the inter-
vention of the psychiatrist. Can confidentiality be broken?

**A patient, in therapy, affirms that he committed a murder in the past. What about
confidentiality? If the patient subsequently denies the act, is the situation changed?

**A minor admits to using "soft" drugs. May confidentiality be broken? If he uses
hard drugs, does the situation change? If the patient is over the age of 21, is there a
difference?

**A patient (bus driver, airline pilot, etc.) charged with serious responsibilities
shows marked impairment of judgment. Can the company or a governmental regulatory agency be notified without the patient's permission?

**In most jurisdictions adultery, fornication, and homosexuality are illegal. Is this
cause for breaking confidentiality/

**A patient working on a project vital to national security is being subverted. Is it
ethical to break his confidence?

**A college student, a company employee, or a government employee is referred by
college, company or government for a psychiatric evaluation. What is the status of
confidentiality? Is there a difference if the patient is self-referred or referred by his
private physician?

(*American Journal of Psychiatry*, 1970, *126*(10), 1549.)

Treating Insanity

More recently, the Selznick case has attracted national attention. In this instance the nine-year-old son of Mr. and Mrs. Selznick was murdered by Vernal
Walford just three weeks after his release from North Hampton State Hospital
in Massachusetts. As portrayed by the television show "60 Minutes," the hospital released Walford with the knowledge that he was dangerous to society. The
parents had been trying to sue the Commonwealth of Massachusetts for the
past eight years for "gross negligence." The state, under the "doctrine of sovereign immunity," has refused the Selznicks the opportunity to bring suit, despite Walford having been found guilty of the murder by reason of insanity.
The parents brought the suit with a stated interest in fixing blame on the treatment practices of the hospital. In their view the hosptial had acted wrongly and
not in keeping with standards of care held by the profession and expected by
the public. The family went to the United States Supreme Court, where the
principle of sovereign immunity was upheld. As a result of the television program, however, the case was brought before the senate, where the vote was 29
to 0 in favor of setting up a special commission to investigate the release of
Walford.

The Selznick case raised the legal question of responsibility on part of the
therapist and the hospital. It makes the point that when the courts become involved in mental health cases, the protective shield of the profession is rendered
less necessary. The courts look at the individual case with respect to what it believes is in the best interest of the public. Despite the evidence that the therapist
may have acted improperly, the court had believed it not in its best interest to

hear the case.

Psychiatry has addressed the issue of judging sanity in many well publicized cases. The case of John W. Hinckley, Jr., the attempted assassin of President Reagan, has received continuing attention. Surely the act of attempted murder is not rational. No person in their "right mind" would engage in such action. However, once a group of experts in the field of mental health determine the individual to be "sick" or "healthy" and this opinion gains acceptance in the courtroom, consequences take on entirely different meanings. A murderer is considered a criminal who may be put to death, while an insane person can be treated, cured, and released. The struggle in defining the difference and prescribing the proper course of action is charactistic of our increasing humane civilization.

Stress

As a result of more readily available and reliable data on mental health, new questions pertaining to the effects of mental stress have arisen. It is recognized that certain occupations are more stressful that others. Air traffic controllers and law enforcement personnel have convinced the courts of this and are granted early retirement and other forms of monetary reimbursement as compensation for illness due to stress.

A less well publicized but potentially more profound case was heard by the United States Court of Appeals for the District of Columbia. The court ruled in January of 1982 that the Three Mile Island nuclear reactor number 1 was to remain closed until the potential harm to the mental health of people living near the power plant could be assessed. This is the first time the Nuclear Regulatory Commission was ordered by a court to conduct an environmental assessment to determine the effects the operation of the plan might have on the psychological health of neighboring residents and on the well-being of the communities surrounding the plant. Experts testifying in court held that residents were being subjected to severe psychological stress from fear of a disaster (Reverson, 1982).

The case establishes a powerful precedence. Not only does it place a value on mental health in relation to nuclear power, but more importantly it demonstrates our sophistication in documenting mental conditions. One might consider, for example, in a similar manner the potentially harmful effects that closing a symphony orchestra, losing a professional sports franchise, or selling of public park lands might have on the public. Moreover, because leisure has the potential of combating stress, this brings us one step closer to expressing the desirability of leisure as a treatment technique. It is only a short step from prohibiting activities that *cause* stress to advocating or requiring activities that *reduce* stress.

Summary and Implications

The discussion thus far has addressed interest in moral theory, ethical guidelines of related disciplines, and the influence of the courts on the implementation of professional ethics. In focusing attention on the implications of this material for the practice of leisure counseling, several directions for future action emerge.

Moral Theory

The first and most pressing need is for the field of leisure counseling to address questions of moral theory. This struggle to distinguish "good" from "bad" actions should serve as a foundation to ethical practices. With the identification of desired outcomes or consequences of intervention, the practitioner will define what "ought" to be done and how. Through the deliberate design of courses of action, the context and consequences of leisure counseling surface. In so doing we reveal who we are and for what we stand. Moreover, from disciplined conduct comes the coherence essential for the advancement of knowledge.

Study in moral philosophy and theory requires application of knowledge from the fields of developmental psychology, humanistic education, human development, and social psychology. From such enlightenment, we gain essential understandings of human behavior from which leisure behavior acquires meaning. This perspective of moral theory helps the practitioner understand how to balance technical and aesthetic competence. Knowing when to conform and when to deviate from accepted practice marks professional excellence. Simply deciding when to do what one believes is "right" without regard for prior experience, conscience, or the welfare of others should be viewed as irresponsible. Yet, without coherent direction from the field of practice as to proper and improper professional behavior, how can irresponsible acts ever be identified?

Related Disciplines

In reviewing related disciplines, issues of ethical import can generally be grouped into areas of the practitioner, client, colleagues, and society. Regardless of the respective profession, statements of ethical practice all share some degree of commonality.

The distinctiveness of any particular set of ethical principles is drawn from the theoretical basis that directs practice. While the counseling professions have tended to achieve this distinctiveness, leisure has not. Unlike marriage counseling, guidance counseling, and rehabilitation counseling, the difficulty in delimiting the practice of leisure counseling is confounded by the variable meanings of leisure. In addition, there has not as yet been a consensus as to the psychological functions that leisure ought to perform or any consensus regarding the role that leisure should play in our society. Questions such as these must be answered before ethical guidelines can be developed.

We have come to understand that a lack of theoretical or practical basis for leisure counseling may be a problem, for it is how one chooses to define the area of practice that governs ensuing discourse. Debate of proper strategies and techniques are secondary to issues of definition. If one considers him/herself a counseling psychologist, vocational guidance counselor, or therapeutic recreator, he/she has by virtue of training and practice delimited methodologies in important ways.

The use of leisure activity involvement as a directed strategy should serve to illustrate this point. Activities involvement is expected in the practice of therapeutic recreation and is reflected in professional literature. This is not the case in the counseling professions, where a bias toward activity participation is absent.

Influence of the Courts

At the point that one's actions interfer with the "life, liberty or pursuit of happiness" of others, our legal system becomes involved. Toward this end all members of society are held responsible for obeying laws. However, those who earn the privilege of membership in a profession are required to conform to additional constraints. The purpose of exercising greater scrutiny over the acts of the professional is largely derived from the public's awareness of the profession's ability to do harm as well as good. The degree to which the public has control over the professional's scope of practice or areas of misconduct is profoundly influenced by the courts. The duty of the counselor to control the behavior of the client, warn the public of potentially dangerous clients, and uphold the confidentiality of the therapeutic relationship are areas in which the courts have ruled. Codes of ethics that do not recognize the record of legal rulings fail to reflect the realities of the world in which we live. Codes that simply mirror existing jurisprudence do little to distinguish the profession.

In conclusion, we may therefore accept the dynamic relationship between professions seeking to enhance the public's understanding of "right" and "wrong" and the courts' responsibility for protecting the rights of others. Through this interaction, society defines its values in a constantly changing fashion.

Implications for Leisure Counseling

In that leisure has not evolved into a unified field of study, but has taken numerous meanings in both normative and etymological ways, definition has remained elusive. To some, leisure is a "state-of-being" that can be achieved in the workplace. Others argue for nonwork time or activity-specific definitions. We are also aware that the meanings of leisure have evolved over time and from civilization to civilization.

However, in a contemporary sense it is possible to isolate a number of issues that should be of some interest to all who study leisure counseling. This speculation is helpful both as a testing ground for defining actual problems and in directing inquiry that subsequently may distinguish leisure counseling from other disciplines. A study of these issues should also be helpful in developing ethical guidelines for the field.

HAPPINESS: Is the purpose of leisure to increase personal happiness and if so should this be the criteria for judging the need or success of leisure counseling? What have the moral philosophers since the time of Mill learned about the "Greatest Happiness Principle"?

PLEASURE: Is the purpose of leisure to create a pleasurable state of being? How much pleasure is needed and within what context? What is the relationship between pleasure and happiness? Can pleasure be defined as simply the absence of pain?

PARENTALISM: Many forms of leisure involve significant risk taking. At what point, guided by what information, does the leisure counselor seek to avoid or alter the experience to protect the individual?

FREEDOM: Leisure is often characterized by the lack of obligation. What are the implications of directing people to actions that require little responsibility or allegiance? What does it mean to choose freely?

ACTIVITY: Does leisure involve activity? Can one be at leisure during work or rest? Is work activity necessarily different from leisure activity, and if so, in what ways? Is it proper for the counselor to participate in leisure with the client, and if so, for what purpose and under what constraints?

TIME: If one defines leisure as nonwork time, does this mean that all those experiences that occur during work are of no concern to the leisure counselor? In what ways does the time of the child differ from the time of the college student, worker, or retiree? How does one differentiate between recreation and leisure with respect to the nonwork characterization?

ENVIRONMENT: Some might argue that leisure should occur in a health-supporting environment. If this is so, what are the implications of the leisure counselor advising against living in a city with air pollution, excessive crime rates, or impure air? Should the leisure counselor advise against listening to loud music because of scientific evidence indicating the likelihood of hearing loss?

EDUCATION: Can a person become educated in leisure? Is this education like any other type of education, or is it uniquely different? What are the values inherent to this subject and through what means should it be taught?

GUILT: Guilt can be a powerful motivator. Within the context of leisure, how can one feel comfort in doing nothing, or not playing the game? Often the depression one experiences from having an uneventful weekend or holiday may be linked to expectations for leisure experience promoted by public images. Because leisure is a personal experience with certain social realities, what is the role of the leisure counselor in mitigating feelings of guilt?

LIFE-STYLE: Questions of leisure are often synonymous with life-style. In an important way, people decide to marry and have children on the basis of perceived life-style. These perceptions affect social policy in the form of laws governing abortion, separation and divorce, and sexual preference. Defining leisure with respect to life-style brings meaning beyond that of vacant time or activity involvement. However, these leisure and life-style questions call for moral philosophy beyond that which presently exists in the field. What is the leisure counselor to do in the absence of this needed guidance?

Conclusions

It is one thing to articulate a social plan and design the improvement on paper. It is quite another to implement it in an actual situation. We have learned — in race relations, environmental pollution, urban affairs, and in a number of other areas of social, economic, and political concerns — that the law can point to change but alone is rarely capable of transforming entrenched institutions, systems, and mythologies.

Regardless of the opinioin that a group of scholars, academicians, or practitioners may have regarding the role, function, and importance of their work, it is the "felt need" of the public, as manifested in the law, that underscores its expressed value. Simply proclaiming that leisure counseling is important because there have been significant changes in the work place or that we now have more time for leisure are not sufficient arguments for public support and, more importantly, do not provide an adequate basis for professionalization.

As a first step, some group in the applied areas of leisure should begin the task of collecting case materials. These cases should illustrate the unique issues confronting the leisure counselor and the kinds of case studies relevant to leisure counseling ranging from confidentiality to environmental stressors. Not until the actual casework is generated will the field take on a unified form. Should insufficient uniqueness of cases be found, then perhaps there is good reason to conclude that leisure counseling has existed solely in the minds of a very few and might in due time disappear as a professional or academic interest. If, however, substantive cases are revealed, combined with heightened "felt need" from the public in general, then leisure counseling could emerge on its own or be adopted as a speciality within an existing discipline.

A related issue to consider is whether leisure counseling is nested in leisure and recreation or in the counseling fields. If, for example, counseling psychology as an academic discipline with licensing mechanisms decided to embrace leisure counseling as a subspeciality, predictable consequences would follow. Curriculum would be based in counseling programs, state licensing as a psychologist would be pursued, and the ethical practices for leisure counseling would be essentially those of any other psychologist. As was noted earlier, the sport psychologists elected a similar course of action.

This would be a considerably different approach from what presently exists. Today it is possible for the "instant expert" with entrepreneurial instincts to claim competence. This obviously is a matter of critical concern to those who teach, practice, or conduct research in this area, particularly to those who teach leisure counseling within the university.

Herein lies a critical concern confronting those who practice, teach, or conduct research in this area. Leisure counseling was appealing in the past precisely because it seem to encourage innovation. Because it lacks structure and definition, there is opportunity for creative involvement on the part of the professional. After reviewing several articles on the topic of leisure, Bordin (1981) may have captured this essence when he said: "I can only express my indebtedness to the contributors. They have shown us that leisure counseling is an area where psychologists can have their own peculiar brand of fun" (p. 77). Accepting this notion that having fun is symptomatic of healthy growth, it would seem essential that the counseling psychologist explore the issues of leisure. Yet others may caution against having fun with someone else's life-style. Here we witness the dilemma of offering potentially hazardous services weighed against the necessary risks of trying to better serve humankind.

However, those responsible for leisure services delivery in recent times have never had significant public support. Volunteers can run programs, high school students can supervise activities, and we can reward the elderly with residence in a utopian "leisure village." The apparent impression that nothing can go wrong in leisure is highly singular and positivistic. As pointed out by John Dewey (1908): "Moral theory cannot emerge when there is a positive belief as to what is right and what is wrong, for then there is no occasion for reflection" (p. 5).

This view, commonly held by the public and adopted by many in the field, has created a dilemma not easily solved. The whistle blowing clipboard toting adult, calling everyone out to play and have fun, is to be expected. The creation of the "do gooder" is paralyzing to those who wish to question. When we expect no negative consequence of action, we demand no accountability for positive outcome. It is not likely that leisure counseling will be taken seriously until the CONSEQUENCES of leisure as discrete and definable human behavior is better understood.

The views of John Dewey remain important. We cannot have a professional field of practice without first understanding the moral foundations for the field. It is not possible, no matter how easy it might appear, to agree on a set of ethical principles without first understanding the ethical and moral foundations of our beliefs. This line of questioning is particularly important when we realize that the nature of work is changing in our society and that the prospects of a "leisure age" are possible. Clearly, we have already begun the challenge of trying to identify the moral basis one calls upon to direct another human being into a job or onto welfare.

"To justify its existence, leisure counseling must begin to SHOW why it is needed in the first place" (Iso-Ahola, 1981). No matter what posturing the field takes, without existence of "felt need," intellectual growth and professional development will not occur. Those who believe that leisure counseling is a powerful approach to solving some of the people problems facing this society in the decades to come must first hold themselves accountable to the idea that IF IT IS STRONG ENGOUH TO HELP, IT IS ALSO STRONG ENOUGH TO HURT.

REFERENCES

American Medical Association, *Principles of Medical Ethics*, 1957, p. vi-viii.

American Psychiatric Association, Position statement on guidelines for problems in confidentiality. *American Journal of Psychiatry*, 1970, *126*(10), 1543-1549.

American Psychological Association, *Ethical Standards of Psychologists*. Washington, D.C.: APA, Revision, 1979.

Bordin, E. The psychologists are coming. *The Counseling Psychologist*, 1981, *9*(3), 75-77.

Dewey, J. *Theory of the moral life*. New York: Holt, Rinehart and Winston, 1908.

Dill, D. Introduction. *The Journal of Higher Education*, 1982, *53*, p. 244.

Ethical principles of psychologists, *American Psychologist*, 1981, *36*(6), 633-638.

Fagothey, A. *Right and reason* (5th Ed.). St Louis: The C.V. Mosby Co., 1972.

Golann, S. Emerging areas of ethical concern. *American Psychologist*, 1969, *24*, 455-459.

Goldman, L. *Research methods for counselors*. New York: John Wiley and Sons, 1978.

Hassett, J. But that would be wrong . . . *Psychology Today*, November, 1981, *15*(11), 34-50.

Hudson, W. *A century of moral philosophy*. New York: St. Martin's Press, 1980.

Iso-Ahola, S. Leisure counseling at the crossroads. *The Counseling Psychologist*, 1981, *9*(3), 71-74.

Kendler, H. Self-fulfillment: Psychological fact or moral prescription/ *Academic Psychology Bulletin*, 1980, *2*, 287-295.

Kindleberger, R.S. How should we live our lives? *The Boston Globe*, May, 12, 1982, p.2.

Koch, S. The nature and limits of psychological knowledge. *American Psychologist*, 1981, *36*(3), 257-269.

Levey, C.S. On the development of a code of ethics. *Social Work*, 1974, *19*, 207-216.

May, W. Code and convenant or philanthropy and contract. In *Ethics in medicine*. Cambridge, Ma.: The MIT Press, 1977.

Miller, N. & Robinson, D. *The leisure age*. Belmont, Ca.: Wadsworth Publishing Co., 1963.

National Recreation and Park Association, *Suggested principles of the code of ethics of the recreation and park profession*. Alexandria, Va., NRPA, 1977.

North American Society for Psychology of Sport and Physical Activity, *Ethical Standards for the Provision of Services by Sport Psychology Consultants*. NASPSPA, 1982.

Reiser, S., Dyck, A., & Curran, W. (Eds.). *Ethics in medicine*. Cambridge, Ma.: The MIT Press, 1977.

Reverson, D. NRC told to study mental health issues at TMI. *Monitor*, American Psychological Association, April 1982, *13*(4), 3.

Robertson, & Grant. Teaching and ethics: An epilogue. *The Journal of Higher Education*, 1982, *53* 345.

Scully, M. Carnegie Council detects ethical delay in higher education, sees it spreading. *The Chronicle of Higher Educaiton*, April 23, 1979, *18*(9), 1.

Sylvester, C. *Toward confidentiality as a code of ethics for the therapeutic recreation profession: An exploratory study of the judgments of therapeutic recreation practitioners toward confidential incidents including clients*, Unpublished masters thesis, University of Maryland, 1981.

Tarasoff v. Regents of University of California, 13 C.3d 177, 529 P.2 553, Cal RpTr. 129

(1974).

Winkler, K. Sharp increase reported in courses of ethics. *The Chronicle of Higher Education* , September 4, 1979, *19*(1), 15.

NAME INDEX

A

Adams, B., 180, 186, 196
Addams, Jane, 288
Adkins, C., 50, 88, 93, 95, 141, 155, 167, 177, 197, 246, 252
Agresti, J. Levi-, 8, 50
Aguilar, T., 210
Aldous, J., 180, 196
Allen, J.R., 114, 124
Allen, L.R., 54, 76, 135, 137, 152, 221 227, 231
Allport, 12
Amick, R.G., 48
Anderson, R., 106, 122
Aristotle, 97, 281
Ethica Nicomachea, 281
Arnhoff, D., 71, 78
Arnold, 12
Atchley, R.C., 159, 160, 167, 168, 175
Ausubel, D.P., 130, 152
Avedon, E.M., 152
Axelson, L., 182, 196

B

Ball, J.D., 131, 152
Bandura, A., 56, 57, 71, 76, 116, 118, 119, 121, 122, 123, 216, 231
Barfield, R., 168, 175
Barrett, T.C., 83, 94, 140, 156
Bateson, G., 23, 48
Beard, J.G., 155, 244, 246, 247, 251, 252
Beavers, W.R., 187, 196
Beck, A.T., 56, 71, 77
Beck, C.E., 61, 77
Beck, D., 180, 196
Bell, R., 196
Bem, D., 64, 77
Benedict, Saint, 10
Bengston, V.L., 160, 173, 175
Bentham, Jeremy, 281
Berelson, B., 16, 48

Berkowitz, L., 77
Berlyne, D.E., 80, 94
Berryman, D.L., 245, 251
Besag, F.P., 138, 152
Bhavini, R., 154
Bieri, 57
Binet, 63
Binstock, R.H., 165, 175
Bishop, D.W., 102, 123, 139, 156
Blasi, A., 64, 77
Blocher, Donald H., 55, 77, 174, 221, 226, 227, 228, 231, 234, 236
Bloland, P.A., 80, 82, 94, 136, 141, 151, 153, 220, 231, 248, 251, 260, 276
Bloom, B.S., 143, 154
Blumen, J. Lipman-, 224, 232
Bodden, J.L., 57, 58, 77, 79
Bolles, R.N., 25, 30, 31, 33, 48, 137, 141, 152
Three Boxes of Life, The, 31
Bottzin, R., 57, 78
Bordin, E.S., 215, 219, 226, 231, 298, 299
Borow, H., 77
Bosse, R., 169, 175
Bowen, G., 181, 182, 197
Bradley, R., 153
Brayshaw, R.D., 85, 94
Bregha, F., 200, 213
Breit, M., 50
Brennecke, J.H., 28, 48
Brenner, J., 100, 124
Brewer, M.B., 100, 123
Briggs, K.C., 193, 196
Brightbill, C.K., 137, 152
Brody, V., 131, 152
Brooks, J.B., 28, 48, 80, 94, 105, 123
Brotman, H.B., 157, 175
Brown, I., Jr., 118, 123
Bruner, J.S., 7, 13, 48, 103, 105, 123, 131, 152, 156
Buffone, G.W., 229, 232
Bundy, R., 234, 251
Bunting, C.J., 229, 232

301

SUBJECT INDEX